Separate Games

**SPORT,
CULTURE
& SOCIETY**

DAVID K. WIGGINS, SERIES EDITOR

Other Titles in This Series

Separate Games

African American Sport
behind the Walls of Segregation

Edited by David K. Wiggins and Ryan A. Swanson

The University of Arkansas Press
Fayetteville
2016

Copyright © 2016 by The University of Arkansas Press
All rights reserved
Manufactured in the United States of America
ISBN: 978-1-68226-017-3 (cloth)
ISBN: 978-1-68226-122-4 (paper)
e-ISBN: 978-1-61075-600-6

24 23 22 21 20   5 4 3 2 1

Text design by Ellen Beeler

♾The paper used in this publication meets the minimum requirements of the American National Standard for Permanence of Paper for Printed Library Materials Z39.48-1984.

Library of Congress Control Number: 2016947891

To all those athletes forced to participate in sport behind the walls of segregation

Contents

III. Organizations

Series Editor's Preface

Sport is an extraordinarily important phenomenon that pervades the lives of many people and has enormous impact on society in an assortment of different ways. At its most fundamental level, sport has the power to bring people great joy and satisfy their competitive urges while at once allowing them to form bonds and a sense of community with others from diverse backgrounds and interests and various walks of life. Sport also makes clear, especially at the highest levels of competition, the lengths that people will go to achieve victory as well as how closely connected it is to business, education, politics, economics, religion, law, family, and other societal institutions. Sport is, moreover, partly about identity development and how individuals and groups, irrespective of race, gender, ethnicity, or socioeconomic class, have sought to elevate their status and realize material success and social mobility.

Sport, Culture, and Society seeks to promote a greater understanding of the aforementioned issues and many others. Recognizing sport's powerful influence and ability to change people's lives in significant and important ways, the series focuses on topics ranging from urbanization and community development to biographies and intercollegiate athletics. It includes both monographs and anthologies that are characterized by excellent scholarship, accessible to a wide audience, and interesting and thoughtful in design and interpretations. Singular features of the series are authors and editors representing a variety of disciplinary areas and who adopt different methodological approaches. The series also includes works by individuals at various stages of their careers, both sport studies scholars of outstanding talent just beginning to make their mark on the field and more experienced scholars of sport with established reputations.

Separate Games traces the history of some of the most prominent and influential African American sports teams, events, and organizations during the era of racial segregation. Edited by Ryan Swanson and myself, the anthology includes twelve chapters written by scholars who are well versed in the interconnection among race, sport, and American culture. The result is a book that makes clear how important sports programs were to African Americans behind the walls of segregation. In addition to helping convince those in predominantly white organized sport of the ability level of individual black athletes, separate or parallel sports programs were important to African Americans because it provided examples of black self-help and organizational skills while at once engendering a sense of racial and community pride.

These sports programs, moreover, were important to African Americans because they served as symbols of possibility and examples of achievement during a period in American history characterized by rampant forms of racial discrimination in sport and society at large.

David K. Wiggins

Acknowledgments

This book was a pleasure to put together, largely because of the opportunity to work closely with the outstanding scholars who contributed essays on various aspects of sport among African Americans behind the walls of segregation during the civil rights period. All of the contributors, chosen for their expertise and quality contributions to the research literature, took the project very seriously as evidenced by their work that is characterized by clear writing, thorough research, and cogent analysis and interpretations. We are forever indebted to them and genuinely appreciative of their time and efforts.

Also essential to the completion of this book was the staff of the University of Arkansas Press. Dedicated to producing quality books that appeal to both a scholarly and more popular audience, Mike Bieker, D. S. Cunningham, and other staff members have been very encouraging and shown unwavering support throughout the entire process of putting the book together. As sport historians, we have also benefited from the commitment shown by the press to publish books that examine sport in its various forms. The press takes sport seriously, recognizing its importance and insights it can provide on other institutions and significant societal concerns and issues.

Lastly, we would like to express appreciation to our families for their support. As all academicians are fully aware, the scholarly process is time consuming and arduous and requires understanding and encouragement from family members at every turn. In this regard, we are most fortunate in having loving wives and children who enthusiastically stood with us as we brought this project to fruition. We are most grateful.

Introduction

In the years immediately following emancipation in 1865 a select number of African American athletes participated in white organized sport at various levels of competition. Some of these athletes realized great success in their respective sports and garnered national and even international reputations for their exploits. For instance, Isaac Murphy, the outstanding jockey from Lexington, Kentucky, captured three Kentucky Derbies and a plethora of other prestigious titles that ultimately led to his selection into the horse racing hall of fame in Saratoga Springs, New York. Boston's Frank "Black Dan" Hart garnered fame as a pedestrian, winning such well-known races as the Rose Belt, Astley Belt, and O'Leary Belt competitions in the late 1870s and 1880s. Moses Fleetwood Walker made baseball history in 1884 when he played for the Toledo Mudhens of the American Association that at the time had major league status. Indianapolis's Marshall "Major" Taylor was perhaps the greatest bicyclists of his generation, capturing many championships and establishing sprint records on the oval during the latter stages of the nineteenth and early part of the twentieth centuries.

The seemingly unlimited possibilities for African American athletes would be shattered by the turn of the twentieth century as a variety of factors would lead to their elimination from many white organized sports. Although a limited number of African American athletes would continue to participate, most notably and successfully in boxing, white college sport, and the Olympic Games, a hardening of the racial lines eliminated many of them from white organized competitions. African American athletes responded to their elimination from white organized sport in two basic ways. Some of them, particularly those in individual sports, traveled overseas to extend their careers and find fame and fortune. Prime examples of these athletes were Marshall "Major" Taylor and the jockey Jimmy Winkfield who found great success in bicycle and horse racing competitions abroad.

The majority of African American athletes, however, were forced to satisfy their competitive urges by participating on the all-black teams and in the leagues and organizations behind the walls of segregation. One of the most vibrant separate or parallel-sports programs were those at historically black colleges and universities (HBCUs). Prestigious schools such as Howard, Lincoln (Pennsylvania), Hampton, Tuskegee, Tennessee A&I, Morehouse, Virginia Union, Grambling, and

North Carolina Central established successful teams in a variety of sports. The sports programs at HBCUs were complemented by a plethora of other separate amateur and professional teams, leagues, and organizations that collectively resulted in a vibrant black national sporting culture. Without question, the most prominent and important of the all-black sports programs was Negro League Baseball. Because of its status as America's national pastime, baseball was particularly significant to African Americans, holding out a measure of symbolic importance far greater than other sports during the era of racial segregation.

Separate sports programs among African Americans were remarkably similar in organizational structure to predominantly white organized sport. Black baseball, for instance, was similar to its major league counterpart in that it was divided into two leagues, held an annual all-star game comprised of the outstanding players from the two leagues, and at season's end sponsored a world series to determine the year's championship team. The sports programs at HBCUs were like those at predominantly white institutions in that they began as relatively informal student-run activities and evolved over time into a highly organized phenomenon under institutional control. They closely resembled programs on predominantly white campuses in that they included a wide variety of sports, were ultimately controlled by elaborate bureaucratic organizations, and were rationalized along educational, athletic, and social lines. Also like the programs on predominantly white campuses, sports at HBCUs were crucial in that they contributed to a much desired sense of institutional pride and national reputation, and engendered school spirit by bringing students, faculty, and alumni together to share in the thrill and excitement of common pursuits.

One distinctive feature of separate sports programs was the style of play. In contrast to white organized sport, separate games behind the walls of segregation was generally more daring, unpredictable, and geared toward improvisation. This was certainly evident in Negro League Baseball, but also apparent in other separate sports both in and outside of educational institutions and at the amateur and professional levels of competition. Another distinctive feature of separate sports programs is that on occasion they were led by whites rather then blacks. Noteworthy examples would be J. L. Wilkinson, the white owner of the Kansas City Monarchs, who signed Jackie Robinson to his first professional baseball contract; Oscar Schilling and Harry Earl, two white employers of the Cincinnati, Indianapolis, and Western Railway, who were founding members of the Colored Speedway Association; and Abe Saperstein, the Jewish promoter and businessman who owned the legendary Harlem Globetrotters basketball team. In addition to some white founders and owners, African American players and teams had occasions to cross the color line and compete against white players and teams. These ranged from the triumph of a Negro League all-star team at the interracial Denver Post Baseball Tournament in

1936 to Jimmy McDaniel's famous 1940 tennis match against Don Budge at the Cosmopolitan Tennis Club in New York City.

Separate sports programs were obviously important because it gave African Americans an opportunity to satisfy their competitive impulses by competing among and against highly skilled and talented athletes. These programs were also meant to showcase the talents of African American athletes with the hope that they would eventually find their way into white organized sport. Perhaps most important, these separate sports programs were especially significant because they provided opportunities to display black self-help, race pride, business acumen, and organizational abilities. Serving as examples of black enterprise, separate teams, leagues, and organizations played a crucial role in the African American quest for equal rights and racial uplift. For African Americans, separate sports programs were ultimately about agency and how best to deal with the seemingly untenable choices among individual success, group faithfulness, and integrationist goals. It was an especially difficult task considering the racialist thinking and discrimination in America.

This anthology, consisting of twelve essays written by noted historians and sport studies scholars, analysis noted teams, events, and organizations that helped make up the world of black sport. The essays cover separate sports programs that have previously drawn attention from scholars as well as those that have received far less coverage and known only to those with a detailed knowledge of African American history and culture. The essays are all characterized by important insights, thorough research, and written in a clear fashion that makes them accessible to both academicians and a more popular audience. Like all anthologies, the collection is not exhaustive, covering carefully selected topics that together provide a more complete understanding of the pattern and role of sport behind the walls of segregation. Limited space did not allow for an assessment of the Harlem Globetrotters, Negro League World Series, West Virginia Athletic Union basketball tournament, Tuskegee Institute women's track and field team, and a host of other separate sports programs that were important to African Americans living in a society that denied them equal rights and freedom of opportunity.

It is our hope as editors that this volume will be of great interest to a large number of readers and encourage more scholarly studies on separate sports organizations among African Americans. Importantly, relatively scant attention has been paid to all-black sports teams, events, and organizations. Separate sports programs among African Americans have been marginalized. With the exception of Negro League Baseball, which has been romanticized by many and held up as a reminder of America's supposed commitment to democratic principles and fair play, separate sports programs behind the walls of segregation have largely been ignored, only occasionally studied in a serious manner by academicians. One possible reason for this neglect has to do with the difficulty in locating and utilizing sources necessary to provide the details and accurate assessment of these programs. The neglect of the subject, however, seems to have more to do with the particular interest that academicians have in studying African American athletes only when directly connected to some aspect of white organized sport. Scholars have been far more interested in interracial athletic contests and the process of integration in sport rather than the individual athletes and various events and organizations integral to the development of a black national sporting culture.

Whatever the reasons for the neglect of separate sports programs, it is unfortunate since a more thorough understanding of them can tell us a great deal about the institution of sport itself as well as the manner in which African Americans, particularly during the interwar years, dealt with racial discrimination and their inferior status. Sport history will always be incomplete if academicians only study African American athletes in relation to their white counterparts and in the context of integration rather than segregation. The Cincinnati Red Stockings are especially important in the history of baseball, but so are the Cuban Giants; the history of the Boston Celtics tells us a great deal about professional basketball, but so does the history of the New York Renaissance Five; the story of the University of Tennessee Lady Vols basketball team is essential for understanding the role of women in the sport, but so is the story of the Philadelphia Tribune girls basketball team; it is difficult to ascertain the status of women in track and field without recounting the exploits of women in the sport at UCLA, but the same holds true for the Tennessee State Tigerbelles; Dick's Sporting Goods High School National Tournament tells us a great deal about the importance of high school basketball, but the same holds true for the National Interscholastic Basketball Tournament; the USC-UCLA football rivalry provides important insights into the popularity of the gridiron game on college campuses, but the same can be said for the Turkey Bowl Classic; the story of automobile racing cannot be told without recounting the history of the Indianapolis Five Hundred, but it is also true of the Gold and Glory Sweepstakes; the Major League All-Star game provides an important glimpse of the popularity of the national pastime, but the East-West All-Star baseball game does the same; the decisions of the National Collegiate Athletic Association makes clear the power of a sports organization, but so do the decisions of the Colored Intercollegiate Athletic Association; tennis cannot be understood without having knowledge of the United States Tennis Association, but it is also true of the American Tennis Association; so much of golf's popularity has been dependent on the success of the United States Golf Association, but the sport's popularity was also due to the United Golf Association; and bowling owes much of its popularity to the American Bowling Congress and Women's International Bowling Congress, but equally important to the success of the sport has been the National Negro Bowling Association.

I
Teams

1

Cuban Giants

Black Baseball's Early Sports Stars

Leslie Heaphy

Since the 1990s baseball fans have become more aware of the history of the game, especially the Negro Leagues. The National Baseball Hall of Fame notes that one of the topics that elicits the most questions from visitors and callers is the Negro Leagues. With the showing of the movie *42* in 2013 new emphasis and interest has been brought to bear on the story of baseball integration and the struggles involved. In 2006, seventeen former Negro League players and owners were inducted into the National Baseball Hall of Fame, bringing the total to thirty-five from the official leagues and pre-1920 era. With all this interest and attention there are still many gaps and stories that have not been told, especially of the early pre-league years. One of the most dominant and well-known teams of the late nineteenth and early twentieth centuries were the Cuban Giants. The Giants built a strong reputation on the field and developed a large following among the fans and the black and white press. Both black and white newspapers provide the history of the team as much of their early play involved white opponents. Their solid play helped lay the foundation for the successful Negro National League created in 1920. Most people, even baseball aficionados, would be hard pressed today to tell you who played for the Giants or where the team came from. How did they become so well known in their day? Why are they significant to the history of baseball? What did they accomplish on and off the playing field? Why does such mystery still surround the origins of the team?

A good place to start is asking where the team came from. Why were they the Cuban Giants? Many stories have been told explaining how the players were not really Cuban; how they tried various tricks to convince people they were not African American but Cuban. The most common story was that they spoke gibberish on the field so fans thought they did not speak English. Given the prevalence of

Jim Crow attitudes and black codes throughout much of the country, these antics were believed to be necessary to attract fans. But is this just a humorous story to tell or is there some truth in what sounds like a tall tale? Historian Michael Lomax suggests this is just a tall tale and that the prevalence of mulatto players and merging of three black teams created the Cuban Giants."[1]

The best evidence still suggests that the Cuban Giants became the first professional black baseball team when they were founded in 1885 at the Argyle Hotel in Babylon, Long Island. A number of newspaper articles indicate that they may have started playing the year before, but there is no solid evidence for this claim. This early professionalism makes the Giants noteworthy and deserving of further study but this is just one reason to consider the Cubans as one of the most important teams in black baseball history. Historian Michael Lomax refers to the Cuban Giants as "the most successful black baseball club of the late nineteenth century—a direct result of economic cooperation."[2] What the team created others wanted to become. The Giants were able to develop a successful product that white and black audiences paid to see.

Argyle Hotel headwaiter Frank P. Thompson collaborated with C. S. Massey, John Lang, and S. K. "Cos" Govern to create a team that would entertain the guests at their resort and eventually at Henry Flagler's hotel in St. Augustine, Florida. The Cuban Giants were likely formed with the best players from the Argyle Athletics, the Philadelphia Orions, and the Washington Manhattans. Bringing together athletes of such high quality guaranteed exciting games and growing fan interest. Since the players were being paid this was a business venture that needed to succeed. Questions still abound about how this team came together, but it is known that John Lang provided much of the financial support and traveled with the ball club. Newspapers sometimes even referred to the club as Lang's Cuban Giants before eventually just calling them by the shorter Cuban Giants moniker. Timing could not have been more perfect for this business venture as the club was able to take advantage of both the increased leisure time people had due to the Industrial Revolution and the growing number of white teams that needed opponents. These independent white clubs needed monetary support and to build their reputations so they were more willing to play any team who could provide a strong enough challenge to attract paying customers.

S. K. "Cos" Govern and Frank P. Thompson may have seemed like a bit of an unlikely pairing due to their background and professions but they both understood promotion and good business. Born Stanislaus Kostka Govern in St. Croix in 1854, Govern made a name for himself as a labor organizer, a journalist and even as a Shakespearean actor. He was a mulatto catholic who came to the United States in 1868 as a cabin boy. Govern ended up in Washington, DC, where there was a large and thriving black baseball community as early as 1868. Though there is no evidence that Cos played, by 1880 he was managing the Washington Manhattans. His role with the Manhattans gave him access to the best black players of the day.[3] Frank P. Thompson was the headwaiter at the prestigious Argyle Hotel in Babylon, Long Island, a resort town. He and Govern were associates since Govern had been a headwaiter in Philadelphia and Atlantic City. Together they created a business model with the Cuban Giants that later teams would try to emulate. Given the time period and racial attitudes of the day, the idea of getting help from white businessmen seemed slim and yet they were able to develop a model of cooperation, a joint venture. First they received the support of John Lang and then in 1886 of Walter Cook followed by John M. Bright. In addition, they developed business ties with clubs at all levels from the Major Leagues to the amateurs. This kind of relationship building made the Cuban Giants a success when so many other teams struggled and failed. Although the money came from white investors, the daily activities of the team were carried out by Govern, Thompson, and team secretary George Van Sickle.[4]

The players invited to join the original 1885 squad were not newcomers to the game. Most of them had played for years on amateur teams around New York, Philadelphia, and Washington, DC. Signing the top players from the Orions to this new club made them the "giants" in black baseball. The Orions had a reputation as one of the best teams on the East Coast so signing their best players was smart business. Sheppard Trusty (p), George Williams (2b), and Abe Harrison (ss) became the nucleus of the new club and helped make it easier to sign other players to the team.

The team began play in the fall of 1885 after pulling together the necessary players and found themselves victorious most of the time. They even played games against the Major League New York Metropolitans and Philadelphia Athletics. They lost both games, but made them close enough contests to prove they were bonafide competition for any club. On October 6 the *New York Times* reported on the game against New York in which the Cubans were beaten 11–9. This account did not treat the game as a serious competition, though the score was close. The opening line read, "There was a farcical game of ball at the Polo Grounds yesterday that served to amuse some 600 spectators." The Metropolitans scored nine of their runs in the first inning, but after that it would appear by the score a more serious game ensued.[5]

A local Pennsylvania newspaper revealed one of the common difficulties of African American teams when it reported in September that owner John Lang had up and left the team, taking all their money with him. This may explain why his name is rarely mentioned in any later accounts of the ball club and even in historical works looking back on the club's beginning. It is still difficult to put all the pieces together from the existing newspaper accounts, both black and white.[6]

With the arrival of winter the team headed south to St. Augustine where they continued to entertain hotel guests, this time at the Hotel Ponce de Leon. While most of their winter games took place in Florida or nearby, the Giants did embark on a journey to Havana, Cuba, to play a series of ball games. This became another important first as they are recognized as the first professional club to play outside the US borders.[7]

One of the leading stars on the original team was pitcher Sheppard "Shep" Trusty. Trusty hailed from New Jersey originally and was early on dubbed by the papers a "phenom." He got his start in 1882 with the Orions. Trusty and catcher Clarence Williams (born Harrisburg, PA) made a great battery with strong pitching and excellent hitting. Williams enjoyed a long professional career, playing until 1905 while Trusty died at the age of thirty. Williams was described as a heavy hitter and fine runner. They were joined on the field by defensive specialist Benjamin Holmes from Virginia, who played the hot corner and pitcher/outfielder Billye White of Providence, Rhode Island. Others on the team included Andrew Randolph (Philadelphia, PA), 1b; Harry Johnson (Burlington, VT), 2b; Ben Boyd, George Parago (Charlottesville, VA), Art Thomas (Washington, DC), c; G. Day, S. Epps, Milton Dabney, and G. Shadney.[8]

The 1886 squad set out to establish a national reputation for themselves and by at least some accounts, they succeeded. In June, Govern lured star pitcher George Stovey to the club. This was quite a coup since he was considered by most to be the most dominant black pitcher of the day. Unfortunately, this led to other teams seeking his services as well and he ultimately signed with the Jersey City Blues. Losing Stovey did not dampen the strong play as at one point during the season the Giants recorded a thirty-five-game win streak and the local Trenton paper reported at the end of the season, "The Giants have done some splendid work on the diamond and have gained a national record."[9] Some of their strongest play came against such teams as the Jersey Blues, whom they beat four out of five times; the Monitors, whom they beat twice; and the Long Island City Stars, whom they also beat twice before losing 6–5. They beat the Princeton college boys 16–1 on 17 hits. In describing their early season victories, the local Trenton paper again gave their team high praise. "The escutcheon of the Cuban Giants still remains unsullied. Thrice have they crossed bats with opponents of no mean reputation, but each time the result has been an increase in the laurels already won."[10] When the Giants arrived in New York to play the Flushing Nine the locals treated their guests like kings. Harry Hill, a wealthy New York businessman and avid sports supporter, paid for them to stay at the Grand Street Hotel and also for their travel to the game at College Point. Unfortunately for Mr. Hill and the local fans, the Cubans did not bow to their hosts and beat them 9–7.[11]

After the conclusion of the regular season many of the Giants went south to play again in St. Augustine and the surrounding area. Before leaving, John Bright presented all the players and S. K. Govern with bouquets of flowers for their fine play and "gentlemanly conduct upon the field."[12] Management planned to keep the boys in shape upon their return to Trenton for the 1887 season. Govern, Bright, and Walter Cook planned to continue with the team, hoping to invest in some improvements for their stadium on East State Street. These included a new grandstand and a separate carriage entrance to make it easier for fans to get in to the park. In order to maintain rights to the name of the club, the team was incorporated as "The Cuban Giants Baseball Club of Trenton, New Jersey." They also bought three different uniforms for the players depending on where they were playing.[13]

When the Giants returned to Trenton in 1887 their success led to an effort to form the National League of Colored Baseball Players which never really got off the ground. The Giants chose not to join this new effort and that helped ensure its failure. Govern determined the club could make more money continuing their independent play. The Cuban Giants continued on their own, opening their regular season on April 11 amid a parade and much fanfare. In their second game they played the Princeton Orange and Black to a 6–6 tie. The game got called early because the Princeton players had to catch a train back to school. This game highlighted something fans would see a lot of during the season, superb and daring base running as well as what some considered antics as the Giants did anything to liven up the game. For example, Ben Holmes would do the cakewalk along the third base sideline or the players would applaud a good call from the umpire.[14] Clarence Williams stole three bases during the game including home plate. When they defeated the Reliance Club of Philadelphia 14–3 the Cubans showed off their ability to score at will. Only four of the fourteen runs were earned and those all came in the first inning. They found continued early success against the Newarks, easily beating them 8–2 and 14–1 in a series to decide the Champion of New Jersey. Billy Whyte got the victory in the first game and Shep Trusty came away victorious in the second game with a ten-strikeout performance. Two days later found the Giants on the right end of a runaway score, beating the University of Pennsylvania club, 24–5 on twenty-four hits. Whyte again pitched the team to victory with Clarence Williams playing a flawless game behind the plate. Syracuse University became the next victim, losing 6–4 with Shep Trusty striking out six. They battered the local Richmond nine 17–1 behind the arm and bat of pitcher George Parago. Parago had five hits to lead a balanced attack with four other Cubans getting four hits apiece.[15]

Reported attendance at Giants' games ranged anywhere from a few hundred to a few thousand depending on the day, the time of the game, and the place. The Cuban Giants had access to playing fields throughout the region from New York to Philadelphia. It was this draw that made them a target for some of the professional leagues approaching the Cubans to join their ranks. Cook and Bright rarely took the bait because they could make more money playing on their own. In fact, in later years when the Giants joined the Middle States League they got themselves in hot water for allegedly paying their players above the league limit.

Another way the Giants tried to promote their play came with the creation of different championship games. For example, in May 1887 Giants management sent out a challenge to the top team in the International League, the Newark Little Giants, with the winner getting to call themselves the Champion of the State of New Jersey. The Cuban Giants put on a show and won 14–1 in the first game and 8–2 in the second game, earning the right to call themselves the state champs.[16]

In early June, the Trenton papers reported a 23–2 win over the Quaker Giants as the Cubans stole four bases and Harrison hit two homeruns to give the win to Selden. A local reporter wrote, "The way the Cuban Giants continue to wipe the ground with all the second-class clubs that have the courage to come here is getting to be a chestnut."[17] The *New Haven Register* reported on the Cubans impressive victories, stating, "The Giants have beaten some of the best teams in the country this season and will give a fine exhibition of ball playing."[18] Playing Indianapolis of the National League again saw the Cubans win. "Their base running was particularly fine and bases were stolen with great ease." They beat Cincinnati as well, playing before a hometown crowd that witnessed the 8–5 win.[19]

Not long after the newspapers gave such glowing accounts of the Cubans play, the St. Louis Browns refused to play the Giants. Team president Von Der Ahe set up the game, even buying tickets for his players to get to the game since it was not part of their regular schedule. In a rare documented move, the evening before the planned contest, Browns players delivered a letter to Von Der Ahe refusing to play. The letter indicated their willingness to play any club but not "negroes." Some researchers have speculated their refusal could have also been due to the Cubans strong reputation and fear of losing to them.[20]

The Cuban Giants did not always win; they led into the fifth inning against the Athletics, but lost 14–9. Their fielding unraveled completely and they could not hit. Fielding and hitting were typically the team's strong points. Ben Holmes was considered "by far the best third baseman who has played in our city since the opening of the season. The Giants are all first-class players and are more than a match for any clubs in the State League."[21] Ben Boyd led the club with four hits in an 8–5 win over a Cincinnati nine. They showed "particularly brilliant play" and "pounding the leather" in an 8–6 win over Binghamton. By early July, their record stood at 40-25 with fifteen games postponed due to bad weather. More importantly, they had outscored their opponents 636 to 378.[22]

The team continued to win through the whole season as they knocked off the Hightown Orientals in early September by a score of 27–0. The Orientals had not lost a game coming in to the contest. George Parago got the win while Charles Williams led the hitting attack with a triple and homerun. They beat a local Baltimore nine 8–2 in October and then as they wound up the regular season before breaking up for the winter they were expected to play in Cincinnati. The local press in Cincinnati stated, "The Cuban Giants, the greatest team of colored players ever organized, will be at the Cincinnati Park next Saturday and Sunday."[23] By the end of the season, the Giants declared themselves the Colored Champions for the year and, according to black baseball historian Sol White, were "the happiest set of men in the world." They actually lost the series to their main rival in black baseball the New York Gorhams, losing the series 2–1.[24]

When the Cuban Giants returned in 1888 they received a number of offers to join existing leagues. This came after a strong winter that included a win streak of 49 straight games and Richard Kyle Fox of the *National Police Gazette* announcing he would book them to play any challenger for a prize of $1000–$10,000 and the claim of an American championship. The strongest possibility appeared to be the Central League, but management said no to all leagues under the National Agreement (those part of organized baseball's national structure) since no Sunday games were allowed. Sunday play brought in the biggest crowds and therefore the Giants could not afford to miss Sunday contests. They opened their new season with a 13–5 victory over Williams College, continuing their pattern of playing any challengers, no matter their rank. Jack Frye led the club with four hits and George Williams scampered across home plate three times. Keeping with the college theme, the Cubans lost to the Princeton boys 5–4 in a sloppy game that saw them make fourteen errors. They beat Lafayette 5–3 behind the stellar pitching of Billy Selden. Other opponents ranged from Trinity to Yale and Amherst College. By June, their record stood at 35-12 with one tie. More importantly, teams could charge more when the opponent was the Cuban Giants, so it did not matter as much if the hometown team lost. The usual price in most places for tickets to the grandstand was 25 cents, but when the Cuban Giants came to town clubs regularly charged 50 cents and still filled the stands.[25]

The Cubans worked hard to promote their reputation with S. K. Govern finding a number of different ways to do this. He created intra-squad games and brought in celebrity umpires such as fighter Jack Dempsey to entice the fans. This new emphasis continued into the 1889 season after the death of Walter Cook. Without his financial resources the team needed new ways to stay afloat financially. Govern may not have had the money, but he clearly was the promotional brains and the man with the eye for player talent.[26]

By the close of the season the Cuban Giants reputation preceded them and they were no longer just an East Coast sensation. A reporter from Detroit wrote the following to describe their play. "None but representatives of a race capable of the most advanced station in the arts and sciences could furnish so marvelous an exposition of the national game as that given yesterday by the dusky diamond experts of

Jersey."[27] At the end of the season the Cubans played the Gorhams, the Pittsburgh Keystones, and the Norfolk Red Stockings for the championship. They beat the Gorhams in a five-game series, 4–1, to win the Eastern Championship while the Chicago Unions were declared the Western champions. Many players then went their separate ways, some teaching and coaching while a number headed south to St. Augustine to work at the Flagler Hotel and play baseball for the entertainment of the guests.[28]

In addition to playing baseball, Thompson and Govern formed an organization known as the Progressive Association of the United States of America (PAUSA) in February 1889. The two served as president and secretary while Giants third baseman Ben Holmes also attended meetings. The intent of the group was to discuss ways to eliminate racial prejudice and to use these efforts to help build business opportunities such as baseball games for their own Cuban Giants.[29]

In 1889, the Giants joined the Middle States minor league as the Trenton Cuban Giants, opening the season at Lancaster, Pennsylvania, on May 1. Joining this league broke with the team's usual pattern of remaining independent. Govern

Team photo of the 1887 Cuban Giants with Manager S. K. "Cos" Govern seated in the center. *Image courtesy of Noirtech Research Inc.*

and Cook thought this league looked more financially sound than previous new leagues. The Middle State League lasted one year with thirteen teams playing, from cities in New Jersey, Delaware, Pennsylvania, and Connecticut. Norwalk, Connecticut, proved the farthest distance for league teams to travel. Throughout the season teams came and went, making it difficult to keep to a schedule. For example, Shenandoah entered the league on July 17 and disbanded on August 6. The Harrisburg Ponies provided the stiffest competition for the Cuban Giants. The Cubans finished the season with a 55-17 record. They played their home games in Hoboken, New Jersey, while the Philadelphia Giants, who were also members of the same league, played in Gloucester, New Jersey. John Bright continued to finance the team after Walter Cook died in June 1888. Losing Cook hurt the Giants because Bright did not have the financial resources and therefore the team never again was as sound financially. Bright and Govern continued to work together, but Bright appeared to be more interested in making money than winning. The other owners in the Middle State League wanted the Cuban Giants for economic reasons and not because they were trying to make any statements about integration.[30]

However, before the season even got underway, the league owners questioned how much Giants players were getting paid. It was suggested in response to the complaints that the club would have to substitute lesser players to comply with the league salary limit of $75. This would lessen their quality of play and they would begin losing, and therefore some owners said they should not be allowed in the league. This supported the argument that the only reason for letting the Cuban Giants into the league was because of their strong reputation and the economic boost they would bring. This kind of tension continued all season, though the newspaper reports seemed to all remain respectful. For example, in May a report in a white newspaper said, "It appears that the colored club has been running things to suit its own sweet will." The league even denied reports from the *Inquirer* that the Giants would be kicked out because of their color. [31]

Opening day saw the Giants lose to Lancaster 7–3 with George Stovey picking up the loss. The Giants recovered the next day to defeat Lancaster 6–1, pounding out 13 hits for winning pitcher Selden. Two days later in Harrisburg the league capitalized on the draw of the Giants with over 3,000 fans in attendance to watch the Giants lose 6–5. Even with the big crowds, the Cubans found themselves in hot water with the league at a meeting in mid-May. They were charged with not using the league-sanctioned Mason balls in their games and paying players above the league approved salaries. The charges were later dropped when John Bright promised they would do better at following the rules. Unfortunately, even though the charges were dropped, the Giants forfeited two games in the standings that they won because they did not use the league ball. At the end of the season these games would be part of a protest over Harrisburg being named league champion.[32]

Throughout the season the Cuban Giants and the Harrisburg Ponies traded first place. One of the opponents that helped the record of the Cuban team was the Philadelphia Giants, who lost regularly and eventually left the league mid-season to be replaced by the Gorhams. The president of the league, Charles Mason, also resigned, leaving the league in disarray. Less than half of the league games scheduled had actually been played due to league issues and inclement weather. By early August when the season ended, Harrisburg was declared the league winner with the Cubans in second place and York in third. John Bright protested the ruling to President Voltz, but his claims were never resolved and Harrisburg went down in the records as the league champion. Bright claimed Harrisburg was credited with too many wins and the Cuban Giants did not get credit for all their victories. In the head-to-head competition between the two teams they played fifteen games, with one later being declared an exhibition game. The Cuban club came out the winner with a 10-4 overall record solidifying their argument that they were the better team. President Voltz simply declared, "Mr. Bright's charges are entirely unwarranted and untrue."[33] The Cubans lost in a short series 2–0 to the New York Gorhams, making them the Eastern Colored Champions. By the conclusion of the season, Govern had determined that joining the MSL had been a bad move for the team as nothing positive seemed to result.[34]

The following season saw the Giants in danger of disbanding due to internal dissension largely the result of changes after Cook's death. A new team playing under the name the Big Gorhams was accepted into league play. Manager Kertie of Harrisbrug got in the middle of the controversy by claiming he had signed away all the Cuban Giants and therefore his team would be the new Cuban Giants located in Harrisburg. John Bright did not accept the invitation to join the Eastern Interstate League (EIL) and held the rights to the team name, playing with a new team except for Harrison and Grant, who stayed with him. The Eastern Interstate League included seven teams, all playing in Pennsylvania. Bright paid out a lot of money to sign away players from the Boston Resolutes and Pittsburgh Keystones for his new club. He had trouble finding a home park to play in due to the controversy and the fact that John P. Murphy, proprietor of the grounds in Trenton, invited the Newark American Association team to use his park. A second team found financial backing in Harrisburg and became the York Monarchs, accepting the EIL invitation and playing the whole season, disbanding in early October. The York club had many former Cuban Giants on their roster. The Big Gorhams team played 100 recorded games and finished at a remarkable 96-4. Newspapers reported a 39-game win streak as part of their 96 victories. For the Cuban Giants club they were reported as the Eastern Champions for the 1890 season with a record of 80-24, after compiling a 41-16 record for the first half of the season.[35]

Following a quiet winter, J. M. Bright brought his team back, playing out of Ansonia, Connecticut, for the 1891 season. In some circles the team was referred to as the Ansonia City Giants, and they officially joined the Central Connecticut League, which merged with the Connecticut State League in late April to form the Connecticut League (CL). John Bright became part of the committee scheduling contests for the league. The team struggled all season as players regularly jumped from the Cubans to the Big Gorhams and back. It appears the players moved around just to keep playing regularly and because Ambrose Davis of the Gorhams had signed away S. K. Govern from the Giants. According to a variety of newspaper accounts, the players liked playing for Govern better than Bright and so when he moved many followed him. This constant bickering between the two teams did not help either of their seasons and led to contests being canceled, complaints being launched against them both by other league teams, and the eventual collapse of the CL in mid-June. This led to the Giants and Gorhams both returning to independent play where they remained. The Cuban Giants played primarily in the greater New York area and limited their challenges for the next two seasons as they could no longer afford to pay large guarantees. They had a few impressive victories reported throughout the season, showing the team name survived even if there was ongoing controversy about which club represented the original Cuban Giants. Newspaper accounts make it hard to tell since they called a number of teams the Cuban Giants. Also, game accounts would call clubs the former Giants or stories would have the Cuban Giants playing, but each week their roster would have different names on it. For example, when they beat Northhampton in July the roster included pitcher Douglass, outfielder Dickman, and second baseman Bell but a week later the roster had Robinson, Barton, and Cato and none of the earlier players.[36]

When the 1892 season opened a Cuban Giants team was again playing independently, almost exclusively throughout the New York area. With the decline of the Gorhams, the Cubans played mostly white semipro teams. They recorded an 11–5 win over the Flushings in early May with George Stovey getting the win. Stovey led a pitching staff that also included Peno, Douglass, and Whyte. The team seemed to give up a lot of runs, but scored regularly too, delighting the fans who came to see them play. One of the best wins of the season came in early October as they beat the Fultons 11–7. The Fultons claimed dominance as the amateur champions of Brooklyn. Jackson, the backstop, led the way going 5–5 in the game and scoring three runs.[37]

As the 1893 season loomed, J. M. Bright called a meeting to try to revive the Middle States League, but this did not happen. After the upheaval of the previous three seasons, Bright needed to reorganize his team and its playing schedule if they were going to continue. Local news coverage is sporadic for the season, but the team did play and won handily throughout the New York area. Sporting new uniforms as part of this effort, they defeated the Paterson club 18–11 in April behind the relief pitching of Catto, coming in for George Stovey. Before a crowd estimated to be about 1,000 fans they beat the Easton club 10–2 as the local press said, "Cubans defeated them with hands down."[38] Their hitting kept them in close games with the Jackson duo hitting and scoring with some regularity. Clarence Williams was still with the team and he was joined by George Stovey, Sol White, Abe Harrison, and the Jackson brothers, Andy and Oscar. Local papers reported the Giants record at 99-12-1, and this success set the Giants up to return to prominence in the next couple of seasons.[39]

The Cuban Giants returned to their dominant form in 1894 and 1895, being declared Eastern Champions at the end of both seasons. Their opponents continued to include amateur, semipro, and professional teams as well as the area college nines. Over the course of their history they played Williams College nine times, with their two strongest wins coming in 1894 and 1895. In beating Williams College in 1894 the news reported, "The Cuban Giants played a sharp game, batted hard and ran bases well." They won 14–5.[40] Their travels took them as far north as Middlebury, Vermont, playing them at least four times in 1893, 1894, and 1898 with the Giants coming out on top in all four games. In the first contest in May 1893 the local college paper reported that over 400 fans came out to see the Giants beat up their boys 17–8. In 1894 the Giants won 11–4 and 14–8 and finished off their wins in 1898 with a 17–7 shellacking. It was said that fans got to see some of the best ball players of the day when the Cuban Giants came to town.[41] They played the Cornell College boys annually and always gave a good showing, "they always give great satisfaction, as a baseball team and as a minstrel show." This newspaper account made reference to the Giants ability to entertain the crowds not only with their excellent play, but also their "shadow ball" routines. Their dominance was supported by the record reported by their manager to the local press at the end of the 1894 season, 124-22-3.[42]

With that measure of success in 1895, two teams developed with similar monikers, the Cuban X-Giants and the Genuine Cuban Giants. Following their records in the newspapers is incredibly difficult simply because reporters either did not know the difference or the results sent in did not specify what team. Edward B. Lamar Jr. became the manager and booking agent for the Cuban X-Giants from 1895 to 1906 while Bright stayed with the Genuine Cuban Giants club. The Cubans success also led to efforts by Bud Fowler to copy their success with the Page Fence Giants, founded in Adrian, Michigan, in 1895 and for William Peters to copy Govern's efforts in promotion with his own Chicago Unions. Peters wanted to elevate his Unions to the dominance of the Cuban Giants and by 1896 the Unions were tops in the West. The other idea Peters followed was breaking out of the Chicago market and looking to build a wider reputation as the Giants had always done.[43]

The Genuine or Original Cuban Giants were generally seen as the inferior team to the Cuban X-Giants for almost the next decade. William Selden continued to lead the pitching staff in 1895 with John Patterson leading the hitting attack. For example, when they beat Chester in early May 1895, Patterson had three hits and scored three runs in the 16–4 victory. Selden garnered victories against teams such as the University of Vermont, Wesleyan College, and Newport.[44] By 1896, Dorsey Robinson seemed to be handling most of the pitching duties as the Giants continued to travel the East Coast playing all comers. They opened the season with a loss to Portland 9–8, that game was followed by a loss to Pawtucket at Dexter Park, 24–3. They lost again the next day to Pawtucket 16–5. They enjoyed some success against the Newport nine, playing them on at least four occasions, beating them twice. At the end of the season, the Cuban X-Giants found themselves playing the Page Fence Giants for the championship with many papers simply calling them the Cuban Giants. They also played in a season ending series with the now-prominent Chicago Unions where the Cuban Giants dominated, but the Page Fence Giants and the Cubans never played each other so no true Colored Champion was declared by the newspapers.[45]

John Bright wanted to remedy that oversight in 1897. Championship series helped promote the ball club and proved to be financially successful so Bright wanted to see a full tournament with all the best teams, East and West playing each other. He hired George Williams, one of the original Cuban Giants from the 1880s, as the team's new manager. Unfortunately, while Bright had a great idea the execution was lacking and the tournament never materialized as he did not invite the Cuban X-Giants or get solid commitments from any of the other teams.[46]

The difficulties between the Cuban Giants and Cuban X-Giants continued into the 1898 season as both claimed the other was stealing their players. E. B. Lamar offered to schedule a ten-game series between the two teams with five games in North Adams, Massachusetts, home of the Cuban X-Giants and the other five in New Jersey. Lamar offered to give the Cubans $100 for every game they won, but also expected them to donate $50 to the Maine Monument Fund when they lost. John M. Bright did not agree because he did not like being dictated to and he wanted more say in the choice of venues and where the money would be donated. This kind of squabbling did not help either team and allowed for the continued rise of newer clubs such as the Chicago Unions and Columbia Giants. In fact, the Cuban X-Giants, not the Cuban Giants, went out west to play the Unions in a series billed as the Colored Championship of the West.[47]

In the 1899 season the Cubans did play an ongoing series with the Chicago Unions, scheduled for thirteen games over the course of the season. In mid-June, the series was tied at four games a piece with William Selden pitching most of the games. This kind of back-and-forth play had always proved a successful promotion in the past and drew decent crowds again. Following this model, they did the same with the Columbia Giants at the end of the season, playing them at least four times in a one-week stretch as they barnstormed through the Midwest. The Cubans won the first two games 7–4 and 17–1 before losing 16–3. Newspapers reported that they planned to play twenty-one games throughout Michigan for a guaranteed $500 plus whatever the gate brought in. Scores have not been discovered for all twenty-one games but the back-and-forth challenge was a return to an earlier successful model of operation for the club.[48]

By 1900 the team makeup had changed as players tended to move around a great deal. Bright set up games just in the New York area and relied on strong weekend crowds to make the payroll with an occasional celebrity entertainer making a surprise appearance as well. Featherweight boxer George Dixon showed up to delight the crowd during a game in June when they played the Chicago Unions. Frank Grant managed the club and even played some second base with Ed Wilson and Williams Bell sharing the majority of the pitching duties. The rest of the infield was rounded out by Knucks James (ss), Johnny Hill (3b), and William Parker (1b). Roaming the outfield for the Cubans were William Kelley, Billy Thompson, and an unidentified athlete named Brown. This team joined the Eastern Interstate minor league and finished with a 40-16 winning record.[49]

Given the rising prominence of Chicago area teams, the number of new teams in the New York area, and the ongoing troubles the Cuban Giants had in keeping players, it is no surprise their play became more sporadic after 1900. Newspaper reports of their local games appeared less frequently and the team tended to stay local with an occasional short trip into Pennsylvania or Ohio. For example, in 1902 the Cubans beat the Kent State University team 12–5 and also Toledo 7–5. They beat a Honesdale, Pennsylvania, nine in 1904 9–4 on twelve hits and a team in Vermont 10–3 with the strong battery of Nelson and Garcia. John Garcia died later that year after having a heart attack during a game in early October. The Giants also continued their efforts to promote a championship series whenever they could. They played the Leland Giants at Auburn Park in September 1904 for the Colored Championship, coming off an 80-30 season. They won the first game 6–1, but that appears to be the only game they won. Again in 1908 the Giants seemed to return to barnstorming outside New York and playing multiple series games against teams such as the Leland Giants, the Gunthers, and the Logan Squares. Victories did not come easily in those series as the Cubans defense seemed to desert them at crucial times. Croxton ended up on the losing end of many of those contests between the errors behind him and the walks he gave up. They recorded victories on their travels through Maryland, Massachusetts, Ohio, and Pennsylvania.[50]

Returning in 1909 the Cubans found themselves again barnstorming around the New York and Pennsylvania area, though the newspapers sometimes confused them with the Havana Cuban Giants playing in the south. The Havana team came to the United States on tour and barnstormed mainly in Texas and surrounding areas, with the newspapers often simply referring to them as the Cuban Giants. This club only lost one game on tour. Meanwhile, the Cuban Giants back East struggled and had more bad news when their second baseman William Bedford got struck by lightning and died while the team was warming up for a game. Others got knocked down but no one else was hurt.[51] A new outlaw league in 1910 tried to sign the Cuban Giants to their league out west; they were the Arkadelphia Cuban Giants. This became another influence of the earlier Giants success, teams copying their name, their business practices, and their promotional successes. When the team lost in 1911 to a Trenton club 17–3, a local reporter seemed to capture the past and present for the club in his comments, "Shades of those old days on YMCA field, when our young men used to quake and tremble at the mere site of the husky swart-faced crew!"[52]

Another way to judge the success and popularity of the Cuban Giants would be to put a slight twist on the idea of copying being the highest form of flattery. Many ball clubs borrowed the name of the Cuban Giants over the years, from the Cuban X-Giants to the Penn Yan Cuban Giants to the Arkadelphia Cuban Giants, the Key West Cuban Giants in 1920, the Florida Cuban Giants in 1929–30 and the Havana Cuban Giants as late as 1941. The Arkadelphia team played in 1910, and though there is no direct tie to the original Cuban club, one could surmise at least that they thought the name might help draw more fans. Their record, in the few games that have been found, was not stellar at 2-7 but none of the games were blow-outs. Most saw the Giants on the short end of a one-run loss.[53] When the Havana team returned to play newspapers made reference to their showmanship (shadowball) and fine play. These were things the original Cuban Giants had always been known for. Satchel Paige even pitched a game for the Giants, losing to the Indianapolis Clowns 9–0. Earlier in the season Paige had pitched in relief against the Havana team and beaten them 11–9.[54] The most interesting of these later teams was the Penn Yan Cuban Giants who played in upstate New York in 1924 and part of 1925.

The Brooklyn Cuban Giants submitted a proposal in 1924 to the chamber of commerce in Penn Yan, New York, offering to come and play two games a week there through the whole summer if they would move the ball field in front of the grandstand at the Yates County Fairgrounds. The businessmen in Penn Yan saw an opportunity to promote the name of their town and bring in tourists and they readily said yes. They kept the name Cuban even though none of the players were Cuban. The roster sported such names as "Beano" Thomas, "Chick" Wells, Rufus Johnson, Wm. "Baldy" Woods, and Richard "George" Washington. The first game was played a week after the decision was rendered. For the Cuban Giants the move made sense financially because there would be less competition for people's money upstate. New York City already had three teams playing in the Negro Leagues at the time. The players came from all over, though none were from Cuba and they played a total of eighty-nine games in 1924, of which sixty-two were victories. Unfortunately from a financial standpoint, the Giants did not make out well, though the County Fairgrounds saw their best numbers as people came from all over to see the team play. The attendance was just not high enough to do more than cover the team's expenses. The 1924 season ended badly when the team's booking agent got arrested for keeping money from the players following a series against the Toronto team from the International League.[55]

Due to the lack of financial success it was unclear whether the Cuban Giants would return in 1925, but seven of the team's players had stayed for the winter, finding jobs in the local area. James L. Robinson approached the players to form a new team called the Penn Yan Colored Giants. This produced a rivalry when the Cuban Giants decided to return. Both teams set out to raise money and the Colored Giants proved more successful, and so by the start of the season the new team became the Penn Yan Colored Giants. The Cuban Giants decided to remain in the south where they had played thirty-five spring training games and played the 1925 season in Cumberland, Maryland, under manager John B. Johnson.[56]

The Cuban Giants are still a team shrouded in a certain amount of mystery, but there is no denying the quality of play of the early teams nor the influence the team had on subsequent teams, players, and leagues. One simply has to look at the number of teams that copied their name all the way into the 1950s or the leagues who sought the original Cuban Giants as members because they would provide an economic boost. Consider some of the players who played for the Cuban Giants, future Hall of Famers in Frank Grant and Sol White, nineteenth-century stars such as George Stovey, Shep Trusty, Clarence Williams, William Selden, and Benjamin Boyd. The influence the team had on the early effort to form the National League of Colored Baseball Players in 1887 and the promotional ideas of both Govern and Bright add to the importance of the Cuban Giants in the nineteenth century and beyond. When Sol White wrote his early history of colored baseball the Cuban Giants figured prominently in his discussion and in the rivalries that developed between the successful black clubs. Although their record against Major League clubs was not outstanding the fact is they played at least ten contests in just 1886 and 1887 alone before the color barrier really took hold. Major League teams saw the benefit of playing a top black team in both paycheck and promotion.

2

Smilin' Bob Douglas and the
Renaissance Big Five

Susan J. Rayl

Though not the first professional black basketball team in the United States, the New York Renaissance Five, or Harlem Rens, proved to be one of the most successful of the first half of the twentieth century, earning an eighty-eight-game win streak in 1933, winning the first World Professional Basketball title in 1939, and serving as the first all-black team in the National Basketball League.[1] Organized and owned by Robert L. "Bob" Douglas, the Rens broke many barriers over twenty-six years, and along with the Harlem Globetrotters laid the basis for much of the play that is now seen on a basketball court, while in a legally segregated America.

Born on the island of St. Kitts in the British West Indies on November 4, 1882, Douglas immigrated to New York City in 1902.[2] He first observed basketball in 1905 when a colleague took him to an upstairs gymnasium in midtown Manhattan. Douglas, who had played soccer and cricket and swam while growing up in St. Kitts, fell in love with the new game. Three years later in 1908, Douglas and two partners, George Abbott and J. Foster Phillips, formed the Spartan Field Club, an amateur organization that offered competition for black youth in soccer, cricket, track and basketball. From 1910 to 1918, Douglas played on the Spartan Braves basketball team, and then took over duties as the general manager of the Spartan Field Club.[3]

By 1921, the Spartan Braves played games as a member of the interracial Metropolitan Basketball Association (MBA), agreeing to rules and regulations concerning amateur sport.[4] When evidence emerged showing some MBA players had received pay for playing baseball, professionalism became an issue in the MBA over the next two seasons. Though he had removed players deemed as professional from his team, Douglas experienced a lack of support from the MBA when two other member clubs failed to follow through with scheduled games. Believing the MBA favored some clubs over others, he decided to turn his amateur Braves into a professional team.[5] Perhaps this was also due to the precedent set in the 1922–23 season by the white McMahon brothers, who established an all-black professional team, the Commonwealth Five, which included players from four of the "amateur" MBA teams.[6]

Negotiations between Douglas and the owners of the newly built Renaissance Ballroom likely began in the spring of 1923. Douglas agreed to adopt the name "Renaissance" or "Rens" in return for practice and playing space. He set his sights on developing a top professional black team, and found tremendous support from Romeo Dougherty, a fellow British West Indies immigrant who served as the first sports and theater editor of the *New York Amsterdam News*.[7] Dougherty, known as the "sage of Union Hall Street," came to know Douglas very well during the days of the Spartan Field Club and used his position to promote Douglas's teams.[8]

The New York Renaissance Five played their first game against the Collegiate Five, a white team, on Saturday, November 3, 1923, at the Renaissance Ballroom and won, 28–22. Inaugural team members included Leon Monde, Hilton "Kid" Slocum, Frank "Strangler" Forbes, Zack Anderson, Hy Monte, and Harold Jenkins. Monde, Slocum, and Forbes formerly played for the Spartan Braves. A large enthusiastic crowd witnessed the first game of a team who would realize great success over a span of three decades.[9]

Over the next three years, Douglas sought to establish his team by seeking opponents that challenged his Rens. Though Cumberland Posey of Pittsburgh sought to schedule games between his Loendi Five and the Rens, Douglas opted to follow the lead of the McMahon brothers and their Commonwealth Five in playing against the top white team, the Original Celtics. Many of the other amateur teams that turned professional found it difficult to turn a profit and went out of business, yet the Rens continued to grow and thrive under the business-minded Bob Douglas.[10] Douglas gained fans and supporters by charging less admission than Commonwealth, 50 cents versus 75 cents, and through the passing and playing ability of the Renaissance players. Though Commonwealth narrowly defeated the Rens, 38–35, in February 1924, and by a large margin two weeks later, Douglas took note of their talented players.[11]

After two seasons, the McMahon brothers dissolved their all-black Commonwealth Five team. Douglas took the opportunity to sign two former Commonwealth players, George Fiall and Clarence "Fats" Jenkins, known as the "Heavenly Twins" for their teamwork on the court.[12] Douglas also took notice of James "Pappy" Ricks, the "Jersey Kangaroo," who had played for Loendi and Commonwealth and in January 1925 signed him to the Rens team. Walter "Longie" Sanders, a standout player for his Atlantic City High School team and the Atlantic City Y Big Five, joined the Rens in the fall of 1925.[13]

In early 1925, the Rens played their first game against a team that would become their greatest rivals, the Original Celtics (Celtics).[14] Though they lost this first game, 43–35, it served as the beginning of a rivalry on the court and friendship between the players off the court. Over the next several months, the Rens lost to the Celtics four more times, both at home and on the road.[15] But in mid-December 1925, the two teams met at the Manhattan Casino. On a cold winter night, 4,000 eager fans came to watch the game, but 1,000 were forced to wait outside for the results. In their fifth meeting, known as the "the battle of the gods," the Rens finally overcame the Celtics, 37–30. The Rens victory over the top professional team was symbolic in nature. "Championships in those lines of sports where the color line is drawn remain with the whites," wrote Romeo Dougherty. "They deny the colored brother a chance to compete with them, but once they let down the bars they prove the fallacy of their claims of a superiority which only the white race enjoys. All Negroes have asked is a fair chance, and when given that chance, they have more than made good."[16] A month later the Rens gained another win over their new rivals, only to then be soundly defeated in a seventh game, 46–21, before the largest crowd to see a black basketball team compete; 10,000 fans, at the 369th Armory in New York.[17]

Although columnist Ira F. Lewis of the *Pittsburgh Courier* questioned black involvement in the professional game, and denounced Cumberland Posey for it, Douglas and his Rens found great support in Harlem.[18] In the midst of the Harlem Renaissance, Douglas's young team represented the possibility of equality for African Americans through their wins against white teams such as the Bronx Five, the Union City Five, and the Assumption Triangles. Basketball served as a vehicle for improved race relations, according to Romeo Dougherty. In a loss to the white Nonpareils in Brooklyn, Dougherty stated, "There were a number of colored fans scattered throughout the gathering and the congenial spirit existing between the races at a game staged and fostered by the whites wherein a colored team was part of the attraction bodes good for basketball."[19] Dougherty credited Douglas and the Renaissance management with not only keeping the Rens financially solvent, but also doing their part to eliminate the color line in sport, drawing attention locally and regionally in the process.[20] By the middle of their third season, the Rens, announced Dougherty, had become "an institution in Harlem."[21] At the end of the 1925–26 season, the Rens held a two-year winning streak on their home court and a 77-15 season record.[22]

Between 1926 and 1929 the New York Renaissance Five entered the ranks of big-time basketball, playing over one hundred games a season against white and black teams throughout the Northeast. In late November 1928, the Rens began playing "home" games in Philadelphia at the Palais Royal on Monday nights, in addition to their Sunday night games at the Renaissance Ballroom in Harlem.[23] Douglas signed twenty-one-year-old Eyre Saitch, who had recently won the 1926 American Tennis Association National men's singles title in St. Louis.[24] The Rens played white teams such as the Catskills, Bronx Professionals, Philadelphia Giants, Brooklyn Dodgers, Atlantic City Buccaneers, Visitation Triangles, and Manhattan Whirlwinds, and a few black teams such as the Bridgeport Professionals, Ritz Club, and Quaker City Elks. But the Rens-Celtics matchups continued to draw the most fans and to be the most meaningful.

To draw larger crowds and increase business, Douglas scheduled the toughest teams for his Rens. "What's the difference?" questioned Douglas, "We are playing big time basketball, and the harder the teams the better we like it. Then too, a glance at our record will show that we haven't fared so bad by meeting the best in the game. Give the fans a run for their money, whether you are on the winning or losing end, and they will be satisfied."[25]

Douglas and the Rens continued to gain respect from black fans. But with respect came responsibility, both on and off the court. Following a loss to the Brooklyn Dodgers at home in late October 1927, Douglas reprimanded his players for sloppy and careless play.[26] The Rens owner also demanded discipline from his players, removing George Fiall from the team when he consistently broke training rules. At the end of the 1927–28 season, the *New York Amsterdam News* reported that, despite a 109-22 record, fifteen games were lost due to carelessness, poor conditioning of the players who broke training rules, and discipline problems. The newspaper believed that because the Rens were now a drawing card, they had a responsibility to their fellow blacks. On the court they represented black America and it was important that they play their best. Yet, the newspaper and fans failed to take into account the physical toll taken on Ren players who suffered from illness and injuries while playing a demanding travel schedule of six games a week over five months.[27]

In January 1929, while Bob Douglas suffered from double pneumonia,[28] the Rens made their first trip to the Midwest, defeating two black teams, the Savoy Five, which included two former Rens, George Fiall and Specks Moton, and the Cleveland Elks. But they also lost games to two white teams, Fort Wayne and the Chicago Bruins. The approximately 500 black fans that attended the Bruins game faced higher ticket prices and segregation in the less popular seats at the George Halas Pavilion. The loss to Fort Wayne and Chicago of the American Basketball League (ABA) did not sit well with fans and black newspapers.[29] Frank Young of the *Chicago Defender* stated, the Rens "looked like world beaters in the first half . . . but in the second half they looked like everything else but." Because the Rens held a 3-point lead at the half, their play in the second half, and eventual loss to the Chicago Bruins, was questioned. Whether the Rens were defeated, or they "laydown," what happened looked questionable.[30]

In their first six years, the Rens earned a 465-95 record, gaining respect and admiration from fans and opposing teams in the process.[31] The Rens now defeated ABL teams consistently, and occasionally the Celtics and South Philadelphia Hebrew Association (SPHA). They not only served as ambassadors for Harlem, but also for their fellow black citizens, a job that made it difficult for the young players to enjoy themselves off the court. Bob Douglas knew his players' actions were under scrutiny, perhaps more so because of their color. As the team gained fame, their responsibility to black Americans increased as reported by black newspapers. Supported by the community of Harlem, the Rens thrived despite the racial and economic challenges they faced.

By 1929, living conditions in Harlem had deteriorated due to overcrowding and an increased black population of 165,000. White landlords charged blacks more than whites for housing, so black families frequently doubled up in one apartment. "People were packed together to the point of indecency," wrote Gilbert Osofsky.[32] Yet, in mid-August 1929, the Renaissance Casino underwent renovations costing $10,000 in order to attract customers. The ballroom now included loges in addition to the private boxes exclusive to the Renaissance, unique decorations, a new lighting scheme, and new carpet.[33]

The 1929–30 season began with a potential split of the Renaissance team. In mid-October, owners of the Original Celtics attempted to secure an injunction to prevent three or four Renaissance players from playing for the Renaissance team. Approached during the summer by Jim Furey, manager of the Original Celtics, these players had signed contracts to play for the Celtics during the 1929–30 season, and the Celtic owners were determined to hold the players accountable. "It is my opinion that they figured we were helpless and would be in no position to fight them when the issue came to a head, but we are represented by legal counsel in whom we have the greatest confidence and the battle will be waged to the bitter end," stated Bob Douglas. Because the players had signed contracts without a release from Douglas, the application for an injunction against the players by the Original Celtics was denied.[34]

In the midst of an economic depression, and despite the lack of income for many in Harlem, the Rens found success on the road, as witnessed by the thousands of fans who patronized their games. In addition to several home games early in the season, the Rens played hundreds of games in the Midwest between 1929 and 1932. Their travels took them to cities such as Philadelphia, Pittsburgh, Fort Wayne, Chicago, Youngstown, Cleveland, Detroit, Atlantic City, Passaic, Syracuse, and Baltimore, where they played teams such as the Chicago Bruins, the Wynn Undertakers, the SPHAs, the Baltimore Athenians, Otto Briggs Tribune, Holy

Cross, and the Cleveland Rosenblums.[35] In the fall of 1931, Douglas signed John Holt, a former player for the Collegians and Orioles, to replace Harold Mayers. In a new advertising ploy for Rens games, Douglas initiated "Ladies Night" at the Renaissance Casino in February 1932. Many women attended the Rens game for free and watched the Rens defeat the New Jersey Hebrews. Also, college fraternity teams began to play at the Renaissance Ballroom while the Rens were away.[36]

One team the Rens did not play in 1932 was the Harlem Globetrotters. Recognizing the success of Bob Douglas's Rens and the financial potential of a professional black basketball team, Abe Saperstein, a young Jewish businessman, organized the Globetrotters from Chicago's Savoy Five and the team made its debut on January 7, 1927, in Hinkley, Illinois. By the spring of 1932 the Globetrotters claimed to be the national basketball champions on the basis of their record of 189-11 in the 1931–32 season. "The team has repeatedly challenged the New York Rens, but the Harlem team has avoided meeting the westerners," stated the *Chicago Defender*, who noted that fans requested a Renaissance-Globetrotter matchup.[37]

The 1931–32 season closed with a win over George Gregory and his team and a benefit game. The benefit game featured the Celtics and the Rens at the Renaissance Ballroom, and supported the Boy Scouts of Harlem and their new thirty-piece brass band. Though the Rens had taken the previous encounter, the Celtics won, 35–30, in a hard-fought game. The Celtics looked in rare form and gave a passing show for the fans. Cab Calloway, an ardent basketball fan and former player, entertained with his jazz band before the game, and the Vernon Andrades Orchestra "set restless feet to motion" after the game.[38]

Poor economic conditions and over 50 percent unemployment in Harlem continued to challenge Bob Douglas, but his Renaissance team stayed afloat through barnstorming in the Northeast, Midwest, and South during the depression of the 1930s. Although the Rens played most of their games on the road, they usually opened the season at home on election day, and played annual Thanksgiving and Christmas day games at home. Between 1932 and 1936, the core Renaissance traveling team included the captain, Fats Jenkins, Pappy Ricks, Eyre Saitch, Tarzan Cooper, Johnny Holt, Bill Yancey, and Willie Smith. In the 1935–36 season Jackie Bethards replaced Pappy Ricks. "The Magnificent Seven" earned a 497-59 record and eventually were elected in 1963 as a team into the Naismith Memorial Basketball Hall of Fame.[39]

In January 1933, just after the Rens announced plans to travel south for the first time, Bob Douglas was named manager of the Renaissance Ballroom. Douglas, a personable man known for his smile and whose handshake was as good as any contract, would now remain at home booking games for his Rens from the Renaissance Ballroom.[40] Eric Illidge took over the Rens financial management on the road, and the team captain, Fats Jenkins, served as a player-coach.

The Renaissance Theater and Renaissance Casino and Ballroom. *Image courtesy of User:Beyond My Ken / Wikimedia Commons / CC BY-SA 4.0*

"Ripping and snorting through the fair land of the south, a veritable northern tornado of a basketball team is spreading havoc among opponents," noted the *New York Amsterdam News*, "and that tornado is the Renaissance Big Five, champions of the world." Welcomed enthusiastically wherever they traveled and drawing large crowds during their 3,000-mile southern trip, the Rens met all-comer, club, professional, and college teams. Both black and white spectators came out to see them play, and they won the admiration of the crowds. After two weeks in the South, the Rens traveled through the Midwest, scoring wins in Illinois, Indiana, Michigan, and Ohio.[41] Heading home through a snowstorm in late February, after their sixtieth consecutive win, members of the Renaissance team narrowly escaped serious injury when their bus crashed into a concrete retaining wall near Albany, New York. Nonetheless, the Rens won their sixty-first game, defeating the Celtics the following night, 25–17, before "a banner crowd" at the Renaissance Ballroom.[42] Another trip to the Midwest garnered additional wins in Ohio, Missouri, and Illinois, including a close 36–35 win against the Celtics in Cleveland, where Ren player Willie Smith received a warm ovation from his hometown.[43] After defeating the Union City Reds on March 26, the Rens held an eighty-eight-game win streak for the season. The streak ended the following night in Philadelphia when the Rens lost to their rivals, the Celtics.[44]

In tremendous demand by the mid-1930s, the Rens averaged six games a week. Renaissance players earned $150–$250 per month in the mid- to late 1930s, with bonuses of $25–$50 for winning games against the Celtics. Top black basketball players such as Fats Jenkins may have earned $1,500–$2,000 in a single season.[45] The Rens developed a strategy on the road that guaranteed a return game. They defeated each team they played by exactly ten points, scoring the points they needed and then allowing their opponents to come within ten points of their score. "Normally what happened when we went out on the floor was we got ten points as quickly as we possibly could," recalled John Isaacs. "That was the ten that the home officials would deny you. And then for every two baskets the other club made, we made one."[46]

The Rens tour in the South in 1935 on their private bus took them to Atlanta, New Orleans, Birmingham, Montgomery, Tuskegee, and Memphis. Black and white fans and white college coaches attended the games in Birmingham, sitting in segregated sections. The Rens easily defeated their opponents, but gave the crowds good games. Applauded by whites for their talent on the basketball court, most restaurants and motels barred the Rens. Instead, players lodged with black families in private homes, in dorms on black college campuses, and in "colored" YMCAs.[47] By early 1936, the Rens drew thousands of spectators to several games in the Midwest, including 7,500 in Muncie, 6,000 in Anderson, and 5,000 in Indianapolis and their travels took them to Pennsylvania, Ohio, Indiana, Illinois, Tennessee, Georgia, South Carolina, and Alabama.[48]

From the fall of 1936 to the spring of 1939, Harlem's economy remained bleak so the Rens continued to play most of their games on the road to remain financially solvent. Still, Bob Douglas spent $15,000 redecorating the Renaissance Ballroom, in preparation for the 1936–37 season. A new neon sign was said to "command the avenue" standing thirty feet high at 138th and Seventh Avenue.[49] Douglas added Zachary Clayton and John Isaacs to the 1936–37 team, and Louis Badger and Al Johnson in 1937–38.[50] When John Holt retired from the Renaissance team, and joined the New York City Police force, Douglas recruited William "Pop" Gates and Puggy Bell for the 1938–39 season, while releasing Jackie Bethards. Lou Badger left to play for the Harlem Yankees.[51]

The Rens found great success on the road in January 1937, playing in the South. With wins over Kentucky State and the Celtics in Louisville, the Rens boasted 10 consecutive victories on the tour. Against Kentucky State, a black college team, the Rens gave the players and spectators from nearby towns an example of "Big Time" basketball. The game against the Celtics was the first ever for the Rens in Louisville.[52] White teams rarely played black teams in the South because of segregation laws. Southern white coaches and teams admired the Rens, though, as they attended the Rens' games and diagramed their plays.[53]

The Rens started training for their 1938–39 season during the last week of October, and opened on election night, November 8, at the Renaissance Ballroom by defeating the Visitations, 28–18.[54] Due to lack of attendance at home, however, Bob Douglas decided to put his Rens on the road for the remainder of the season.

The Rens drew only a couple hundred spectators for the game against the Visitations and not many more when the Celtics visited. The Rens left in early December for Philadelphia, with plans to return to the Renaissance Casino for a Christmas night game against the SPHAs. The SPHAs had defeated the Rens a couple weeks earlier, so the Rens wanted revenge.[55] Fans and reporters continued to speak highly of the Rens and the teamwork that set them apart from most other professional basketball teams. "For a perfect picture of precision and timing, watch the Renaissance floor machine clicking on all five," wrote *Pittsburgh Courier* sportswriter Chester L. Washington Jr. "Here you have harmony, color, skill, and showmanship all blended into a brilliant combination. Here one sees the rarest artistry of the courts at its best."[56] Many fans agreed that the Rens earned "a most enviable record." In many cases, the Rens were capable of doubling a score, but chose to make a game out of each and every contest. The Rens won twenty-six consecutive games in January 1939 against teams in Ohio, Pennsylvania, West Virginia, Indiana, Illinois, and New York. In a game in Chicago against the Sheboygan Redskins, a white team, about 3,000 spectators attended despite a heavy snow.[57]

The Rens grew accustomed to long hours on the road, while they endured the racism prevalent in American society, never knowing what restaurants or hotels would welcome them. Traveling by bus in the Midwest, the Rens centralized their operation, according to John Isaacs. "If we were in Indiana, we stayed in Indianapolis and played all the surrounding towns," recalled Isaacs. In this way, the Rens frequently traveled 200–400 miles one way to night games. "We played every night of the week and twice on Sunday, with our losses usually on Mondays," stated Isaacs.[58] "Traveling down south, you eventually had to get used to the 'N' word," he recalled. "In my first experience in traveling with the Rens down south, I wasn't used to anyone calling me a nigger, simply because that was cause for immediate war, or a fight." And, the young ball player wasn't used to signs that said "white" and "colored." "The word 'colored' was always spelled backwards, as if we were so stupid we wouldn't even know how to spell it," explained Isaacs. In one incident in Knoxville, Tennessee, a white ticket man refused to sell Isaacs a train ticket when he went through the door labeled "white." Called a "nigger" and "boy," Isaacs was forced to go back out the "white" door and enter the dilapidated door labeled "colored" in order to purchase a ticket to Atlanta, Georgia.[59]

Traveling through the year's biggest blizzard in early February, the Rens stayed over in Pittsburgh on their way south.[60] Traveling secretary Eric Illidge stopped by the offices of the *Pittsburgh Courier* to brag about the team. When asked by sportswriter Wendell Smith about a possible game against the Globetrotters, Illidge stated, "We will play the Harlem Globetrotters anytime, anywhere. They've been going around telling folks how good they are, and how they will beat us, but we issued them a public challenge and they're afraid to answer it." Smith supported

Illidge in suggesting that "For the last time, Mr. Saperstein should answer this challenge or forever more hold his peace."[61] In mid-March, following their defeat of the Celtics at White City Stadium in Chicago and a record of 103 straight wins, the Globetrotters responded by calling for a game with the Rens. Yet, the inability of Bob Douglas and Abe Saperstein to agree on financial terms, as well as an acceptable date for a game, ended any challenge between the two teams to play.[62] Ironically, it was a third party that brought the two teams together on the court in Chicago.

Considered top professional teams, the Rens and Globetrotters were two of the twelve teams signed by white co-promoters Harry Hannin and Harry Wilson to play in the first-ever World Professional Basketball Tournament, March 26–28, 1939, at the Madison Street Armory in Chicago.[63] In their first contests, the Rens defeated the New York Yankees, 30–21, and the Globetrotters defeated Fort Wayne, 41–33. With the Globetrotters' defeat of the Chicago Harmons, 31–25, the Rens and the Globetrotters were scheduled to meet in a semifinal game.[64] Described as "a fancy passing and shooting team of Negroes," the Rens defeated the Globetrotters, 27–23. Approximately 7,000 spectators witnessed the Rens defeat of the Globetrotters, including Bob Douglas, who came in from New York to see the game. According to the *Chicago Daily Tribune*, "The Globetrotters were no match physically for the rangy, heavy Renaissance quintet." Nonetheless, both teams received several ovations from the crowd for their skill.[65] After defeating the Globetrotters in the semifinal round, the Rens faced Oshkosh for the championship title. Three thousand fans, mostly Oshkosh fans, witnessed the Rens' 34–25 win.[66] The defeat of Oshkosh fulfilled Douglas's lifelong dream of seeing his team at the top of the professional game. Following the championship game, Bob Douglas hosted a banquet for his team at the Hotel Grand where the team stayed during the tournament. At the end of the 1938–39 season the Rens sixteen-year record stood at 1583-239, with the Rens victorious in at least 100 games each season over the previous fourteen years.[67]

From 1939 to America's entry into World War II, the Rens maintained their reputation as one of the top professional barnstorming basketball teams despite the loss of players to retirement, new teams, and the war industry. Just as the 1939–40 basketball season was getting underway, Clarence "Fats" Jenkins retired from the Rens. Douglas named Eyre Saitch as captain.[68] In their seventeenth season, the Rens continued to barnstorm, and their games in Washington, DC, against the Heurich Brewers, a white team, attracted both black and white fans. Noted the *New York Amsterdam News*, "Fully one-half the crowd which packed the gymnasium was colored—and they sat where they pleased with no difficulty from the whites who attended the same show."[69] On the eve of World War II, professional basketball served as a catalyst for the integration of spectators, and eventually of teams.

The Renaissance team broke many attendance records in early 1940 as they gained wins against teams such as the SPHAs, Detroit Eagles, Akron Firestones, and the Dayton Pros, as well as all the National Basketball League (NBL) teams and most of the top teams in the East. In the South, the Rens played South Carolina State, Morehouse, Tuskegee, Xavier, Arkansas State, and Alabama State, followed by several games in Illinois.[70] In the quarterfinals of the second World Professional Basketball Tournament, the Rens led at the half 18–16, but the Globetrotters came out on top defeating the Rens, 37–36. A win over the Syracuse Reds put the Globetrotters in the final game against the Chicago Bruins. With the Rens cheering for them on the sidelines, the Globetrotters won the 1940 tournament by defeating the Chicago Bruins in a close game, 31–29.[71] The Rens had lost to the Globetrotters, but they lost little prestige in the basketball world.

Despite winning the professional championship without any comedy, the Globetrotters disappointed many black Americans. Bob Douglas referred to Abe Saperstein's team as "clowns," and though he applauded their basketball talent, he had little respect for their style of play, according to his brother James Douglas. Bob Douglas favored exhibitions of passing, but he refused to allow his Rens to be known as black comedians.[72] Still, the Rens wanted to make up for their loss and they looked forward to their next game with the Globetrotters. Though both owners continued to make efforts at several junctures, Douglas and Saperstein failed to arrange any games between their two teams.[73]

The fall 1940 season opener witnessed the SPHAs, 1939 ABL Champions, defeating the Rens by eight points, before a crowd of 2,500. In his first game as a Ren, Wilmeth Sidat-Singh, a graduate of Syracuse University, scored seven points, as did Pop Gates. In addition to Singh, Douglas signed Charlie Isles from the Detroit Big Five. Saitch, Cooper, Smith, Gates, and Bell rounded out the 1940–41 team.[74] Following a bitter loss to the New York Jewels of the American League, the Rens toured the Midwest, playing games in Pennsylvania, Ohio, Indiana, and New Jersey. On Christmas night, the Rens met the SPHAs at the Renaissance Ballroom.[75]

Over the next three months, the Rens defeated several teams in the Midwest, such as the Waukegan Ahapas, the Indianapolis Kautskys, and the Michigan All-Star Five.[76] The *Chicago Defender* announced the Rens, the Globetrotters, and the Toledo White Huts, an integrated team, as three of the sixteen teams invited to the 1941 World Professional Tournament in Chicago.[77] Tarzan Cooper rejoined the Rens for the tournament, and Bob Douglas came from New York City to watch his team. While the Globetrotters lost in the second round, the Rens qualified for the semifinals.[78] Losing a close game to Detroit, the Rens then defeated the Toledo White Huts, 57–42, for third place.[79]

In the summer of 1941, Bob Douglas was worried that the military draft would drain off his stars, but it was retirement and moving to other teams that threatened to change the face of the Rens.[80] Because of the war and uncertainty of availability, Douglas did not require contracts for his players. Wilmeth Sidat-Singh joined the military; John Isaacs, Dolly King, and Pop Gates worked at Grumman Aircraft on Long Island; and Tarzan Cooper put in time at a naval yard in Philadelphia.[81] Therefore, Douglas signed Hillary Brown, Sonny Boswell, and Duke Cumberland, all former Globetrotters, as well as newcomer, Sonny Woods of New York's Benjamin Franklin High School, for the 1941–42 season.[82] In mid-December, the Colored Intercollegiate Athletic Association (CIAA) banned all association teams from playing professional teams.[83] While the CIAA did not represent all black college teams, the Rens no longer traveled south. Instead, they appeared in several states in the East and Midwest, defeating such teams as the Chicago Bruins and the Club Star of Gary.[84]

At the end of February 1942, both Randy Dixon of the *Pittsburgh Courier* and Al White of the Associated Negro Press revealed the membership of several eastern teams. White stated that the nucleus of five of the top professional black basketball teams in the East—the Bears, Harlem Yankees, Paterson Crescents, Toppers, and Mets—was made up of a small cohort who played on different nights for different teams, using their own names. Dolly King, Tarzan Cooper, Pop Gates, John Isaacs, Bricktop Wright, and Wilmeth Sidat-Singh played for more than one team and their names had been seen on several different team rosters.[85] Free agency in professional basketball appeared to be thriving during World War II, and it negatively affected the strength of the Rens team.

With Isaacs, Gates, King, and Cooper all playing for Grumman, the Rens entered a young team in the 1942 World Professional Tournament. They earned a first-round win over the Northern Indiana Steelers, with Sonny Boswell setting the individual tournament scoring record of 32 points, but lost to Oshkosh, the eventual tournament champions, 44-38, in the second round.[86] Making up for this loss, the Rens won the Cleveland Invitational Tournament in mid-March by defeating Fort Wayne, East Liverpool, Ohio, and the Chicago Bruins.[87]

At the end of the 1941–42 basketball season, Sam Lacy stated that the Lichtman Bears management had "all but spoiled" the members of the Washington Bears team. The Bears players earned a minimum of $500 apiece, for a twenty-three-game season, and received bonuses of $50 each at the final banquet. The barnstorming Globetrotters and Rens played over one hundred games per season, and the players for the two teams averaged a monthly salary of $125, with an overall salary of $500. Referred to as "Basketball, Inc.," by Al White, revolving players put in time with several eastern teams, but they always scheduled the Washington Bears first.[88]

Following their defeat of the College All-Stars in the fall of 1942, the Rens looked forward to playing the New York Jewels of the NBL on Christmas night at the Renaissance Ballroom. Douglas had changed the lineup for the All-Star game and the midwestern tour because most of the veteran Rens could not get away from their defense jobs to travel with the team, adding Tom Seeley and John Williams to the squad.[89] The Rens attracted 2,000 fans for the game, due to holiday visitors to Harlem and servicemen on furlough, in their 54–34 defeat of the Jewels.[90]

Douglas entered his Rens, who had won an overwhelming number of their games during the season, in the 1943 World Professional Tournament in mid-March. Though it is unclear why, he gave the players permission to represent the Washington Bears in the first round. Shortly before the tournament, though, the top Renaissance players decided to make more money playing just for the Bears. Believing promoter Harry Hannin had encouraged Washington to "steal" the Rens club, Douglas withdrew his Rens from the tournament. With a line-up that included nearly all former Rens, the Washington Bears defeated Minneapolis, Dayton, and before 12,000 spectators, Oshkosh, 43–31, for the Professional Tournament title and $1,500 in prize money.[91]

Over the next two years, because of wartime travel restrictions, Douglas scheduled the Rens in the New York City area and planned for games every Sunday night at home. With a nucleus of Puggy Bell, Pop Gates, and Zach Clayton, former Rens often played as well. Douglas, "the fox of 138th Street," planned to present teams equal to previous Renaissance squads. "I've got a few surprises in store for the fans this year," stated Douglas about the 1943–44 season.[92] To that end, Douglas signed Hank DeZonie, who had played for the Harlem YMCA and Clark College. The Rens proceeded to maintain a winning streak at home, playing against teams such as the Celtics, Detroit Eagles, SPHAs, Brooklyn Jewels, New York Americans, and Union City Reds; that is, until the annual Thanksgiving night game against the SPHAs. An overflow crowd witnessed the Rens first loss at home in seven years, and to one of their rivals, the SPHAs, 57–52. Douglas delighted, however, in election night wins over the Celtics in 1943 and 1944, as well as his Rens 50–42 defeat of the Detroit Eagles in 1943. Coached by former Celtic Dutch Dehnert, the Eagles reportedly withered in the second half, while the Rens looked as if they were in mid-season form.[93]

Beyond their Sunday night games in Harlem, the Rens traveled to the Midwest each March to play in both the Cleveland Tournament and the World Professional Tournament in Chicago. Winning their third consecutive title in Cleveland in 1944, the Rens lost the following year to the Detroit Mansfields.[94] In Chicago, the Rens defeated the Detroit Eagles and Chase Brass, but lost in the semifinals to the Fort Wayne Zollners, and then to the Harlem Globetrotters in the consolation game.[95] Having played three times, the Globetrotters led the Rens with a 2-1 record. In 1945, the World Professional Tournament proved again to be a challenge for the Rens. After defeating the Indianapolis Stars and the Pittsburgh Raiders in the first two rounds, the Rens ended their tournament play when they lost in the semifinals to the Fort Wayne Zollners and also to the Chicago Gears in the consolation game.[96] Stated Bob Douglas, "We just aren't up there like we once were, because we haven't the ball players we had in other years. All of our top players have reached their peak, and many of them are now on the downgrade. Every time we get a new man who is any good we lose him to the Army."[97] What had affected the play of the Rens was not so much a decrease in talent, but player movement and constant changes in the team roster due to the war.

Despite continued player movement, Bob Douglas formed a competitive Renaissance team in the fall of 1945, with several veteran and two rookie players, Benny Garrett and Lenny Pearson.[98] November and December brought several wins for the Rens against teams such as the Jersey Reds, the SPHAs, the Brooklyn Jewels, the Celtics, and the Visitations.[99] The Rens stayed close to home and played fewer games, but with a 65-3 season record, Douglas was confident of a Rens victory at the 1946 World Professional Tournament in Chicago.[100] In their 82–39 defeat of Toledo, the Rens set a new tournament record for high scoring. An overconfident Rens team then lost to Oshkosh, 50–44, in the second round. Fans from the south side of Chicago, who had followed the Rens team for years, blamed the loss on late-hour celebrations by players on two consecutive nights.[101]

Seven months later, in October 1946, two former Rens, William "Dolly" King and William "Pop" Gates, signed contracts to play for two National Basketball League (NBL) teams: the Rochester Royals and the Buffalo Bisons (Tri-Cities Blackhawks), respectively, for the 1946–47 season. King's contract included a $7,000 salary and an additional $2,000 in bonuses while Gates's salary remained unannounced. Bob Douglas advocated integration and so gave his blessing to King and Gates.[102] In deference to the NBL, the newly organized Basketball Association of America (BAA) refused to include black players or teams in its league, rather it used the Rens and the Globetrotters in preliminary games to draw crowds for its games. For example, in a Rens game against the SPHAs in Philadelphia, 7,000 fans attended, while an average of 2,000 fans attended the Philadelphia Warriors games without the Rens.[103] Rick Hurt of People's Voice noted, "The lily-white BAA will gladly use the Globetrotters or the Rens to draw in the crowds, but draws a rigid line on Negro players or Negro teams playing in the league."[104] Despite the obvious exploitation, Bob Douglas scheduled his Rens in preliminary games, believing the BAA would eventually admit black players or teams.

With the addition of Nathaniel "Sweetwater" Clifton, Hillary Brown of Chicago, and Jim Usry of Atlantic City, Douglas believed his 1946–47 team would be the most versatile Rens team since the mid-1930s.[105] Competition for top players continued between Bob Douglas, Abe Saperstein, and other black professional basketball team owners. In late December, Abe Saperstein filed an injunction to restrain Nathaniel "Sweetwater" Clifton from playing basketball with any team other than the Globetrotters, stating that Clifton had signed a contract with the Globetrotter organization. Three weeks later though, Judge Lloyd Church denied Saperstein's petition for an injunction. Evidently, Clifton had signed contracts with at least four teams, as he also played games with both Dayton and Detroit.[106]

A month earlier, a large crowd of former Harlemites, believing the Rens could not be beat, had watched their team lose two games, 47–43 and 46–25, to the integrated Red Devils, led by Jackie Robinson at the Olympic Auditorium in Los Angeles. Robinson had just completed his first season with the Montreal Royals baseball team. For the first and only time in their history, the Rens had flown across the country to play two games. The Rens blamed their poor play on the long plane flight, which arrived several hours late.[107] Jack Duddy, the white owner of the Red Devils hoped for a west coast franchise in the NBL for his team, and Douglas sought league affiliation for the Rens as well. Perhaps national exposure of both teams could demonstrate the high level of play desired by the NBL.[108] The one benefit of the two losses to the Red Devils, however, was the addition four months later of Red Devil player, George Crowe, a former 6'4" University of Indiana star, to the Rens line-up. Douglas also signed Bill Brown, who had played for the Washington Bears, to compensate for the loss of Clifton and Bob Powell.[109]

Soon, fan attention turned to the Rens' game against the SPHAs at Madison Square Garden, in the first game of a doubleheader, with the BAA Knickerbockers against Providence in the second game. Such a contest was rare for Madison Square Garden, as black teams had been banned from the venue. Leading up to the March 26 contest, the SPHAs and Rens had split eight games, but in this much-publicized preliminary game, the Rens defeated the SPHAs, 49–35.[110] With this significant victory, Douglas and his Rens looked forward to the annual World Professional Tournament in Chicago. On the way to Chicago, the Rens displayed brilliant shooting in their defeat of the Oshkosh All-Stars, in Oshkosh, giving the Rens a 96-13 season record. Before 10,000 fans, however, Toledo upset the Rens, 62–59, in a close contest, eliminating them from the tournament.[111]

In the fall of 1947, BAA league owners met in Philadelphia to discuss the possible admission of the Rens into the league. With the support of his friend and New York Knickerbocker coach, Joe Lapchick, Douglas drove to Philadelphia and was invited to sit in on the discussion. Though Douglas felt confident that his Rens were in, a majority of the owners voted no. Lapchick threatened to quit the BAA, but with Douglas's encouragement he remained, believing he could be a catalyst for change in bringing down the color barrier.[112]

A disappointed Douglas returned to New York to prepare his Rens for another season on the road. Douglas re-signed Dolly King and Pop Gates, the only two blacks in the NBL, after they received releases from Rochester and Tri-Cities, respectively.[113] Throughout November and December, the Rens earned several wins and a twenty-two-game winning streak, playing to capacity crowds while barnstorming in the Midwest. Returning to the Renaissance Ballroom on Christmas night, the Rens defeated the Washington Bears, 53–37, before a sold-out crowd.[114]

Despite the integration of a few ABL teams, black teams such as the Rens and Manhattan Nationals faced problems with Ned Irish in finding arenas in which to play. Irish, Madison Square Garden executive vice president and founder of the BAA Knickerbockers, refused to allow some of the top pro white teams in the NBL such as the Indianapolis Kautskys, Toledo Jeeps, Syracuse, and Oshkosh, to play black teams in Harlem. These teams had working agreements with his BAA, which had an "anti-Negro" rule. Irish maintained a monopoly on New York basketball, and he sought to eliminate any attempt by black sport promoters to run a basketball arena in Harlem by disallowing top white teams from playing there. Black teams, such as the Rens, were forced to stay on the road to survive, preventing the fans in the New York area from seeing them play.[115] Nonetheless, the Rens served as one of eight teams in the tenth World Professional Tournament, held April 8–11, 1948. With a 110-10 record going into the tournament, the Rens beat Bridgeport in the first round and, led by Sweetwater Clifton, Tri-Cities in the second round. In the finals, George Mikan scored 40 points to lead his Lakers to victory over the Rens, 75–71, despite Sweetwater Clifton's 24 points.[116]

In the fall of 1948, while Abe Saperstein signed Sweetwater Clifton for $10,000, the highest salary ever paid to a Globetrotter, Bob Douglas turned the Renaissance basketball team over to Eric Illidge, after managing the team for twenty-five years. Though Douglas maintained ownership, Illidge leased the team and ran it on his own.[117] Under Illidge, the Rens began their twenty-sixth season with three notable and prophetic wins. Six hundred fans watched the Rens defeat the SPHAs, 75–67, on November's election night.[118] In mid-November the Rens defeated a new professional team, the Toledo Collegians, in Dayton, Ohio. A week later, only 366 fans came out for the Rens' game against the Detroit Vagabond Kings in Dayton. The Rens won by six points in a close game, the second win for the Rens in Dayton that season. By then Detroit had lost many league games in the NBL. By early December, the Rens had a 12-2 record, with both losses to the Anderson Indiana Duffy Packers.[119]

On Friday, December 17, history was made when Ike Duffy, NBL president, admitted the Rens to the league. Though the Toledo Jim White Chevrolets and Chicago Studebakers broke the color barrier by adding black players in 1942, the Rens served as the first all-black team in an organized league, accepting an offer to represent Dayton, after having won 2,078 games as the New York Rens.[120] The Rens replaced the Detroit Vagabond Kings, who reportedly withdrew because of poor attendance and an $11,000 debt. They also adopted Detroit's 2-17 record and their schedule. In addition to league play, the Rens continued an extensive traveling schedule. Admittance of the Rens into the NBL was significant. "For years, the Negro cagers have traveled the country, beating the best in the various pro leagues, but were never admitted to membership," stated *Pittsburgh Courier* sportswriter Wendell Smith. "But times insist on changing and now they are in—a Negro team representing a city of white and colored people, which is unique if nothing else." Smith believed the Rens had a tough road ahead, as the team was not as strong as it once had been. But, like Douglas, Smith had great visions for the future. He knew a good performance in the league could mean a successful future for other black players.[121]

On Sunday, December 19, the Dayton Rens began their new journey, losing to the Anderson Packers, 83–61, in their first league game. The Rens used only six players against Anderson, as Jim Usry was in the hospital for an operation, and substitute players failed to arrive in time. With two new players, John Brown and Herb Beasley, they won their first NBL game, 53–50 in overtime, against Hammond Indiana, on December 23 in Indiana.[122] The day after Christmas, the Dayton Rens lost to Tri-Cities, while a team called the New York Rens won against the Chicago Stags in an exhibition game in Chicago. Evidently, previous commitments split the team in two, one against Tri-Cities and the other against Chicago. The following night, Oshkosh beat the disabled, but reassembled, Dayton Rens by 11 points in Milwaukee.[123]

Through the second week of January 1949, the Dayton Rens ranked at the bottom of the NBL with a 4-20 record. February and March found them attempting to climb the league ladder with little success. Because Dayton was unable to obtain a gymnasium for games as frequently as needed, home games were played in various locations.[124] The Dayton Rens finished the NBL season in last place with a 16-43 record (14-26 without the Detroit record), the worst ever for a Renaissance team. Financially the team went under, and within two months, the NBL revoked the Rens contract.[125] Competition in the NBL had proven much tougher than Eric Illidge and Bob Douglas had expected. With an increasing number of black players going to mostly white teams, Douglas realized he could no longer compete financially with the top white teams.

On May 25, 1949, sixty-six-year-old Bob Douglas shocked the professional black basketball world, and leased his Renaissance team to his greatest competitor, Abe Saperstein. Over the next two years, the Rens, with all new players, served as the undercard, or "B" team, to two touring Globetrotters teams. Two years later, however, Douglas brought his Rens back to New York, and while retaining ownership of the team name asked Johnnie Walker, manager of the amateur "Snookies and Sugar Bowl Five," and Pete Petroupolos, head of Greater New York Sports Promotions, to rebuild the Rens and continue their tradition. After a year of rebuilding, Walker hoped for a successful one-hundred-game season for the team, now called the Original Renaissance Five.[126] This rebuilt Rens team barnstormed, mainly in the Northeast, until the mid-1950s, but with the integration of the National Basketball League their prestige as a top team remained in the past.[127] Like the Negro Leagues, the very ideal that Bob Douglas strove for, the elimination of the color line, killed the team he had created and dedicated his life to for over a quarter of a century.

The legacy left by the Bob Douglas and the New York Renaissance Five remains enormous. In 1963, the Naismith Memorial Hall of Fame enshrined the Renaissance team, followed by Bob Douglas in 1972, Charles "Tarzan" Cooper in 1977, and William "Pop" Gates in 1989 and John Isaacs in 2015.[128] Players such as Clarence "Fats" Jenkins should surely be considered in the near future. While the Rens made many contributions to the professional game, the greatest was in race relations. By breaking down stereotypes, the Rens demonstrated that blacks and whites could compete equally on the basketball court and also work together for a common goal. The New York Renaissance Five, among other black teams, laid the foundation and paid the price for the black and foreign athletes now playing in the National Basketball Association. Despite the numerous challenges they faced, with hard work and perseverance, Bob Douglas and his New York Renaissance Five found success on the basketball court.

3

The Philadelphia Tribune Newsgirls

African American Women's Basketball at Its Best

J. Thomas Jable

Considered the greatest African American women's basketball team of all time by the leading African American newspapers, the Philadelphia Tribune Girls' Basketball team dominated play during its eleven years of existence. From 1931 to 1942, the Newsgirls, as they were commonly called, compiled a sparkling record, rarely losing to African American teams, which enabled them to claim the mythical National Colored Girls Basketball Championship in each year of their existence.

The Newsgirls' unparalleled achievements give rise to a number of important questions: How and why were the Newsgirls created? Why and how did a newspaper, the *Philadelphia Tribune,* organize and support the team? What was its formula for producing and maintaining the Newsgirls' dynasty and championship teams for more than a decade? Those are some of the questions that this essay attempts to answer. In that no legitimate mechanism existed to determine a national championship, such as a national tournament or national rankings, championships, though mythical, were generally based on a team's won-lost record and the caliber of its opponents. There seemed to be widespread acceptance of this process, giving credibility to teams that proclaimed and displayed a championship moniker.

A multitude of interacting led to the creation of the Newsgirls. Philadelphia's African American population increased enormously following World War I as a result of the Great Migration. The number of African Americans residing in Philadelphia rose from 84,459 in 1910 to 219,599 by 1930. The black migrants came mostly from Virginia, Maryland, and North Carolina and settled in African American neighborhoods in south and north Philadelphia and Germantown. Employment opportunities for most newcomers were limited to menial jobs in which males worked as day laborers and females did housekeeping chores.[1] As southern blacks poured into Philadelphia's African American communities, they not only taxed an already acute housing shortage, but they also strained the city's resources and increased the need for expanded social services.

One institution that was instrumental in helping newcomers, as well as resident blacks, adjust to urban life was the Colored YM and YWCA. These institutions provided educational programs and recreational activities for African Americans of all ages, but their emphasis on mental, physical, and spiritual development was directed primarily toward youth. The Colored YWCA offered programs in the industrial and domestic arts for young women. Classes in sewing, cooking, crocheting, knitting, and millinery were useful to young women and girls not only for potential employment opportunities, but also for their own homemaking edification. In some cases the Colored YM-YWs helped their members secure employment. These institutions also provided recreational activities, such as swimming, basketball, and volleyball for enjoyment purposes as well as for developing their members' physical attributes. In a large number of Colored Ys, basketball became the featured sport.[2]

The growing popularity of basketball during the 1920s led YM-YWCAs to organize basketball teams for competitive play against teams from sister Ys and community organizations. The situation in Philadelphia was unique in that an African American newspaper, the *Philadelphia Tribune,* organized women's and men's basketball teams. Serving Philadelphia's black community, the *Tribune* was the primary messenger to keep African Americans abreast of current economic, political, and social issues, particularly race relations, civil rights, and economic opportunities. As the woes of the Depression spread across America, Philadelphians began to suffer. Survival seemed like the only priority, and the *Tribune* was not exempt. It tapped into sport and promoted basketball to increase its circulation and to generate revenue. Its several basketball teams, particularly the Newsgirls, were highly successful and contributed to the newspaper's sustenance. This essay examines the role of the Philadelphia Tribune Women's Basketball team in the history of women's and African American sport. An ancillary purpose is to examine the team's impact on Philadelphia's African American community.

Newsgirls' Precursors: Quick Steppers and Hornets

In 1928 Inez "Pat" Patterson, swimming instructor at the Catherine Street Colored YWCA and physical education major at Temple University, organized a girls' basketball team at the Y. The girls adopted the name "Quick Steppers," possibly because they were considered "the fastest colored girls court team in the East." With only one season under their belt, the seventeen-year-old Patterson predicted that the Quick Steppers 1929–30 campaign "should place basketball on the highest pinnacle ever reached in this city." Patterson built her team from among Y members and such basketball stalwarts as Rose Wilson, known as "poison" because of her effective play at forward with great speed, and Lillian Cooper, both of whom migrated to Philadelphia from Virginia after leading their Hampton High School team to the state championship. Joining this duo were Helen Laws, a fast forward from Germantown; Dorothy Lewis, another fast forward and all-around athlete; and Anna Mae Coley, a brilliant center from the local McCoach Playground team. The team's sparkplug was Patterson herself, a guard "who is a whiz with the basketball." All of them played basketball on the high school level.[3]

The Quick Steppers worked hard in preparing for the 1929–30 season, practicing against boys' teams. Although they were prudent and conservative during their first year of operation, losing just two games, they planned to "run wild" in their second season because they believed they had "the material and ability to make any girls team in or out of town take notice." Paced by Wilson, considered the fastest girl in basketball, Laws, and Patterson, the Quick Steppers compiled an 11-1 record in 1929–30, losing only to Dunmore Central of Scranton, purported white champions of Pennsylvania. Their sterling record gave them a rematch with Dunmore and a shot at the Pennsylvania state championship. Dunmore agreed to the rematch because its star player, Nora Thompson, had not played in the first encounter between these two teams. Thompson's presence, however, did not matter, as the Quick Steppers walked away with the victory and "established themselves as one of the greatest castes [*sic*] of feminine basketeers that ever aimed the big oval at the rim." This victory enabled them to lay claim to the Eastern if not national colored women's basketball title.[4]

The following season the Quick Steppers battled the Hornets of the Germantown Colored YWCA for the city championship. The Quick Steppers opened the season at Scranton against the Anthracite A.C., a white team. The Hornets, in the meantime, boasted a roster headed by the great Ora Mae Washington and Lula Ballard, both of whom had just returned from Chicago after playing for the Savoy Colts of that city. Both were also whizzes on the tennis court. Ballard at age eighteen won the Colored Singles Tennis title in 1927 and 1928 before Washington, ten years her senior, wrested it from her in 1929 and held and defended it another seven times. On the basketball court, too, Washington had no equal. A rugged, competitive, and highly talented athlete, Washington, according to her nephew, James Bernard Childs, eschewed practice, but delivered when it counted, leading the Hornets and later the Newsgirls to multiple national titles. Then, as the 1930–31 season progressed, Helen Laws switched colors and joined the Germantown squad, a common practice among professional and semiprofessional basketball players of this era.[5] With no established organizational structure to monitor play, enforce rules, and adopt and administer policies dealing with player contracts and team stability, a player was virtually free at any time to offer services to any team that wanted her.

In some cases, she might want to join her close companions on another team, while in others, she might abandon one team for a better financial arrangement offered by another. Laws's motives for jumping to the Hornets is not known.

The Hornets, coached by Joe Rainey, former Lincoln University track coach, was anxious to snatch the city title away from the Quick Steppers and lay claim to a national crown. The opportunity came in February 1931, when the Hornets defeated the Quick Steppers twice in two weeks. In winning the second contest, 23–14, the Hornets outscored their opponents by 13 to 4 in the second half after settling for a 10-all tie at halftime. The Hornets shut down the Quick Steppers from the field in the second half allowing them just four free throws. Washington's 14 points equaled the total output of the Quick Steppers, while newcomer Laws chipped in with 5 points. The victory improved the Hornets record to 12-1.[6]

In stripping the Steppers of the Eastern crown, the Hornets now set out to capture the national title. Defeating all comers in and around Philadelphia as well as in New York, Baltimore, and Washington and running its record to 21-1, the stage was set to play for the National Negro Women's Basketball Championship. To earn that title the Hornets would have to beat the Rankin Club of Pittsburgh, which had not lost a game in three years. Crossing the snow-covered Allegheny Mountains, the Hornets journeyed to Pittsburgh and defeated Rankin, 23–19. Ora Washington dominated play, scoring 17 of her team's points and giving the Hornets a legitimate claim to the national title. Washington's prowess on the basketball floor surfaced that year as she scored over 200 points in leading her team to a 23-1 record.[7]

Newsgirls Created

Just as the Hornets were laying claim to the 1931 championship, the *Philadelphia Tribune,* a weekly African American newspaper, decided to organize a women's basketball team. A long advocate of sports with a voluminous sports page, the *Tribune* had been covering girls' and women's sports for at least a decade. Since the fall of 1929, the newspaper had been sponsoring a men's team, commonly hailed as the Tribune Big 5. The brain child of Otto Briggs, former Hilldale baseball star and *Tribune* circulation manager; Randy Dixon, *Tribune* sports editor; and Joseph H. Rainey, Lincoln University track coach and *Tribune* sports writer, the Big 5 inaugurated play on December 7, 1929, and played competitively against prominent black teams including the Harlem Renaissance. Briggs's effort to promote and bring high-caliber basketball to Philadelphia was reflected in a November 1931 *Tribune* column that praised the success of last year's Big 5. Pleased and appreciative of local fan support, Briggs decided that "depression or no depression, he was going to give the fans of Philadelphia and West Chester, who gave him real support, another first-class team."[8]

The success of the Tribune Big 5 also led local basketball fans to clamor for a girls' team. Among them was Selena "Teeny" Bailey, who expressed her desire to see a girls' team in a letter to the *Tribune* editor: "I do hope that there will come a time when the TRIBUNE will have a Girls Tribune Five. There are quite a few girls interested, too. Will that time come?" It did in the fall of 1931 when Briggs, taking his cue from local fandom, hired Inez Patterson, swimming director at the Catherine Street YWCA and "foremost girl athlete in the city," to select players for the team and to tutor them. Most of the players she chose played for her Quick Steppers team, namely Ruth Lockley, Ann Carrington, Rose Wilson, Louise Hall, Gladys Walker, and Louise "Dick" Hill.[9]

The Tribune Girls, or Newsgirls as they were popularly known, was a misnomer because most of the players were women in their twenties and thirties. Quasi-professional female basketball players "earned small salaries or worked at other jobs to make ends meet."[10] During this period, black women worked mostly as maids, housekeepers, or servants. Ora Washington, for instance, is listed as a waitress for a private family and a servant to the head of household in the 1920 census.[11]

The Newsgirls made their debut on November 13, 1931, in a preliminary tilt before the Big 5's season opener, defeating Bryn Mawr, 59–8, behind the hot shooting of Rose Wilson and Dickie Hill. By Christmas the Newsgirls had rung up six straight victories, the most notable coming over the Lampeter, Pennsylvania, white squad, 43–30. Gladys "Twig" Walker and Wilson tossed in 15 and 13 points, respectively, while Inez Patterson "led a passing attack that practically dazed their opponents." Then, in January they won two games on the same day, whipping the newly organized Argonne Girls, 31–2, and Howard Hi of Wilmington, 26–4, before bowing to Trenton, 16–14.[12]

The pinnacle of the 1931–32 season came in the best of five series with the Germantown Hornets, 1931 National Colored Champions. The Hornets got the jump on the Newsgirls, winning the first encounter by a 20–15 score. With Germantown nursing a 2–1 lead at intermission, most of the scoring came in the second half as Ora Washington led the Hornets with 12 points and Helen Laws dropped in 4. Rose Wilson had 10 points for the Tribune squad in a losing effort. Following their loss to the Hornets, the Newsgirls went on a victory spree, winning four games in four days, avenging an earlier loss to Trenton and defeating the Anthracite Girls of Scranton, a white team, and the Bridgeton, New Jersey, Nesco Comets twice.[13]

To get his team ready for its second contest against the Hornets, Otto Briggs hired Emanuel "Shorty" Chappelle, Tribune Big 5 player, to coach the Newsgirls. Under Chappelle's tutelage, the Tribune girls displayed precision passing, slick floor work, and sharp shooting that enabled them to tie the series with a 33–24 victory. Dick Hill of the Newsgirls led all scorers with 12 points, while Washington was close behind, tossing in 10 for the losers, but it was Patterson's play in the third quarter that brought the crowd to its feet with her brilliant passing along with a sensational shot that extended the Newsgirls' lead to 23–14 after three quarters. Washington's play and shooting ignited a late Hornet rally that closed the gap to two points, but then Patterson and Hill hit three straight baskets to ensure the victory. The Newsgirls triumph snapped the Hornets forty-five-game winning streak compiled over the past two years.[14]

The third contest saw the Hornets forge ahead, 2–1, in the five-game series. Laws and Washington played spectacularly for Germantown. Laws's shots "were revelations. Three were one-handed shots made in full flight, while the other was a shot from mid-floor. All dropped clean as whistles." Washington, however, sealed the victory during the closing minutes "when she twice executed bulls-eyes on difficult chances." The Newsgirls came back to win the fourth game, 33–27, behind the sharp shooting of Patterson (13 points) and Hill (11 points), knotting the series at two wins apiece and setting the stage for a fifth and deciding game for the national championship.[15]

The fifth and final game was "the most thrill-saturated game played here this season, barring none," wrote Randy Dixon, sports editor of the *Tribune*. For three quarters, the Tribune girls outplayed and out-hustled the Hornets. "Not one person in the hall gave a tinker's damn for the Hornets chances," continued Dixon. "Had it not been for the masterful exhibition of Ora Washington, the Hornets would have been slaughtered." The Newsgirls took a 20–13 lead into the fourth quarter, but then "the fireworks exploded." After the Hornets' fleet forward, Helen Laws, hit a shot from the side, Washington "let go a humdinger from way back beyond the center of the court." Dixon described it as "an awe provoking effort [that] . . . gave the Hornets the necessary impetus to inaugurate a rally." Then after shaking off two defendants, she hit a "heart-twistor [*sic*]" closing the deficit to one point. Louise Penn and Laws connected on two uncanny shots to put the Hornets out in front, 23–20 with less than a minute to play. But with fifteen seconds remaining, Patterson hit a field goal and Helen "Midge" Davis followed with a clutch free throw in the closing seconds, knotting the score at 23 and sending the game into overtime. In the extra stanza, Rose Wilson and Dick Hill hit two shots apiece giving the 31–23 victory and the National Colored Championship title to the Newsgirls. The final whistle brought instant mayhem, for "it was fully ten minutes before order could be restored. The cash customers fanned to fever heat by the ardor and closeness of combat gave outlet to all kinds of riotous impulses," Dixon exclaimed. "They stood on chairs and hollered. Others hoisted members of the winning team upon their shoulders and paraded them around the hall. They jigged and danced and readers, believe me, they were justified. It was just that kind of a game." The victory improved the Newsgirls' season record to 31-5 to go along with their newly christened national colored championship banner they could now proudly display.[16]

Ora Washington Joins Newsgirls

Newsgirls coach "Shorty" Chappelle sounded an optimistic note as he prepared his team for the 1932–33 season. Pleased with the turnout of several newcomers along with many old stars including captain Inez Patterson, Chappelle predicted that the Tribune girls would "make new records and set new standards for women's basketball in the Eastern U.S." while challenging for the "world title." His confidence received an astronomical boost three weeks later when thirty-three-year-old Ora Washington, hailed as "the greatest individual performer in the girls ranks," left the Hornets to sign on with his squad. It is not clear whether Briggs orchestrated a coup in signing her, or if she voluntarily jumped ship to play with the reigning champs. Whatever the case, the Hornets lost its star player who last season averaged 6 field goals and 15 points per game. Unable to fill the void created by Washington's departure, the Hornets would never again play at the championship level. But the Hornets' loss was the Newsgirls' gain, and Chappelle planned to move Washington from center to guard in order to team her up with Patterson, dubbed the second-greatest female basketball player next to Washington.[17]

The Newsgirls opened the 1932–33 season at the Catherine Street Colored YWCA on Thanksgiving night. The big question was how well Washington and Patterson would play together. The answer came quickly as both stars scored at will—Washington tallied 9 points, while Patterson finished with 5 as the Tribune ladies defeated the Bridgeton, New Jersey, Omega Girls 32–16. After racking up several lopsided wins in December and in early January 1933 that led to a string of victories, the Tribune girls faced stiff challenges in upcoming games against the St. Nicholas Girls of Harlem led by tennis star Isadore Channels and Blanche Winston and against the Leavittsburg, Ohio A.C., a white team that compiled a 123-7 record since its inception three years earlier.[18]

Business manager Otto Briggs welcomed the challenges because he wanted the Tribune girls to become undisputed national and world champions. Rising to the occasion, the Newsgirls played their best game of the year in routing St. Nicholas, 30–5, for their fifteenth straight victory. Following their eleventh consecutive win over the white Lampeter club near Lancaster, Pennsylvania, a couple weeks earlier, the *Pittsburgh Courier,* alluding to the Harlem Rens great men's team, called the Newsgirls "a Renaissance in Girls basketball." Although the Tribune femmes' claim to the 1932 mythical national championship had some standing among African American teams, it had little validity in nationwide basketball circles. A case in point was their 34–28 loss at home to Leavittsburg in the first of a three-game set that the *Tribune* advertised as being for the "world's title." Led by their captain, Susie Sponseller, who had been compared favorably with Babe Didrikson, the Ohioans handed the Newsgirls their second defeat of the season. Five days earlier, the Tribune club, playing girls' rules, which hampered their style of play with no shooting guards or center jump, suffered its initial defeat at the hands of the Easton, Pennsylvania, Pals. Then in late February, Briggs took his girls' squad to Ohio where it lost all three games on this road trip—two to Leavittsburg and the other to Pat Young Service Girls at Cleveland. In the Leavittsburg matches, Sponseller, once again, destroyed the Newsgirls, scoring 26 and 23 points in the two contests.[19]

Following their winless road trip, the Newsgirls returned home and began another winning streak, finishing the 1932–33 season without another loss. Their first encounter back at home was a three-game series with the Colonial Maids, Philadelphia's white champions, for the city's women's basketball title. The Newsies won the first two games behind the stellar play of Washington and Rose Wilson. Afterward, Otto Briggs wasted little time in claiming the city championship for his Newsgirls. The Tribune ladies then went on to pin defeats on the St. Nicolas Girls at Harlem, the Honesdale, Pennsylvania, white team, and the Belmar, New Jersey, Specials, whom they defeated twice. Their first victory over Belmar was the Specials first loss on their home floor, and the second victory over them pushed the Newsgirls 1932–33 record to 30-6. Most of the games were played before packed houses. The Honesdale game drew a reported 1,500 fans, while at Asbury Park where the Tribune's men's and women's teams played a doubleheader, the capacity crowd spilled onto the court, causing officials to rope off a segment and thus reducing the size of the playing area.[20]

Patterson's Departure and Regional Tours Bring National Recognition

Less than three weeks before the Newsgirls opened the 1933–34 season, Inez Patterson accepted a position at the Orange, New Jersey, YWCA. In addition to her duties at the Orange Y, she was elected chair of the New Jersey Basketball League of the Council of YWCAs. Patterson's departure created a vacuum that would be difficult, if not impossible, to fill. Not only was she a versatile athlete with superb basketball skills, but she was also an exceptional leader on and off the court. Initially counting on Patterson to fortify the Newsgirls' play on both offense and defense, coach "Shorty" Chappelle had high expectations of reaching a higher plane this season, one of which was defeating last year's nemesis, the Leavittsburg, Ohio, team led by Susie Sponseller. Even though her vocation's calling took her away from Philadelphia, Patterson continued to maintain a close relationship with the Newsgirls from her new post in New Jersey.[21]

The Newsgirls moved ahead without Patterson, opening the season with a traditional Thanksgiving night game followed by a dance. The game-dance format, billed as a full evening of entertainment, was a common practice during the Depression to induce more spectators to attend basketball games. The season opener attracted a large crowd and Otto Briggs, the engaging entrepreneur and promoter that he was, added an additional feature. To show the public his appreciation for its support of the Newsgirls, Briggs offered everyone who attended the game a free ticket to his new roller-skating rink, Palais Royal Deluxe, proclaimed the "finest colored rink in the East." Briggs's gesture not only enhanced the Newsgirls' image and his benevolence among the public, but it also increased the public's awareness of his new enterprise. To promote the roller rink even more, Briggs scheduled the Christmas night game against the New York Girls, white champions of New York, at his Palais Royal Deluxe. He advertised the event as a full night of pleasure for 35 cents (25 cents for children). Fans could see the game and enjoy roller skating before and after the contest.[22]

Several weeks prior to playing at the roller-skating rink, the Tribgirls played an exhibition game against the Hornet All-Stars, a team comprised of original Hornet players—Ora Washington, Ruth Lockley, Lillian Fountaine, and Evelyn Mann temporarily defected from the Newsgirls. To the surprise of most fans, the All-Stars could not find the hoop in the early going and trailed 8–3 at the half. But they rallied in the second stanza, tying the score at 11 with thirty seconds to go. Then in the waning seconds, Helen "Midge" Davis hit a shot that "cut the cords at exactly the same second the timekeeper's whistle sounded" to eke out a 13–11 victory for the Tribs. Davis's timely basket was very reminiscent of her clutch free throw that sent game five of the 1932 Hornets-Tribune championship series into overtime. With Washington and the other defectors back in the Tribune's fold, the Newsies whipped the Woodbury, New Jersey, Darts, 38–18, before a standing-room-only crowd at West Chester. Playing only in the second half, Washington poured in 14 points, repeatedly bringing the crowd to its feet with her accurate shooting. The captain did not have to leave the bench for the next game, a 23–5 Tribs's triumph over the Princeton Rhythm Girls. The Newsgirls lost just one game in two years to an African American team, and since their inception in 1931, they won 97 of 109 games.[23]

The Tribune Girls' sterling record prompted the Allied Social Clubs of the East to hold a "monster Testimonial Dance and Vaudeville Show" in their honor on February 9, 1934. The organizers "promoting this monster testimonial . . . will spare no pains in making this affair one of the outstanding affairs of the season. All bona fide clubs that have contributed news to the *Philadelphia Tribune* and those known to the Allied Clubs of the East are invited to attend." The organizing committee lined up two bands—Charlie Gaines and his WCAU Orchestra and

Syl Nash and his Rhythmic Maniacs—to play. Subfreezing February temperatures, however, put a chill on the Tribs's testimonial. Although frigid weather kept most of the allied club representatives at home, a number of local dignitaries and Newsgirls' supporters attended the affair in spite of the cold spell. All of the players, except Evelyn Mann who was ill, braved the zero degree temperature to attend. "All of the champs were prettily gowned. Miss Ora Washington looked well in pink silk. . . . Miss Rose Wilson was stunning in baby blue lace. . . . Red moire was Miss Helen Davis' most becoming choice, . . . while Miss Ruth Lockley was beautiful in black chiffon trimmed in silver."[24]

With the testimonial behind them, the Tribune Girls looked forward to their first southern tour that would take them to North Carolina and Virginia in March. In tuning up for their southern trek, the Newsies scheduled games with Inez Patterson's new Quick Steppers, the Anthracite Girls, white champions of Pennsylvania's coal region, and teams from Washington and Baltimore. *Tribune* sportswriter W. Ardee's pregame analysis gave the Quick Steppers a better than even chance of beating the Newsgirls because Patterson, "who once labored under the *Tribune* banners, has harnessed a select cast of femme individuals who rate as being capable of toppling the heretofore all powerful news-marms from their throne." But the Newsgirls carried the day until they met the Baltimore Y team in late February. The Marylanders pinned a 12–11 loss on the Tribgirls, snapping their long winning streak with a controversial field goal at the final whistle. Some observers believed the whistle blew before the final shot was taken, while others thought that the ball hit a ceiling rafter before descending into the hoop. Whatever the case, it did not matter as the officials counted the Baltimore basket, allowing the Marylanders to take home the victory.[25]

The Newsgirls returned to their winning ways on their trek to Virginia and North Carolina. Prior to defeating Fayetteville State and the Lynchburg, Virginia, YWCA, the Tribune Girls swept a three-game set from Bennett College of Greensboro, North Carolina, the undefeated 1934 collegiate champions. In front of 1,000 fans at the Sportsarena in downtown Greensboro where colored teams seldom played, the Newsgirls handed the collegians their first loss. "Ora [Washington] broke loose in the waning moments to rack up goals at crucial stages." She tallied 13 points to lead the Newsies past Bennett, 31–22, while leaving her mark on the college players, most notably Lucille Townsend, the Bennett center. On jump balls, Washington would hit Townsend in the stomach. The collegian complained to the referee about Washington's tactics and later revealed that "he caught her when she hit me one time . . . I doubled over and went down." Townsend described her opponent as the "worst ruffian you ever wanted to see." She also recalled several Tribune players sipping corn liquor at halftime which she observed as both teams shared the same locker room during intermission.[26] Those impressions of the Newsgirls and Washington were a far cry from the idealized versions of them reported in the black press.

For the second game, the two teams changed the venue, playing the contest at High Point, North Carolina, before a packed high school gymnasium. In a much closer encounter, the Newsgirls came away with an 18–13 victory. In this nip-and-tuck contest, the collegians showed their superiority early on, holding the Tribs to one point in the first quarter and carrying a 4–3 lead into intermission. It was 9–all at the end of the third quarter; then in the final frame, the lead changed hands several times. Bennett's Vic Jackson scored 7 of her team's 13 points, while Washington could make only two. Then in the last three minutes the Newsgirls made some "almost supernatural shots . . . [to] put the game on ice." At that point, Dick Hill "sank impossible shots in the basket terminating the greatest exhibition ever staged in North Carolina." The teams returned to Greensboro for the third tilt as fans within a one-hundred-mile radius of the city packed the Bennett College gymnasium "to marvel at a great duel between two sharpshooters[,] Dick Hill of the Newsies and Vic Jackson of the home horde." Hill outshot Jackson to bring home a 31–20 victory for the Newsgirls.[27] This victorious southern tour brought widespread national recognition of the Tribune Girls as a championship-caliber basketball team.

Upon returning to Philadelphia, the Newsgirls found no rest for the weary. Just a week after returning from North Carolina, the Tribgirls set out for Ohio in late March to tackle their old nemesis, Susie Sponseller, now playing for the McKenzie Tire Girls. Having traveled several thousand miles in three weeks, the Newsies faced fatigue and went 2 and 3 on this western trip. Susie Sponseller's McKenzie Tire team defeated the Tribs 43–40 in a hard-fought contest in Youngstown and again several days later in Warren, Ohio, 37–31. In between the two McKenzie contests, the Tribune Girls found some solace in defeating the Scherr Tailor Girls with Sponseller also in their line-up, 22–19. On the last day of the tour the Tribs played two games in one day, winning the afternoon contest against the Riggs LeMar Girls at Akron before bowing to the 12th Ward Dems in Cleveland that evening.[28]

As the calendar turned to April, the Newsgirls closed out their season at the Jersey shore. They played the Atlantic City American Legion Girls, South Jersey Champions, and the Belmar Specials. The Atlantic City contest, held on Friday, April 13, ended in a 13–all tie. Rather than play overtime, management of both teams, in search of greater profits, decided to call the game and resume play on the following Friday because the Tribune Girls were an outstanding drawing card. The *Philadelphia Tribune* reported that the suspended game was completed on Monday, April 16, in which the Newsies won by a 17–13 score, their fifth consecutive victory over the Legion girls. After finishing the season on a high note with a string of impressive victories, particularly their undefeated southern tour, the Newsgirls were rewarded with their third annual dinner party and dance.[29]

Local Challenges, Expanded Entertainment, and a Disputed Championship

As the Newsgirls prepared to open their fourth season on Thanksgiving night, now a tradition, against Sarah Pollard's New York Defenders, a new African American girls' basketball team appeared on the Philadelphia sports scene. The Challengers, a club comprised of high school and college girls, was organized by Chester Buchanan, a well-known Philadelphia sportsman. Buchanan owned and coached the team that he hoped to guide to the city championship. The Challengers opened their initial season on the same card as the Newsgirls, playing the Paramount Girls, an Otto Briggs junior-level team, in the preliminary contest.[30]

The Tribune Girls handed Sarah Pollard's outfit a 36–26 setback before a capacity crowd at the Catherine Street YWCA. Heavy rainfall could not keep the fans away. In addition to the basketball doubleheader, the fans were treated to an entertaining show by Baby Selma Headspeath, radio star of the "Colored Kiddies Hour," who "took the crowd by storm with her extraordinary dance numbers and singing. The number which Baby did on skates proved to be a thriller." Two other members of her radio program did a "soft shoe and toe dance which drew rounds of applause." Following the game and show, the crowd "danced to the smooth but hot rhythm of Ike Hopkins and his High Hatters Orchestra." All of this entertainment for the admission price of 35 cents! The *Tribune,* in an effort to keep readers interested in its newspaper, published the following declaration: "the Tribune Girls and management wish to thank their many friends and followers for their encouraging support and hope that they will watch the Tribune each week for their next game."[31]

Following their victory over the Defenders, the Newsgirls played an exciting game against the white Lampeter team. Playing without Washington on Lampeter's home court, the Tribgirls trailed the home club by five points with forty-five seconds to play. But then the Tribs "snatched the game from the locals" with the sharpshooting of Rose Wilson and Dick Hill.[32] Wilson hit two "sensational shots" and Hill threw in the winner—a whistle-beater just as time expired to give the Newsies a 28–27 victory. Then they traveled to the anthracite coal region of northeastern Pennsylvania and defeated two more white clubs, the Mayfield Girls and the Nanticoke Monarchs. Again without the services of Washington, Wilson and Hill paced the Newsgirls to a 51–40 win over Mayfield, while Hill, Helen Davis, and Sarah Latimere, Trib newcomer and recent graduate of basketball powerhouse Downingtown (Pennsylvania) Industrial School, led the charges over the Monarchs before an overflow crowd at Wilkes-Barre. In a January return match with the

Defenders in New York, the Newsgirls behind the play of Washington, Latimere, and Wilson defeated them for the second time that season. Former Trib star Inez Patterson played a strong game for the New York club, but her effort could not match the dominating play put forth by the Tribunes' trio. Later that week the Tribs whipped Asbury Park by the lopsided margin of 48–5. Then near the end of the month, they won their twelfth straight game, drubbing the Mystery Girls of Rutherford, New Jersey, 25–9, holding them scoreless in the second half. Patterson refereed the game that was played on her Orange, New Jersey, YWCA court.[33]

As the Tribune quintet continued its winning ways in February of 1935, the upstart Challengers compiled a string of fourteen straight victories. One of their more impressive wins came over the Camden YWCA, whom they defeated 63–3 behind the sharp shooting of sixteen-year-old Dot Ballard, who tossed in 50 points. Ballard's older sister, Lula, teamed with Ora Washington to win the American Tennis Association doubles championship in 1925, a title Washington would share for twelve straight years. The younger Ballard has been described as "the flashiest player in girls['] basketball today." The strong showing of the Challengers earned them a shot at the city championship against the Newsgirls. Fans who have seen the Challengers play believed they could give the Newsies "plenty of fun for their money and some go so far as to believe that they have a good chance to defeat the national champions." Challenger fans, however, underestimated the Newsgirls, as they watched the Tribs paste a 39–6 licking on the young upstarts.[34]

In late March the Newsgirls took their 24-1 record to Atlantic City where they faced their fiercest rival, the American Legion Girls, who had won fourteen games in a row. Before a packed house at the Jersey shore, Washington and Helen Davis staked the visitors to a 9–8 halftime lead. Then in the second stanza the Tribs expanded their lead, defeating the Legionnaires, 22–16, thanks to Washington's and Davis's continued hot shooting and the defensive play of Inez Patterson who, wearing the Tribune uniform for this game, held the Legion's top player to one point. A month later, the Tribune Girls returned to Atlantic City for a rematch. Again paced by Washington and Davis along with support from Wilson and Hill, the Newsgirls jumped out to a 14–0 advantage at the half. The Tribs's "unusual defense" confused the Legion players and enabled the Philadelphia squad to coast to a 23–14 victory.[35]

The intense Tribune-Legionnaire rivalry carried into the 1935–36 season. Playing at Atlantic City in mid-January, the Newsgirls defeated the Legion team 29–27 in "one of the most hectic battles ever witnessed on the Soldiers Home Court." The Legion Girls took a small lead into the fourth quarter, but then Washington, Wilson, Inez Bovell, and Bernice Robinson uncorked some uncanny shots that pulled the Tribs even and finally put them ahead for good. The victory extended the Newsgirls' unbeaten streak, which attracted even more national attention. Applauding their achievements, Al Monroe of the *Chicago Defender* wrote, "the Philadelphia Tribune Girls . . . have awakened us with a string of victories that have overshadowed anything done by any other bunch of girls in either race."[36]

The return match with the Legionnaires was set for January 24 in Philadelphia, and the *Tribune* newspaper hyped the game with multiple advertisements, commending Philadelphians for supporting the best: "Their Champion B. B. Team" and "Their Champion Tribune Paper" with the underlying slogan, "you get your money's worth when you see the Newsgirls play." Admission was 35 cents for adults and 25 cents for children for the game and dance that followed. To encourage the Tribs's local followers to attend the contest, the ad contained an announcement that "loads of fans from Atlantic City are arranging to accompany their team here, to root for them to stop the Tribune Girls' winning streak." The ad's announcement was an ominous portent as the spunky Legion team knocked off the Newsies, 22–21, handing them their first loss in three years. The setback was quite a shock to the champions who were outplayed by a much smaller team "in a tussle which was one of the best of the season." In a third tilt at Atlantic City, the Legionnaires erased an early 7-point deficit to win a thrilling contest, 29–27. In an uphill battle in which both teams traded baskets in the final stanza, the smaller Jersey shore team gradually caught and toppled the champions.[37]

After their second victory over the Tribs, the Legionnaires proclaimed themselves the national colored champions, and celebrated their self-anointed title at a banquet and reception before four hundred followers, dignitaries, and local officials. Otto Briggs objected vehemently to Atlantic City's proclamation, which prompted him to send a letter of clarification to newspapers around the country. In the letter he charged Atlantic City and its backers with laying claim to a national championship title that they did not earn because the contests between the Newsgirls and Legionnaires were exhibition games. To win the championship, Briggs argued, a five-game series must be arranged just as the Tribunes had done with the Germantown Hornets back in 1932. In all of his correspondence with the Atlantic City club, Briggs reported there was no mention of a championship series. Moreover, championship matches normally were officiated by qualified referees on neutral basketball courts. If the championship was at stake, Briggs declared, he would not have allowed his team to play two games in Atlantic City using the Legion's home referees, nor would he have allowed a local fan to referee one of the games in Philadelphia. In the previous three years, the Newsgirls defeated the Legionnaires eleven times, lost two, and tied one. The two tainted victories by the Legion in 1936 did not give them a legitimate claim to the national title.[38]

The disputed championship and the two losses to Atlantic City, however, did not mar the Newsgirls' 1935–36 campaign. Before the season began, Coach

Chappelle and Briggs fully expected the Newsgirls to retain the national title. Their optimism was apparent in a *Tribune* newspaper column in which Chappelle assessed his team. The coach praised the incomparable and indomitable play of team captain Ora Washington as "outstanding in every instance." Dick Hill, he maintained, "is still playing a bang-up floor game," while sharpshooter Helen Davis "can be seen in every corner of the court and is making points from any angles, although she never allows her opponent to score. Rose Wilson, the 'snake-hips' of basketball is still twisting away making field goals." Newcomers, Sara Latimere, the Downingtown star who joined the Tribs last year, "is giving the newspapers['] writers something to write about," and Bernice Robinson, former Woodbury Darts star, "is putting so much pep in the rest that I think the team will be able to compete with any of the opposite sex."[39]

With such a star-studded array of players, the Newsgirls met the challenges of the 1935–36 season. They whipped Inez Patterson's Orange, New Jersey, YWCA team in their traditional Thanksgiving night home opener minus Dick Hill, who left the Newsies to play for a team in Chicago. The Tribs defeated Patterson's squad for a second time on New Year's night. Other prominent victories came over the Pure Oil Girls of Scranton, white champions of the anthracite coal region, and the hometown challengers—Germantown Hornets and Chester Buchanan's Challenger Girls. The Newsgirls continued success made them a popular attraction as "they rank next to the world's colored champions, the Renaissance, in being a drawing attraction." The Tribune Girls' popularity and the growing interest in women's basketball generated talk of an intercity Girls Basketball League composed of Atlantic City, Asbury Park, Trenton, Harrisburg, and West Chester, among several others. Otto Briggs, ever the entrepreneur in search of new sources of revenue, welcomed the league concept as one plan called for his Newsgirls to play a game with one of the teams in each of the league's cities. The girls' league, however, never got beyond the discussion stage.[40]

New Coaches, White Opponents, and a Dixie Tour

As visions of the girls' league evaporated and Briggs began to prepare the Newsgirls for their sixth season, he decided to make a coaching change. He brought in Tom Dixon, all-around athlete and standout on the Tribune's Big 5 men's team, to replace "Shorty" Chappelle, whom Briggs assigned to coach the newspaper's men's squad. For the second time in three years, Sarah Pollard's New York Colonial Deer provided the opening night opposition for the Newsgirls, and, in spite of Pollard's prediction that her "fast combination" of players would hand the Tribgirls their first setback, the Newsgirls won again. Fans packed the Catherine Street YWCA beyond capacity, reducing the playing court to two-thirds of its normal size; dozens more stood outside unable to get in. Then, too, New York rooters, accompanying their team to Philadelphia in two buses and private cars, swelled the attendance. With the game, show, dance format in use for this event, radio star Baby Selma Headspeath again "thrilled the large crowd with her performances and the work of her pupils." Samuel Lucas Jr., also a local entertainer of radio fame, followed suit with his song-and-dance routine. At 35 cents for adults and 25 cents for children, the *Tribune* marketed the event as an entertainment bargain "for less than one dollar, a family of three can enjoy this evening of pleasure." At the end of the night the Newsies prevailed, winning their sixth-straight home opener.[41]

The Newsgirls also began 1937 on a winning note, defeating the Monarch Girls of Nanticoke, the Pennsylvania white champions, 25–12, in a contest played at the Catherine Street YWCA. Then in late January they traveled to Poughkeepsie where they handed the white Beckwith A.A. their first loss in twenty games, 30–20. Rose Wilson and Washington paced the Tribgirls with 8 points each, while Inez Patterson, donning Trib colors for this game, played brilliant defense.[42]

The following fall, the Tribs invited the Bucktown Girls, another white champion club from the Scranton area, to open the 1937–38 season with them on Thanksgiving night. In making their first appearance in Philadelphia, Bucktown pressed their hosts to the end before bowing in a close contest, 19–17. Bernice Robinson and Ora Washington tallied 15 of their team's 19 points. For Washington, too, it was sweet revenge. She described her opponents as "a crack array of white girls who know what to do with the ball. After four years of trying to trip this touted combination, . . . [we] came through with flying colors." Several weeks later the Newsgirls traveled to Scranton for a return match. Playing without Washington and no available substitutes, the Newsies handed Bucktown its first defeat on its home floor in several seasons, 38–27. Trib veteran Rose Wilson tossed in 13 points, but newcomers Mildred "Sis" Lowery from New York City and Trinidad-born Marie Leach from Montclair, New Jersey, paced the winners with their "great floor work and accurate gunning."[43]

Sandwiched between the Bucktown victories was a 27–15 loss to another white team, the Caseyette Girls, on their home court in Brooklyn. Playing in preliminary games before all the big contests in New York City, the Caseyettes have "absorbed most of the trick stuff of the best pros," putting their passing attack "on par with any boys team in this city." The Caseyettes also received training from the Original Celtics, and in some circles they were rated the best female basketball team ever. But Otto Briggs disagreed, maintaining that he had assembled his best female squad, particularly with the addition of "Sis" Lowery and Marie Leach, who joined the Tribgirls after their loss to the Caseyettes. Not content with just the "National Colored Girls' Championship," he wanted his Trib team to be the undisputed champion of all female basketball teams. With that goal in mind, he scheduled a return match with the Brooklyn club for New Year's night in Philadelphia because he believed "a victory over the Caseyettes would go a long way in strengthening these visions." With Lowery and Leach in fold, the Newsgirls defeated the Gotham squad, 39–22, a triumph that the *Philadelphia Tribune* hailed as the "Tribgirls biggest victory." *Tribune* sportswriter Dick Sun (Randy Dickson) attributed the Tribs's victory to sharpshooting Rose Wilson, who buried 16 points, tricky offensive schemes, and the guard play of Lowery and Leach. "To be truthful," Dick Sun wrote, "the Tribs either played far over their heads, or have suddenly discovered some hidden power that's always been there, but just came out." The loss sustained by the Caseyettes was their first in two years and their first ever to a colored team. It also enabled the Newsgirls to begin making claims for the female basketball national championship.[44]

Although Lowery and Leach were important new components in the Tribune girls well-oiled 1937–38 basketball machine, Briggs's second coaching change in as many seasons made a huge impact. He signed Chester "Buck" Buchanan, owner-coach of the Challengers, to coach the Newsgirls. In moving to the Newsgirls, Buchanan brought over the Challengers' best players—Myrtle Wilson, Hazel Pettus, Lavinia Moore, and Vivian Brown. Buchanan's hiring no doubt strengthened the Tribune team, but it also removed the upstart Challengers as a possible threat to the Tribs's local supremacy on the court and in the press.[45]

A year earlier, the Challenger Girls, under the tutelage of Buchanan, began to gather momentum on the home front. At a time when the Newsgirls experienced a midwinter lull in their 1936–37 schedule with only a few games on the docket, the Challenger Girls grabbed most of the local newspaper headlines. Coach Chester Buchanan was confident that his girls had the ability to challenge for the national title, and after they got off to a 6 and 2 start, his confidence swelled. Buoyed by their rout of the Ajax Girls of Coatesville, Pennsylvania, 37–16, in early February, the Challengers began to prepare for a series against the Tribbies. In the first game Buchanan's squad was no match for the champions as the Newsgirls built a 13–4 halftime lead behind the play of Washington, Latimere, Bovell, Robinson, and Wilson. Their "passing and team work along with their great defensive playing . . . completely baffled their opponents." The champs used their younger players in the second half, which enabled the Challengers to close the gap, making the final score a respectable 24 to 17.[46]

The Newsgirls, now with Buchanan as their coach, continued their success with impressive wins during the first half of the 1937–38 season. In addition to their victories over Bucktown and the Caseyette Girls, the Tribs whipped their staunchest foe, the Atlantic City American Legion, on the loser's home court in early January of 1938. The Tribune Girls' rivalry with the Legionnaires was clearly "the deepest and fiercest feud in sepia [Philadelphia] basketball ranks, male or female." Pregame rhetoric generally reflected the intensity of this rivalry as the Legion squad, mincing no words prior to the return match in Philadelphia, announced "they were coming with blood in their eyes and are bringing the wherewithal to back it up." The Legionnaires showed up ready to play with fire in their bellies if not blood in their eyes. They quickly jumped out to a 13–4 halftime lead. Washington made the only Trib field goal in the first half, but she took control of the game in the second stanza. When the pressure was on, she hit two baskets to knot the score at 15 and then tossed in the winning bucket to preserve a 17–16 Tribs's victory. A third game with the Legionnaires was set for February 18, the day before the Newsgirls' scheduled departure on their southern tour. But when the shore femmes "hoisted their guarantee demands at a late moment," the Tribgirls replaced the Legion team with the New York Deer, whom they defeated in a lackluster performance.[47]

Following their victory over the New York Deer, the Newsgirls departed on a projected 4,000-mile southern tour with stops in South Carolina, Georgia, Alabama, Mississippi, and Louisiana. They played their first game on February 21 against South Carolina State Agricultural College at Orangeburg, a team coached by Lula Ballard, Ora Washington's longtime friend and foe on and off the tennis court. Prior to the basketball game, Washington and Ballard played an exhibition indoor tennis match "to give fans in this section [of the country] a chance to see these tennis stars in action." The Tribgirls played boys rules, but for some contests, like the one at Orangeburg, they were required to play girls rules, which hampered their style of play, reducing their effectiveness. They did, however, play a brief exhibition fray against the boys squad coached by a Mr. Dawson, who experienced a rather uncomfortable moment during team introductions. Ric Roberts, *Atlanta Daily World* sports columnist, reported the incident, indicating that one of the Trib players "tossed a kiss" to Coach Dawson. The coach "blushed, looked around and sighed: 'She must have meant one of you guys up here beside me!' . . . His lady friend sat beside him, a certain look in her eyes."[48]

From Orangeburg, the Newsgirls traveled to Atlanta to take on the Atlanta Ladies Tennis Club in a two-game set. Pregame publicity ran high as the *Atlanta Daily World* sang the praises of the Tribune team and its superstar, Ora Washington. "The world champion women performers will have the best known colored feminine athlete in America in their lineup in Ora Washington, eight times national women's tennis champion. She is one of the greatest jumpers of her sex in the world, a fact which makes it well nigh impossible to get shots over her head in tennis or to pass over her in basketball." Describing Washington as an "unspoiled gentlewoman," Ric Roberts wrote, "Miss Washington, unlike most females, effects the burden of national prominence with dignity and grace. She is wholly unaffected, has the most obliging and pleasing personality and is a favorite of all of her associates." Another *Daily World* columnist, Lucius Jones, classified the Tribune girls as "the best colored feminine professional basketball outfit in the world." To counter the stalwarts from Philadelphia, the Atlanta club recruited the top local college basketball players to play for them. But the local college all-stars, however, were no match for the champions. The Newsgirls won the first game, 26–19, behind the long-range shooting of "Sis" Lowery, the inside play of Bernice Robinson, and the ball-hawking of Washington. In the second contest, Washington, "a basketeer with unusual ability," hit shots that put the Newsies up early. Then in the second half, the Tribs pulled away as Rose Wilson heated up to join Washington in a shooting spree that led them on to a 27–16 victory. Commenting on the abilities of the Newsgirl players, Lucius Jones wrote, "The Tribune girls have a girl who sinks long shots with uncanny ease in Mildred Lowery, a sensational all-court player in Ora Washington who also can drop those long ones, and a corking good under-the-basket duo in Miss Wilson and Miss Robinson. Rose, the former girl is versatile, being one of the best dribblers, passers, and form shot specialists on the team. However, that Marie Leach is also a sweet performer."[49] The Tribs's Dixie tour ended abruptly and without explanation in Atlanta, but initial plans called for the team to play opponents in Alabama and Mississippi before culminating in New Orleans with a contest against Mother of Sorrow girls, champions of Dixie.[50]

African Americans, traveling in the segregated South during the 1930s, experienced severe discrimination as Jim Crow prohibited blacks from using most hotels, restaurants, and gas station restrooms. Alice Coachman, the great Tuskegee athlete, revealed in an interview with Pamela Grundy that the color line forced her and her teammates to take bathroom breaks along the roadside with males and females on opposite sides of the bus, of course.[51] Although incidents, such as this, made travel in Dixie difficult, black athletic teams endured blatant discriminatory practices to participate in challenging athletic competitions or to honor or fulfill contractual obligations. Whatever discrimination the Newsgirls may have faced on their southern tours either went unreported or did not make the *Tribune*'s sport pages.

The Newsgirls returned home to face the unbeaten Woodbury, New Jersey, Darts, a team composed largely of teenagers. Bernice Robinson, current Trib standout at age twenty and an original Dart, joined her younger sister, Mildred, on the Woodbury club to help them beat the Tribs in two straight games to finish their season undefeated. The Newsgirls used three subs in the first game, but critics conceded that Woodbury would have won no matter who was playing for the Tribune Girls. The Darts won a squeaker in the second game as the elder Robinson hit a one-hander from the corner with less than thirty seconds remaining for a 30–28 Dart victory. Then in April the Newsgirls closed out the 1937–38 season with a lopsided drubbing of the New York Deer headed by Inez Patterson. Rose Wilson and Marie Leach were the top guns for the Tribs. Their strong performance in the season's finale prompted the *Tribune* to report the victory as the Newsgirls best play of the season.[52]

Ora Mae Washington, 1939. *Courtesy of John W. Mosley Photography Collection, Charles L. Blockson Afro-American Collection, Temple University Libraries, Philadelphia, PA*

Coaching Carousel, Mounting Championships, and the End of an Era

As the 1938–39 season rolled around, the Newsgirls found themselves with another new coach, their third in three years. Freddie Mooch, prominent south Philadelphia athlete, replaced Chester Buchanan, who returned to coach his old team, the Challenger Girls. Mooch had the colossal task of preparing his players to defend their newly proclaimed title of "World Champions." This year's squad was a blend of seasoned veterans and talented newcomers. Superstars Washington and Rose Wilson were surrounded by veterans Marie Leach, Myrtle Wilson, Bernice Robinson, and Sara Latimere, who missed the 1937–38 season due to an illness. A host of newcomers headed by Vivian Coleman of Philadelphia's top amateur club, St. Mary's Hawks, were expected to contribute significantly.[53]

The Tribbies began the season on a high note, whipping the Caseyettes Girls, 27–19, at their traditional Thanksgiving night home opener. The following year they defeated a strong Queens County Girls Team of Jamaica, Long Island, winning on Thanksgiving night for the ninth consecutive year. Trailing at the half, Washington and Rose and Myrtle Wilson put on an offensive show, while Robinson, Iona Burton, and Gladys Walker shut down the opposition with stellar defensive play. The Tribs's victory over Queens County was followed by a surprise loss to the same team on New Year's night of 1940. Later that week, the Newsgirls rebounded with an impressive win over the New York Whippetts. Washington played a "spectacular game which brought rounds of applause," while Rose Wilson, Barton, and Robinson provided plenty of support. They had the challenging task of countering the play of Mildred "Sis" Lowery, their former teammate who was instrumental in helping the Newsgirls chalk up victories on their 1938 southern tour. In February 1940, the Tribgirls traveled to Rochester to take on the Filaret Girls, renown white champions. The Filarets proved to be tough opponents as they defeated the Newsies for the second time in three years. The Newsgirls returned to their winning ways in mid-March, defeating the Whippetts, New York City champs, 25–23, in Harlem. The hosts took a five-point lead with six minutes remaining, but Washington and Rose Wilson led the comeback with 7 points to ensure the Newsgirls' victory. Then they came home to take on the St. Mary's Hawks, local amateur titleholder, for the championship of Philadelphia. The Hawks were on a seven-game winning streak and had won forty-two of their last forty-three games. In the first of a three-game set, the Tribs defeated the Hawks, 40–20. As usual, Washington and Wilson led all scorers, pacing the Newsgirls to victory.[54]

The year 1941 signaled dramatic changes for the Newsgirls. Several weeks before the basketball season began, Otto Briggs resigned as circulation manager of the *Tribune* and business manager of the Newsgirls due to poor health. In his absence, the Tribs prepared for the 1941–42 campaign under their fifth basketball coach, Robert "Panicky" Bryant, former Lincoln University football and basketball star. Bryant was optimistic about his team's chances with most of the star players returning and performing in practice as if they were in mid-season form. On top of that, the development of second-year player Marion Stevenson, a recent graduate of Cheney Teachers College, was cause for more excitement. Four hundred fans packed the Catherine Street YWCA to see the Tribune Girls open their eleventh season on Thanksgiving night against the Freedman Hospital Nurses of Washington, DC. Riding a twenty-four-game winning streak, the undefeated nurses came to Philadelphia prepared to extend it, but the Newsgirls refused to cooperate. In a close and thrilling contest, they defeated the nurses, 28–21, snapping their winning streak. Stevenson, the Tribs's budding new star, tossed in 13 points, while longtime veteran Gladys Walker followed up with 8. Conspicuously missing from this triumphant event were Ora Washington and Otto Briggs, a clear signal of the changes in the air.[55]

The changes experienced by the Newsgirls were minute compared to those that would sweep the United States following the Japanese attack on Pearl Harbor. As the ides of World War II cast a dark shadow over the entire country, the flames of sport barely flickered. Within weeks of the Japanese raid, Trib coach Bryant, an ordained minister, was called to active duty as an army chaplain. The team, nevertheless, continued to play and finished out the 1941–42 season, compiling a commendable record, including wins over local rivals Lansdowne and Woodbury. Ora Washington, though still captain of the Tribs, played sparingly during that season. With Briggs fighting a chronic illness at a veterans hospital, William T. Coleman and Reginald Fosque ran the team in his absence. They continued the Tribs's policy of admitting servicemen in uniform free to Newsgirls' games. The Tribune Girls concluded their season with a victory over the Long Island Pantherettes, a decisive win for the Newsies as the two teams had split two contests earlier in the year. With wartime needs and demands taking precedence, the Newsgirls decided to disband for the duration of the war. They canceled their 1942–43 season, which included a trip to Mexico, and never suited up again.[56]

Otto Briggs died on October 27, 1943. His death both symbolized and signaled an end to an era. Briggs's passing and the dark clouds of World War II smothered African American women's basketball from which the Tribune team never recovered. Briggs, however, not only left his mark on the *Tribune* and on the city of Philadelphia, but also on African American women's basketball. He used sport, particularly basketball, along with other forms of entertainment (shows and dances), to increase the circulation of his newspaper and generate revenue for his enterprises. Just as the *Tribune* promoted sport, sport also promoted the *Tribune*. Briggs's basketball teams, men's and women's, were well known throughout the country, primarily due to the black press, but every time his players put on their uniforms with the word *Tribune* sprawled across their chests, the audience was exposed immediately to the *Philadelphia Tribune*.

Briggs's success as an entrepreneur and promoter often brought mixed results. The Newsgirls had "such good players, they had difficulty securing games. Other teams were afraid to match them. The attendance receipts at Briggs' games sometimes suffered also. Fans knew the Tribune girls were going to win; so many times they didn't bother to see the game. Other times, Thanksgiving and Christmas, crowds of fans overflowed onto the playing floor."[57]

Otto Briggs and the *Philadelphia Tribune* are only half of the story. The other half belongs to Ora Washington and her teammates, whose drive, dedication, skill, and effort kept the Newsgirls atop the women's basketball world for more than a decade. Washington, a nonpareil on both the basketball and tennis courts, demonstrated her ability and tenacity year in and year out. The black press could not praise her enough, variously describing her as kind, reserved, and unassuming, among other things. Her opponents, however, at least the players at Bennett College, held a different view, castigating her as an unkempt ruffian. To be sure, she was highly competitive, enjoyed the heat of battle, and knew how to win, all of which contributed to her enviable record of superlative achievements.

During a time when superb female basketball players could offer their services to the highest bidder for more lucrative financial remuneration, Washington remained with the Newsgirls throughout her career after joining them in 1932. Other talented players, Inez Patterson, Helen Davis, Marie Leach, and Mildred Lowery, played for several different teams. Washington and teammate Rose Wilson, nevertheless, spent almost their entire careers wearing a Tribune uniform.

As quasi professionals, Washington and her cohorts had to supplement their small salaries with other jobs, most of which were menial and servile in nature. Washington, as great an athlete that she was, toiled as a housekeeper during most of her working years. The 1920 census shows her in Philadelphia working as a servant to the head of household and as a waitress to a private family. Ten years later she was living in Chicago and working as a hotel maid. By 1940 she was living with her younger sister, Christine Hill, and her sister's son, along with her brother, Larry, and her cousin, Grace Jeffries. No occupation was listed for Washington in the 1940 census.[58] As the elder statesperson of the Tribune team, Washington played basketball well into her early forties for which she received little remuneration. In fact, her nephew, James Bernard Childs, and her grandniece, Brenda Hogue, have indicated, in a recent interview, that Washington was not paid as a player.[59]

Lula Ballard, Washington's tennis doubles partner and teammate on the Germantown Hornets, came from a well-known Germantown family. The 1930 census shows her with five siblings—two sisters and three brothers. Her younger sister, Dorothy, played on Chester Buchanan's Challenger Girls team. Her father was a blacksmith at an auto shop and owned his own home on Pike Street that was valued at $5,500. The Ballards were not found in the 1940 census.[60]

Inez Patterson, a contemporary of Lula Ballard and thirteen years younger than Washington, began playing on semiprofessional teams in her late teens. Patterson's widowed mother, Alice, was the proprietor of a store on 83rd Street in West Philadelphia. The 1930 census, shows her real estate to be worth $2,200. She had sufficient resources to send Inez to Temple University where Patterson's preparation in physical education led to a professional career with the YWCA.[61]

Four age cohorts of Patterson's from New Jersey—Lavinia Moore of Cape May, Frances Butler of Pennsauken, Bernice Robinson from Woodbury, and Marie Leach from Montclair—joined the Tribune team after Patterson left Philadelphia. Moore, with a college education, was a secretary at the YWCA where she earned an annual salary of $1,100 in 1940 at age twenty-six. Butler at age twenty-seven worked as a domestic and Robinson at twenty-two served a private family as a maid. Their 1940 earnings were $240 and $416, respectively. Leach, the daughter of a landscaper who owned his own home valued at $15,000, attended the Bordentown Industrial School for Girls. No occupation was listed for Leach.[62]

Unfortunately, the contributions of Leach and her teammates have gone unnoticed. But an even greater injustice has been dealt to Ora Washington, whose life and great career was hardly recognized beyond the African American community. Racial barriers doubtless prevented her from getting the recognition and remuneration that she deserved. Following her athletic career, she spent most of her life working as a housekeeper in Philadelphia; a champion athlete deserves better. But the tentacles of racial discrimination also hampered the entire Tribune team as well as its management. Rose Wilson, relatively unknown, was a dominant forward on the Newsgirls and led them to victory after victory throughout their existence. Her play was nearly as pivotal as Washington's. Inez Patterson, Helen Davis, Louise Hill, Bernice Robinson, and Sarah Latimere are just a few of the other outstanding players and unsung heroines who never got the attention or recognition that their careers warranted. Perhaps, in a small way, this tribute to the Tribune Girls shines some light on the players and their careers that have lingered far too long in the shadows of darkness.

4

The Tennessee State Tigerbelles

Cold Warriors of the Track

Carroll Van West

In the lore of Tennessee sports history, few names are more evocative and lionized than the Tennessee State Tigerbelles, a group of women sprinters who dominated track and field events in the nation and world from the mid-1950s to mid-1980s.[1] Scholarly interest in the impact of the Tigerbelles has multiplied in the twenty-first century, with dissertations and books addressing how these women track and field stars shaped mid-twentieth-century images of African American women, women involved in sports in general, and issues of civil rights and international affairs.[2]

The story of the Tigerbelles and their significance to American sport and culture must center on the great talent and dedication to excellence of these young women. But as media coverage of their athletic exploits intensified from the early 1950s to the 1960s, the Tigerbelles were swept up in American preoccupation with the role of women in contemporary sport, the impact of race in American sport, and the role that amateur athletes could play as pawns in the propaganda posturings of the United States and the Soviet Union during the Cold War.

Track and field at Tennessee Agricultural and Industrial State College (renamed in 1968 as Tennessee State University) began in the aftermath of Jessie Owens's success at the 1936 Olympics. The college's first women's track team formed in 1943 under the direction of Jessie Abbott, succeeded by Lula Bartley in 1945. Abbott brought with him a commitment to excellence gained at Tuskegee Institute, home to the first nationally dominant African American track and field program. Abbott's Tuskegee model shaped what happened at Tennessee State for the next generation of sport.

In 1946 college president Walter S. Davis aggressively implemented a state mandate to make Tennessee A&I the equivalent of the University of Tennessee in all aspects, including athletics. Tom Harris, formerly of Wilberforce University, became the men's and women's track coach, training his athletes on a hastily built track around the football field. Tennessee State found success early, with both men and women placing third at the annual black college track and field championships at Tuskegee Institute. Then at the 1948 London Olympics, the program tasted its first international success as Audrey Patterson won a bronze medal in the 200-meter race. The college celebrated her success with a parade on Centennial Boulevard, one of the central avenues in the segregated African American section of Nashville.[3]

The 1950s witnessed the rapid rise of the Tennessee State program to national and international acclaim and grudging recognition in the Jim Crow South.

Coach Ed Temple proved to be the catalyst. He became the women's track coach in 1950 and established what became known as the Tigerbelles Women's Track Club. At the track club's beginning, Temple recalled a hurried meeting with college president Walter S. Davis, where Davis offered a deal that a recently graduated student could not refuse: "Go to grad school, run the post office, coach women's track—for $150 a month."[4]

Without any scholarships to offer women athletes—an impediment to recruiting that would not change until the 1970s—Temple used work aid to offer students support. The athletes worked two hours a day somewhere in the college in addition to the demanding practices Temple implemented. Patterning his new program on the established and successful track program at Tuskegee, Temple instituted an Amateur Athletic Union–endorsed summer program to attract top high school talent to train with his college sprinters. The AAU summer program was the key to his recruitment efforts (since he hardly had a travel budget otherwise) and graduates from the summer program produced almost all of his Olympic gold medal winners. Temple designed the summer program to mesh with his goals and training regiments at the college so that the athletes once enrolled at Tennessee State already knew the "Ed Temple way."[5]

Other athletes came to Tennessee State due to rising reputation of Temple as a gifted coach. Mae Faggs, for example, started at Tennessee State in the fall of 1952, after competing as a teenager in both the 1948 and 1952 Olympics. Cynthia Thompson from Jamaica also participated in the 1952 games. At that competition in Helsinki, Finland, Barbara Jones and Faggs both took gold medals, the program's first.[6]

In the 1954–55 track season, Temple's athletes continued their winning ways and received national recognition when Tennessee State freshman Isabelle Daniels defeated her teammate and former Olympian Mae Faggs at the Washington Evening News indoor track meet in the District of Columbia. The *Chicago Defender* reported that the "Tennessee Tigerbelles broke three records and took two trophies, five first and one second place medal before a near capacity crowd."[7] In October, the Tigerbelles dominated at a meet held at Madison Square Garden in New York City and won the AAU Women's Championship, an important first since the AAU meet was not segregated and white and black runners competed against one another. The Tigerbelles would dominate AAU competitions for years into the future.[8]

National acclaim turned to international fame during 1956 Olympic-year competitions. As early as January Earl S. Clanton III of the *Chicago Defender* was reporting Ed Temple as a possible coach for the women's track team due to the "scintillating runaway of the Tennessee State club in the national AAU outdoor meet last summer."[9] That streak continued at the segregated Tuskegee Relays in May when the team took goal medals in each event they entered. The *Chicago Defender* account of the Tuskegee competition, however, also introduced a new theme that would follow the Tigerbelles for years: they were graceful, beautiful women not muscle-bound, unattractive athletes. The reporter described Yvonne Macon, who won the shot put, discus, and baseball throw competitions, as "the shapely 19 year old New York born field eventer."[10]

Temple admitted that he wanted attractive women in his program, ones who would prove that women athletes could be feminine and attractive. He remarked: "I had a motto. I said, I don't want oxes, I want foxes. I want nice looking girls" to counteract the assumption women who participated in sports could never be married, or have children, to fulfill the image of a proper American woman who so permeated popular culture in the 1950s. In 2007 Temple elaborated on his "I don't want oxes theme": "A lot of people black and white believed that if girls got muscles they could never have babies. So, playing sports was okay in grade school, but black folks got funny about their daughters playing sports as maturing young women."[11] Temple added that he was "absolutely determined to prove to the world that you could be a very feminine young woman and still get the job done on the track."[12]

Eight Tigerbelles competed at the 1956 Olympic qualifying events, and Mae Faggs was part of the US "Goodwill" squad that traveled to Africa. As Tennessee State University historian Bobby L. Lovett has emphasized, the success of the Tigerbelles came from women who "had to unload from cramped car seats and perform against college teams that had scholarships, hot food, and first-rate travel and housing."[13]

In interviews, Temple also has discussed not only challenges posed by Jim Crow laws and ethos of the 1950s but the resistance of the men who administered the college's athletic programs. He felt that administrators were jealous of the rapid success of the Tigerbelles in national and international competition, a benchmark of success that the mainstream men teams at Tennessee A&I struggle to match in the 1950s.[14]

The crumbling but still stout walls of Jim Crow did not stand in the way of the six Tigerbelles who competed at the Melbourne Olympics during the summer of

1956. Four Tigerbelles, including Isabelle Daniels, Mae Faggs, Margaret Matthews, and the high school junior Wilma Rudolph, composed the 4 x 100 relay team and took the bronze medal while another high school star competing with the Tigerbelles, Willye B. White, won the silver in the long jump. Temple, however, was not chosen as an American coach and did not make the trip; he charged veteran Olympian Mae Faggs to take the six Tigerbelles to Australia. Fagg, insisted Temple, "was the spitfire. I mean, she put the fire in 'em."[15] Despite Temple's absence, the women acquitted themselves with honor both on the track and within the Olympic Village, where they could freely mix with their white teammates and athletes from around the world. After the Olympics, the State Department chose Faggs to be the single woman member of a US track and field squad that traveled to Africa as part of its effort at cultural diplomacy in addressing "the growth of nationalism in Africa."[16]

The Tigerbelles continued as Cold War ambassadors for the United States during trips in 1957 to Cuba and then in 1958 to the Soviet Union as officials searched for people of color to represent the flag in a suddenly more diverse world. The Soviet threat in athletic competitions was both on the track and in the press room. American officials wanted to win, and to show that American women were ladies, as part of the larger cultural campaign to prove the superiority of the United States over the communist system of Soviet Russia. Not wanting to be embarrassed at the forthcoming Olympic games in Rome, US track and field officials began to seriously consider a role for Ed Temple on the national squad. When the 1958 event did not end well for the United States, a reporter in the *Washington Post and Times Herald* asked, "Where are the Babe Didricksons and Stella Walshes of yesteryear?" The reporter provided Ed Temple's answer: "We have the material but we don't give it a chance to develop. Our women just need more opportunity." Temple backed up his observation by pointing out his Tigerbelles won all sprint races because "the sprinters had proper training."[17] At the Chicago-hosted Pan American Games in 1959, Tigerbelles won twelve events, further solidifying their program as the nation's best for women's track and field.[18]

The nascent civil rights movement framed the success of the Tigerbelles in the 1950s. When these women toured the free world and behind the Iron Curtain, they enjoyed freedoms unavailable in the Jim Crow South, especially Nashville, where groups like the White Citizens Council held sway. Parades and on-campus celebrations of the Tigerbelles could happen in the African American section of the city, but the rest of Nashville, including its sports pages, paid little attention, at least until the bronze medal success at the Melbourne Games in 1956. After that the *Nashville Tennessean* assigned one of its cub reporters, David Halberstam, to write a story about the Tigerbelles. Willye White recalled: "The Olympic games introduced me to the real world. Before my first Olympics, I thought the whole world consisted of cross burnings and lynchings. After 1956 I found there were two worlds, Mississippi and the rest of the world."[19]

The 1960 Olympics in Rome became a focus for every training session and meet that the Tigerbelles accepted that year. Temple had his most talented athletes ever, and the team dominated all national competitions, winning its fourth consecutive AAU national title at the April competitions in Akron, Ohio.[20] In July, the Tigerbelles dominated track events at the Olympic trials in Abilene, Texas, as they also endured the pervasive racism of Texas. The women almost missed one race because the driver refused the assignment; a hurried replacement got the team to the competition just in time. After the trials, the US Olympic committee named Ed Temple as the women's track and field coach for what commentators around the globe considered a showdown Olympics between the two superpowers, the United States and the Soviet Union.[21]

As Temple prepared his national team for the September Olympics, the backdrop of the Cold War loomed ever larger, what author David Maraniss called "one of the hottest summers of the cold war."[22] The backdrop of racial expectations also hindered the preparation of his team, especially the Tigerbelles. The lack of mainstream media coverage meant that few in the American press, along with their European counterparts, thought the US team would be a force in women's track and field. Olympic officials seeded some athletes, such as Wilma Rudolph, lower than expected in preliminary heats because they would not believe the recorded times that Coach Temple reported.

Once the races began, however, the Tigerbelles roared past most competitors, a storyline even reported in depth in the college's hometown of Nashville by renowned *Nashville Banner* reporter Fred Russell.[23] Barbara Jones took an individual bronze while teaming with Martha Hudson, Wilma Rudolph, and Lucinda Williams on the 400-meter relay team that won the gold medal, setting a new world record time. Wilma Rudolph, a native of Clarksville, Tennessee, won three gold medals and became an international sports celebrity.[24] The *New York Times,* for instance, profiled her after her wins in the 100- and 200-meter sprints, calling her "This queen of the 1960s" who was "a slender beauty whose eyes carry a perpetual twinkle, as if she were amused, and a little puzzled, at what is going on around her."[25] Three days later, with a photograph from the competition along with an individual photo, the *Times* picked up on its theme with the article, "World Speed Queen." It also called Tennessee State "the cathedral of women's track in this country," with Coach Ed "Temple the high priest."[26]

The print media was one thing; the unprecedented coverage that the 1960 games had on American television was another. Images of the Tigerbelles in their red, white, and blue USA uniforms (regrettably shown only in black-and-white film) arrived in prime time in American living rooms, courtesy of CBS's commitment to twenty hours of coverage. The image of these African American stars must have been startling since the networks at that time still kept African Americans by in large off the television screens.[27]

Television made the American winners national heroes. From this lofty international stage, Temple and the Tigerbelles began to tour other European locales, beginning in Athens, Greece, where the media played up the look of Rudolph as much as her achievements. At the Empire Games in London, the Tigerbelles again dazzled the crowds and media with their speed and grace. An infatuation with Rudolph began there that has never really ended. When the *Guardian* prepared a special blog on the most stunning Olympic moments as part of its coverage of the 2012 London Olympics, it chose Rudolph's 1960 performance at Rome as #35 of 50. And the writer observed that the Olympic achievement made Rudolph an international star: "The Italians called her La Gazzella Negra (the Black Gazelle) the French La Perle Noire (the Black Pearl) and the English, where she won the 100m dash at an invitational, the Tennessee Tornado."[28]

Back in the States by the end of the month, the Tigerbelles, with Rudolph garnering the most press, toured New York City, Detroit, and Chicago before a triumphant return to Nashville, where Mayor Ben West presented the team with a congratulatory proclamation—this event occurring in the same calendar year that sit-in demonstrations had rocked downtown businesses.[29] In her hometown of Clarksville, Tennessee, Rudolph presided over a huge community celebration, which became, at her insistence, the first integrated public event in the city since Reconstruction.[30]

Success bred more competition for the Tigerbelles in the 1961 track season. It began with the late January announcement that Rudolph was the recipient of the annual Associated Press designation of "Women Athlete of the Year." The following month, Tennessee A&I stars were the featured attraction at the inaugural Mason-Dixon games in Louisville, Kentucky. The team was now considered one of the greatest in all sports, and ever-growing crowds wanted to see the women run, while corporate sponsors lined up to be associated with these athletes. In April 1961, the All-American Homemaker of Tomorrow banquet at the snazzy Statler-Hilton Hotel in Washington, DC, hosted both white Miss America Nancy Anne Fleming and Wilma Rudolph as its honored guests. General Mills corporation gave Tennessee A&I a $1,000 scholarship in Rudolph's name. The attention, Ed Temple admitted to a reporter covering the event, was "more than we imagined."[31] Rudolph also met with President John F. Kennedy and Vice President Lyndon B. Johnson at the White House's Oval Office during that visit to DC. The leaders of the free world embraced the opportunity for a photo opportunity with the internationally famous Olympian, her mother, Blanche Rudolph, and Coach Ed Temple.[32]

Through it all Temple marveled at Rudolph's charisma: "Here's a person so great, but still so feminine, looks so nice, has a smile—she had everything." He told one scholar: "She would be the same person walking down Jefferson Street [in Nashville] or in Clarksville as she would meeting President Kennedy, or kings and queens, or ambassadors, or anything else." Here, Temple believed, is the reason why Rudolph "opened up the doors for women's sports period. I ain't talking just about track and field."[33]

Naturally the acclaim directed at Rudolph distracted then disappointed some of her Tigerbelle teammates. Certainly they understood that Rudolph's inspirational story of becoming a track star after having polio and wearing braces and special shoes until she was almost a teenager, and she did win all of the races. But they also knew the image was carefully managed—no one knew or at least acknowledged that Rudolph was a mother, already having a daughter named Yolanda, whom her parents cared for. In 1961 she married William Ward and was acknowledged as Wilma Rudolph Ward when she received the prestigious Sullivan Award for amateur athletic excellence in early 1962. By 1963 Rudolph had divorced Ward and married Yolanda's father, Robert Eldridge.[34]

Media coverage of Rudolph's brilliance dwarfed that of the Tigerbelles until Rudolph stopped competitive track and field in the summer of 1962. In one final meet against the Soviet Union's best at Palo Alto, California, Rudolph and other Tigerbelles defeated their Soviet rivals, leading a reporter from *Sports Illustrated* to write: that it was "the best track meet of the year, but also was the prettiest. Soviet women athletes have always seemed more attractive than Soviet women clerks or housewives, and now the Americans are catching up in this new respect as well as in the events on the field."[35]

Once competitive track was over, Rudolph hit the exhibition circuit. The US Information Service, one of the nation's Cold War propaganda arms, sponsored a trip to Ghana and Senegal in 1963. Tigerbelles continued to carry the torch, as columnist A. S. "Doc" Young observed, in annual competitions with women teams from the Soviet Union. Young wrote that the thought that competitive athletics were somehow improper for young women was passing as was the day that Soviet athletes routinely dominated American women. He gave credit where credit was due, first to Tuskegee Institute and then to the Tigerbelles, especially Rudolph. Young wrote that Rudolph "was probably the first Negro girl athlete to be described as being 'beautiful' in the general-circulating daily press. She proved that a girl didn't require a face by Frankenstein to qualify for the world of track and field."[36]

The Tigerbelles image only improved with the team's results in the 1964 Olympics in Tokyo, where Wyomia Tyus took gold and silver medals and Edith McGuire won one gold and two silver medals. US Olympic officials finally relented to the obvious and in 1967 named Temple as the coach for both the men's and women's teams. Then in the 1968 Mexico City Olympics Tyus took two more gold medals and Madeline Manning took another. Coach Temple later told Jennifer

Wilma Rudolph at the finish line during the 50-yard dash at a track meet in Madison Square Garden, 1961. *Image courtesy of Library of Congress, Prints & Photographs Division, NYWT&S Collection [LC-USZ62-115646].*

Lansbury that he felt Wyomia Tyus's achievements had been neglected, in large part because she was quiet and lacked the charisma of Rudolph. "People don't realize. Tyus did more great things than Wilma on the track. Wilma won 3 gold and a bronze. Tyus won 3 gold and a silver," Temple observed, and then emphasized, "Tyus was the first person, man or woman, to repeat in the sprints. Jesse Owens didn't repeat, Wilma didn't repeat. Tyus was the first person."[37]

Nor was the team's image damaged by the controversial protest by US men sprinters John Carlos and Tommie Smith at the Mexico City Olympics. After receiving their medals, Carlos and Smith raised clenched fists in a Black Power salute as the national anthem played over the loudspeakers. Their silent protest sparked a national outcry: track stars were to enhance the US international image, not burnish it. The six Tigerbelles who participated in the games did not join the protests, but Wyomia Tyus said she would give her medals to the two male sprinters if the Olympic team stripped them of the honors they had earned. The Tigerbelles' lack of civil rights activism did not mean that they were only sports figures and took no notice of the turmoil that swirled around them in the 1960s American South. Lucinda Williams remarked: "Look we had all experienced racism. Most of us came from the segregated South. We knew what it was like . . . we also knew why we had bag lunches and had to go to the bathroom in the fields when we traveled. At the end of the day we knew Mr. Temple had it right, we needed to get our degrees, compete hard, and be young ladies, we were going to get equality through our hard work."[38]

Racism was not the only barrier in the 1950s and 1960s; gender expectations and sexism were constant challenges. In interviews with historians Lansbury and Salisbury, Ed Temple consistently expressed his frustration with college administrators who always favored men's teams, no matter the international success of his program. He understood the South was football country but the achievements of the Tigerbelles were extraordinary. Temple told Lansbury that it really made him mad that after the success of 1960—and the national tour of his tired track stars that brought unprecedented positive publicity to the Tennessee A&I—college administrators still refused to provide scholarships to the women athletes.

The sexism of the age is most glaring today. It was more than the college administrators and the sports writers cited earlier—it extended to Olympic officials and even male teammates at TSU and on the Olympic team where male athletes would harass their female teammates and keep training equipment out of their reach. Even as the 1968 team dominated the AAU National Championships, a newspaper account called the women the "Tennessee Cindercuties."[39] As the work of Sara M. Evans and other scholars have shown over the past generation, those who advocated civil rights for African Americans often struggled with extending those same rights and considerations to African American women.[40]

The Olympic fortunes of the Tigerbelles changed in the 1970s. As more and more university systems across the South integrated, some track stars went to better funded formerly all-white universities. Also the congressional approval of Title IX of the federal Education Amendments of 1972 led more universities to invest new or enhanced funds into women's sports, furthering accelerating that process. Then in the South particularly state legislatures cut funding for formerly all-black public colleges and universities, claiming that such designated funding was no longer necessary. Despite the challenges, Temple's Tigerbelles still remained a power. Madeline Manning took a silver at the 1972 Munich Games and Kathy McMillan also won a silver medal at the 1976 Montreal Olympics. Then a promising team for the 1980 Moscow Games, with Mims, McMillan, and newcomers Brenda Morehead and Chandra Cheeseborough, lost their chance at international fame when the United States decided to boycott the games in protest of the Soviet invasion of Afghanistan.[41]

The 1984 Olympics at Los Angeles, however, became a platform for another remarkable Tigerbelle performance as Chandra Cheeseborough won two gold medals along with a silver medal. Times had changed, however; Cheeseborough never received the international or national acclaim afforded earlier Tigerbelle stars as Mae Faggs, Wilma Rudolph, and Wyomia Tyus. The Cold War was at a far different place that year. The Soviet Block boycotted the Los Angeles games, in reaction to the previous American boycott of the Moscow Olympics four years earlier. Many commentators felt that the winners had not faced the best competition, and slighted the athletes' achievements, even when medalists like Cheeseborough had set new national records in their recorded times.[42]

For over thirty years, the Tigerbelles had been standard setters for women track and field programs in the United States. Ed Temple orchestrated that achievement by recruiting, training, and retaining the best athletes he could find. His teams of the 1980s and early 1990s were skilled and competitive but no longer dominated on the international stage. Temple retired in 1993—with over forty years of shaping a legacy that even in the twenty-first century equates the word Tigerbelles with athletic excellence. His teams won a staggering thirty-four national titles, along with thirty-one Olympic medals. His successor as Tigerbelles coach was his last great sprinter, Chandra Cheeseborough. TSU historian Bobby L. Lovett observes: "no other institution in Tennessee had come close to matching these achievements."[43]

Cheeseborough continued the "Temple way," with her own modifications as TSU track coach into the 1990s. Wilma Rudolph, however, died from cancer a year after her coach's retirement. Obituaries from across the country emphasized not only her achievements at the 1960 Rome Olympics but her post-track career as a teacher, an inspirational speaker, and a role model. In the *New York Times*, Ira Berkow called Rudolph, "America's black Cinderella."[44] LeRoy Walker, then president of the US Olympic Committee, called Rudolph "one of the greatest sprinters of all time."[45]

Mae Faggs received similar praise after she too died of cancer in 2000. Recognized as the "mother" of the Tigerbelle tradition, Faggs later took an MA from the University of Cincinnati and then coached track and tougher physical education at various Cincinnati-area high schools.[46]

Indeed, most of the Tigerbelles found success outside of the world of TSU track and field. Some, like Wyomia Tyus, stayed close. Tyus raced professionally in the 1970s, served as an expert commentator at the 1972 Munich Games for ABC-TV, was a founder of the Women's Sport Foundation, and then taught and coached track at schools from the elementary to high school levels.[47]

Tyus's good friend and competitor, Edith McGuire Duvall, quickly retired from competitive track and field and became a schoolteacher and coach. But then she took up a second career as owner of several McDonald's restaurant franchises. Big Macs made her a rich woman, and she and her husband gave TSU $1 million, half of which they designated for the Charles and Edith Duvall Endowment for Excellence in Women's Track at TSU. The endowment gives TSU athletes a better chance to compete against major college track and field programs, providing funding that Ed Temple only dreamed of.[48]

One wonders, in this far different world of collegiate athletics of the twenty-first century, if any track and field program will ever match the excellence, or the cultural impact, of the Tigerbelles Women's Track Club of Tennessee State University. TSU officials in 2004 dedicated an Olympic Plaza, completed with a four-story-tall sculpture dedicated to the university's many Olympians. The plaza is a daily reminder of a four-decade-long legacy of excellence established by a coach and a group of dedicated women athletes. Twenty years after Temple's retirement as Tigerbelles coach, Nashville *Tennessean* writer Dwight Lewis remarked: "If there's anybody in America who has ever achieved success at the highest level in the area of track and field, it is Temple. His Tennessee State Tigerbelles opened the door for women, not only in track and field, but in all sports."[49] That is why the story of the Tigerbelles will continue to burn brightly in the history of college sports well into the twenty-first century.

II
Events

5

The National Interscholastic Basketball Tournament

The Crown Jewel of African American High School Sports during the Era of Segregation

Robert Pruter

The National Interscholastic Basketball Tournament was one of the premier black high school athletic competitions of the twentieth century. Organized and conducted by African American educators from 1929 to 1967, an era of intense racial segregation, the tournament was intended to provide a sporting experience for black youth equivalent to what their white educator counterparts were already providing through a well-developed array of mostly segregated state, regional, and national tournaments across the United States. The National Interscholastic Basketball Tournament, or NIBT, which was the initial designation of the black high school tournament, covered a number of different tournaments under different sponsorships and under slight variations of name during its nearly four decades of existence. This essay examines the history of the NIBT and the accompanying development of the various league, state, and regional tournaments that black educators established in support of it. The NIBT was the crown jewel in African American high school sports during the era of segregation, and served as the vehicle by which black educators also worked to broaden sports offerings to male and female athletes.

The NIBT began in 1929, but there is a long history of African American high school sports competition that led up to its founding at Hampton Institute in Washington, DC. Black interscholastic sports grew significantly during the 1920s, but the level of participation and organization depended on the area of the country. In the Deep South, black high schools suffered from rigid segregation and a white establishment that kept them impoverished. The development of athletics in black high schools in states such as Mississippi, Alabama, and Georgia lagged far behind white schools in the South and their black counterparts in other areas of the country. In the northern and western states, African Americans who attended integrated schools, notably in Chicago and New York, had the opportunity to participate in interscholastic sports on predominantly white teams. Also, predominantly black schools in the North (through de facto segregation) had the opportunity to compete against predominantly white schools. Most significantly, in the border regions—notably the District of Columbia, Missouri, and Kansas—segregation was still a fact, but economic support for black schools was far superior than in the Deep South and interscholastic sports especially thrived there in the 1920s.[1]

Border States Give Rise to Black Interscholastic Sports

Interscholastic sports for black high schools originated in the border states and sections, namely Washington, DC, West Virginia, Virginia, Kentucky, Missouri, and Kansas, as well as Indiana and southern Illinois. In this region of the country where de jure segregation existed, black high school teams were barred from competing against white schools and denied membership in state interscholastic associations and participation in the state meets sponsored by those associations.

The border states presented certain advantages to African American high schools over the Deep South. According to black sports historian Charles Herbert Thompson, border states were better able to finance their schools, supporting high schools with designated taxes from the black population. He noted that as "residential compositions" changed, many African American high schools in the border states inherited superior structures with more athletic facilities. The locus for the first black high school athletic programs was the Washington, DC, area. High school sports developed there because of the high concentration of African Americans in the area (more than a quarter million in a fifty-mile radius counted in the 1910 census), plus a favorable tax situation, which required that 10 percent of all taxes paid by blacks in the District of Columbia go to black schools. Thompson believed the number of schools, their proximity to one another, and their better facilities were especially conducive to the development of a highly organized interscholastic program in DC's black high schools.[2]

After several years of informal athletic competitions among such schools as Colored High of Baltimore, Wiley Bates of Annapolis, and M Street High of DC, six black DC educators in 1906 formed the Inter-Scholastic Athletic Association of the Middle States. The organization was the brainchild of Edwin Bancroft Henderson, who had joined the DC school district in 1904 as its first African American physical education instructor. Notwithstanding the organization's name, Henderson and his colleagues created a broader organization that included African American colleges along with local high schools, plus affiliated athletic clubs. Henderson envisioned the association as a means to provide training and opportunity for black Americans, especially high school students, with the idea that African Americans could help break down racial barriers through their athletic achievements.[3]

But the development of character through sports was also on the founders' minds, seeing athletics as a means toward "improvement of the youth, physically, mentally and morally." Unlike their white counterparts, black educators also desired to use interscholastic sports to build the mental and physical strength of African American youth so they could handle everyday impediments, slights, and hostilities from a prejudicial and discriminatory white society.[4]

The inaugural competition of the new athletic organization was a track and field meet held on Memorial Day in 1906. In the 1907–8 season, the association added a basketball competition. The initial association consisted of eight teams—Howard Medical, Howard College, Crescent Athletic Club, Oberlin Athletic Club, LaDroit Park, and the three secondary schools of Armstrong, M Street, and Howard Academy. Colored High of Baltimore and Commercial High of DC later joined the association. Other sports added to the schedule were baseball and football. In 1910, the Inter-Scholastic Association canceled its league format and became a sanctioning body.[5]

In December 1910, Henderson founded the Public Schools Athletic League (PSAL). The league was modeled after the New York PSAL, and thus encompassed both the District's high schools and elementary schools and was designed not only to provide competitive sports but also to provide a physical fitness program for all the District's children, boys and girls. By 1911, the PSAL was organized into eight grammar schools and four high schools (two outside the District), conducting competition in basketball, football, baseball, and indoor and outdoor track and field. By the 1920s, the high school league was called the Interstate High School Association, and included schools from DC, Baltimore, and Virginia. This league was supplanted by the South Atlantic High School Association in 1930.[6]

The development of African American high school sports in the DC area laid the foundation for their expansion into border states in the 1920s. West Virginia educators created one of the earliest athletic associations for black high schools, when they formed in 1925 the West Virginia Colored High School Athletic Union, and as a result the activities of their athletic association received considerable coverage in the national African American press. The league was launched with a basketball tournament, which drew eleven of the state's twenty-four black high schools. This number increased to seventeen by 1927, and twenty-two by 1930. The West Virginia association also later sponsored a state meet in track and supported baseball but not a tournament competition.[7]

Missouri and Kansas were typical border states, with histories of segregated school systems but a bit more enlightened tendencies in terms of race relations. As a consequence, black high schools received sufficient support to provide robust athletic opportunities for their students, and they could compete occasionally against white high school teams. Most of the schools were equipped with gymnasiums, which helped to foster outstanding basketball competition. The Missouri Valley Interscholastic Athletic Association (MVIAA) was formed in 1918 among African American schools of Kansas and Missouri. The initial membership included six schools, three from Missouri and three from Kansas. In basketball, the MVIAA pioneered league competition for both boys and girls. Basketball for girls had a particularly early development in Kansas, holding annual state championship competition. On the eastern side of Missouri was the Mississippi Valley Interscholastic Athletic Association, founded in the 1920s to provide athletic competition among the segregated schools in the St. Louis area of Missouri and Illinois.[8]

Illinois shared with Indiana the dubious distinction of being the only two northern states that had legal segregation in their schools, and as a result the black schools in southern Illinois and throughout Indiana were forced to establish their own state organizations, Illinois in 1919 and Indiana in 1920. Indiana had a state-wide organization, but in Illinois, approximately fifteen black schools in an area of southern Illinois known as Egypt, formed the Southern Illinois Conference of Colored High Schools (SICCHS). The schools had played basketball and other sports since before World War I, and being excluded from competition with white schools and membership in their leagues resulted in the need to organize their own sports and award championships. Basketball was the first sport contested, but the first postseason tournament was not staged until 1925. In 1922, the league initiated an annual track and field meet.[9]

The SICCHS schools were not initially members of the Illinois High School Athletic Association (IHSAA), but in 1928 they adopted the eligibility rules and conditions of competition as established by the IHSAA, and in return the association furnished the SICCHS with team trophies and individual awards for the league's basketball and track and field competitions. In November 1928, the IHSAA Board of Control voted to admit schools of the SICCHS to membership in the state association, but that membership did not allow the black schools in Egypt to compete in the IHSAA state tournaments.[10]

Development of National Tournaments by Negro Colleges

African American colleges in the border states were naturally aware of the plethora of interscholastic tournaments sponsored by the major white universities. While many of the predominantly African American schools in the North participated in university-sponsored track tournaments, the legally segregated all-black schools in the South and the border states were barred from such participation. In response to this situation, several Negro colleges in the 1920s, notably Howard University and Hampton Institute, began sponsoring interscholastic meets, first in track and field and later in basketball. Howard University inaugurated an annual interscholastic track and field meet in 1920 at the same time it began its intercollegiate meet for Negro colleges.[11]

In 1922, Hampton Institute inaugurated its new athletic field with a combination intercollegiate and interscholastic track meet. The meet was the brainchild of Hampton's physical education director, Charles H. Williams. The interscholastic competitions, along with the intercollegiate competitions, grew slowly at first, attracting only a handful of schools, but by the mid-1920s the meet took off, and became the preeminent track and field invitational for black high schools. In 1925, schools from North Carolina and South Carolina joined the usual entries from DC, Virginia, Maryland, and New Jersey.[12]

While the African American schools in the border states in the East had their annual Hampton Institute intercollegiate and interscholastic track meet, the Midwest border states had no comparable meet until Lincoln University of Jefferson City, Missouri, established the Middle Western Interscholastic in 1930. This May track meet attracted segregated black schools in the border states—mainly Missouri, Kansas, and southern Illinois—and the socially and legally segregated black schools in the northern cities, notably Detroit and Gary. Also in 1931 Lincoln sponsored its first interscholastic tennis tournament for black schools, and in 1933 initiated a midwestern tournament in basketball, inviting schools from Illinois, Missouri, Kansas, and Oklahoma.[13]

Track and field meets historically in high school sports had been used to launch high school leagues or to serve as the seed event around which a sports program could be expanded. Football and basketball lend themselves to one-on-one competition, but track and field usually calls for more than a dual meet—for participation by a whole group of schools. The Public Schools Athletic League in New York, for example, was launched with a giant indoor meet in Madison Square Garden in 1903. Mentioned earlier was Edwin Bancroft Henderson's launch of the Inter-Scholastic Association with a track and field meet in 1906. Similarly, Charles H. Williams had thus used the Hampton national track meet to pave the way for the establishment of the National Interscholastic Basketball Tournament (NIBT). Williams founded NIBT in 1929, with the hope of encouraging greater interest in and development of basketball in African American high schools, and also to encourage greater infrastructure for the sport with the creation of leagues and state associations. The racial exclusion policies at the University of Chicago and other university-sponsored basketball tournaments forced the African American community to develop its own national tournament to give recognition to schools with black student bodies.[14]

Williams persuaded Hampton to finance the costs of the tournament and to provide the meals and lodging for all the participants. He also had to find sponsors for the entertainment and the awards for the tournament and was able to get help from local merchants as well as from the A. G. Spalding & Bros. sporting goods company. An invitation went out in February 1929, and Williams requested records of the schools and stipulated that the schools must be in good standing with their state associations and that no player be older than twenty years of age. The first year's tournament—a two-day affair on March 22–23—drew only ten teams, and they were limited to the eastern seaboard, coming from Washington, DC, North Carolina, Virginia, and West Virginia. Perennial power Armstrong Technical of DC beat Douglass of Huntington, West Virginia, to garner the first championship.[15]

The following year, the tournament drew a larger field, hosting teams from Florida, South Carolina, and Kentucky. The title game outcome was a repeat of the previous year, with Armstrong Technical again defeating Douglass High. The national meet was still in its formative stages, but it was having the impact that Williams envisioned, if the *Chicago Defender* March 1931 report can be believed. The paper noted that the tournament "has served to awaken a keener interest in the cage sport than ever before. There has been not only greatest interest in state tournaments since the inception of the meeting [at Hampton], but numerous sectional tournaments are being held this season in several states."[16]

In 1931 the tournament became more national in scope when Phillips from Chicago and Roosevelt from Gary participated. The field was the largest ever, consisting of fifteen schools from seven states and DC. The participation of Phillips resulted from their exclusion the year before from the National Interscholastic Basketball Tournament of Amos Alonzo Stagg, sponsored by the University of Chicago. Phillips was the first black team to win the Chicago Public High School League's heavyweight (equivalent to varsity today) title, defeating Morgan Park High in the championship match. The *Chicago Defender*, in its extensive coverage of this breakthrough for the black community, publicly asked Stagg to invite Phillips to its national interscholastic tournament. In 1930 the biggest postseason tournament in Chicago was not the state tournament, which was largely a tournament of downstate schools, but Stagg's national tournament. Every year the Public League champion was an automatic entry into the Stagg tournament—that is, until 1930, when the color line reared its ugly head. Second-place finisher Morgan Park High, a predominantly white member of the league, received the invitation that should have gone to Phillips. The Stagg tournament in 1930 was facing increasing resistance from educators, and many states, especially those from the North, refused to send their champions. The southern states were still eager participants, and barring Phillips was an obvious but reprehensible way to keep the tournament alive. The *Defender* pointed this out, noting that "the university athletic department had bowed to the will of the ex-Confederates and their offspring."[17]

In 1931, the Phillips heavyweights were rated as the favorite to again win the Public League championship. The Stagg tournament had been discontinued, but Phillips wanted national recognition and decided to enter the Hampton tournament. The scheduling, however, required Phillips to participate in the NIBT prior to the city title game. Thus, based on their prior 1930 city championship, Phillips was invited by Hampton to participate. The Phillips team, coached by Julius Norman and led by future amateur and professional star Agis Bray, easily prevailed at Hampton, beating their competition by an average of seventeen points. The other northern team, Roosevelt High of Gary, was participating at Hampton, because the Indiana state tournament was segregated. Roosevelt took third place, setting the stage for future domination of the tournament by the school.[18]

The Depression exacted a toll on the NIBT, which was not helped by widespread flooding in the mid-Atlantic states in 1932. Charles H. Williams, believing that adverse weather conditions would prevent many teams from participating, canceled the 1932 tournament. Hampton sponsored the 1933 event, but it attracted only eleven schools representing just five states and DC. The tournament was won by Roosevelt High. For the first time, the tournament selected an all-star team, something that had been done in the national tournaments held in Chicago. Roosevelt was coached by one of the best of the early African American coaches, John Smith, and went on to dominate the tournament during the 1930s.[19]

Roosevelt did much to sustain the NIBT during the Depression years. When Hampton Institute decided it could no longer afford to sponsor the tournament, Charles H. Williams found a willing sponsor in Roosevelt High, which along with the city of Gary, agreed to host the tournament. Roosevelt's coach, John D. Smith, served as its director. The 1934 and 1935 tournaments were played at Municipal Auditorium in Gary, and the players were housed in the high school, which was supplied with cots by the United States Steel Corporation. Roosevelt High worked to make the tournament an eventful one, with a parade through the downtown streets of Gary, a water show by the school's Aquatic Club, a social to bring the teams together, a tour of the city, and free movie passes to the local theater. Roosevelt also provided for the first time a comprehensive tournament program of twenty-eight pages, with pictures of the participating teams and a history of the tournament. The more geographically assessable Midwest location helped expand the tournament, away from an East Coast predominance, with entries for the first time in 1934 from Arkansas and southern Illinois and in 1935 from Missouri. Roosevelt High won the 1935 tournament for the third year in a row over a field of eleven teams, in which the two-day tournament set a record for attendance, at 12,000.[20]

In 1934, when the NIBT came under sponsorship of Roosevelt High, the organizers formed the National Interscholastic Athletic Association (NIAA, but completely separate from today's National Association of Intercollegiate Athletics). Their intention was to create an equivalent to the National Federation of State High School Athletic Associations, a national governing body representing all sports and composed of all black state associations. The NIAA, however, never became an all-embracing national organization as envisioned by its founders.[21]

After an absence of three years, Kentucky returned to the NIBT in 1934. This event makes clear the challenges that African American schools in the South faced in forming interscholastic associations. Most of the state's growth in black high schools occurred only after World War I, and initially many were only two-year institutions. Such schools were only able to provide interscholastic sports programs after their conversion to four-year institutions during the late 1920s and early 1930s. Support from the state and local governments was anemic for black schools, and most were direly impoverished and small, without gymnasiums and other sport facilities. At many of the schools, basketball was played on an outdoor gravel-surface area. Only a handful of the schools could support a football team.[22]

By the mid-1920s, fewer than twenty black high schools in Kentucky were competing against one another, but during the late 1920s and early 1930s an additional thirty schools were soon engaged in sports competition. This rapid increase in numbers came from several factors—growth in support of black education that resulted in the founding of many new high schools, increased enrollments, the change from two-year to four-year programs, and the increased facilities afforded the schools, much of it due to support from Julius Rosenwald, the head of Sears Roebuck. Kentucky black schools received considerable support from northern philanthropy, notably from Rosenwald, who during the 1920s contributed to the construction of 5,357 schools, shops, and teachers' homes in black areas of the southern states. Local blacks contributed 17 percent to the cause, and local white officials were shamed into providing 64 percent from public funds. At least five Kentucky high schools serving an African American population were named after the famed philanthropist.[23]

As a result, in 1932 leading African American educators in the state formed the Kentucky High School Athletic League. Membership was limited to only four-year schools, and approximately fifty joined in the first years, eventually reaching a high of sixty-nine. The league regulated competition in three sports—basketball, football, and track and field. The only state championship sponsored by the Kentucky League, however, was the annual basketball tournaments for boys, held at the Kentucky State College in Frankfort. Girls' basketball was not supported by the Kentucky League, but the schools sponsoring girls' teams would sometimes compete for a state championship. This pattern of development of interscholastic athletics in Kentucky was replicated throughout the South during the 1920s and 1930s.[24]

The 1936 tournament was played at Roanoke, Virginia, with Lucy Addison High serving as sponsor and the Roanoke Municipal Auditorium serving as the venue. The tournament had fourteen teams competing, from six states. The 1937 and 1938 tournaments were canceled, but Williams revived the NIBT in 1939 at Fayetteville State College, North Carolina. In subsequent years, however, a rival tournament at Tuskegee Institute, Alabama—which had established itself as the Southern Interscholastic Basketball Tournament in 1935—grew rapidly to emerge as the de facto national tournament, if not in name. The emergence of the Tuskegee Tournament reflected the belated growth of high school sports in the Deep South states in general. This growth was marked by the establishment of African American state high school associations in North Carolina (1930), Georgia (1932), South Carolina (1934), Tennessee (1934), Louisiana (1935), and Mississippi (1940).[25]

The border region of DC-Maryland-Virginia, however, experienced the most robust growth in sports programs for black high school youth in the country, providing an array of sports that rivaled their white counterparts. In most regions of the country, African American sports were usually limited to four at most—basketball for boys and girls, track for boys and girls, football, and baseball. But in the border region's middle Atlantic states, black schools formed a variety of leagues and state associations, which sponsored an array of sports beside the above-mentioned four. The South Atlantic High School Conference, which served schools in DC-Maryland-Virginia, also sponsored tennis, golf, and swimming; and the Public Athletic League of Baltimore sponsored soccer, rifle, girls field ball, swimming, wrestling, bowling, and boxing. The black high schools in the region also participated in the NIBT tournament throughout its existence, but never traveled south to Tuskegee.[26]

Southern Interscholastic Basketball Tournament

In 1935, the Tuskegee Institute augmented its nine-year-old national track and field tournament for girls and boys with a basketball tournament, in which there were separate competitions for boys and girls. The tournament was held indoors, which was a novelty for many African American high school teams in the Deep South. Tuskegee's expansion of its high school sport programs is indicative that the South was making progress in bringing interscholastic athletics up to the level provided blacks in the border states. The meet drew ten boys teams and six girls teams. The tournament was initially called the Southern Interscholastic Basketball Tournament (SIBT), and beginning in 1937 grew more national in scope when the competing National Interscholastic Basketball Tournament was canceled during the years 1937 and 1938. By 1939, the tournament was drawing twenty-five boys teams and fourteen girls teams. In contrast, the NIBT, held in Fayetteville, North Carolina, in 1939, attracted only fourteen boys teams. The SIBT clearly superseded the revived NIBT in 1939 as the authentic national tournament.[27]

In 1940, the *Chicago Defender* represented the prevailing sentiment that the Tuskegee event was the new national basketball tournament. The paper completely ignored the national tournament that took place in Fayetteville, North Carolina, which was won by Gary Roosevelt. Instead, the paper gave extensive coverage to Tuskegee and the championship won by Lincoln High of Evansville, Indiana, not calling the tournament national but treating it as such. This coverage aroused the ire of Gary coach and one of the principals of the Fayetteville tournament, John D. Smith, who wrote a strong letter to the *Chicago Defender*'s influential sports columnist, Fay Young, who had been a longtime supporter of the NIBT since it began in 1929. In his column, Young quoted Smith comments that the Fayetteville event was the "national" tournament and that the Tuskegee was not, and then Young acidly responded, "Since the Fayetteville tournament was called 'national,' it ought to be national in scope. It is not national when 14 of the 16 teams are from the Carolinas and West Virginia," and then pointed out that Fayetteville is "too far for most high schools to send teams."[28]

Smith was probably displeased that another Indiana school, Evansville, which competed in a southern Indiana tournament, went to Tuskegee rather than to Fayetteville. The following week, the *Chicago Defender*, to apparently assuage Smith a little, ran a photo of the Roosevelt champs, referring to the tournament as "national," but also pointedly noting that fourteen of the sixteen entrants came from the Carolinas and West Virginia.[29]

In 1940, the Southern Illinois Conference of Colored High Schools petitioned the association they belonged to, the Illinois High School Athletic Association for $75 to pay for a trip of its league champion, Attucks High of Carbondale, to participate in the Tuskegee national tournament. Although members of the IHSAA, the SICCHS schools were excluded from the association's state tournaments. Attucks received the funds in 1940 to go to Tuskegee, but the following year the IHSAA turned down the Southern Illinois Conference petition for funds, because it had always disapproved of intersectional contests. The state association no doubt realized that it put Egypt's segregated schools in an unfair situation, both denying them entrance into the Illinois state tournament and keeping them from playing in the end-of-season tournaments. Thus, after 1940 SICCHS schools no longer participated in any national black tournament, and the IHSAA seemed unwilling to integrate the black schools of Egypt into their programs.[30]

In 1942, the IHSAA board came up with an arrangement that only heightened the segregation problem. The board had the two top teams of SICCHS play for the "colored high school basketball championship" as an adjunct to the regular state tournament. The IHSAA arranged for the league to conduct a tournament each year to pick out the two contenders for the state championship. The SICCHS championship game was played in the afternoon between two quarterfinal games. The SICCHS schools continued to protest their exclusion from state tournaments, and in 1946, the IHSAA finally acceded to their wishes and forced integration into southern Illinois, in both state-sponsored track and field meets and basketball tournaments.[31]

Indiana, on the other hand, despite having a long history of virulent Ku Klux Klanism throughout the state, proceeded with integration more cleanly than Illinois, ending its segregated system in one year, 1942. The year before Gary Roosevelt participated in its last national tournament, at Fayetteville. In 1942, two other African American Indiana schools took part in the Tuskegee tournament, but thereafter all black Indiana teams participated in the integrated state tournament in lieu of the national black tournament.[32]

National Invitational Interscholastic Basketball Tournament

Tuskegee recognized that its tournament was truly more national in scope, and in March 1941 changed its name to the National Invitational Interscholastic Basketball Tournament (NIIBT). In the 1941 tournament, a total of eighteen boys and sixteen girls teams representing twelve states competed for the national championship. The tournament recognized the huge numbers of African American schools sponsoring basketball for girls throughout the South, particularly in Kentucky and North Carolina where they competed for state championships, and in Tennessee where they competed in eastern and western sectional tournaments.[33]

In its first year, the NIIBT only attracted schools from the Deep South and Southwest states, and the final in the boys bracket was between two Oklahoma schools, with Sand Springs Booker T. Washington (OK) beating Seminole Booker T. Washington (OK) 38–24, for the title (virtually all the black high schools in Oklahoma were called Booker T. Washington at that time). Marques Haynes, who became the famous dribbler for the Harlem Globetrotters, played for Sand Springs. In 1942, twenty-seven boys teams and twenty-one girls teams, representing fourteen states, participated. Because of gasoline and tire rationing during World War II, Tuskegee was compelled to cancel its 1943 tournament.[34]

The National Interscholastic Basketball Tournament continued to struggle at Fayetteville, attracting only ten teams in 1941—five from North Carolina, two from Virginia, one each from Georgia, District of Columbia, and Indiana (the long loyal Gary Roosevelt). The following year, the tournament was moved to Durham, North Carolina, with twelve schools, again with a heavy concentration (eight of the schools) from the Carolinas and Virginia. For the first time since 1931, Gary

Roosevelt was no longer participating. A considerable plus for the tournament was the participation of two schools from Missouri and Kansas, two states that had been ignoring the national tournaments since their founding, both states long satisfied with their interstate competition in various sports since the early 1920s. Missouri schools would participate in future national tournaments, but this was Kansas's only participation. It proved to be a good one, as Sumner High of Kansas City, Kansas, beat a Virginia school and two West Virginia schools on route to its title win. The travel restrictions of World War II ended this tournament after 1942 as it did at Tuskegee.[35]

National Tournament Resumed in Nashville in 1945

In 1945, the national black interscholastic basketball tournament entered a new phase, coming under new sponsorship by Tennessee A&I State College (later called Tennessee State University) in Nashville. Dr. W. S. Davis, president of A&I, and Henry Arthur Kean, the school's athletic director, together founded this new competition, which they formally called the National Invitational High School Basketball Tournament (NIHSBT). This was a last-minute change in the name. The tournament was originally envisioned as the Midwestern Invitational High School Basketball Tournament, but when Davis and Kean began getting entry requests from Arkansas, Oklahoma, and West Virginia, the name was changed to reflect its increasing national scope. No schools from the East Coast attended the first year, however. The *Chicago Defender* ran a story as late as March 24, 1945, on the impending Midwestern Invitational tournament. Because the gymnasium at Tennessee A&I was deemed inadequate, organizers used the nearby gymnasium at Pearl High School, deemed the best athletic facility for blacks in Nashville. The new national tournament excluded girls from the competition, making it an all-boys affair as Davis and Kean found sponsoring both a boys and girls tournament financially unfeasible. Thirteen teams from five states participated in the event.[36]

Davis and Kean also decided the time was right to establish a new national organization to oversee the tournament, the National High School Athletic Association (NHSAA). Kean was elected the organization's first president. Although a parallel organization to the National Federation of State High School Athletic Associations, the founders of the NHSAA knew that with fewer resources it was "not designed to achieve functional status" with the predominantly white organization. Charles Herbert Thompson claimed that the NHSAA became the "most significant organizational structure in the history of black interscholastic athletics."[37]

In 1946, the organizers increased the NIHSBT's appeal by adding a consolation bracket to allow first-round losers at least another game before heading home. Sixteen teams participated, among them twelve state title holders, including the first representation from an eastern seaboard state, Maggie Walker High of Virginia. The addition of the consolation bracket gave the national interscholastic contest the largest field since the 1942 tournament in Tuskegee. Oklahoma continued its string of champions at four, when Booker T. Washington of Cushing defeated Tampa Middleton (FL), 44–40, for the 1946 title. In the 1947 tournament, Booker T. Washington of Tulsa continued the Oklahoma string of championships.[38]

The NIHSBT faced a number of troubling issues in 1947. President Kean asked that the NHSAA take on greater financial support for the tournament, which had been supported almost solely by Tennessee A&I. Kean asked each school to pay an annual fee of one dollar to their associations. Charles Herbert Thompson also reported that the NHSAA also voted to eliminate the consolation bracket, deeming it was "no longer needed," a decision that appears mystifying given the success of the 1946 tournament. The NHSAA realized the consequences of integration in 1947, when the black schools in Kansas merged with their white counterparts and took themselves out of the Nashville tournament.[39]

The 1948 NIIBT saw the entry of a new basketball power, St. Elizabeth, from Chicago, Illinois. The school, a member of the Chicago Catholic High School Athletic League but not the Illinois High School Athletic Association, competed against other Catholic league members, as well as against other high schools during barnstorming tours in the South on Christmas and Easter breaks. The *Chicago Defender*'s Fay Young, who also served as the commissioner of the NHSAA, used his influence and position to bring St. Elizabeth into the tournament, which brought northern state representation into the tournament. St. Elizabeth was eliminated in the first round, but the tournament had not seen the last of the school. Tulsa Washington (OK) repeated as the tournament champ, defeating Don Thompson, of Tampa, Florida. The next three years of the tournament were won by St. Elizabeth. In 1949, seventeen teams, fifteen of them state champions, participated. The next year a more logical sixteen teams participated, and thereafter the tournament settled on that sized field. Also, a rule limiting players to under twenty-one years of age was imposed.[40]

The eastern states had three representatives in the 1949 national tournament —Armstrong Technical of Washington, DC; Booker T. Washington of Norfolk, Virginia; and Avery Institute of Charleston, South Carolina. Many of the eastern schools, however, chose not to participate, including those from North Carolina, because they regularly competed in regional tournaments. One regional was the Eastern Scholastic Tournament in Hampton, Virginia. Another was the Invitation High School Tournament in Fayetteville, North Carolina, sponsored by Fayetteville State College, which the school considered to be a continuation of the national tournament it sponsored from 1939 to 1941. To avoid competition with the Nashville tournament, Fayetteville scheduled its tournament a week earlier.

Armstrong Technical (DC), for example, won the Fayetteville tournament in 1949 and the following week was eliminated in Nashville with a one-point loss to the eventual champion, St. Elizabeth.[41]

In the 1950–51 basketball season, St. Elizabeth continued to exert itself as a perennial national power in basketball, in touring the southern states during the Christmas holidays, winning all eight of its contests, and then sweeping through the national interscholastic tournament for the third consecutive time. The school, however, was forced to forfeit its title for using an ineligible player, who had already completed eight semesters of high school prior to participation in the tournament. Runner-up B. T. Washington High of Cushing (OK) was awarded the first-place trophy. St. Elizabeth was put on probation for the 1952 tournament, and that year the school won only one game in a season in which they played only twelve league games. The action against St. Elizabeth was important for the NHSAA, because it helped combat the belief that African American high school basketball had loose academic standards.[42]

In 1952, the historic Louisville Central (KY) High School, coached by Willie L. Kean, brother of Henry Arthur Kean (cofounder of the Nashville tournament), defeated another historic school, Wheatley High of Houston, for the national title. The Nashville tournament had always been handicapped by inadequate facilities, and patrons of the tournament had to be turned away for lack of seating in both the college and high school gyms. Finally, in 1953, Tennessee State University (formerly A&I) opened a 4,000-seat arena, and every tournament game was now played in the new facility, making the tournament a much more attractive event befitting its national prestige. This ended the Pearl High School automatic participation in the tournament. Tennessee State worked to create a memorable event for the participants with TSU coeds as queens, providing a basketball variety show, and feting the coaches at a special pretournament breakfast. Paris Western (KY) beat Montgomery Booker T. Washington (AL) for the 1953 championship.[43]

The Impact of *Brown v. Board of Education*

In 1954, the United States Supreme Court, in its historic *Brown v. Board of Education* decision, outlawed segregation, notably public school segregation, across the land. Before 1954, only Indiana (1942), Illinois (1946), Kansas (1947), and Missouri (1953) had integrated their state high school basketball tournaments. After *Brown*, integration gradually crept across the United States, and black schools closed their doors as students enrolled in integrated institutions and African American state high school athletic associations disbanded to join the heretofore-white state athletic associations. The tournament at Nashville felt this impact by 1956.

Prior to the 1956 NIHSBT, the Oklahoma schools merged their black state high school athletic association with the white state athletic association, which prevented them from sending any teams to the national tournament in Nashville. The loss of the Oklahoma teams dealt a severe blow to the prestige of the tournament as many of the best teams in the national competition hailed from that state. The 1956 national tournament was dominated by Louisville Central (KY) High School, which won its third straight under Coach William Kean. The team had dedicated their championship run to Henry Arthur Kean, the late brother of their coach and one of the founders and past presidents of the NHSAA. As an indication of how integration was affecting coverage of the tournament by the African American press, the *Afro-American*, in Baltimore, failed to report the results of the 1956 Nashville tournament but gave a sizable story on Crispus Attucks High winning the Indiana state tournament for the second straight year. In 1957, West Virginia, one of the founding states in the national tournament and with a rich tournament history, ended its participation. Almost immediately after *Brown v. Board of Education*, West Virginia began integrating its schools, so by March of 1957 the West Virginia Athletic Union held its last state tournament with a rapidly dwindling number of schools, sending Park Central High of Bluefield to the national tournament before disbanding.[44]

St. Elizabeth of Chicago—which after their tournament disgrace of 1952 had participated in the 1953, 1954, and 1955 tournaments, winning only one game each time—returned to their championship ways by capturing the 1957 tournament. This would represent the team's third national championship (the stripped title of 1951 not included). Coached by Art White and led by its great center, Arthur Hicks, St. Elizabeth beat McKinley High of Baton Rouge, Louisiana, for the title. The team was presented the newly created Henry Arthur Kean Memorial trophy, donated by the Universal Life Insurance Company of Memphis. St. Elizabeth was awarded permanent possession of the trophy as a three-time winner, and the tournament had to create another Kean trophy for the following year. The 1957 tournament represented St. Elizabeth's last participation in the Nashville tournament, thus ending northern state participation. At the end of the 1961 season, St. Elizabeth became an all-girls school, but not until after winning the Catholic League title.[45]

The 1958 Nashville tournament was a grand one for Pearl High of Nashville, which won national basketball honors with a win over Carver High of Dotson, Alabama. As a host school from 1945 to 1952, Pearl had the participation record for the largest number of tournaments, so winning the national title was that much sweeter. Behind their star player, Ronnie "Scat" Lawson, Pearl posted a perfect season record in 1958. The tournament, however, was diminishing, as only nine state champions were represented, all from southern states. North Carolina and Texas did not participate, even though those states had not yet begun integration of their high schools. The tournament paid tribute to the late Fay Young, legendary sports writer from the *Chicago Defender* and the NHSAA commissioner who had died some months earlier. At the business meeting of the NHSAA, John H. Cooper of Wilberforce, Ohio, was elected new commissioner to replace Young.[46]

The 1959 NIHSBT again consisted of only nine schools, with Pearl High repeating as champions. The title game between Pearl and Scipio Jones of North Little Rock, Arkansas, featured two outstanding athletes, Ronnie "Scat" Lawson and Eddie Myles, of the two schools respectively. Both made the tournament all-star team, and the two players, according to Charles Herbert Thompson, were the most highly recruited players in the history of the tournament, Lawson ending up at UCLA and Myles ending up at Seattle University. Two juniors on the Pearl team, Vic Rouse (another tournament all-star) and Les Hunter, went on to lead Loyola University of Chicago to the National Collegiate Athletic Association title in 1963. That all four went on to play at predominately white schools rather than the Negro colleges is indicative of the level of integration that was taking place on college teams in this period.[47]

While the African American community took pride in their athletes' success in integrating basketball, many foresaw the impending decline in their own sports institutions. Bill Nunn of the *Pittsburgh Courier*, for example, noted that in the

Pearl High School basketball team, Nashville, Tennessee. National Champions, 1959.
Image courtesy of Pearl High School Alumni Association.

recruitment of Rouse and Hunter, Loyola coach George Ireland took players that rightly should have played at Tennessee A&I State University, calling it "one of the biggest thefts since the Brinks bank job."[48]

The *Pittsburgh Courier* correctly reported on African American sentiments of the day, but did not get the story quite right. Tennessee A&I State University's legendary coach John B. McClendon, considered by many the "father of black basketball," fielded teams renowned for their fast break and up-tempo style of play, and the Pearl High players learned that style of game practicing in the Tennessee State facilities. According to Les Hunter, McClendon showed no interest in Hunter or Rouse. Hunter speculated that McClendon, because he was "on top of the basketball world," waited for players to come to him rather than to actively recruit them.[49]

In 1960, Pearl High, led by Rouse and Hunter, made it three national titles in a row, beating Roosevelt High of West Palm Beach, Florida, before the largest crowd ever to see the title game. When Pearl High won its fourth title in 1963, that made the sixth consecutive time a Tennessee high school had won the championship. Only 2,500 spectators witnessed the title game, a low number compared to the crowds in recent years, which ran approximately double in size to the 1963 crowd. The title game had to compete with the television broadcast of the NCAA tournament, which featured Loyola University of Chicago, which had four African American starters (including the earlier mentioned Pearl graduates Rouse and Hunter). Integration across America was making the national interscholastic less special for African Americans. The 1963 tournament saw membership in the NHSAA dwindle to eight teams and eight states, with the withdrawal of Louisiana from the competition. Charles Herbert Thompson reported that "expenses and travel distance" were cited as the "stated reason" for Louisiana's withdrawal. He said that this erosion of the tournament "made its future uncertain."[50]

The 1964 NIHSBT saw Parker High of Birmingham (AL) end the six-year reign of Tennessee winners when it eliminated Pearl High in the semifinals, and went on to take the national title. A Tennessee school would never win another title, because a few months later, the Tennessee Secondary School Athletic Association (TSSAA) voted to accept as affiliate members the black schools belonging to the segregated Tennessee High School Athletic Association and the Middle Tennessee Athletic Association. This action brought integrated competition to Tennessee high schools, but not yet the state tournament. The TSSAA conducted a separate "affiliate" state championship in 1965, won by Pearl; but in 1966 the state tournament was integrated with the participation of three black high schools, plus four formerly white schools with integrated squads. Pearl High made extraordinary history that year, stunning the high school basketball fans across the state by winning the TSSAA championship, marking integration in Tennessee with an exclamation mark.[51]

End of the Tournament

The integration of Tennessee high school basketball would effectively exclude the state from the tournament and Nashville as the host site. A new venue for the national tournament was found at Alabama State College in Montgomery. The NHSAA membership was down to seven states in 1965, and the future of the tournament was the main topic of the group's annual meeting. Some of the delegates from states close to integration voiced the opinion that the tournament should not continue, but in the end the membership voted for the tournament's continuation. The following year, however, the NHSAA lost another member when the Arkansas black schools merged with the white schools. Only eight southern states still had dual systems for white and black schools, and of those Louisiana and Texas were no longer participating in the tournament. Again at the annual meeting, the NHSAA had to deal with the tournament's future, and Charles Herbert Thompson said the delegates came to the conclusion that "until all vestiges of segregation were erased, the NHSAA felt it had a definite purpose to serve."[52]

The 1966 championship saw only eight schools representing six states competing for the national title. When South Carolina withdrew in 1967, membership was down to five states. The NIHSBT, again held on the campus of Alabama State College, consisted of only six teams, the lowest total ever. Before the 1968 tournament was scheduled, the president of the NHSAA, C. T. Smiley, requested that each eligible state association make known by February 1, 1968, whether or not they planned to attend the national tournament. After Florida, Alabama, and Georgia, however, merged their black state associations with the white associations, membership was down to two, Mississippi and Virginia, and the NHSAA reluctantly canceled the 1968 tournament.[53]

The executive committee of the National High School Athletic Association made the decision that the end had come, and on June 16 convened and in what Charles Herbert Thompson said was "probably a solemn occasion" agreed unanimously to dissolve the organization. While integration indicated progress in the country, the downside was that many black institutions, such as the National Interscholastic Basketball Tournament (and all its permutations), born of segregation, were forced out of existence. The great legacy of the tournament is that it was a wonderful athletic event for African American students, educators, and public, who, while kept out of the mainstream of the high school sport world, created their own sports institutions, which they could look on with great pride and with sense of accomplishment and fulfillment.[54]

6

The Black Heart of Dixie

The Turkey Day Classic and Race in Twentieth-Century Alabama

Thomas Aiello

Robert Russa Moton, the president of Tuskegee Institute, and J. Council Trenholm, president of Alabama State Normal School, didn't like each other very much. They had very different ideas about education, about civil rights, about everything. But they were, despite their differences, allies in both education and civil rights. Racism gave them little choice. And so in 1924 they formalized an athletic rivalry between their two schools by creating an annual neutral-site game that would celebrate black Montgomery and black education in Alabama.[1] The two schools' football teams had been playing each other since 1901, but now they would be playing the first game that became known as a "classic."

Classics between historically black colleges were more than just annual football games between rivals. They included parades, dances, and alumni gatherings. By the late twentieth century, they included job fairs and other contests between groups of competing students. The most influential of these early classics pitted Howard University and Lincoln University, which drew coverage from the black press throughout the country, serving as a touchstone for the race to demonstrate athletic and academic success. Classics were events. They were happenings. And they served as a staging ground for politics, culture, and class in the communities they represented.[2]

The 1924 Alabama classic game was contested between the two most prominent teams in the state—one the home of the Tuskegee Machine, the other a liberal facilitator of civil rights activism. Thus, the game's dynamics mirrored the various divisions in black life. One university was urban, one rural. One was largely absent the hardened conservative hierarchy that often dominated black colleges in the twentieth century, the other was not. The Classic then served not only as a center of Alabama's black sports, but also as a theater for the debates of black fans who

supported them. Despite the tumult of Jim Crow and the long civil rights movement in Alabama, there was always the game.

That game was the nation's oldest continuously played black college "classic,"
but the rivalry between the two schools had its genesis in the post-Reconstruction
nineteenth century, well before either attempted to field a football team.

In fall 1886, tensions were high in Marion, Alabama, between the local black
public college, Lincoln Normal School, and the local white Baptist one, Howard
College. That semester, a group of more than twenty Howard students surrounded
a Lincoln student after he refused to leave the sidewalk and allow his white counterparts to pass. The Baptists began beating their Lincoln counterpart, but the
Lincoln student was able to fight back, defending himself and escaping before
any more harm could be done. The incident gave Howard trustees leverage in
their continued effort to have Lincoln removed from Marion, if not all together
destroyed. "This question of self-defense must be settled and the sooner the better," wrote William B. Paterson, the normal school's white president, in a letter to
Tuskegee's Booker T. Washington. "An educated man will not and can not take the
abuse that an ignorant one will."[3]

Washington, for his part, supported Paterson with full throat in the school's
battle with Howard. But he wouldn't go much farther than that. The incident convinced local Marion whites that the black school needed to leave, and so Paterson
began scouting locations and lobbying the Alabama legislature for a change of
venue. Ultimately, the choice would come down to Birmingham or Montgomery.
Washington did everything he could at that time to lobby against Lincoln's relo-
cation to Montgomery. That was, he argued, Tuskegee's sphere of influence. He
didn't want any further competition. The school should move to Birmingham.
"My object," he argued as early as February 1887, "is to prevent the Marion school
from being located here."[4]

Later that month, on February 25, 1887, the legislature approved two measures
that would grow the rivalry between the two schools. The first chartered Alabama
Colored People's University from the ashes of Lincoln Normal and appointed a
board of trustees to relocate the school from Marion. The second gave the Tuskegee
board of trustees the power to purchase land for school use, thus removing a mod-
icum of power from state commissioners and putting it in the hands of Tuskegee
itself. On that day, February 25, the state legislature laid the foundation for mod-
ernizing its black colleges, while simultaneously giving birth to the modern versions of Tuskegee and what would become Alabama State University.[5]

It also created a legitimate rivalry between the two schools, re-founded (as
it were) on the same day. Washington continued to make the argument over
the coming months that Tuskegee's reach extended less than forty miles away to
Montgomery, corresponding regularly with influential friends in the capital to

convince them of that fact.[6] Paterson, meanwhile, also had an interest in the final location of his Marion school. "The whites of Bgham," he told Washington, "are at work to get a Baptist College there and will probably oppose the Colored."[7] It was a not subtle warning to his friend and colleague. We might be coming to Montgomery against our will.

In July 1887, the Baptist leadership of Marion announced that Howard College would be leaving for a larger city. Though the school produced no formal plan, it was clear to most that Birmingham wanted the school, and that the feeling was mutual. The location became official later that week, allowing the white Baptists of Birmingham to argue against locating the black state college near the school that originally caused so many problems. With the white Marion school coming to Birmingham, the black Marion school was coming to Montgomery. It was coming to Tuskegee's backyard.[8]

Washington, for his part, would remain close to Paterson after the conflict. Such was the nature of black college life in the Heart of Dixie. There was a healthy nineteenth-century rivalry between Tuskegee, Lincoln, Talladega, and Alabama A&M, but the schools remained allies and coalesced around one another when threatened by the creeping hoard of white supremacy.[9] Still, the ordeal hurt Washington's pride, and his paranoia would ensure that the Tuskegee leader would keep Paterson at arm's length. And his friends knew it. "I may some times seem to be with Paterson," wrote Cornelius Nathaniel Dorsette, the most prominent black doctor in Gilded Age Alabama, "but never fear its only to keep posted and to be prepared to work for Tuskegee and unless I loose my grasp on this people, you shall always have the major part of its pupils." William Jenkins, a member of the Tuskegee faculty, reported to Washington after visiting Alabama State that it was one of "the most miserable excuses I have ever witnessed." Paterson, for his part, "occupied most of the time in his usual style of braggadocio and mean insinuations."[10] Years before the schools began playing football, the rivalry was on.

Throughout the early 1890s, the schools jockeyed for influence with the legislature, mainly to receive the largest possible shares of the state's meager resources for black education. There was predictable politicking, glad-handing, and the common backstabbing that comes with competition for state funds. Tuskegee had the benefit of longevity at its current location and the growing fame of Washington. Alabama State had the benefit of a location near the capitol and a white president.[11] In 1897, the rift grew greater, when one of Tuskegee's white board members attacked Paterson and Alabama State for hiring white teachers along with black teachers, thus encouraging an illegal "social equality." A frustrated Paterson wrote to Washington that "I believe the desire to have peace and good-will between our Schools is mutual," but that he was not above a fight.[12] And so, in the wake of Washington's 1895 Cotton States Exhibition address, the white head of Alabama

State was arguing for the validity of social equality with the black head of Tuskegee. The foundation of the rift between the two schools would continue along those same poles for decades.

For the student bodies, however, such bureaucratic bickerings were angels dancing on the heads of pins. The advantage for the students, as of 1893, redounded to Tuskegee, because in 1893, under the leadership of Coach Clarence Matthews, Tuskegee fielded its first football team. Of course, the team itself was a tenuous thing. Matthews wasn't just Tuskegee's coach. He was also a freshman student who had just arrived on campus. He would serve as coach until his graduation in 1897.[13]

The team played its first collegiate game in January 1894 against Atlanta University. Tuskegee lost in a shutout. It lost in a shutout in 1895. And in 1897. And in 1899. That fourth shutout loss was significant, however, because for the first time, Atlanta came to Tuskegee. "We are about [to] introduce a new feature in the social and Athletic side of Tuskegee," James Washington wrote to his brother Booker, "and I must write you for your support, both financially and morally. On the 15th of December we are to engage Atlanta University on our grounds in a game of foot ball, and of course we need co-operation from you." Sponsoring a game was something different from simply traveling to play one. "I hope to impress those Atlanta folks as to how to be received and treated, a point which all who have visited there will say, they are weak on. We are aiming to make their trip here, one of pleasure, also profitable, in fact it is intended to make the day a gala one."[14]

And so Tuskegee had its first experience with the gala event that is an annual college football rivalry. The team lost again in 1900, but for the first time, Tuskegee scored points. And so, prior to 1901, Tuskegee was 0-5, with all of its losses to Atlanta University. It was clear to then-coach Charles Winter Wood that the team needed an easier opponent. And so, in 1901, Tuskegee did for its local rival what more established Atlanta had done for it—it gave Alabama State a chance to play. State was still catching up to Tuskegee and only recently had created a football team. Its 1901 game would be its first. But even though its rival began a football program in 1893, Tuskegee had only played five collegiate games of its own; it had only hosted one previous contest; and it had only scored twelve meager points.[15]

Despite that lack of success, there is something to be said for experience. The Montgomery upstarts were no match for the Golden Tigers. They lost 37 to 0.[16]

That first game, however, would be played under a shadow that would reach through most of their twentieth-century games. That November, as the teams took the field, Alabama was writing, approving, and ratifying a new state constitution that would almost uniformly disenfranchise black voters in the state. It included a poll tax, a literacy test, and, perhaps most importantly, a "descendants" clause that served to exempt white voters from undergoing such rigorous tests for voting. While the local school was winning its first collegiate football game, the white *Tuskegee News* was urging ratification. "If the intelligent and worthy negro could only realize the wonderful blessings which the new constitution brings them they would all vote for ratification," a typical editorial surmised. But "if the new Constitution should fail of ratification it will be solely because of the indifference of the white men who in all the battles for right, heretofore have borne the brunt of the struggle."[17]

Such was the racial climate in Alabama, ensuring that though there was a legitimate tension between the administrations of the two schools, and though their athletic rivalry would grow to match those bureaucratic tensions, they would often remain allies in the face of the racism that surrounded them. Still, the differences between Paterson and Washington as to what constituted "social equality" and the best means of achieving it were real, and in a climate of heightened racial tensions, those differences would exacerbate the sense of rivalry between the schools, particularly in sports like football.

The next season, 1902, with the new constitution ratified and the black vote all but eliminated in Alabama, Tuskegee and State played again. State lost 85–0. Alabama State didn't field a team in 1903, but in 1904, they played Tuskegee again. Again it was the only game on their schedule. Again they lost, this time 65–0.[18]

Less than a month prior to the 1904 game, on October 23, a bombshell article appeared in the *New York World* roundly criticizing Washington and Tuskegee and using Paterson and Alabama State as its counterexample. "The Negro Normal and Industrial School at Montgomery," the article claimed,

with a white man, W. B. Paterson, as President, had last year within 100 pupils as many as Tuskegee, with an income of $13,000, compared to the stated income of $71,933 and actual receipts of $155,000 of the Washington school, yet it has never been said that the students of the former were not well equipped to take care of themselves.

The two schools illustrate the argument as to management for some time prominent, i.e., that the negro cannot manage successfully where great executive ability is required. If Paterson can do good work with $13 a pupil, why does it take $155 for Washington?[19]

The article's race baiting was an annoyance, but nothing that black leaders like Booker Washington weren't already accustomed to. What rankled Washington was the assumption of equivalency between Tuskegee and State, and the notion that he was doing far less for students with far more resources. The opinions could be brushed away, but the numbers were correct. The rivalry between the two schools continued to grow more significant as the stakes continued to rise. It was surely little consolation to Washington that his football team had trounced its rival 187–0 over the preceding four seasons, but advocates of the schools understood football scores far more than they did line-item budget projections and cost-per-student descriptions.

The numbers were simply clearer (and more readily available) in football. Tuskegee continued to dominate the series in the coming years, but it was evident that Alabama State was improving. The team lost to both Tuskegee and Talladega in 1905, but its loss to Tuskegee in 1906 was coupled with a tie with Talladega. In 1907, State again lost to Tuskegee, but it managed to beat Talladega twice. In 1908, the Montgomery squad defeated Talladega, Atlanta, and Florida Normal and Industrial, again only losing to Tuskegee. Finally, in 1909, Alabama State had defeated everyone on its schedule when it again met Tuskegee on December 3 in Montgomery. The years of frustration faded in a defensive struggle that allowed a single safety to win the game. Under the leadership of Coach John Hope, Alabama State defeated Tuskegee 2–0.[20]

The win would be an anomaly in the early years of the rivalry, with Alabama State only winning one other contest in the next twenty-four years, a 13–0 victory in 1915. But 1915 would be more important to the schools for another reason. That year, both Booker T. Washington and William B. Paterson passed away. The relationship of the two had improved in their later years. Washington, for example, used his influence with Andrew Carnegie to help Paterson secure funds for a campus library in 1909.[21] Their schools, however, had become entangled with the identities of their leaders and had grown in relation to the state of their rivalry. That being the case, rivalry would be one of the principal legacies that continued after their deaths.

In the years after 1915, Tuskegee not only returned to its winning ways, but it dominated Alabama State, leading by large margins in games that were not very competitive. Importantly, however, people still came to watch. It was a popular game, and white sports promoters in Montgomery realized that there was money to be made. Chief among them were sporting goods salesman Cliff Green and his friend Fred J. Cramton, the owner of a local lumber business.

Cramton, born in 1868 in Michigan, moved after his high school graduation from his hometown of Hadley, Michigan, to Montgomery, Alabama, where he worked as a wood planer in a local excelsior mill. He wasn't a man of means when he arrived, but he worked hard and took advantage of opportunities along the way. He married an Alabama girl, Abbie, and together, in 1901, they had a daughter, Hazel. During that first decade of the twentieth century, Cramton was able to parlay his success and connections into the creation of his own firm, and the lumber company would only grow in the years to come. By 1921, Cramton had moved his family to the exclusive Cloverdale neighborhood of Montgomery. He and Abbie toured Europe together.[22] Both, however, would return in time to witness the grand opening of the side project that had occupied Cramton through much of the late 1910s.

That project had begun when Cramton donated a landfill he owned to the city of Montgomery for the construction of a baseball park. It was the kind of civic donation that helped grow many of the metropolitan areas in the Sunbelt, affluent businessmen growing their bottom lines by growing the infrastructure and capabilities of their cities. Cramton worked with the city to develop the stadium, but after a series of bureaucratic handwringings, Montgomery gave the land back, deciding that the project was too ambitious and expensive. A frustrated Cramton, in turn, decided to build the stadium himself. He worked with the local Jaycees to raise $33,000. He already had access to lumber. By 1922, the new venue was able to host its first event, a college baseball game between Auburn and Vanderbilt.[23]

Cliff Green, like Cramton, came from relatively humble beginnings. Born in Atlanta in 1882, Green came to Montgomery to become a clerk in a sporting goods store. He married into a wealthy family, however, and he and his wife Wilsie promptly moved in with her widowed father, William A. May, and his black servant, Rachel Bradley. In the early 1910s, however, Green rose quickly, probably with May's money, to own his own sporting goods store. With the exception of military service in World War I, nothing interrupted his rise to local prominence. By 1920, Green had his own home, he had four daughters, and he had his own black servant, Julia Robinson.[24]

Green, like Cramton, had a vested interest in the development of sports in Montgomery. He sold sporting goods, Cramton owned the stadium that quickly became known as Cramton Bowl, and the occasional collegiate baseball game would not be enough to provide an adequate return on Cramton's investment and create a culture of sports to fuel Green's business. And so the two worked to find other games for the new venue.

There was, of course, a clear racial line in Jim Crow Montgomery, and wealthy business leaders were a part of it. Montgomery was a segregated city, the capital of a stiflingly racist state. Neither Cramton nor Green was a pioneer in racial cooperation and equality. Both were part of the class of high-ranking whites that supported the apartheid system that dominated Alabama. At the same time, however, both were sports fans with a vested financial interest in well-attended events at Cramton Bowl. And so they looked to the two local rivals, both with strong black fan bases who attended games even when the contests were not close.

For their part, both Tuskegee and Alabama State also had an interest in creating an annual neutral-site game. They understood that by playing the game at a neutral site, they could generate fan interest, thereby increasing revenues. Tuskegee was close enough to Montgomery to make the contest fair for both teams, and with much of the alumni base of the schools largely remaining in the area after graduation, it would serve as a celebration and showcase of their alma maters in the heart of segregated, racist Dixie. The colleges signed with Cramton and Green in 1924, and the concept of the classic—an annual neutral-site contest accompanied by broader celebrations of both universities and their alumni—was born.[25]

On November 15, 1924, 2,182 fans entered the new arena to see Tuskegee's Tigers take on the team still known in the 1920s as the Yellow Jackets. Alabama State was obviously an underdog, considering its history, but the team surprised everyone by taking the opening drive for a touchdown. That success, however, would prove an anomaly, and Tuskegee would simply overpower State for the rest of the game, ultimately winning 28–7. It was an outcome most fans expected. Under the leadership of second-year coach Cleveland L. "Cleve" Abbott, the Tigers would go on to win the championship of the Southern Intercollegiate Athletic Conference and would be named the mythical Black College National Co-Champions, the first of six such titles in the following seven years.[26]

That first game deemed a classic was neither called the Turkey Day Classic nor was it played on Thanksgiving, but it would establish a precedent for the years to come.[27] Writing the following year, Will Rogers described arriving at the Birmingham train station and being shocked by the number of black customers waiting for the train. "Well here is what it was," he explained in his own stammering, racist way.

> "The entire Bent Haired population of Birmingham was going to Montgomery, Alabama, to a Football game. Tuskegee Institute was to play Alabama State Normal that afternoon, and they were going on the same train that I was. (Black, High Brown, Chocolate, dark bays, Low yellows, ashy, every shade in the world.) There wasn't nothing else but—"[28]

The most immediate precedent, however, was the dominance of Tuskegee. That was the way the games had gone prior to the neutral-site classic; that was the way they would continue. Though Alabama State would manage two ties in 1927 and 1928, the team would win no games against the Tigers in the 1920s. The Hornets would win three in the 1930s and only one in the 1940s. Attendance had grown from the small crowd in 1924 to 13,257 fans in 1947. Though the rivalry was fierce in those years because of the proximity of the schools, it was by no means as prominent as many of the other budding "classic" games in black college football simply because of the lopsided nature of the contests. The game moved to Thanksgiving Day in 1928, for example, but until the 1950s, the game was known principally as the Dixie Classic. When fans of the 1930s and 1940s talked about the Turkey Day Classic, they were referring to the annual rivalry game between Atlanta schools Morris Brown and Clark University.[29]

In the 1950s, however, the dynamic between Tuskegee and Alabama State would change. Cleve Abbott, who had seen so much success for the Tigers in the 1920s, was finishing his career. His last season would come in 1954, and it would not be a good one. Tuskegee had only three winning seasons in the 1950s. Their struggles, however, only strengthened the rivalry, because Alabama State finally had a legitimate shot at winning. The Hornets won six games against the Tigers in the 1950s. From 1952 to 1955, they won four games in a row, a feat the school had never managed before.[30] The games in the 1950s, however, would take on a new hue less because of Alabama State's success, and more because of the civil rights maelstrom swirling around the games.

As the decade opened, the Supreme Court's decisions in *McLaurin v. Oklahoma* (1950) and *Sweatt v. Painter* (1950) ruled against segregation in American graduate schools and law schools. Four years later, the Court's *Brown v. Board of Education* (1954) decision would cite both of those cases in ruling against segregation in primary and secondary public education. In May of the following year, the Court demanded compliance in *Brown II* (1955). The system that had sustained the white South since well before the Turkey Day rivalry began—and the system, to be fair, that had created the conditions for the existence of both Alabama State and Tuskegee—was crumbling, and whites were not going to passively accept such indignities. Three months after *Brown II*, for example, Roy Bryant and J. W. Milam murdered Emmett Till in Mississippi.[31]

There had been, in the years since Tuskegee and Alabama State first played, dozens of Emmett Tills in Alabama, dozens of unpunished murders of black boys and girls, men and women, at the hands of racist vigilantes. But in the wake of such massive social change, the black South, and black Alabama in particular, would begin to fight back. In March 1955, Claudette Colvin refused to leave her seat on a bus in the Capital Heights section of Montgomery, less than two miles from the Alabama State campus. Her case would ultimately become *Browder v. Gayle* (1956), which would formally declare Montgomery's bus segregation unconstitutional.[32] Colvin's activism, however, would not exist in a vacuum, and its proximity to Alabama State would be fitting, as the area's response to racism was fed largely by the university whose version of "social equality" was much different from that of its regional counterpart.

As early as 1943, E. D. Nixon founded the Montgomery Voters League. Nixon, a former Pullman train porter who had risen to become the president of the Alabama chapter of the Brotherhood of Sleeping Car Porters, was also the president of the Montgomery branch of the NAACP. He designed the Voters League to help register black voters, still suffering from the restrictions put in place by the 1901 constitution. Coming on the heels of the group's creation, the Women's Political Council was founded in 1946. Mary Frances Fair Burks was chair of the Alabama State College English department, but when she was unable to participate in the local chapter of the League of Women Voters, she created her own organization. It was middle class and all female. It was small, but it was incredibly influential.[33]

This wasn't rare—the history of activism coming from black colleges, often led by faculty members. But the involvement of Burks was unique in that Alabama

State didn't seem to mind. For the most part, the administrations of historically black colleges and universities were incredibly authoritarian and conservative. When students at Fisk protested a local lynching and picketed the local segregated theater, for example, President Thomas E. Jones expelled the leader of the protests for actions that were "detrimental to the best interests of the University." Lincoln University (Pennsylvania) and Alcorn A&M also witnessed such protests. Similarly, when the student council president of South Carolina College for Negroes helped organize a post-*Brown* desegregation petition, he was expelled, touching off campus-wide protests that culminated in the expulsion of more students and the dismissal of several members of the faculty and staff. "It must be reported as one of the bitter ironies in the civil rights movement in the South," wrote William P. Fidler, president of the American Association of University Professors in 1965, "that the administrations of some Negro institutions have exercised autocratic control over the actions and utterances of their faculties and students."[34]

But that autocratic control wasn't happening at Alabama State. And after World War II, the Montgomery Voters League and the Women's Political Council worked together to challenge white hegemony in Montgomery. Four days after *Brown*, for example, Council member Jo Ann Robinson, another Alabama State professor, wrote a letter to Montgomery's mayor bemoaning the segregation on the city's buses. The mayor ignored her letter, of course, but, more importantly, she was able to pen the letter without consequence, a reality that most likely didn't exist for professors at Tuskegee.[35]

In the wake of such activism and race controversy, on November 24, 1955, a massive parade choked the downtown area. It wasn't a protest march. There was no anger. It was simply the pregame celebration for the Turkey Day Classic. "None of the games or the parades can equal that in Montgomery each Turkey day," wrote *Chicago Defender* sports editor Fay Young. But even more impressive to Young than the parade, more impressive than the eight-page game-day insert in the local black newspaper, the *Alabama Journal*, was the coverage of the events in the race-torn capital's white newspaper. "Time and again we have marveled at the spirit displayed by the Montgomery Advertiser," wrote Young, "the day prior to the game, the day of the game, and the morning following the Dixie classic."

> Down in Montgomery it is quite a bit different. Alabama is the home of both Tuskegee Institute, founded by Booker T. Washington, and the Alabama State College. Alabama is Alabama and that means exactly that State is looked upon as an Alabama institution.
>
> Thus the 5,000 or more white fans, who delay their turkey dinner each year to pull for the hometown boys, weren't bothered where the players came from as long as they wore the uniforms of State.[36]

The white fans did not attend the alumni parties, the festival, or any of the student events sponsored by both universities that made the classic a happening. But coverage of the event always included the parade and parties that accompanied the game, those elements of Thanksgiving week that drew together the black community in and around Montgomery. The game that followed the revelry in 1955 ultimately ended in a 19–13 win for Alabama State, its fourth in a row, and that recent success surely helped local white attendance.[37] But the significance of Young's report cannot be overstated. The race antipathy in Montgomery was intense. Alabama State had been the prime mover behind a series of organizations designed to capitalize on Supreme Court decisions to overthrow the apartheid system that had existed for the entirety of the lives of many if not most of those living in the city. And yet thousands of whites attended the game. The local paper, whose editorials railed against *Brown* and its consequences, reported heavily on the game and its attendant festivities.

The temptation is to assume that somehow sports was able to trump racial discord and bring disparate peoples together, but such is the stuff of popular movies. The struggle for racial equality in Montgomery was still, as of Thanksgiving 1955, theoretical in the minds of whites. The schools were still segregated, as were the buses. Rights organizations had formed, letters were mailed, but there was, as of yet, no legitimate threat to white hegemony in the city, and therefore there was no problem with traversing the racial line for the sake of a good game.

One week after the Alabama State win, the threat would become real. On December 1, Rosa Parks refused to give up her seat on a Montgomery bus to a white man, just as Colvin had done earlier that year, and the Montgomery Voters League and Women's Political Council sprang into action. Nixon bailed her out of jail. Robinson, with the tacit support of her university, wrote and distributed a flyer. "Another Negro woman has been arrested and thrown in jail because she refused to get up out of her seat on the bus for a white person to sit down," it said. "This has to be stopped. Negroes have rights too, for if Negroes did not ride the buses, they could not operate."[38]

She was right. On Monday, December 5, with the help of the publicity provided by those flyers, black Montgomery quit riding the buses.[39] The bus boycott would last 381 days, which meant that the next time Alabama State and Tuskegee met on Thanksgiving, the racial conflict in Montgomery would no longer be theoretical. "It was on Monday, Dec. 5, 1955, that a stick of moral dynamite exploded in the faces of lily-white Montgomery officialdom," reported the *Pittsburgh Courier*'s Ric Roberts, "and now, a year later, that it is now certain the dynamic persistence of the bus boycotters has severed the iron grip of the past." And white officials knew it. State attorney general John Patterson watched with a scowl from his third-floor office as the Classic parade moved through downtown. There were twenty-six high school bands participating, up from twenty the previous year. The mile-long procession moved slowly past the Dexter Avenue Baptist Church, home to boycott leader Martin Luther King. Unlike the previous year, the tension was thick, overwhelming the normal feeling of celebration. The *Courier* explained, "It was being whispered among the Negroes that 7,000 members of the Ku Klux Klan would be marching along Dexter St. Sunday." And they would.[40]

It wasn't simply the presence of the Klan that would set the crowd on edge. White Montgomery police were clearly there to harass just as much as protect. "Two young police officers," Roberts reported, "strangely keeping rival football factions apart, narrowed their flint-hard eyes and one commanded, firmly, 'Get back in them stands, Boy, and quick.'" Tuskegee won the game 19–13, ending the Alabama State win streak, but that was hardly the story following the event.[41] The world had simply changed. It wouldn't be the same again.

The boycott could have gone on much longer. Most of the white anger directed at the football fans existed because the boycott was having the intended effect. The city was losing 65 percent of its bus business. It cut schedules, laid off drivers, raised fares to try to compensate. White merchants also suffered. But the city government wouldn't capitulate. The frustration among protesters was palpable, and there was talk about calling it off and chalking the whole thing up as a failure. But on November 13, 1956, almost a year after Parks's arrest and nine days prior to the Classic, *Browder v. Gayle* trumped white Montgomery's intransigence. The bus company agreed to integrate. It agreed to black drivers. On December 21, 1956, black citizens boarded the buses.[42]

The following Thanksgiving witnessed a record-low attendance by white fans in the history of the Classic. The Hornets would win that 1957 contest, and for the rest of the decade, the two teams alternated victories, but the overwhelming progress of the civil rights movement had severed relations between the races even as desegregation had brought them closer in physical proximity.[43] The tension would ultimately boil over at the 1960 Classic.

In 1957, while the Classic was experiencing a record-low white attendance, there were a series of black Baptist church bombings that rocked Montgomery. Bell Street Baptist, Mount Olive, Hutchinson Street, and First Baptist all experienced bombings. So too did First Baptist's parsonage, where its pastor and leading civil rights organizer Ralph Abernathy lived. In a climate of white retribution, a climate that even kept white fans from attending a football game, it should come as no surprise that the indictments following the crimes either ended in acquittals or dropped charges. Three years later, in the week prior to Thanksgiving, the Ku Klux Klan and other groups posted signs around Montgomery urging "10,000 white people" to meet at Cramton Bowl on Thanksgiving. Those whites who "care about your children and their future" should come and come armed.[44]

Such anger wasn't occurring in a vacuum. Earlier in 1960, following the birth of the sit-in movement by students at North Carolina A&T in Greensboro, student demonstrations at Alabama State protested the continued intransigence of segregation and discrimination in Montgomery. Here again the rare willingness by the Alabama State administration to tolerate race activism set it apart from the administrations of schools like rival Tuskegee. There would, of course, be many Tuskegee students who would join the Student Nonviolent Coordinating Committee, but Tuskegee's student activism would not be sanctioned by its administration, and thus would not draw white anger to the school. Still, it would feel such anger by default because of the school's rivalry with State. In the days before the game, the Klan tied a group of sticks wrapped in brown paper to mimic the appearance of a bomb to the main gate at Cramton Bowl along with a Klan banner and a note that warned, "This could be real Thanksgiving Day at Cramton Bowl."[45]

In response to the threats, both the Hornets and the Tigers agreed to cancel the parade for the first time since the rivalry became a "classic." A local restaurant with a liquor license was ordered closed for gameday. Still, five armed white men were arrested in the restaurant parking lot prior to kickoff, men clearly there to foment the race riot that the Klan had been promising. Two of those arrested, Henry Alexander and Sonny Kile Livingston, had been indicted for participating in the 1957 Montgomery church bombings.[46]

Though Montgomery's police commissioner, L. B. Sullivan, blamed the tensions on student demonstrations at Alabama State and actually recommended the cancellation of the game, his force, to their credit, ensured that no violence occurred that Thanksgiving. The Tigers won the game that day, the first of what would become their own four-game winning streak. The story, however, was the threat of riot that loomed over the day's proceedings.[47] It demonstrated that though sports could serve as a binding agent and a refuge from the race antagonism swirling around them, that antagonism could also seep into the function of those sports, could make them a theater for all of the broader problems in society at large. Whites had returned to Cramton Bowl, but they had returned with guns.

Games between the two continued. While Alabama State would begin its own three-game winning streak in 1964, Tuskegee would dominate the late 1960s and early 1970s. That sustained period of success would lead to eleven NFL draft picks from 1967 to 1971, including linebacker Walter Johnson, tackle Fritz Latham, defensive end Otis McDaniel, and receiver Alvin Griffin. In 1971, the teams would not play each other for the first time since fifty years prior in 1921. The absence was the result of a feud between Alabama State president Levi Watkins and his Tuskegee counterpart Luther Hilton Foster. The dispute arose after Tuskegee agreed to play an additional game in Cramton Bowl, which the Hornets claimed as being under their own sphere of influence. The resulting bickering led to each president feigning

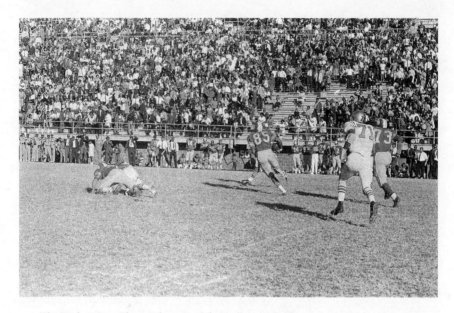

The Turkey Day Classic, the annual football game held in Montgomery, Alabama, between Alabama State College and Tuskegee Institute. *Image courtesy of Alabama Department of Archives and History, Montgomery, Alabama.*]

innocence and outrage at the other. "Charges and counter-charges have brought the two fine Alabama institutions into an almost unsolvable en passé," reported the *Atlanta Daily World*'s Marion Jackson, "which has created almost calamitous trepidation among friendly neighbors." Fortunately, however, the anger would subside. But in the three years that followed, the Classic between the two was the last game on the schedule, placing it in December, rather than on Thanksgiving. Such is the nature of advance collegiate scheduling in the middle of a feud. When the game returned to Thanksgiving in 1975, Alabama State began a long streak of success, winning fifteen of the next seventeen games.[48]

State had grown to nearly twice the enrollment of its longtime rival, which certainly aided its ability to further develop the football program. In 1973, the NCAA began dividing university athletic programs into divisions, and with the smaller Southern Intercollegiate Athletic Conference schools like Tuskegee claiming a place in Division II, the larger Alabama State found itself at a crossroads. In 1976, the Hornets abandoned their affiliation with the SIAC, and later that decade they began playing many of the schools that made up the Division I Southwestern Athletic Conference. In 1982, the Hornets officially joined the SWAC, and the scheduling problems associated with the changes left Tuskegee and Alabama State suspending the Classic again for 1986 and 1987. Tuskegee ended its season well before Thanksgiving for those seasons, while Alabama State supplemented the Tigers with Clark Atlanta in 1986 and Johnson C. Smith in 1987. Frustrated fans of both schools, however, convinced the administrations to bring the game back. Johnson C. Smith would never be an adequate replacement for Tuskegee.[49]

The year 1987 also served as a milestone for Alabama State because that year it hired a new coach, Houston Markham. The early 1980s had been difficult for the Hornets, who consistently finished in last place in their new conference. But they managed in 1987 to woo longtime Jackson State assistant Markham, who would turn the program around. "I see a big hill," he told reporters upon his arrival in Montgomery. "I'm a climber, and I'm determined to climb that hill." Markham would win sixty-eight games in his eleven seasons at ASU, earning more wins than any coach in the school's history, including six consecutive wins against rival Tuskegee from 1988 to 1995. Markham's tenure would feature many of the school's most decorated players, including Eddie Robinson, Zefross Moss, Brad Baxter, and Reggie Barlow.[50]

In 1990, the game reached another milestone when BET broadcast a tape-delayed version of the game. Seven years later, Tuskegee became the first historically black college to reach five hundred victories, and the Tigers did so against their rival in the Turkey Day Classic. Not only would Tuskegee's 1997 victory provide them such a milestone, it would also usher in a long period of dominance through the late 1990s and the twenty-first century. In 2009, the schools would sign a broadcast contract with ESPNU, which still holds the rights to the Classic.[51]

The final Turkey Day milestone occurred in 2012. Since the Classic began in 1924, the one constant in the game had been Cramton Bowl. It was the stadium's creation that allowed for the development of the Classic in the first place. Even when the Ku Klux Klan placed mock bombs and warning signs on its gates, the Hornets and Tigers had always met at the iconic Cramton Bowl. But 2012 witnessed the completion of Alabama State's new on-campus stadium, complete with luxury boxes, shops, and a restaurant. Unlike most schools that debut new facilities at the beginning of athletic seasons, the Hornets chose to debut theirs at the end. Their most important game, after all, happened on Thanksgiving. "Make no mistake about it. Thursday was Alabama State's day," argued reporter Nick Birdsong, noting the sold-out crowd at the debut of the new stadium. "But it was their guest's game." Tuskegee won 27–25, taking the first game in State's new stadium and ensuring that the fire of the rivalry would have plenty of fuel for generations to come.[52]

Still, as intense as the rivalry remains, that fuel has fundamentally changed. No longer are the two schools uneasy allies against white supremacy with different notions of "social equality" and the best methods of achieving it. No longer are fans riding on segregated buses to arrive at the stadium. No longer are Klan members threatening to bomb the stadium. Or churches. Or houses.

The racial problems of Montgomery and the broader South, of course, have yet to be fully solved. But the institutionally sanctioned terrorist violence that accompanied an earlier version of that racism has largely dissipated, making the stakes game between different ideas of how best to accomplish black equality less important. And that, in turn, has reshaped the contest between Alabama State and Tuskegee. "Both schools and their alumni know that the game is a much anticipated and beloved event," said Alabama State president C. C. Baker in 1993, "and the city of Montgomery knows the game brings revenue to city businesses and city tax coffers."[53] Through the late twentieth century and into the twenty-first, the rivalry between the two schools has grown, but it has grown as a game between a set of otherwise friendly adversaries, rather than one between ideological foes using football as a surrogate for broader debates about Patersonian or Washingtonian versions of "social equality."

And such is for the best. As those debates—and their necessity—have faded, there has always been the game. Whether at Cramton Bowl or the Alabama State campus. Whether known as the Dixie Classic or the Turkey Day. Whether a battle for SIAC supremacy or an intra-conference, intra-division rivalry whose only consequence is pride.

There has always been the game.

7

Gold and Glory Sweepstakes

An African American Racing Experience

Todd Gould

In 1991, Willy T. Ribbs became the first African American to qualify for the Indianapolis 500-Mile Race. His accomplishment was historic. And yet, it was only one thrilling moment in a remarkably rich, yet largely forgotten, black auto racing legacy that preceded Ribbs by nearly seven decades.

During the 1920s, when groups like the Ku Klux Klan wielded tremendous influence within Indiana's social and political circles, and sports venues like the Indianapolis Motor Speedway were segregated, a dedicated group of individuals created a sporting event exclusively for African Americans—a racing spectacle so grand it attracted the attention of national newspaper and newsreel agencies, as well as thousands of spectators from all over the country. The event was the Gold and Glory Sweepstakes, a freewheeling, dust-raising, 100-mile grind around the dirt track at the Indiana State Fairgrounds in Indianapolis.

"The Gold and Glory Sweepstakes was the race that belonged to the colored people. It was *ours*," noted Boniface Hardin, historian and president emeritus of Martin University. "It was something our community could take joy in. And there was truly glory attached to winning it." Former driver Leon "Al" Warren remembered, "We drew great crowds all the time, up to 10,000 to 12,000 people. The stands would be overflowing." Another driver, Joie Ray, recalled, "We were treated like heroes. It was really our time to shine."

The Queen of Central Western States

In 1903, the *Indianapolis Star* debuted as a new daily newspaper in the Hoosier capital. A column from one of the paper's early issues quoted a national business journal that viewed the state of Indiana and its capital city as a land of great potential.

The article noted that "[Indiana's] wealth and trade increase materially day by day." The column concluded that Indianapolis, and the Hoosier state in general, "must be considered as the coming city, the Queen of Central Western States."[1]

A number of prominent railways crisscrossed the city, helping to bring unprecedented growth to the area—a population growth of more than 250 percent in three short decades from 1870 to the turn of the century. Several key industries fueled the fires of free enterprise that burned brightly in Indianapolis during the early 1900s. At the heart of this rapid expansion was a burgeoning automobile industry. Celebrated Hoosier author Booth Tarkington made a sweeping prediction about the growing number of midwestern auto manufacturers in his novel, *The Magnificent Ambersons*, "They [automobiles] are here, and almost all outward things are going to be different because of what they bring."[2]

During this era, Indiana was the nation's top auto producer, creating nearly twice the amount of vehicles of other major cities, such as Detroit and Cleveland. Hundreds of different makes and models of autos were being produced in the Hoosier state, including fifty lines in Indianapolis alone. By 1921, the local chamber of commerce boasted that Indianapolis and the Hoosier state led the world in the manufacture of "better grade automobiles," including many renowned brands, such as Stutz, Duesenberg, Waverly, Auburn, Cole, and Studebaker.[3]

Jobs in this new industry were plentiful during the early twentieth century, as more and more people poured into Indianapolis looking for promising new employment opportunities. These new jobs were not only limited to white Americans. At the time, America was in the midst of the Great Migration, a cultural movement that sparked a major exodus for many African Americans who left the rural South for new opportunities in the large factories in northern metropolises, such as Chicago, Detroit, and Cleveland. Auto manufacturing jobs in Indianapolis were some of the most lucrative and highly sought after jobs in the midwestern United States for many African Americans. By 1920, the city's black population skyrocketed to more than 10 percent of the city's total citizenry, the highest percentage of any city north of the Mason-Dixon line during the era.

The growing African American population sparked some rising racial tensions in the city. James Madison, historian, author, and professor emeritus of the Department of History at Indiana University, analyzed the social climate of the Hoosier state during the early 1920s, "Nearly 95 percent of all Hoosiers were born in Indiana, and statewide, nearly 97 percent were native, white persons living in Indiana. There was a prevailing attitude among this vast majority of white, native-born Hoosiers that in order to maintain the integrity, safety and prosperity of life in Indiana, there must be an effort to keep the state '100 percent American.' And in the minds of this ethnic, religious majority, there was a group of 'others' who threatened this way of life, most notably African Americans, Catholics and Jews, who were considered 'less than 100 percent American.' And many in the state felt that these 'others' were out to undermine all the moral principles that the majority held near and dear."

Many in this lily-white majority banned together in various statewide groups and local neighborhood associations to combat perceived threats from these "others." One of the most visible organizations throughout the nation, and especially in Indiana, was the Ku Klux Klan. Indiana became a regional headquarters for the KKK starting in 1922, and one of the Klan's top leaders, D. C. Stephenson, managed the organization from offices in downtown Indianapolis. Historian Richard Pierce, chair of the Africana Studies Department and an associate professor at the University of Notre Dame, noted, "Indiana became a segregated state during the 1920s in a way it had not been before and to a much larger extent than it had ever been before that time. For African Americans and other 'outside' groups with entrepreneurial interests, it got a whole lot tougher to succeed during the 1920s than in [previous] decades."

Prez

Despite the social pressures of the day, Indianapolis's African American community experienced a cultural renaissance during the 1920s, marked by smooth jazz sounds that emanated from the clubs up and down historic Indiana Avenue, which ran through the heart of Indianapolis's bustling African American cultural district. Many black businesses also thrived, following the earlier success of visionary leaders, such as Madam C. J. Walker, one of the nation's first black millionaires. As well, the decade gave rise to an exciting sports scene, as the Indianapolis ABCs became a charter member of the Negro National League during the early part of the century.

William Rucker was a product of this social renaissance. As a successful entrepreneur, Rucker created several notable business ventures, including opportunities as a business contractor and a consultant to manufacturing firms and the railways. Rucker earned the respect of both whites and blacks in Indianapolis. The well-dressed businessman who seemingly always sported a straw hat and a 5-cent cigar, had the uncanny ability to bridge the city's broad social gaps, which made him a strong ally to white politicians who recognized the growing importance of the black vote in the city. "If whites needed a voice in the black community, or if blacks needed their voice to be heard by the white community, they all came to him," explained Rucker's grandson, Paul Bateman. "One year he might support the cause of the Democratic candidate. The next year he might support the Republican's cause. It didn't matter to him, as long as the needs of the black community were being met."

Rucker was also an ardent auto racing fan. Since 1911, the city had played host to the annual Indianapolis 500-Mile Race, the world's most famous auto race, where powerful race cars roared over a paved, brick surface at a pace of more than 60 miles per hour . . . a speed one *Indianapolis Star* reporter called "death-defying" in May 1911. Richard Pierce noted, "Race car drivers were kind of like the outlaws of the Old West, living on the edge of their seats . . . unpredictable, tough. They were a combination of brains and brawn, which was a new, evolving definition of manhood during the early 20th century. They were trying to manipulate the physical environment, especially the mechanical, physical environment. But they were also conquering the mental, courageous aspect of [the environment]. In a special way, they were the maestros of both worlds."

The speed and thrills of the Indy 500 fascinated William Rucker. "He wanted so badly to see a black driver race at the '500,'" noted Bateman. "He knew a lot of good black mechanics in the area, and he knew they would make good race car drivers. Of course, blacks weren't allowed at the [Indianapolis Motor] Speedway in those days."

Segregation cast a long, dark shadow across the social landscape in most of Indiana. Persecution of "outsiders" was prevalent in the sporting world, just as it was in practically every aspect of social, religious, racial, and political life for most Hoosiers. Joie Ray, a former driver on the colored auto racing circuit, remembered, "A lot of the white mechanics and drivers got along just fine with all of us. Blacks and whites, we all respected each other and we respected the sport. We got along just fine. But it really was the promoters who sanctioned and operated the events. They were the ones who made sure it stayed separate. At that time, there was really no way whites and blacks were going to race together."

Controversy over the notion of whites and blacks in competition together first erupted in 1910 during an unusual racing event between Erna Eli "Barney" Oldfield, America's top white racing champion, and Jack Johnson, the famed black boxing champ of the era. As a promotional stunt, the two staged a match race to attract greater interest in the sport and to reap a hefty profit on the sensational hype created by promoters of the event. In their respective fields, both men had larger-than-life personalities and egos to match. Johnson, the boisterous fighter, once boasted, "I'd be happy to beat Mr. Oldfield at his game as easy as I best Mr. Jeffries [the former heavyweight champion] in the ring. In fact, I've got $5,000 that says I'm a faster driver on any track." To add to the hype, the *New York Times* printed a statement, which noted that Johnson "won several victories the previous winter in a southern California racing carnival," and that "he knew how to handle himself in four-wheeled competition."[4] Oldfield, the burly, cigar-chomping speed champion, could not resist the challenge. He issued a public reply: "I note in today's paper a challenge made by Jack Johnson to race me for $5,000 . . . Automobile racing is my business, and if Johnson or any other man in the world has $5,000 to bet he can beat me, I am ready to meet him."[5]

Most racing events during the early twentieth century were loosely organized affairs, typically organized between entrepreneurial promoters and drivers eager to compete. The closest thing the sport had to an official governing body was the American Automobile Association. When officials from the AAA heard of the race organized between Oldfield and Johnson, representatives called it a "farce" and publicly forbade Oldfield from competing in the event.[6]

Oldfield, always the rebel, ignored the AAA's mandate and scheduled the race with Johnson on October 25, 1910, on a dirt track at Sheepshead Bay, New York. Thousands of spectators lined the track to take in the spectacle. Both racers posed for a number of interviews, photos, and newsreel highlights of prerace warm-up laps.

The actual match race hardly lived up to the hype. Oldfield, the seasoned racing veteran, easily outpaced his rival, winning by more than two laps. As Barney crossed the finish line, reporters flocked to his car. He gloated during his postrace interview, "I can tell you this. When they took old Jack outta' that car, he sure wasn't smilin'."[7] After the event, the AAA reportedly suspended Oldfield for agreeing to continue with the race, despite their protests. Oldfield was hardly fazed by the incident. The renegade driver had great disdain for several actions of racing's governing body and was infamous among members of the group for his long history of disagreements and run-ins with it. The following season, the AAA reinstated Oldfield, as more and more spectators demanded to see him. In the short term, the stunt did little to diminish the meteoric careers of both Oldfield and Johnson in their respective fields. In the long term, however, the dispute appeared to make the AAA more leery of the types of events it would sanction, especially those that might involve whites and blacks in mixed competition.

Boniface Hardin explained, "By 1924, William Rucker was pulling together the folks he thought he needed to get black drivers involved in big time auto racing. But it was made very clear to these organizers that racing's governing body was not going to endorse colored drivers. Even if white and black drivers wanted to compete against each other, those who raised the money and promoted the white drivers were not about to have their top competitors going up against black drivers in any sort of sanctioned competition. They didn't even want any special 'match races' or any other stunt that would involve a white driver against a black driver. Most white drivers relied on that promotional money to continue racing, and they couldn't 'buck the system,' so to speak. So the white drivers and mechanics had to stay away from these potential competitions. When William Rucker and his partners discovered that they couldn't get black drivers into the Indy 500, or any other race that was considered a 'whites only' race, they began working on the next best thing."

Rucker's "next best thing" took root on January 12, 1924, when he and his new partners, both black and white, came together to create the Colored Speedway

Association. The group included Harry Dunnington, a writer and promotional wizard who hyped black sporting events throughout the region, and Robert Brokenburr, one of the region's most highly respected black attorneys, who served as legal counsel for the organization. Together with Rucker, these black businessmen joined forces with a white racing promoter by the name of Harry Earl, known as "the Baron of Ballyhoo" in midwestern auto racing circles, and Oscar E. Schilling, a successful railway executive and auto racing promoter who helped bankroll the organization's initial undertakings. Oscar's son, Jack Schilling, remembered, "Harry and Dad were always looking for new investment opportunities in racing. They would round up investors and maybe even use a little of their own money to get a race circuit organized and promoted. They could then take a percentage of the gate receipts to earn money back on the events."

Schilling continued, "My dad was not as big an auto racing fan as Harry, but I think both of them saw the popularity of racing and the strong investment potential in the sport." The articles of incorporation noted that the purpose of the Colored Speedway Association was "to perpetuate the interests of sportsmanship in race driving and other associated activities."

The group appointed Rucker president. To the organization, and eventually to the black community, he was known simply as "Prez." Hardin explained, "Prez Rucker didn't have the money he needed [to start the organization.] However, he had the charisma and the personal strength to pull together the right people to make things happen. White or black, it didn't matter to him. He just wanted the best people he could find to get the Colored Speedway Association off the ground."

"There's really an interesting confluence of social change that begins to take effect in American society right after the First World War," commented auto racing historian Joe Freeman. "Black Americans are staking a new claim on their heritage and on their rights in society. This also included the major sporting events of the day. And in Indianapolis, a town with a strong automotive heritage and a strong racing heritage, it made perfect sense that African Americans would want to pursue those passions in great earnest and create opportunities for themselves."

Gas-Snorting, Rubber-Shod Monsters of the Speedway

At the start of 1924, the Colored Speedway Association set up its headquarters in the 600 block of Indiana Avenue, in the heart of Indianapolis's African American district. Plans for the association's first big event commenced that spring. By July 1 the CSA announced plans for its inaugural race, an event to be staged on the one-mile dirt track at the Indiana State Fairgrounds on August 2. A quarter-page advertisement in the *Chicago Defender* on July 27 trumpeted the upcoming festivities: "Get Your Reservations Now to See the World's Fastest Colored Drivers Dash for $2,500 in Prizes in the First Annual 100-Mile Auto Race—Daredevil Stunts, Fireworks, and other Events Included."[8]

The black press, including the *Indianapolis Freeman,* added to the prerace hype by displaying one of the entrant's cars in front of the association headquarters on Indiana Avenue near two of the district's most popular jazz clubs, where foot traffic and an excited buzz were the thickest. The *Freeman* blared on August 2, "Indianapolis is ready for the world's greatest event, the first 100-mile auto race featuring all our men at the wheel. The hotels and lodging houses are now being crowded, and the management states that they have received letters from all over the country asking for reservations. Indianapolis now without a doubt is the birthplace of the world's greatest and largest auto races."[9] Frank A. "Fay" Young, the sports columnist from the *Chicago Defender,* colorfully penned, "All America must be turning its eyes and ears toward Indianapolis for this event, attempting, as it were, to catch a fleeting glimpse of chocolate jockeys spurring their gas-snorting, rubber-shod speedway monsters to fame and fortune or to faintly hear the fascinating hum of racing motors. And this being no stretch of the writer's fertile imagination, for many states are represented among the gaily-painted chariots of steel and the assemblage of nervy, nervous, castor-fumed drivers on hand to flirt with death and danger . . . in hopes of winning gold for themselves and glory for their Race." The paper dubbed the event "the Gold and Glory Sweepstakes."[10]

Joe Freeman noted, "Promoters during the time were really a wild bunch. The truth was often bent beyond belief. There were all sorts of tricks they used to get fans into the stands. Many drivers were billed as 'the greatest in the world,' or something really far-fetched, like 'the Russian dirt track champion,' even though Russia never had a dirt track champion at the time. There was an enormous amount of hype similar to the circus coming to town . . . 'Thrills, chills and spills' . . . 'Death-defying acts' . . . 'Drivers skidding on the edge of disaster' . . . All that type of language was used to add to the mythical stature of these drivers."

Paul Bateman recalled the stories his grandparents shared about the festivities surrounding the first Gold and Glory Sweepstakes. "Days before the race, people started coming to the fairgrounds. There was a tremendous fervor about the whole thing. People who didn't have a place to sleep actually camped out near the State Fairgrounds. By the time race day arrived, my grandfather estimated that there were over twelve thousand people in the stands."

Fifteen African American drivers took their places on the starting line for the inaugural Gold and Glory Sweepstakes. The vehicles were a menagerie of makes, models, and styles. Driver Leon "Al" Warren remembered, "There really weren't any rules about car size or engine size at the time. You'd have some Fords and Duesenbergs entered. But then you'd have some really wild-looking cars . . . Some drivers, the ones who were the best mechanics, made their own cars from scratch.

They worked in garages and took old, discarded parts and put them into a chassis they'd mold themselves. I recall one fellah, Bill Jeffries from Chicago, was a real big guy. He built a special chassis that would fit around his large waist. Other guys customized their cars to their own needs."

Flashbulbs popped and reporters stood poised as several of the nation's leading African American newspapers covered the history-making event. Hollywood's *Pathé News* sent a camera crew to film highlights of the race. Soon the thundering sounds of revving engines and roaring applause overtook the scene, and the race began. The *Indianapolis Freeman* noted that afternoon that "12,000 strained and eager faces" in the crowd struggled to catch a glimpse of the speeding cars amid the thick blanket of dust and smoke.

"Of course the big problem was always the dust," noted Al Warren. "The cars in front of you would always kick up so much dirt and dust you couldn't see right in front of your face." Indianapolis Motor Speedway historian Donald Davidson expanded on the trials many race car drivers battled during the era, "The dust would keep them from seeing directly in front of their cars. There were these light poles that ran around the inside of the track. Often the only way a driver could tell how close he was into a turn was to look up at the poles on the inside railing and then see how the poles banked around the corners. Of course, if the wind was blowing, the drivers were just guessing." Davidson continued, "There were no seat belts or safety harnesses of any kind at the time. Often drivers simply had a rope to tie them into the car. Others didn't use a rope, because they actually felt safer being thrown clear of the car during an accident, rather than attempt to ride it out in the car." "Everything from your waist up was completely exposed," explained Joie Ray. "Rocks and clods of dirt would be pelting you all the time. It was like someone was picking up handfuls of rocks and throwing them at you constantly throughout the race."

Another Gold and Glory driver, Sumner "Red" Oliver, remembered the ornery nature of his fellow competitors on the track: "It was dangerous out there. They'd just cut you off and keep on going . . . Often we'd get so close to one another, we could practically reach out and touch each other. We were just inches from each other. A lot of times we'd yell names at each other. We were all good friends off the track. But on the track, it was something else."

Ten laps into the inaugural Gold and Glory Sweepstakes, an Indianapolis mechanic, William Buckner, took the lead when several drivers pulled into the pit area for minor mechanical adjustments. Chicago's "Wild Bill" Jeffries was in second place and pressing Buckner hard. Soon, several of the lesser makes and models of cars began to fail, with engines smoking, as sportswriter Frank A. "Fay" Young described it, "like a 'Big Bertha' gun after it has been discharged."[11] Buckner continued to fight through the thick smoke and dust until his car hit a large chuckhole along the back straightaway. His car lost a tire, and he spun off the track and out of the race.

Jeffries was now in the lead. As he passed by the grandstand, he waved to the crowd. "Isn't that just like 'Big Jeff'?" quipped a journalist from the *Indianapolis Freeman*. His lead was short lived, however. Four laps later he signaled to his pit crew that his car was malfunctioning. On lap 53 of the hundred-lap affair, he pulled into the pits and never pulled out again. A large rock had shot through his engine and severed the main water line. The crewmen could not repair his car in time to allow him back into the competition. Young lamented of his fellow Chicagoan, "Our city's best hope for a championship just went goodbye."[12]

With ten laps to go, many of the fifteen cars that started the race had succumbed to hard driving and the elements. There were only three remaining drivers in the race, all Indianapolis drivers. The limited competition, however, did not seem to dampen the enthusiasm of the crowd. As the three cars came down the final straightaway, the crowd was raucous. Young claimed that he, too, was "daffy with excitement."[13]

Crossing the finish line a mere seventy-five yards ahead of the competition that first year at the Gold and Glory Sweepstakes was Malcolm Hannon, a former chauffeur who once worked for owners and executives at the Graham Motor Company. Aboard a 1923 Indy 500 car, a "Barber-Warnock Special," Hannon paced the pack in 1:45:42, an average speed of 63.5 miles per hour. According to the *Chicago Defender,* Hannon's speed was considered one of the top times for dirt-track auto racing.[14] The *Indianapolis Freeman* viewed Hannon's win as a victory for *all* African Americans: "The roar [of the crowd] was the dawn of a new opportunity, another step forward, the brushing away of another barrier, another obstacle met and surmounted by our group in the realm of sports."[15]

The Negro Speed King

On the south side of Indianapolis, several young men gathered every afternoon at a local garage. They were there to watch the skilled hands of a vehicular virtuoso, Charlie Wiggins, a slightly built, genial garage owner who earned a reputation as one of the most gifted mechanics in the city. Leon "Al" Warren was one of those youngsters enamored by Charlie's engaging smile, entertaining stories and automotive savvy. "My brother and I used to hang out at his garage whenever we could," Warren said. "Even race car drivers and mechanics from the Indianapolis 500 knew of Charlie and knew of his expertise with cars. Everybody in town knew that Charlie could make one strong, fast car."

Red Oliver was another curious spectator who marveled at the mechanical genius of Charlie Wiggins. "He often let me come down to the garage and help put race cars together," Oliver mentioned. "I never saw anything like it. His hands were like magic under the hood."

Charlie's wife, Roberta, reflected, "He was really good at what he did. He made a lot of money during those early years at his shop . . . Even white car owners came to Charlie's garage, because he had such a good reputation with cars."

Wiggins got his start as an auto mechanic with the Benninghof-Nolan Company in Evansville, Indiana. Henry J. Benninghof and Eugene E. Nolan operated an automotive sales and service company on Main Street in the southern Indiana town and hired Wiggins as one of the city's first black mechanics. Mildred Overton, Wiggins's niece, stated, "Those two boys, those owners, were both barely in their twenties. At the time they broke with a lot of tradition and social norms of the day. They decided to give Uncle Charlie a chance as an apprentice in their repair shop. At the time it was very rare for a black man to work as a mechanic. But those two boys didn't care. They recognized Uncle Charlie's talents right away and put him to work. [Working for them] changed Uncle Charlie's life forever."

Historian Joe Freeman noted, "Superb mechanical ability was really a great American art form. And this was as much, certainly, a part of the black community as it was of American society as a whole . . . Automobiles were still a 'new frontier' at that time. There were no rules, so to speak. Guys who worked in garages were always trying to invent 'the better mousetrap,' trying to come up with a slicker and better solution to make their cars run better . . . And Charlie Wiggins, in particular, proved that his practical skills were enormous."

In 1922, Wiggins and his wife, Roberta, left Evansville for the racing capital of Indianapolis. He worked as the chief mechanic for a Jewish garage owner, Louis Sagalowsky. Soon, his reputation expanded, and he was helping drivers and mechanics at the Indianapolis Motor Speedway work on their ultra-powerful race cars. As well, he honed his skills on his own racing machine, a race car he dubbed "the Wiggins Special." In 1926, he decided to enter his speedster at the Gold and Glory Sweepstakes. He made special adaptations to his car. Wiggins was a mere 5'5" tall and weighed only 120 pounds. He found it necessary to raise the cockpit and extend the controls of his "Wiggins Special" to accommodate for his small stature. His custom-designed engine churned effortlessly, aided by his own, specially mixed oil concoction of part STP Motor Oil and part castor oil. He also used a low-grade airplane fuel to power his racing machine.

When the Colored Speedway Association held time trials for the 1926 Gold and Glory race, Charlie Wiggins sped to one of the fastest qualifying times in the field and earned eighth place in the preliminary qualification heats. The entire purse for the event, the largest of any African American auto race in the country at the time, totaled $2,550.

Attracting nearly 12,000 spectators, the 1926 Gold and Glory Sweepstakes was one of the largest sporting events in the midwestern United States. As they had done the previous two years, Prez Rucker and the Colored Speedway Association had once again created a spectacular event that celebrated the ingenuity and courage of the African American spirit. The prerace festivities, which included fireworks and a parade, added to the hype, as the *Chicago Defender* noted with grandiosity: "The fastest cars in the land will make the first lap of the big grind, and the race will be on. Many will remember the exciting finish during the first race two years ago, when Hannon, the fierce champion, pushed his steed to a finish so thrilling that several women fainted and had to be carried from the stands . . . [This race] should prove to be a great success, stamped as one of the biggest sports events of its kind in the world."[16]

After all the sensational prerace festivities, the green flag dropped. The engines roared. The adrenaline flowed. And the race was on. "Wild Bill" Jeffries, in a pure white Fronty Ford with a bold number "1" painted on the side, stormed to an early lead. The crowd sent up an enthusiastic roar. Drivers reacted to the cheers and gunned their engines as they passed the grandstand. "As a little girl, I can remember the start of those races very well," Mildred Overton recalled, as she accompanied her uncle Charlie Wiggins to the Indianapolis Fairgrounds races. "The roar was so loud and deep, you could feel it in your stomach. It was thrilling."

Sixty laps—sixty miles—into the one-hundred-mile affair, and Bill Jeffries still maintained the lead. But a sudden roar from the Indianapolis crowd caused "Wild Bill" to look back. Charlie Wiggins, who at one point had been nearly one lap behind the leaders, was now gaining on Chicago's premier black driving talent. For ten laps, the two drivers battled for the top spot. By lap 70, Jeffries held only a slim, one-car-length lead. Then, in the fourth turn, Wiggins revved his engine to full power and overtook Jeffries. By lap 75, miles of hard driving caused Jeffries to pull into the pits for refueling and new tires. He was five laps behind Wiggins by the time he finally reentered the track. By lap 90, Wiggins had coasted to an easy lead. Despite a valiant effort by Jeffries to gain three laps on the field by the end of the race, he still could not catch Wiggins.

When the dust settled at the end of the race, Charlie Wiggins pulled into the winner's circle. At an average speed of 66.7 miles per hour, the Indianapolis driver and mechanic captured his first Gold and Glory trophy. The *Indianapolis Recorder* explained how the driver was able to garner a lead he would never relinquish, "Charlie Wiggins, driving his own make of racing automobile, a Wiggins Special, never going to the pits once for gas, water, nor oil, never stopping for tire changes and driving a steady pace, won the third annual Gold and Glory Sweepstakes, which carries besides a beautiful silver cup and a large cash prize, the national dirt track championship for 100 miles."[17]

The *Chicago Defender* reported, "A wild burst of applause greeted [Wiggins] from his home towners, some of whom lost their heads and broke like a bunch of wild steers, women and men, running across the track, despite the yells from the cooler heads warning them of the impending danger of getting killed as [other drivers] were still in the race for second, third, and fourth place honors."[18]

Joe Freeman noted, "One hundred miles on a rough, rocky, dusty track is a long way. And it will tire out even the strongest of guys. And when you have somebody like Charlie, who only weighs just over 100 pounds, and such a small, wiry fellah, that one hundred miles had to be a real experience. The fact that he even survived is an accomplishment. To win the race is truly spectacular."

"He was just like a hero around town," Al Warren commented. "I remember them putting up posters all up and down Indiana Avenue with Charlie's picture on them. He was a local boy, and he was the champ." The *Indianapolis Recorder* dubbed Wiggins "the Negro Speed King."[19] Charlie Wiggins went on to capture second place in the 1929 Gold and Glory Sweepstakes, as well as back-to-back-to-back championships in 1931, 1932 and 1933. He was the only four-time champion on the African American racing circuit.

23-Skidoo

The success of the Gold and Glory Sweepstakes inspired promoters in other midwestern cities to organize their own "Colored Speed Classics." Flyers and newspaper advertisements from Chicago to Akron to Langhorn, Pennsylvania, and even as far south as Atlanta and Fort Worth, all promoted a "Square Deal to All" with special applications sent directly to "Colored Drivers Only." Because of the popularity of the annual event in Indianapolis, many in the press referred to the national colored racing series as "the Gold and Glory Circuit." Al Warren remembered, "We'd get notices in the mail all the time to go to one town or another. Sometimes the top prize was only $100. Other times it was more. All the drivers knew each other, more or less. A lot of us would travel together. Some of the guys, like Charlie, had their own cars they'd bring to these events. Others of us had to find someone to loan us a car for the race."

The drivers and mechanics on the Gold and Glory circuit dared to run a dusty gauntlet, traveling from small town to small town, attempting to steer clear of large ruts, bumps, and unfriendly whites along their way cross country. Almost no hotel would host them. Almost no restaurant would serve them. Yet, with their race cars and hopes in tow, they left their regular jobs and their families behind each weekend to chase their dream of racing on the professional colored racing circuit. "Things weren't quite as bad here [in the Midwest] as they were down South," Warren recalled of his travels with fellow drivers. "We learned which routes were the safest to go. Often they wouldn't be the most direct routes into town, but they were considered the safest."

"They didn't have interstate highways back then," noted Red Oliver. "The roads were tough and really bumpy. We'd go to Iowa or Pennsylvania or somewhere down South, and many of those trips were really long. And we'd have to get back Sunday night for our regular jobs on Monday." Joe Freeman added, "It was a time of great experimentation in the automotive industry, not just for race cars, but for passenger cars, as well. A lot of these cars were not made for driving a long way on a hard, bumpy road. Tires blew and engines overheated. Getting from town to town was often quite an adventure."

Columnist Frank Young traveled with some intrepid drivers on a trek from Chicago into Indianapolis for one Gold and Glory race. He made the following diary entries along the way:

> Saturday morning, 6 AM . . . Just outside of Hoopston, Illinois and raining like the devil. The front tire of our car goes "gaflooey," rim and all coming off. 9:00 AM . . . Raining pitchforks, and we make a highway change in Danville, Illinois. Commandeered the cook's stove in the kitchen of one restaurant to dry out. Called up the Colored YMCA in Indianapolis to get latest weather report. Things look not so good at the moment.
>
> 11:00 AM . . . Hit Indianapolis Route 33, eighteen miles out of Lebanon, Indiana . . . Another blowout without a spare. Four miles to nearest garage on the flat, which cuts the tire to a frazzle. Get fixed up, after paying the man and thanking him, we notice sign on his barn: "Kleage Realm, K.K.K.," and we move on in a hurry. Not scared, but just got a darn good move on us![20]

Some white car owners and mechanics were sympathetic to the cause of African American drivers and loaned their cars to black drivers for many of these races. Many agreed to loan their cars to African Americans for a share of the winnings. Still other white drivers and mechanics greatly admired and even modeled their careers after some of the most successful Gold and Glory competitors. Harry MacQuinn, noted Indy car driver and mechanic, and "Wild Bill" Cummings, one of the most celebrated white drivers of the era, both worked alongside Charlie Wiggins and gained valuable advice from his mechanical expertise. Cummings ultimately won the 1934 Indianapolis 500-Mile Race. For years after his accomplishment, Wild Bill credited much of his success to several of his mentors, including Wiggins, whose mechanical skills and driving know-how boosted Cummings's interest and enhanced his mechanical prowess.

Wiggins often lent his own race cars to both white and black drivers in races throughout the Midwest with an agreement to split any prize monies won. All of Charlie's cars sported the number 23, short for the phrase "23-Skidoo," a popular phrase of the decade that typically indicated an opportunity to leave in a hurry. Whether he was competing in the race or simply loaning his car to another driver, Wiggins typically insisted on driving the prerace qualifying laps himself, in order to pinpoint any potential engine malfunctions. More than once this caused a ruckus in races where the regulations declared that the race was limited to "whites only." Boniface Hardin recounted one incident in Louisville, Kentucky: "The white crowd was watching all the drivers taking their test laps. But then they saw a black man getting out of one of the cars, and several in the crowd became infuriated. They charged out on the track after Charlie. Promoters had to call in the Kentucky state police to calm things down. The police arrested Charlie for his own protection and kept him at the jail until the hubbub died down. Eventually they released Charlie, allowing him to return home safely. Later he glanced at a copy of the official police report that listed a reason for his arrest: speeding!"

With the Tenacity of a Determined Fighter

The Gold and Glory Sweepstakes was the stage for many highs and lows on the colored speed circuit. Barney Anderson, a mechanic from Detroit, captured the 1929 event aboard a Model-A Ford he reconfigured into a winning racing machine. However, the most significant—and frightening—moment that year occurred during the twenty-seventh lap, when Edward Grice, a veteran of the Great War and a three-time Gold and Glory participant, collided with another driver, William Walthall. The crash sent Grice's car airborne more than twenty feet and flipped the vehicle four times before it landed. Ambulance drivers rushed Grice to City Hospital in Indianapolis, where he was admitted unconscious with a fractured skull and severe internal injuries. Friends and family initially held out hope for recovery. By the following day, however, Grice had still not regained consciousness. Finally, at 10:00 P.M. on Sunday, July 8, four days after the race, Grice, a thirty-six-year-old mechanic and father of two young children, died at City Hospital, the first-ever death recorded at the Gold and Glory Sweepstakes.

One race official told the *Indianapolis Recorder* that Grice was "a mighty fine fellow," and added, "His death is to be greatly regretted, as we found him always for fair play and true sportsmanship."[21] Barney Anderson, 1929 Gold and Glory champion, told the press, "Negro race drivers lost a true sportsman with the passing of Grice. He was a credit to the game." The *Recorder* eulogized, "He was from his early childhood decidedly of mechanical bent . . . He constantly dreamed of piloting a machine at a dizzy pace while breathless and admiring spectators gazed in dazed amazement . . . On Thursday, July 4, with the tenacity of a determined fighter, Grice, undaunted by two previous futile attempts, tried again for the last time evermore."[22]

Another travesty beset the drivers and mechanics of the 1935 Gold and Glory event. Often smaller dirt-track auto races around the country during the era had a difficult time finding the legitimate funding and promotional support needed to put on a good show and provide an attractive purse for the top finishers. Indianapolis Motor Speedway historian Donald Davidson explained, "It was a very common thing in the 1920s and '30s to have unscrupulous promoters abscond with the funds [primarily earned from ticket sales and entry fees] during a race.

Some drivers got wise to these scams after a while, however, and created a plan to stop them. While different races were going on, a driver who was not competing in a particular heat would stand outside the office door and watch to ensure that no one came running out the back door with a satchel in his hand. Occasionally that did happen, and there were cases in which drivers actually chased a promoter down the road to try to catch him and retrieve the money."

Unfortunately, the participants of the 1935 Gold and Glory Sweepstakes were not aware of such scams. Typically the Gold and Glory races were headed by William Rucker, Oscar Schilling, Harry Earl and the rest of the Colored Speedway Association. But in 1935, the annual Indianapolis colored auto race was organized by an outside promotional group from Dayton, Ohio. The local press offered no reason why the CSA did not coordinate and promote the 1935 event.

During a prerace "daredevil" stunt car exhibition, the crowd began to settle into their seats for the big race. Meanwhile, members of the Dayton organization were quietly gathering up the funds from nearly 10,000 paid customers and more than twenty entry fees and making a quick exit out of town. As the prerace events drew to a close, tradition at the Gold and Glory events demanded that the promoter appear at the starting podium to signal the beginning of the main race. But as drivers made final race preparations, several noticed that the promoters were not at their typical station near the starter's podium. Soon the joyous applause from the crowd turned to murmurs of curiosity, then shouts of confusion. The drivers looked up from their cockpits. Some left their cars and made their way to the podium to investigate.

By the time many of the drivers and mechanics figured out what had happened, there was no trace of the Dayton promotional group anywhere near the Indiana State Fairgrounds in Indianapolis. While some drivers took off in a futile attempt to find the scoundrels, most other racers began to pull their cars back onto their trailers and prepare for a disappointing trip home. At the last moment, however, members of the crowd agreed to pass the hat to collect an impromptu purse for the drivers who still wished to compete.

Several drivers had come from Chicago, Cleveland, and even as far as Tulsa, Oklahoma, for the competition. Not to race would have seemed a remarkable shame and a terrible waste of time, energy, and money. Eventually all of the twenty-three participants agreed to lace up their helmets and rev up their engines for a shortened affair, a fifty-mile sprint race to determine a champion . . . a "winner-take-all" affair with the champion collecting the limited funds that were gathered quickly through the crowd that afternoon. Amid the melee, the press failed to document the winner of the event or the total winner's purse.

"Auto racing was pretty raw in all aspects during that era," motor sports historian Joe Freeman noted. "Races often were loosely organized events throughout the country. It was not like today, where you have structured racing bodies that govern the entire sport and all aspects of promotion and financing. These were more like the old medicine show men who would set up a 'fly-by-night' shop and 'flim-flam' a few bottles of snake oil, and then slip out of town. [Some promoters] saw an opportunity for a scam. Unfortunately for many unsuspecting drivers who simply loved to race, they lost their entry fees, as well as the opportunity to win funds to make much-needed updates and repairs to their race cars. If there was a dark underbelly to the racing game in the early days, it would be the dishonest nature of many promoters."

A Bad Premonition

Amid the financial struggles of the Great Depression, many racing circuits, white and black, ceased operations. However, the Gold and Glory Sweepstakes continued its successful run for twelve years. The 1936 race promised to be the Colored Speedway Association's grandest affair to date, featuring fireworks and aerial stunt pilots, as well as a postrace dance at Tomlinson Hall in Indianapolis, a famed dance palace that hosted many jazz greats of the era, such as Louis Armstrong, Joe "King" Oliver, Bix Beiderbecke, and Hoagy Carmichael. The Gold and Glory Gala Ball, as it was dubbed by the *Indianapolis Recorder*, would feature a "battle of the bands" competition between "the well-known Clarence Paige and his aggregation of musicians hailing from Cincinnati," and "the nationally famous Windy City dance band headed by the inimitable maestro Erskine Tate of the Savoy Ballroom."[23]

The race itself also garnered great interest, with, as the local press dubbed, "ebony pilots shooting around the turns at breakneck speed,"[24] including four-time champion Charlie Wiggins pitting his skills against two of his former pupils, Sumner "Red" Oliver and Leon "Al" Warren, as well as many other top black drivers throughout the United States, including former Gold and Glory champions "Wild Bill" Jeffries and William James, both from Chicago. A whirlwind of excitement and anticipation swept over the crowd as the public address announcer introduced each driver that entered the track during a short prerace parade around the one-mile dirt oval.

The *Indianapolis Recorder* reported that a popular Indianapolis 500 driver of the time, Howdy Wilcox, would be there to help promote the Gold and Glory event. The paper noted, "Drivers of our race are barred from participating in all AAA races . . . Wilcox, famed for his showing in past Memorial Day [Indy 500] races, announced that he will go to the battle line for our boys in the bigger racing game if we come out and support them in the Gold and Glory race . . . Your own interest may cause the promoters to allow Negro pilots to enter the races for big money. If you support your own drivers, that will be reason enough, for they want that type of backing for every driver in their classic."[25]

The roar of the crowd rose as the drivers made their way to the starting line for the beginning of the 1936 race. Before the green flag dropped to signal the start of the race, however, an argument ensued between the promoters of the event and a couple of the drivers regarding some technical specifications with one of the racing vehicles. By the time the shouts were quelled, the argument had lasted two hours, infuriating nearly all in attendance. Promoters were anxious to get the race underway quickly, but some drivers, including Charlie Wiggins, grew concerned that the long delay, in the midst of the summer sun, had caused the dirt track to dry out too much, which had made the driving surface unsafe.

Prior to races on paved surfaces, very little maintenance is required to prepare the track before the event. Traditionally, for races on dirt tracks like the Indiana State Fairgrounds oval, the dusty surface must be coated with a mixture of oil and water prior to the start of the race in order to keep down the blowing dirt and debris and make the surface safer for the drivers.

At the 1936 Gold and Glory event, promoters understood that patrons were growing increasingly impatient after the long, two-hour argument. Despite protests from the drivers to prepare the track adequately, the promoters did not wish to delay the race further. They demanded that the drivers take their places immediately to start the race. Before Wiggins left the pits and went to his position at the starting line, he looked at his wife, Roberta, shook his head, and told her that he had a bad premonition: "Somebody is going to get hurt today."

Roberta remembered that the comment haunted her. She recalled that she could barely stand to watch as the green flag dropped and the race started. Red Oliver remembered, "The cars were running really fast that day. Two laps into the thing, the dust was kicking up something terrible. Charlie was in first place. I was in third at the time. Suddenly I heard the crowd screaming. Then I thought I heard the announcer say that there was a wreck on the northwest end of the track."

Roberta recalled, "Charlie was really bearing down hard to stay in front. But the dust was so bad that he could not see that there was another car from the back of the pack that had stalled in front of him. He burst through the thick dust at the last second, but by that time, he did not have time to react to the stalled car. He tried to swerve, but it was too late."

The ensuing crash sent one car airborne into the infield. Thick, black smoke engulfed the far end of the track. Eight, then ten, then thirteen cars skidded out of control and slammed into a swelling inferno. More than 8,000 spectators watched in disbelief. Drivers, mechanics, and distraught fans rushed to the accident. One by one they began to pull drivers out of the fiery scene. Al Warren was one of the drivers trapped under the wreckage. He recalled, "Someone yanked the steering wheel out of my car so that I could crawl out of there. Once I got out, I headed back into the pile to help some of the other drivers. The first person I saw was Charlie. He was lying on his back with a car on top of him. He kept screaming, 'Take it off my leg! Take it off my leg!' So I jumped out on the track and tried to lift the car off him. That's when I turned around and heard the roar of the other engines bearing down on me. I had to jump out of the way fast. When I looked up again, I saw

Officials, drivers, and mechanics at the Gold and Glory Sweepstakes, 1936.
Image courtesy of Indiana Recorder *Collection, Indiana Historical Society.*

another car slam into Charlie's car. He and the car went flying into the air. It was an awful thing to see."

Breaking through the restraints of race officials, a sobbing Roberta Wiggins dashed into the infield toward the wreckage. "Somebody had told me he had been killed. I couldn't believe it. I had to find Charlie."

Race officials eventually pulled Wiggins's limp, unconscious body from the crash. An ambulance rushed Charlie and other wounded drivers to a local hospital. Several competitors suffered minor injuries. By late afternoon, most of the drivers had been treated and released. By nightfall, Wiggins was the only driver remaining in the emergency ward. Doctors listed him in critical condition.

Several hours later, Charlie was still in surgery. Roberta sat uncomfortably on a wooden bench in a hospital hallway. She remembered, "They finally came in and told me that Charlie was going to live, but they had to amputate his right leg. In my whole life, I never saw Charlie cry. But that day we both sat and held each other and cried and cried. Racing meant so much to Charlie. And now we knew that his racing career was over."

Weeks later Charlie Wiggins returned to his garage. He had fashioned a wooden prosthesis using a lathe in his workshop. And then, with the same cheerful

determination that defined his character, he went back to work building and repairing cars. Until his death in 1979, Charlie Wiggins continued to impart his stories and his automotive know-how to generations of young mechanics and race car drivers.

These Men of Grease and Grit

The 1936 race not only marked the end of Charlie Wiggins's career, but the end of the Gold and Glory Sweepstakes, as well. For twelve years the Colored Speedway Association overcame racial prejudices and financial challenges to create new opportunities for African Americans in the realm of sports. Eventually, however, the organization could not overcome the immense monetary struggles brought on by the Great Depression. After years with limited profits, the Colored Speedway Association and the Gold and Glory Sweepstakes ceased operations at the end of the 1936 racing season.

In 1926, *Chicago Defender* sports columnist Frank Young reflected on the legacy the Gold and Glory organizers and participants were carving into a growing sports landscape, "Of what will younger generations speak when they talk of the accomplishments of these great colored racers? Will it be that with heart and heavy foot, they might become the fastest in the land? Or will it be that they did something far greater? For these men of grease and grit are a celebration of all that is grand for our Race. Let us hope that our children speak of the latter. For it is in this moment that we have achieved true greatness."[26]

William Rucker's grandson, Paul Bateman, commented, "My grandfather believed that a black man could race just as well as a white man. And through the Colored Speedway Association, he and the other organizers were able to give black drivers and mechanics an opportunity to prove that . . . The Association helped bring a lot of people together, both black and white. There was a mutual respect there."

The *Indianapolis Recorder* newspaper once noted in a 1929 sports column, "The Gold and Glory Sweepstakes is negro auto racing's greatest spectacle . . . where drivers flirt with danger in a quest for national fame for themselves and for their Race." As celebrated drivers and mechanics, these dedicated African Americans embodied the essence and ardor of the event. Pierce commented, "They forged a fascinating legacy in the relentless pursuit of their dreams. In that way, they truly raced for gold and glory."

Boniface Hardin reflected, "The Gold and Glory Sweepstakes represented the very best of what the colored people could accomplish. It belonged to more than just the drivers and mechanics that participated in it. It belonged to the entire community. It brought us together in celebration. At a time when we needed heroes, these men were our heroes. Theirs is a great story of courage and one that exemplifies the best of the human spirit."

8

The East West Classic

Black America's Baseball Fiesta

Rob Ruck

"We saw a baseball epic unfold itself on this historic field," *Pittsburgh Courier* sportswriter William G. Nunn wrote following the East West Classic in Chicago on a late summer day in August 1934. And the center of attention was black baseball's most iconic figure, Leroy Robert "Satchel" Paige. When the gangly righthander, who had spurned the previous year's inaugural contest, slowly walked to the Comiskey Park mound in the sixth inning, the West squad had a runner on second base and three outs to work with in order to break the scoreless tie. For Nunn, who played for the Homestead Grays before becoming one of black America's premier newspapermen, the game did more than buff Paige's soon-to-be-legendary profile. It "once again demonstrated to the world at large that [black ballplayers] are on a par with major league performers."[1] He could have gone even further. The East West Classic showcased the verve and creative energies of the African American community writ large that had germinated with little notice on the other side of the color line.[2]

That Sunday, Nunn raved, was a peerless baseball day, with the South Side ballpark's double-decker grandstands bathed in azure-blue skies. Stellar pitching, acrobatic fielding, and a great peg by catcher Josh Gibson to catch a runner trying to steal second base meant that no runners crossed home plate during the first five innings. But in the sixth inning, Harry Kincannon, who had played for the Pittsburgh Crawfords since the late 1920s when they were still a team of young sandlotters from the city's Hill District, surrendered a lead-off double to future Hall of Famer Willie Wells.

That set the stage for Paige, who relished moments like this. As he desultorily warmed up, Oscar Charleston pawed the dirt around first base, Cool Papa Bell and Vic Harris talked in the outfield, and Gibson squatted behind home plate. Third baseman Jud Wilson and Dick Lundy, who managed the East squad in addition to playing shortstop for it, conferred on what they would do if Ted "Double Duty" Radcliffe, the next batter, tried to bunt Wells over to third. They had no need to worry. Eleven pitches later, the side retired, Paige ambled off the mound and back to the East dugout. He struck out five batters during four hitless innings, rarely throwing anything but fastballs. In the eighth inning, Paige's Crawford teammate centerfielder Cool Papa Bell walked, stole second, and scored on a ball that lazily drifted over second base. That was all Paige and the East squad needed to win the second Negro League all-star contest.

Later that evening at the Grand Hotel, the center of the off-the-field festivities surrounding the game, John Henry Lloyd held court in the lounge. The greatest Negro Leaguer of the early twentieth century, Lloyd offered an indisputable post-mortem on the game: "You can't beat unbeatable pitching." And on that day, like so many other days, Paige was unhittable. Rollo Wilson, the dean of black sportswriters, writing about the contest's larger impact, noted that: "thousands of fans who had never seen baseball played by high-class colored teams have been converted."[3]

The Comiskey Park crowd of about 30,000 fans, of whom 4,000 were white, was the biggest crowd to watch two black squads play to date. East West Classic crowds would surpass that number in subsequent years, topping 50,000. It's possible that no other event brought more African Americans together at one time during the 1930s and 1940s. The attraction was baseball, but there was more to it than that.

With nine future hall of famers and several other players worthy of consideration for Cooperstown on the field in 1934, the players comprised one of the greatest aggregations of baseball talents to meet on the diamond. Such displays of baseball brilliance would be repeated almost every time the Negro National League's all-star game took place. But more than just a ballgame, the East West Classic was a black *fiesta* whose effect extended beyond a single game.[4] While fans enjoyed the Sunday afternoon contest each year, they had also anticipated the Classic for weeks beforehand, and would relish it for some time after it was played. The audience for the games came from black America's archipelago of urban neighborhoods and towns, as well as the rural hinterlands where most African Americans still resided. Many had read of the impending game in the black press and then listened to stories told and retold for months to come afterward. Whether or not they were in Chicago mattered less than the sense that the game made them feel a part of something bigger and more important than their daily lives. That counted for something during the 1930s.

During the half century that segregation disfigured American sport, African Americans had built a sporting world of their own. This athletic infrastructure of sandlot and college teams, local athletic clubs, and the Negro Leagues offered

African Americans the chance to craft identities defined by competitive grace. On ballfields, gridirons, and basketball floors, in boxing rings, and at the Olympics, African American athletes became their community's paladins. As their exploits were hailed and cherished, sport became a catalyst to forging a more cohesive sense of a national black community. Given that the Great Migration had disrupted black America and often exacerbated class and geographical differences among African Americans, sport played critical if decidedly nonathletic roles. No annual event better displayed sport's ability to celebrate this emerging identity and national consciousness than black baseball's annual all star game, the East West Classic.

The event tapped the entrepreneurial and organizational energies that had been central to the black game since clubs like the Pythians, Mutuals, and Cuban Giants formed in northern cities after the Civil War. These clubs and the Negro National League that began play in 1920 underscored the image of respectability and excellence that black baseball sought to project. Though the first Negro National League did not conceive of an all-star game, the second NNL, which commenced play in 1933, seized the opportunity it offered and made full use of it.

From 1933 through the early 1950s, the East West Classic showcased black baseball's best players and black baseball itself. But what happened off the field mattered as much as what happened on it. In the stands, politicians and musicians flirted with ladies dressed to kill. Men who worked in Chicago's nearby stockyards and steel mills sat amidst black doctors, lawyers, and shopkeepers. In the press box, sportswriters for the *Chicago Defender* and *Pittsburgh Courier* joked with correspondents from the *Baltimore Afro-American*, the *Kansas City Call*, and a few intrepid white writers, and got to work on their sidebars. For African Americans, there might not have been a more celebrated annual event. Negro Leaguer Buck O'Neil was a mainstay at the Classic during his career. "Let me tell you a little bit about the East-West Game," he said, "because for a black ballplayer and black baseball fans, that was something very special."[5]

The Classic's larger setting amplified the game's impact. The annual contests attracted an eclectic mix of sportsmen, fans, musicians, gamblers, politicians, celebrities, and African American leaders to Chicago, where most of the games were held. As a result, these affairs both celebrated black accomplishment and helped to build the social and cultural cohesion that would allow African Americans to mount a campaign for civil rights in the wake of World War II.

The genesis of the East West Classic dates to the spring of 1933 when Roy Sparrow, the Pittsburgh Crawfords' traveling secretary, and William G. Nunn, the *Pittsburgh Courier*'s editor, approached Homestead Grays owner Cumberland Posey Jr. with the idea of staging a black all-star game. Major league baseball had just scheduled its first all-star game as a midsummer promotion at Comiskey Park. With the United States experiencing the nadir of the Great Depression in 1933, both white and black professional leagues scrambled to find new promotional angles to help them overcome the financial pall threatening the sporting industry. *Chicago Tribune* sports editor Arch Ward, who had already helped to create the Golden Gloves boxing tournament and the college all-star football game, persuaded major league baseball to introduce an all-star game to complement the celebration of Chicago's Century of Progress Exposition being held later that summer. For their part, Sparrow and Nunn thought that a black all-star game would focus attention on the Negro Leagues' revival. Their preferred venue was Yankee Stadium, where the game could be promoted as a fundraiser for the New York Milk Fund. When that idea did not gain traction, Sparrow and Nunn solicited Gus Greenlee's backing.

Big Red or the "Caliph of Little Harlem," as journalists sometimes called Greenlee, was Pittsburgh's leading numbers baron and a larger-than-life character. His Crawford Grill was a Mecca for jazz, and Greenlee Field, the ballpark he built in the city's Hill district, was home grounds for his ballclub, the Pittsburgh Crawfords. Greenlee spent a considerable amount of his numbers game profits on sport, particularly the Crawfords. The squad might have been black baseball's best team ever, but Greenlee's vision extended well beyond Pittsburgh. In 1933, after bringing in Satchel Paige, Oscar Charleston, and Cool Papa Bell, and getting Josh Gibson back from the Homestead Grays, he resurrected the Negro National League, which had collapsed due to the combined blows of the Great Depression and its founder, Rube Foster's, deteriorating health.[6]

Greenlee quickly recognized the marketing possibilities that an all-star contest might afford his fledgling league and brought Chicago American Giants owner Robert Cole in on the planning. He knew how much Chicago mattered, to both black baseball and black America. Robert Cole, despite leaving school after the fifth grade, had become one of the nation's leading African American entrepreneuers. With wages saved from his work as a Pullman porter, he opened up a funeral parlor and later an insurance company. The numbers and the insurance business were two of black America's biggest businesses. Like Greenlee, Cole recycled his some of his profits back into the community by backing black basball.

Greenlee risked $2,500 to rent Comiskey Park for the first game, and Sparrow worked his press connections. Reaching fifty-five black weeklies and ninety white daily papers, Sparrow ensured that whatever the size of the crowd in attendance, the game would reverberate through the nation's sporting press. He even got Oscar Charleston and Willie Foster, two future Hall of Famers, on to Chicago radio stations before the game to talk it up. While Sparrow labored behind the scenes, Gus was the center of attention. "That was the greatest idea Gus ever had," Buck O'Neil argued almost sixty years later, "because it made black people feel involved in baseball like they'd never been before."[7]

East-West All-Star Game at Comiskey Park, Chicago, August 6, 1939. Members of the West team, *from left to right:* Ted Strong (SS, Kansas City Monarchs), Parnell Woods (3B, Cleveland Buckeyes), Dan Wilson (LF, St. Louis Stars), Neil Robinson (CF, Memphis Red Sox). Wilson, held aloft by his teammates, hit a three-run home run in the eighth inning that enabled the West to take the lead. *Image courtesy of National Baseball Hall of Fame Library, Cooperstown, NY.*

The East West Classic, which Greenlee and Cole controlled for the next few years, would be played for twenty-one seasons, until 1953. For five of those seasons, two games were played, with either New York, Cleveland, or Washington, DC, hosting the second contest. Chicago, however, was the Classic's mainstay and Comiskey Park its venue for at least one game during each of those twenty-one seasons. Given the size and vibrancy of the African American community in Chicago, and the role that the city played during the great migration out of the South, there was no more appropriate venue for this yearly black *fiesta*.

The great migration of African Americans out of the South during and after World War I had made Chicago the city with the second-largest black population in the country. Indeed, Chicago's African American community had grown apace with the great migration. From 44,000 African Americans in 1910, its black population grew to over 100,000 by 1920, doubled again by 1930, and exploded, to 492,000 in 1950 and 813,000 in 1960. Only New York City was home to more African Americans when the Classic commenced in 1933, and only Harlem, with its celebrated artistic renaissance in the 1920s, could rival the African American neighborhoods in Chicago that many called Bronzeville. Chicago had the only black congressman in the nation, William Dawson, its largest black congregation, the Olivet Baptist Church, and the man who would soon be the most important African American of all, heavyweight champion Joe Louis. Chicago drew African Americans during these years because of its geography and its manufacturing infrastructure. Many African Americans headed there because the city was the terminus of several of the nation's most important railroad trunk lines as well as home to slaughterhouses, factories, and steel mills.[8]

Though "crossing Jordan" into the North had not brought the redemption from segregation and sharecropping in the South that many African American migrants had at first envisioned, Chicago and other northern urban areas were a relatively liberated zone. African Americans were freer to vote there, to gain an education, work in industry, and build a sporting world that they defined and controlled. In Chicago, tickets to the game were sold at department stores, tailors, and shops on the Southside, boosting attendance as well as walk-in traffic.

Given its geographic centrality, Chicago was as ideal a venue for the East West Classic as it was for African Americans seeking to leave Jim Crow behind. "People could get there from all over," Buck O'Neil recalled. "The Illinois Central Railroad would put on a special coach from New Orleans to Chicago. They would pick up people all through Mississippi and Tennessee, right on into Chicago. The Santa Fe Chief would be picking up people in Wichita and Kansas City. The New York Central would come in from the East."[9]

The weekend of the game, both city natives and visitors went clubbing. They might see Lena Horne, Ella Fitzgerald, Louis Armstrong, Duke Ellington, or Count

Basie perform, or find them at the next table at the Regal club, the Savoy Ballroom, the Grand Terrace Café, the Rhumboogie, or the bar at the Grand Hotel. All were located within a few miles of Comiskey Park with a half dozen of the top night-spots within a brief walk from each other along South Parkway (now MLK Junior Drive). "If you were anybody, you were at the East-West Game," Buck O'Neil attested.[10] "It was a holiday for at least 48 hours," veteran sportswriter Sam Lacy recalled. "People would just about come from everywhere, mainly because it was such a spectacle." And it was one where "the interest was focused purely on black folks." And these black folks, Lacy assured his readers, performed at the high-est levels of sport. That elicited the crowd's heartfelt response. "At the East-West Game, we just raised hell from the first pitch, right on through to the end of the game."[11] For Lacy, raising hell came from the sheer exuberance of watching black baseball at its best. For others, it might have been listening to an array of the best entertainers in the world, or displaying their agility at the Texas Tommy, the Lindy Hop, and the jitterbug.

If you wanted to see or be seen, Chicago during the East West Classic was the place to be. Not only were the best African American baseball players on the planet in town, so were the top black athletes from other sports. Heavyweight champ Joe Louis was there; so was Henry Armstrong. While Louis was the best known black boxer of these times, Armstrong was also hugely popular with fight fans and the larger community and his presence added luster to the event. Armstrong was among an elite group of fighters to hold titles in three different weight classes when there were only eight classes overall. Moreover, he held them at the same time. And Armstrong and Louis were not the only athletes drawing attention. Harlem Globetrotters like Goose Tatum and Marquis Haynes, and their owner Abe Saperstein, Olympic broad jump gold medalist DeHart Hubbard, and Olympians Mable Landry and Barbara Jones mingled with politicians and peformers like Bill "Mr. Bojangles" Robinson. Leaders of the Elks and Alpha Phi Alpha, the nation's oldest black fraternity, solidified their social connections, while white politicians, attentive to the increasing number of votes cast by black Chicagoans, also made sure to make their presence noted.

Buck O'Neil's charismatic remembrances of baseball beyond the color line have done more to popularize the game's history than any of the academics, writers, and filmmakers who have helped to retrieve this sporting past. He told Steve Wulf and David Conrads, who captured that spirit in *I Was Right on Time*, that to black players and fans, the Classic was simply "special." The very fact that fans could vote for players by casting ballots printed in the *Chicago Defender* and the *Pittsburgh Courier* mattered, O'Neil emphasized. "That was a pretty important thing for black people to do in those days, to be able to vote, even if it was just for ballplay-ers, and they sent in thousands and thousands of ballots. It was like an avalanche."[12]

For the players, no other games compared. They might have performed before large and enthusiastic crowds in Havana and *Ciudad* Trujillo, or played against white major league all-stars in barnstorming contests in the off-season, but this was an all African American contest that showcased the best baseball players then playing the game, with the eyes of black America upon them.

O'Neil contended that these Negro Leagues all-star games meant more to black fans and players than it did for their white counterparts. Few, if any, have contradicted him on this point. While major leaguers considered the World Series the ultimate goal each season, the Negro League World Series carried less significance. The first black postseason championship took place in 1924 when the Kansas City Monarchs beat the Philadelphia Hilldales in a nine-game series. The Negro League World Series remained fairly successful until the combined blows of league founder Rube Foster's incapacitation and the onslaught of the Depression brought an end to the Negro National League. When the league reformed, the postseason series was revived. But as Donn Rogosin argues, it "never captured the imagination of the black public like the East-West game." The reasons were largely economic. Black fans lacked the money and time to attend a lengthy postseason series. The league often scheduled a few Negro League World Series in cities other than those with teams in it, but even this ploy did not bring in enough fans to make the contests financially viable.[13] For white major leaguers, a cut of the winner's or loser's share of the Series was a substantial year-end bonus; the Negro League World Series did not pay nearly as well. Nor did it generate the publicity for a player that the World Series often did for its contestant. For all these reasons, the Negro League World Series never gained comparable stature among players, fans, and the sporting press. It paled in comparison to both the major leagues' championship and the East West Classic, an annual showcase of the best black baseball had to offer. "For black fans," O'Neil said, "the East-West Game was a matter of racial pride." "That was the glory part of our baseball," Sammy T. Hughes told Rogosin. "It was an honor even if you were just jonna sit on the bench."[14]

Fans were able to vote for players via the black press, to which the East-West Classic was inextricably tied. No institution did a better job of connecting African Americans during the middle decades of the twentieth century than these weekly newspapers. Though the best circulating papers—the *Pittsburgh Courier*, the *Chicago Defender*, and the *Baltimore Afro-American*—were located in northern cities, the papers were widely read in the South, whether the majority of African Americans still lived in the 1930s and 1940s. Often times, Pullman porters carried the papers along their routes, distributing them along the way. The black press promoted the Negro Leagues and other sports, which in turn boosted newspaper sales and advertising. When it came to the East-West Classic, the black press printed ballots for the team and urged their readers to cut them out, vote their preferences, and mail them back.

The East West Classic was not without critics. Those who assessed black base-ball's credibility in terms of how well it measured up to major league baseball often found fault with the African American game. They stressed that contests took too long due to frequent arguments and poor umpiring, that statistics were poorly recorded or even invented, and that too many players lacked schooling in the fun-damentals of the game. Owners and players fought over how much players were paid, owners fought with one another over how the proceeds were to be split, and more than a few took potshots at white booking agents like Abe Saperstein for their fees.

Disputes between the owners and players were the most serious to erupt at the East West Classic. Dismayed by the small sums offered to them as compensation for participating, the men chosen for the game threatened to strike a couple of times unless the owners agreed to pay them more. In 1944, they refused to take the field at Comiskey Park until their demand for $200 per player was met. The August 13, 1944, contest had drawn over 46,000 fans, more historian Neil Lanctot points out, than attended any major league ballgame played that day. Given the $56,000 that the owners grossed, the players demanded more money. Two years later, at Griffith Stadium in Washington, DC, they used their leverage again, at the second of the two East West Classics played that season.[15] These conflicts were part of a larger pattern in which sportswriters criticized league officials for poor communi-cations and rulings that blatantly favored one owner or club over another. Players jumped contracts and might even disappear during the season. Paige was notorious for such behavior.

Most of these criticisms had some validity and from this vantage point, the East West Classic's inaugural contest was fatally flawed. The West club in 1933, they pointed out, was Robert Cole's Chicago American Giants with a couple of other players mixed in. The Crawfords, meanwhile, dominated the East team. How could a contest between a team made up mostly of the Giants, dressed in cream-colored uniforms with "WEST" emblazoned across the breast, and an "EAST" squad in blue and gray uniforms composed mostly of Crawfords be judged a genuine all-star game? Nor did the game result in a charitable contribution, as advertised. Moreover, the quality of play that first game was uneven, and some writers questioned the accuracy of the votes reported by the press. "I know several baseball bugs here and there but I never yet have talked with one who had sent in a list of his favorite players," Rollo Wilson wryly reported. Another sportswriter, Ed Harris, wrote that everyone "knows that Cum Posey sits in his den and makes up all these statistics," a claim that Posey, the longtime owner of the Homestead Grays, later acknowledged to be true.[16] Like Negro League statistics in general, the vote tallies announced by the Negro National League would not have held up to close scrutiny. In 1939, the league announced that over seventeen million ballots had been cast, an astronomical increase over previous seasons. But few seemed to care. Sportswriters used the vote tallies as fodder for columns in which they debated the merits of those selected for the squads and those left off, and baseball *aficionados* debated the lineups at barbershops and on street corners.

John L. Clark, who covered political and social concerns for the *Pittsburgh Courier*, offered a full-throated defense of the game.[17] "Provincial criterion on things beyond their comprehension insist that an affair so stupendous, spectacular or idealistic should never be touched by our brothers of the sepia tint, and behind all of these opinions, one will find somewhere a smallness of character and divided racial spirit as the motivating cause." In his rebuttal of the naysayers, Clark called attention to the event's economic contribution, and "that great American principle and standard—the dollar." He pointed to the staff of ten who had worked for months to prepare for the game, the additional workers who staffed the event, the fifty ballplayers, managers, coaches, and umpires who took part, and the fifty to one hundred boys who worked the game. "The venture last year found over $7,000 turned over before the gates were opened," he noted. Most of all, he stressed, over three-fourths of this amount "passed through the hands of Negroes." Clark lauded the promoters' entrepreneurial courage. "Seven thousand dollars is only 'a drop in the bucket' for some people. But you can count all the Negroes and Negro organizations who will take the same course as the East-West promoters, with only one day, and one chance to recover the investment, on the one hand."

But most fans did not hold the Negro Leagues or the East-West Classic to such a metric. "This was the weekend," Buck O'Neil underscored. "It was near the last weekend before school started, so a lot of kids would save up their nickels and dimes." And not just children and baseball fans relished it. "That weekend was always a party," O'Neil recollected. "All the hotels on the South Side were filled. All the big nightclubs were hopping."[18] Nor did they need the sort of rationale that Clark provided to back the East West Classic. For them, black baseball was fun, and in some intimate social and psychological fashion, meaningful in ways that much of daily life was not.

If sport mattered, then the East West Classic was a valued event. No other black baseball game meant so much to African Americans. Neither the Negro League World Series, a league match-up, nor a Thanksgiving football game between Howard and Lincoln, drew the attention that this once-a-year fiesta of black sport routinely generated. Although the players chosen for the game were extraordinary ballplayers, their game resonated with every African American who had ever played the game on an urban sandlot, mine patch, milltown ballfield, or throughout the rural South. The only sporting event that was more meaningful to African Americans during these years was a night when Joe Louis fought, but those events were experienced for most African Americans by radio, not in person. Although no statistics exist on the racial breakdown of attendance at a Joe Louis fight, it's likely that there were fewer African Americans present at his fights, where the crowd was predominantly white, than at the East West Classic, where it was mostly black. There was another difference between a Joe Louis fight and the Classic. Though white booking agents played a part in the games, the Classic was mostly controlled by African Americans. That was rarely the case when Joe Louis fought; white promoters and managers still called the shots.

The annual East West games drew so well in the 1940s that Wendell Smith wrote that "baseball is the No. 1 sports attraction in so far as Negroes are concerned. Not even Joe Louis—as great as he is—has ever been able to attract 50,000 Negroes at any of his great fights."[19] In 1935, the East West Classic was followed by a Joe Louis fight just two days later. Louis took only two minutes and twenty-one seconds to knock out King Levinsky that evening. The bout, also at Comiskey Park, took place two years before Louis would dethrone heavyweight champion James Braddock and as a result, make him the most widely celebrated African American in the world. But Louis was already drawing support among both black and white fans as worthy of fighting for the title, something no black fighters had been allowed to do since Jack Johnson lost the crown. Having Louis fight two days after the Classic only extended the off-the-field celebrations.[20]

The East West Classic offered a unique platform to black baseball. At no other time did the game command as much attention. In August 1942, Satchel Paige became the target of the black press for his answer to the question: how would you would feel about playing baseball in the major leagues? "It wouldn't appeal to me," Paige responded, much to the dismay of black sportswriters and editors who sensed that World War II was energizing the campaign for integration. Paige forthrightly said he would not relish the hostility of white major leaguers nor would he welcome what for him, at least, would have been a cut in salary. Paige, who made $37,000 in 1941, then earned far more than all but a handful of white major leaguers. The firestorm his candor ignited convinced Paige that he needed to confront the question in a public forum; he chose the 1942 East West Classic. He missed his chance to explain himself before the game when he showed up late and Hilton Smith started in his stead. The game was tied 2–2 when Paige arrived at the ballpark and he was not sent in to pitch until the seventh inning. But Paige had something to say before he threw his first pitch. Using the Comiskey Park public address system, he told the 42,000 fans there that he had been misquoted. Not only did he not object to black players joining the major leagues, he slyly suggested that major league baseball would be even better served by accepting an entire black team.[21] Paige, who understand the economics of baseball as well as any player, probably realized how far-fetched an idea that was. Major League Baseball owners were not eager to share their revenues with one another, much less newcomers.

Historically, the equation of slavery and work on the one hand, freedom and play on the other, had all but defined African Americans out of the mainstream of American sport. And when increasing numbers of immigrants from Europe used sport as a way to Americanize, African Americans had been largely left out. Though the failures of Reconstruction and its legacy of sharecropping and segregation, as well as Social Darwinism, did their worst to prevent African Americans from negating this binary, the Great Migration allowed many African Americans to finally gain both more leisure time and enough political space to pursue sport. In that sense, the East West Classic was all about play, a pulsating, joyous, recognition of African American freedom. The *fiesta*, Roberto Gonzalez Echevarria argues in his *Cuban Fiestas*, involves an array of activities, from "games, music, and dancing to acting, cooking, eating, and drinking, all happening in a special place to mark an exceptional time."[22] With ballpark food during the game, and jazz and the blues afterward, the East West Classic became a secular holiday for African Americans able to get to Chicago for a couple of days each summer.

No other moment during the 1930s and 1940s bathed black baseball in more flattering light. The Classic not only demonstrated black sport's drawing power, the brilliance of its players, and its ability to pull off an event equal to that of the major leagues, the game infused black consciousness across the nation with a sense of collective self-esteem.

It attracted some international attention, too. Although the East West Classic did not garner as much coverage in the baseball-playing Caribbean as it did in the United States, Latino ballplayers were a mainstay of the East West Classic, as they were in Negro League baseball overall. Their contributions to both were recognized in Cuba, Puerto Rico, the Dominican Republic, and throughout the circum-Caribbean baseball world. Over a score of Latinos appeared in the Classic, including Dominican Horacio Martínez, Cubans Martín Dihigo and Luis Tiant Sr., Panamanian Pat Scantlebury, and Puerto Rican Pancho Coimbre.[23] In 1947, in a game held at the Polo Grounds, seven members of the New York Cubans, including future major leaguers Orestes Miñoso and Luis Tiant, represented the East squad in a game played at the Polo Grounds in New York before over 38,000 fans.[24] Appearing in the Classic burnished a player's historical stature. When the Hall of Fame held a special election for African American and Caribbean ballplayers in 2006, East West Classic appearances were discussed in committee deliberations.

Black baseball's success, in the spotlight at the East West Classic, proved to be its undoing. These all-star contests showed that black baseball could put extraordinary athletes on the field and draw large crowds. This was not lost on all baseball executives. As the league achieved record attendance during World War II, Dodgers president Branch Rickey began scouting darker-skinned players. The war had energized the struggle for civil rights and Rickey realized that the first club to tap black and Latino talent would gain an edge on the field and at the box office. Soon after the conflict ended, he stunned the nation by announcing the signing of Kansas City Monarch Jackie Robinson in October 1945. Robinson, who played only one year in the Negro Leagues, represented the West squad at shortstop in the 1945 East-West Classic. After spending the 1946 season in Montreal with the Dodgers' top farm club, he debuted in the major leagues in April 1947.

The Dodgers won the pennant and set attendance records at home and on the road. As the *Pittsburgh Courier* put it, "Jackie's nimble, Jackie's quick. Jackie makes the turnstiles click."[25] But black fans deserted the Negro Leagues and focused on Robinson and the other black players who followed in his footsteps. So did the black press, which had long fought to integrate major league baseball. Independent black baseball was soon on death watch. The Negro National League collapsed after the 1948 season. As Buck Leonard once said, "After Jackie, we couldn't draw flies." Though the Negro American League continued for another decade, largely as a midwestern circuit, the East West Classic could not survive integration. It was last played in 1953.

Though mostly forgotten, black baseball's history would be retrieved in later years. The Negro Leagues and the East West Classic, once viewed as somewhat embarassing artifacts of segregation, are now perceived differently. They signal what African Americans were able to accomplish despite racial discrimination and the degree to which black sport was then rooted in the black community. African Americans would achieve much in integrated professional baseball, but their communities lost control over their own sporting lives as a result. The Negro Leagues and the East West Classic suggest that integration could have come about in more optimal ways, incorporating African Americans in positions of power and embracing their creations as part of a more inclusive sport.

III
Organizations

9

Creating Order in Black College Sport

The Lasting Legacy of the Colored Intercollegiate Athletic Association

David K. Wiggins and Chris Elzey

Black college sport realized significant growth during the twentieth century. Black institutions of different sizes and reputations, including Howard University and Hampton Institute in the upper South and Tuskegee Institute and Morehouse College in the lower South, expanded their athletic programs, resulting in more competitions in a greater number of sports. But increased emphasis on intercollegiate athletics also had a downside. Accompanying the growth were many problems, such as a greater number of injuries, inadequate coaching, poor officiating, inappropriate fan behavior, player eligibility concerns, and game scheduling issues.[1]

The problems associated with burgeoning sports programs at black colleges caused serious concerns among faculty and administrators. In the aftermath of the football crisis of 1905 in which dozens of players were either seriously injured or killed—the crisis eventually led to the establishment of the National Collegiate Athletic Association (NCAA) in 1906—a number of prominent individuals suggested the creation of a national organization to oversee black college sport. In 1906, Samuel H. Archer, football coach, dean, vice president, and later fifth president of Morehouse College, penned an essay titled, "Football in Our Colleges," in *The Voice of the Negro*. In the piece, Archer declared a "pressing need" for an "Intercollegiate Athletic Association" to govern sport among black colleges. Claiming that "most of the charges made against the game (football) are general and might well apply to any of the sports that appeal to young and vigorous manhood," the future Morehouse president advocated for a national organization with a "constitution and printed rules" that would "promote every kind of outdoor sport, prevent the establishment of uncertain precedents, create a wholesome athletic enthusiasm, and maintain a uniform rule in all the colleges concerning professionalism and eligibility of players."[2]

Archer's colleague at Morehouse College, and later secretary of the Colored Men's Department of the International Committee of the YMCA as well as president of the University of Arkansas at Pine Bluff, John Brown Watson, also argued for a national organization to oversee black college sport. In a 1907 essay entitled "Football in Southern Negro Colleges," Watson wrote, "an institution in demand now is an Intercollegiate Athletic Association affecting all the colleges of the whole South." Such a group was needed. "With intercollegiate organization," Watson noted, "many evils connected with the choice of officials and the playing of games could be done away with and the whole matter of college athletics given a higher tone."[3]

Although a separate national organization to govern black college sport never materialized, several regional black athletic associations did come into existence during the second decade of the twentieth century. One of the first regional associations was the Colored Intercollegiate Athletic Association (CIAA). In 1912, Ernest J. Marshall, professor of chemistry and football coach at Howard University in Washington, DC, convened a meeting of representatives from several well-known black colleges at Hampton Institute in Hampton, Virginia, to discuss the creation of an organization to govern sports at their respective schools. Attending the meeting from Shaw University in Raleigh, North Carolina, were W. E. Atkins, H. P. Hargrave, and C. R. Frazier. From Virginia Union University in Richmond came J. W. Pierce and J. W. Barco. George Johnson, a professor at Lincoln University in Oxford, Pennsylvania, also attended. Acting as the conclave's de facto hosts were Hampton's Charles H. Williams and Allen Washington.[4]

United in their belief that a governing body was needed to bring order to black college sport, the men established the CIAA. Over two days of intense discussion and debate, they drafted a "Constitution and By-Laws," which each member institution—Hampton Institute, Howard University, Shaw University, Virginia Union University, and Lincoln University—pledged to follow. The five schools became the original members of the CIAA.

The educators meeting at Hampton in 1912 were all prominent men who, like many middle-class black Americans, believed in the principle of racial uplift. Experiencing various forms of racial hostility, forced to live in a segregated society, and suffering the indignities of Jim Crow laws, the founders of the CIAA emphasized through sport positive images of highly educated and assimilated African Americans who carried themselves with unimpeachable character. To the founders, the new athletic organization would represent the very best sport could offer—characterized by strict adherence to rules, sportsmanship, fiscal transparency, and impeccable organizational structure. In this way, they believed, the CIAA would provide optimal conditions for athletic competition and, by extension, combat deeply entrenched stereotypes of black inferiority and moral degradation. Providing high-quality sports programs and achieving respectability, however, would be difficult. In an era that denied African Americans equal rights and freedom of opportunity while condoning racialist thinking irrespective of educational attainment, cultural background, and social status, the CIAA, like other black institutions at the time, was engaged in a constant battle to prove its worth, conquer social marginalization, and gain recognition in a society that viewed African Americans as being inferior to whites.[5]

Highly detailed and written in unambiguous language, the "Constitution and By-Laws" provide insights into the new organization's priorities and the issues confronting black college sports more generally. Perhaps nothing generated more concern than player eligibility. Like officials at predominantly white schools, the founders of the CIAA wanted to eliminate "tramp athletes," physically gifted players who were known to extend their college football career beyond four years by transferring from one institution to another with little regard for academics.[6] To rein in tramp athletes, the CIAA stipulated that no student would be eligible for athletics until satisfying the "entrance requirements of the department in which he is enrolled, has completed a full year's work equivalent to that required of candidates for a degree, and is taking during his year of competition a full year's work in the institution."[7]

In addition, the CIAA proclaimed itself to be the national governing body of black college sport, specifying that "no student shall participate in inter-collegiate athletics more than four years in the aggregate" in nineteen black colleges and universities, "and [in] many other institutions hereafter approved eligible for membership in the association."[8] But after other black athletic associations were established—the Southeastern Intercollegiate Athletic Conference (SIAC) in 1913 and the Southwestern Athletic Conference (SAC) in 1920, for example—and after the CIAA joined the NCAA in 1921, the regulations were modified and the association ceased to speak for black college sport as a whole.[9]

The rules set by the CIAA were rigidly enforced. Claiming itself to be "the pioneer organization for the purpose of raising the standard of athletics in the negro schools and colleges," and recognizing the importance of exhibiting skills of self-organization and business acumen in a racially segregated America, the CIAA punished member schools for violating the association's written policies.[10]

Howard University and Lincoln University, two of the most prestigious historically black colleges and universities (HBCUs) in the United States, were among the first to feel the sting of the young organization's ire. In 1923, a student named Robert Miller played football for Virginia Union. The following year, Miller transferred to Dunbar High School in Washington, DC, and then to Howard University, where he also played football. Virginia Normal and Industrial Institute (later Virginia State), Lincoln University, and Hampton Institute all protested, arguing that Miller should have been declared ineligible for the 1924 season because he had violated CIAA guidelines that specified students who transferred from high school to college were required to sit out a year before returning to competition. Howard University officials, in a telegram sent by Edward P. Davis, president of the university's Board of Athletic Control, responded by withdrawing the school from the CIAA, noting that "we regret that we are forced to this step by the impossibility of reconciling collegiate and high school standards in the association and hope that our pleasant relations with the member institutions may continue."[11] The CIAA accepted the university's decision, claiming "that the association feels that it is incumbent upon it to say to Howard that it has done its duty in attempting to carry on the spirit and letter of our association, and in furtherance of that policy cannot in justice to our ideals of true sportsmanship arrange athletic contests under conditions which destroy the integrity of the association."[12]

Having withdrawn from the CIAA, Howard was forbidden to play other conference teams. Even though Lincoln University was one of the three schools to have protested Miller's eligibility, it went ahead and played Howard in the annual Thanksgiving Day football game that year anyway—also a clear violation of CIAA rules. As a result, Lincoln was dropped from the conference in 1925. By not showing favoritism to such prestigious institutions as Howard and Lincoln, the CIAA was able to garner much respect, ultimately giving the conference more power, and thus greater control. After much discussion with athletic leaders of both institutions, and after both schools made changes to their academic policies, the CIAA reinstated Howard in 1929, and Lincoln in 1932.[13]

Another incident occurred in 1941. On March 7, Virginia Union played the Harlem Globetrotters in a basketball exhibition in Richmond, Virginia. It was not unusual for CIAA schools to play such exhibitions, but Virginia Union had violated conference rules by not seeking permission from the association to compete against a professional team. In what it claimed was an effort to keep its players "from being contaminated or from losing their proper amateur standing," Virginia Union had instead obtained permission from the Virginia Association of the Amateur Athletic Union (AAU), having agreed that proceeds from the game were to be donated to a building fund at the school.[14]

The CIAA, however, was not persuaded. According to J. L. Whitehead, then secretary-treasurer for the CIAA, the AAU's sanctioning of the game had not invalidated the regulations of the league. Consequently, the CIAA, on recommendation from its eligibility committee, suspended Virginia Union for the remainder of the academic year, though the association was quick to point out "that the amateur status of the union's 1941 basketball team was not affected because the University, and not the players, had violated the CIAA code." A message, though, had been sent. Meting out harsh punishments bolstered the association's efforts to upgrade the integrity of its sports programs, while ensuring that all athletes were treated fairly and given the best opportunity to realize a positive educational experience in the classroom.[15]

The CIAA scrupulously applied attention to all aspects of college sport. No matter the task—the proper scheduling of games; the maintenance of records; fostering good sportsmanship; generating appropriate publicity and media coverage; and improving the quality of coaching, officiating, and administrative leadership—the association strived to be the very best.

Such meticulousness was displayed in the *C.I.A.A. Bulletin*. First published in 1923 and printed and distributed by Hampton Institute, the *Bulletin* was a detailed account of the organization's yearly activities. Each issue typically consisted of the names of delegates and minutes from the previous year's two-day CIAA meeting; essays on a variety of sport-related topics; comprehensive financial statements; lists of certified officials for each sport; a chronicling and cataloging of scores and team champions; and photographs of tournament participants and victorious squads in each sport.[16]

The 1924 *Bulletin* illustrates the seriousness with which the association conducted its business. Only the second *Bulletin* ever published, the issue listed the delegates of the previous year's meeting held at the Virginia Theological Seminary and College (later Virginia Union of Lynchburg) and the names of officers, including William H. Rogers of Virginia Normal and Industrial Institute (president); Louis L. Watson of Howard University (first vice president); and Charles H. Williams of Hampton University (secretary-treasurer).[17] In the issue, Charles H. Williams penned a brief introduction, reemphasizing the purpose of the CIAA and noted that three schools—Virginia Theological Seminary and College, Virginia Normal and Industrial Institute, and St. Paul's College—had recently become CIAA members. William A. Rogers provided a "review of the season of 1923 in athletics" for each sport, noted the various accomplishments of the association, and offered recommendations to improve the organization.[18] The issue also listed detailed minutes of the annual meeting and the organization's financial statement, which revealed that the CIAA had paid dues of $25 to the NCAA, contributed $75 to the United States Olympic Fund, and spent $89.65 to publish the *Bulletin*, leaving the association a balance of $147.90.[19]

In addition, the 1924 issue featured seven essays. Topics ranged from the impact of Greek societies on sports to interscholastic basketball to issues of athletic eligibility. J. H. Lawrence, director of athletics at Virginia Theological Seminary and College, contributed a piece, and Edwin B. Henderson, director of physical education for the segregated public schools in Washington, DC, wrote an essay entitled, "How Can Schools Co-operate with Officials to Develop Greater Efficiency."[20]

Perhaps no piece was as thought provoking as Henderson's. An educator and civil rights activist who would go on to write the first books on the history of African American participation in sport, Henderson made the obvious but unspoken observation that for many years "the leading qualifications for [a sports] official was that he be a white man."[21] Henderson pointed out that while more African Americans were hired as officials, they still received less money than their white counterparts. He ended by expressing his philosophy of college athletics and sport more generally. "Even if presidents cry out for victories," Henderson wrote, "no matter the cost, our profession cannot hope to be considered for its real worth and value in education unless we teach the presidents themselves, if need be, the real virtue in well-played games with victories and defeats as secondary matters."[22]

Subsequent issues of the *Bulletin* were similar. Essays addressing the organizational structure of the association, issues of amateurism, and improvements to the quality of play for all participants were published. After 1924, however, the *Bulletin* added several important sections, including summations of one-day coaches and officials conferences, reports of presentations by members of the black press, testimonials from former CIAA athletes, and a section called "In memoriams" for athletes and others who had been affiliated with the organization.[23] The 1933 *Bulletin*, for example, gave an account of the first "C.I.A.A. Coaches Officials Conference at Hampton," held the previous year. Attended by sixty officials, coaches, and journalists from the *Norfolk Journal and Guide* and the *Baltimore Afro-American*, the conference—which included keynote addresses and question-and-answer sessions—was designed to ensure optimal officiating and that CIAA football coaches understood the rules of the game. Over time, other conferences would be held for basketball. The football and basketball conferences eventually broadened participation by inviting team captains from league schools, as well as high school coaches.[24]

Unsurprisingly, black journalists attended the coaches and officials conferences. Members of the black press were frequent participants at CIAA meetings and regularly wrote columns about the association. Moreover, prominent journalists often gave presentations at the meetings, which were then published in the *Bulletin*. The relationship between the black press and the CIAA was mutually beneficial. Black newspapers provided extensive coverage to the association, disseminating news about sporting events and programs that were usually not covered by the mainstream press, while the black press enhanced its credibility and, in turn, increased readership and the price of advertising space by covering a principled organization.[25]

The *Bulletin* was strengthened by the inclusion of published testimonials from league players. Seeking to garner positive public relations while making clear the association's view of sport, CIAA officials asked selected players to discuss their athletic careers and what the league had meant to them. In the 1936 issue, Otis E. Thorpe, quarterback at Morgan College in Baltimore, extolled the virtues of athletics and, by extension, the association. To Thorpe, sports inculcated values necessary for good citizenship. "After four years of development along the lines of sportsmanship, team play, SELF-CONTROL and SELF-CONFIDENCE," Thorpe wrote, "the athlete finds himself better fitted to become a citizen. Respect for the officials of the game and the rules of the game, one will carry over and will have due regard for the governing body and the laws they enact."[26] In the 1938 *Bulletin*, Junius L. T. Jeffries, a sprinter from Hampton Institute, discussed the goodwill and friendships established through athletic competition. "There is created a spirit of goodwill and fair play among men in competition," noted Jeffries. "The personal contacts made with men we have met for the first time, although we are trying to beat one another, are of inestimable value in our attempt to play life's game fairly."[27]

The "In Memoriams" published in the *Bulletin* paid respects to athletes, administrators, and other key figures who had contributed to the success of the association. An especially poignant memoriam recalled the life of John Borican, the outstanding track star from Virginia State who died unexpectedly in December 1942 from a mysterious case of pernicious anemia. Written by CIAA president George G. Singleton, the memoriam noted that Borican's sudden death "caused deep grief in the hearts of his many admirers throughout the sports world in general and among the coaches, former competitors and present and future track luminaries of the Colored Intercollegiate Athletic Association in particular." Borican, who was just twenty-nine when he died, was remembered not only for his AAU titles in the pentathlon, decathlon, and 800 meters, but also for his famous victory in 1939 over Glenn Cunningham in the 1,000-yard run. In addition, Borican's brief yet highly successful postathletic career as a portrait artist and illustrator was recalled. At the time of his death, Borican was a PhD student in the arts program at Columbia University.[28]

The *Bulletin* was only superseded in quality by the association's leadership, organizational structure, and various sports programs. CIAA leadership consisted of a president, three vice presidents, a secretary-treasurer, and an assistant secretary-treasurer—all elected yearly. The men who held each office occupied important professional and administrative positions at their respective institutions. Ernest Marshall, for example, one of the founders of the CIAA and its president from 1912 to 1915, was a professor of chemistry at Howard University. William A. Rogers, president of the CIAA from 1920 to 1924, was secretary of Virginia State University, and chaired the school's athletic committee for twenty years. Walter G. Alexander, president of the CIAA between 1925 and 1928, graduated from Lincoln

University in 1899 and would go on to become a medical doctor in Orange, New Jersey. H. C. Perrin, president of the CIAA from 1939 to 1941, was a professor at Shaw University, and George C. Singleton, president of the CIAA from 1943 to 1945, was a professor and director of the Department of Business at Virginia State University.[29]

Under the guidance of such men, the CIAA would expand. In 1920, Virginia State University became a member, followed by St. Paul's College three years later. North Carolina A&T College joined the association in 1924, Johnson C. Smith University in 1926, and North Carolina Central University and Bluefield State College in 1928. By 1945, five other schools—Morgan State University, Livingston College, St. Augustine's College, Delaware State University, and Winston & Salem State University—had signed on. Boasting sixteen teams, the league was divided into three regional districts: northern, central, and southern.[30]

In addition to enduring player-eligibility issues and rules violations by member institutions, the CIAA was forced to weather circumstances beyond its control, namely the Great Depression and two world wars. Fortunately, the conference emerged from the crises relatively unscathed. But it had been tested. The Depression, for instance, demanded that the CIAA be extra vigilant in safeguarding its money. In 1931, Charles H. Williams, then secretary-treasurer, deposited association funds in the "Farmers and Merchants Bank, Lawrenceville, Virginia, and in another bank in another city of his selection" because, in his view, it "was the prudent and safe procedure to follow until conditions get back to normalcy."[31] The following year, CIAA president James T. Taylor of North Carolina Central University suggested that to help save money, the number of football officials be reduced. Having fewer officials, Taylor wrote, "is in keeping with the general trend in wages and salary. Most of our institutions are finding it rather hard to finance athletics and it would seem only fair that the 'hen' that lays the golden egg should be given due consideration."[32]

Far more problematic were World Wars I and II. As a result of the United States' entry into World War I in 1917, the CIAA, for the only time in its history, held no annual meeting and canceled the football season. World War II would test the CIAA even more. Since many CIAA athletes were entering the military, team rosters became depleted. Transportation was also an issue. During the war years, the cost of traveling increased, making it more difficult for schools to complete their schedules. The smaller and less financially endowed institutions were hit the hardest. St. Paul's College, for example, canceled its 1942 football season. Smaller schools, such as Shaw University and St. Augustine's College, were forced to withdraw from some contests after receiving permission from the association to do so.[33]

Despite the difficulties caused by World War II, the CIAA maintained the quality of its sports programs. There was a tradeoff, however, the association relaxing many of its academic policies. For instance, it took the unprecedented move—albeit for one year—of altering its eligibility requirements to ensure that member schools could field teams. It even gave permission to St. Augustine's College and Shaw University to organize a "joint football team," because of the shortage of players. In addition, member schools were allowed to play opponents more than once, and teams were encouraged to play opponents within their districts, thereby adhering to the wishes of the Office of Defense Transportation.[34]

World War II also led the CIAA to enlarge program offerings. Exhibiting patriotism, the association felt compelled to expand both its physical education and intramural programs "so as to reach more students and thus to make the maximum contribution to the nation's war job."[35] The CIAA's contribution to the war effort reflected its belief that sports developed healthy bodies, courage, respect for authority, and other traits essential for success on the battlefield. Perhaps Virginia State's George G. Singleton best expressed such a view in his presidential address at the 1943 convention. Evoking Abraham Lincoln's famous Gettysburg Address, Singleton spoke of the importance of the CIAA, and the valuable role it played in developing upstanding young men. "One score and eleven years ago," Singleton said, "our founders brought forth upon this continent a new association converged in sportsmanship and dedicated to the proposition that clean athletic activities are essential to the physical, moral, mental, scholastic and cultural development of the negro youth of the land. Now we are engaged in a great war threatening that association to its very foundation and testing whether that association or any association so concerned and so dedicated can long endure."[36]

The CIAA, of course, did. Helping the association survive was football. Like many predominantly white institutions, CIAA schools embraced the gridiron game because it toughened young men, built character, made money, generated alumni support, and contributed to institutional spirit and loyalty. The CIAA featured several outstanding players and teams. At first, a committee determined the yearly champion. Eventually, though, the Dickinson Rating System was used. (The Dickinson system was named after Frank G. Dickinson of St. Paul's College. Dickinson, at the request of John Whitehead, assistant secretary-treasurer of the CIAA in 1920 and 1921, devised a ranking system based on points that decided conference champions in both football and basketball.) Several rivalries, which drew national attention and thus generated additional publicity for the CIAA, defined league competition.[37]

Arguably the most intensely followed rivalry was the one between Lincoln and Howard Universities, especially between 1919 and 1929, the so-called Golden Age of sports. Each year, on Thanksgiving Day, the two most northern and prestigious institutions in the conference squared off against each other on the gridiron. Alternating yearly between Philadelphia and Washington, DC, the game, otherwise known as "The Classic," drew huge crowds. Specially chartered trains would bring a multitude of fans from across the country—many of which were members of the black upper class—to the host city. In addition to watching the game, Classic goers attended dances, receptions, parties, and pep rallies sponsored by the two institutions. To African Americans, the Classic was just as significant as Harvard vs. Yale and other football rivalries in white college sport.[38]

The CIAA offered other sports, including baseball, boxing, and wrestling. But track and field, tennis, and basketball proved to be more popular among CIAA institutions. The first formally recognized CIAA track meet was held in 1922 at Hampton Institute. Organized under the direction of Charles H. Williams and held at Hampton's new Armstrong Field, the meet included athletes from every CIAA institution. There was also a high school division. Athletes representing Huntington High School in Newport News, Virginia; Booker T. Washington High School in Norfolk, Virginia; and Dunbar High School and Armstrong Tech High School in Washington, DC, competed. The inaugural meet was a huge success. For the next seven years, the league held its track meet at Hampton. In 1930, it was switched to Howard University. In the years that ensued, the meet was held at various locations.[39]

The CIAA track meet would grow in importance and stature, requiring greater oversight and organizational structure. The meet at Morgan State College in 1942 is a prime example. Hundreds of athletes—college as well as high school—competed in events that ranged from the 100-yard dash to the mile run to the shot put and javelin. Howard P. Drew, the one-time record holder in the sprints who starred at the University of Southern California, served as the meet's formal starter. Jesse Owens, the famous Ohio State track star and Olympic hero, was featured in an exhibition of the 100-yard dash and broad jump. A special one-mile relay race was held among several military service teams. Honorary referees for the meet included such local dignitaries as Edward S. Lewis, executive secretary of the Urban League in Baltimore; Carl J. Murphy, editor of the *Baltimore Afro-American*; Dr. David E. Weglein, Baltimore superintendent of schools; Dr. D. O. W. Holmes, Morgan State College president; Howard W. Jackson, mayor of Baltimore; and Maryland governor Herbert R. O'Connor.[40]

In 1924, the CIAA expanded its sports program by holding its first tennis tournament. Four schools—Howard University, Hampton Institute, St. Paul's College, and Virginia Normal and Industrial Institute—took part. Howard was victorious, capturing both the singles and doubles titles. Later, the winner of the CIAA singles title competed against black champions from the Southern Intercollegiate Conference, the Southern Athletic Conference, and the Mid-Western Athletic Association at the annual American Tennis Association (ATA) tournament. The winner was given the Williams Cup. The Williams Cup tournament revealed the cooperation shown not only among black athletic conferences but also between the ATA and HBCUs. Founded in 1916 by more than a dozen black tennis clubs, the ATA staged several early national championships at HBCUs because the tennis courts on campuses were in good condition and because players would not encounter discriminatory policies regarding lodging. University administrators, for their part, recognized the benefits—financial as well as political—of hosting the ATA tournament. Large numbers of African Americans would be on campus sharing in the excitement of tennis matches and attending tournament parties and other social events.[41]

The CIAA held no tennis competition for women. While women from CIAA schools may have played in other tennis tournaments, there is no evidence that they competed in CIAA events. In 1928, Charles H. Williams noted that the CIAA had made provisions for women's participation, "but this innovation has met with little success."[42] In fact, there were no CIAA competitions for women in any sport, and only a few participated in events sponsored by other HBCUs and by black athletic organizations. Such nonparticipation reflected the biases of the CIAA and the United States more generally. Reinforcing such views was the attitude of the African American community itself. Some influential black organizations opposed highly organized sport for women, encouraging instead the playing of intramural games, which, the thinking went, were less likely to inflict physiological damage, cause emotional harm, and violate acceptable notions of black femininity and womanhood. One such organization was the National Association of College Women (NACW), a prestigious group founded in 1910 by Mary Church Terrell.[43] As historian Rita Liberti notes, the NACW in 1929 and 1940 declared its opposition to highly organized college athletics for women, "urging the substitution of intramural contests and intercollegiate non-competitive play activities."[44]

Despite such opposition, there were many African American women who played organized sport. Lucy Diggs Slowe, the first dean of women at Howard University and one of the original founders of Alpha Kappa Sorority, captured the women's single title in 1917 at the first ATA national tournament in Baltimore. Ironically, Slowe, who won the championship nine years after graduating from Howard University and five years before becoming dean at the university, was the first president of the NACW.[45] Tuskegee Institute, competing in the SIAC, had the best women's track team in the country for decades. Coached by Cleve Abbott, then Christine Petty, and finally Nell Jackson, Tuskegee captured multiple AAU national championships in the 1930s and 1940s.[46] Bennett College, a coeducational institution founded in 1873 in Greensboro, North Carolina, by the Methodist Episcopal Church, featured some of the top black women's basketball teams during the Depression years. Showcasing tremendously skilled players, such as the great Ruth Glover, Bennett competed against such powerhouse clubs as the Philadelphia Tribunes—and more than held their own.[47]

No women played organized basketball in the CIAA. (It would not be until 1975 that the association held a postseason women's tournament.) Only men did. And it was hugely popular. Howard University, Hampton Institute, Virginia Union, North Carolina College for Negroes (later North Carolina Central University), and Morgan College especially embraced the sport, though the number of conference games played each year was modest by today's standards. For example, Howard announced a twelve-game schedule for the 1933–34 season. Twelve years later, St. Augustine's College played a scant six conference games. Most CIAA institutions, however, listed as many as twenty contests per season. North Carolina College's schedule for 1941–42 totaled thirty games. But in each of the next three seasons, the most games the school played was twenty-three, in 1942–43. Just as it did to other universities, World War II forced the college to curtail its sport schedules.[48]

CIAA schools did not just play basketball against other association teams. On occasion, they also played athletic clubs and predominantly white institutions. In 1938, CIAA titleholder Morgan College traveled to New York to play Long Island University (LIU), a perennial power coached by the legendary Clair Bee. That same year, Virginia Union also played LIU in the Big Apple, but lost, 57–40. In late March 1939, Virginia Union, champions of the CIAA, again took on Bee's squad, in Harlem—LIU had just won the coveted National Invitation Tournament (NIT)—and this time prevailed. The victory, however, was fleeting. Several days after the game, Tristram Walker Metcalfe, the head of LIU, announced that the team Virginian Union had defeated consisted of only seniors, and therefore did not represent LIUs actual varsity squad. The following year, Virginia Union returned to Harlem and played Brooklyn College. The Panthers, whom the *New York Times* described as "speedy," routed the Brooklynites, 54–38.[49]

In 1946 the CIAA held its first postseason basketball tournament. Organized by association members Talmadge Hill, John B. McLendon, John Burr, and Harry Jefferson—all except Hill were head basketball coaches—the tournament grew to become arguably the most significant athletic event among association schools and HBCUs more generally. William M. Bell, president of the CIAA in the 1940s, would later call the tournament "the greatest indoor attraction in the United States which is sponsored by predominantly black institutions of higher education."[50]

Not that other black conferences shied away from organizing postseason basketball tournaments. In 1934, for instance, the SIAC began sponsoring an annual conference tournament, and seven years later, the inaugural National Invitational Intercollegiate Basketball Tournament (NIIBT) gathered six HBCUs in Cincinnati to determine the unofficial black college champion. But the SIAC tournament never achieved the kind of fame that the CIAA's did, and the NIIBT was a fiscal train wreck—so few people attended games. *Baltimore Afro-American* columnist Art Carter wrote, "The fans stayed away as if the scene of the tournament . . . was a leper colony." When Kentucky State College president R. B. Atwood tried to organize a black college national basketball tournament the following year, there were no takers. Officials of black athletic conferences claimed that the ongoing war effort made participation impossible. The troubles associated with the NIIBT may have also helped convince them.[51]

At first CIAA officials were lukewarm to the idea of staging a postseason tournament. The matter had been raised as early as 1937. In the years that ensued, the idea would again be debated at least twice, and each time it was rejected. Opponents fretted over the cost and questioned why a tournament was needed. Would it be the only factor determining the league champion? If so, what about the games played during the regular season? Would they not count for anything?[52]

But tournament supporters pressed on. Their hard work eventually paid off. In December 1945, at the annual CIAA gathering in Washington, DC, representatives agreed to organize a tournament—after initially deciding not to. Part of the reason why officials changed their mind was because of money. CIAA coffers were almost bare. At the end of 1944, the association had only $165.75 in the bank. Making things worse, several schools were having difficulties paying dues. A basketball tournament, officials argued, would provide a much-needed infusion of cash. Delegates also believed that a tournament would promote the conference while showcasing the league's best players and teams. Morgan College's Talmadge Hill was appointed tournament committee chairman. Joining Hill were John Burr of Howard University, John B. McLendon of North Carolina College, and Harry R. "Big Jeff" Jefferson of Virginia State.[53]

By early 1946, a host city and venue had been selected. Turner's Arena, at Fourteenth and W Streets, NW, in Washington, DC, sat two blocks away from the city's famous U Street, aka Black Broadway. A former auto service shop, Turner's could seat roughly 2,000 spectators for basketball—not a huge number, but big enough, particularly for such an unknown commodity as the CIAA tournament. Turner's was well known among black Washingtonians. Many black events—sporting and otherwise—had been held in the arena. The Washington Bears, for example, a popular all-black professional basketball team that captured the World Professional Basketball Tournament in 1943, played their home games at Turner's. Black boxers, including future World Light Heavyweight titleholder Archie Moore, also fought there. Among the African American entertainers who performed in Turner's were Duke Ellington, Ella Fitzgerald, Jimmie Lunceford, and Paul Robeson.[54]

The inaugural CIAA basketball tournament began on Thursday afternoon, March 7. Of sixteen league teams, half were invited to participate. Because league schools had played a different number of conference games, officials used the Dickinson system to determine which teams would take part. Lincoln University received the top seed, followed by Virginia Union, Morgan College, and West

Virginia State University. Seeded fifth through eighth, respectively, were North Carolina College, J. C. Smith University, Virginia State, and Winston-Salem State University.[55]

From the outset, the tournament yielded the unexpected: North Carolina College, coached by John B. McLendon, defeated West Virginia State, 60–56, and then beat the number-one seed, Lincoln University. Meanwhile, the other half of the bracket unfolded according to the rankings. On Thursday evening, Virginia Union eked by Virginia State, and the next night, overpowered Morgan College, 42–37. The championship game was set. It would be the fast-breaking North Carolina College Eagles versus the Panthers of Virginia Union.[56]

The league could not have hoped for a more exciting final. *Norfolk Journal and Guide* columnist Lem Graves Jr. called it "my all-time sports 'thrill-of-a-lifetime.'" Spectators attending the sold-out game that Saturday afternoon were left feeling as if they had just finished riding the Cyclone at Coney Island. Virginia Union started quickly, building a 7-point margin in the first half. McLendon's team, however, battled back, and by halftime, it was 23–all. For much of the second half, the score was close, but in the final minutes of the game, Virginia Union moved in front, 46–40. Once again, the undersized Eagles rallied, scoring three straight baskets, including one, incredibly, as time ran out. Each team tallied a bucket in the first overtime, and then added eight points apiece in the second. In the third extra period, the Panthers failed to score, and the Eagles went on to win, 64–56. Players and fans were exhausted. "North Carolina College Surprises to Win CIAA Tourney in Hectic Tilt with Union," the *Baltimore Afro-American* headlined. Approximately 75 percent of the sports page in the *Norfolk Journal and Guide* was devoted to tournament write-ups.[57]

The inaugural tournament surpassed almost every expectation. Fans came away enthused. Newspapermen applauded the high level of play. Many coaches were pleased. CIAA authorities gladly welcomed the money generated by the three-day affair, which altogether generated almost $934—more than five times the amount the association had had in reserves fifteen months earlier.[58]

But not everyone was satisfied. Lincoln University's basketball coach Manny Rivero, whose team finished the regular season atop the CIAA, strongly opposed the decision to crown tournament winner North Carolina College conference champion. Rivero minced no words, labeling CIAA president John H. Burr, who also served on the tournament committee, "weak-kneed." Rivero had a point. Back in December, when league representatives first agreed to organize a tournament, it was determined that the team with the highest rating based on the Dickinson system—which Lincoln was, at the end of the 1945–46 season—would be named CIAA champions. In the intervening months, however, a poll taken by the league indicated that a majority of association members believed that the decision should be reversed. Some officials feared that without having the conference title up for grabs, the tournament would be a flop. Nine months later, at the 1946 meeting in Institute, West Virginia—home of West Virginia State University—the issue was finally resolved. Delegates ruled that the poll could not override the preceding year's vote. Consequently, Lincoln was named CIAA champion, while North Carolina College claimed the tournament title.[59]

The black press gave fairly wide coverage to the basketball squabble. The Negro Newspaper Publishers Association reported the story, and Sam Lacy, the acclaimed sports journalist for the *Baltimore Afro-American*, wrote lengthy pieces detailing the issue. Several black papers, including the *Atlanta Daily World* and *Norfolk Journal and Guide*, also covered the wrangle. Because of the reporting, readers not only gained further insights into how the CIAA operated, they also learned, once again, that the conference took matters seriously. Such a view bolstered the image of the association.[60]

In 1947 and 1948, Turner's again hosted the CIAA tournament. Like the inaugural competition, both tournaments—Virginia State won in 1947; West Virginia State prevailed in 1948—played to large crowds. Higher earnings reflected the tournament's growth. In 1947, the association banked $1,566. The next year, the sum totaled $1,300. One reason for greater interest was because of the electrifying finish in 1946. In addition, black newspapers promoted the tournaments, and Howard University played several home games at Turner's. Sponsors, too, got the word out, and supported the tournament financially. The black-run North Carolina Mutual Life Insurance Company sponsored a trophy, as did the Southern Aid Society, the Afro-American Newspapers, Inc., and the Guide Publishing Company, publisher of the *Norfolk Journal and Guide*. The 1947 and 1948 tournament programs contained dozens of ads, the majority of which were placed by establishments along U Street, including You and Me Luncheonette; Three Score Drug Store; Club Bengasi, the self-proclaimed "Mecca of Cafe Society"; and the Hotel Dunbar, where four of the eight tournament teams stayed.[61]

Pragmatic in their approach, organizers believed the tournament could effect lasting change in sport. In the 1947 tournament program, CIAA president John H. Burr wrote: "The 1946 Basketball Tournament set the stage for the realization of one of the more ambitious projects of the CIAA; the recognition of our association, and its inclusion into the NCAA regional and national basketball tournaments. We are hoping that this recognition will come with the 1947 tournament." Several days after the 1948 tournament, Lin Holloway, columnist for the *Norfolk Journal and Guide*, admitted that while basketball played by white institutions was "plaudit-evoking," it "was no better than that seen at Turner's for three days last week and on numerous sepia college basketball courts during the past few years." The comparison, Holloway added, "presents the question whether Negro basketball as

Cover of the program for the third CIAA basketball tournament in 1948.
Image courtesy of Art Carter Papers, Box 170–24, Folder 25, Moorland-Spingarn Manuscript Division, Howard University.

such can long endure, or whether the factions advocating separation of races in sports events will continue to prevent Negro athletes from taking their rightful places in the national scope of sports."[62]

In 1949, the tournament was moved two miles across town to the much larger Uline Arena. Completed in 1941, the venue was named after its seventy-four-year-old owner, Michael Uline, Washington's ice magnate. For years, Uline's squint-eyed views of race relations dictated that African Americans be barred from events he deemed inappropriate for black viewership: rodeos, ice shows, basketball games, hockey matches, anything considered middlebrow. Events blacks could watch were baser, coarser—such as boxing. The arrangement reflected negative assumptions about African Americans.[63]

For much of the 1940s, black Washingtonians chafed under the discrimination. Outraged, they held demonstrations and boycotted arena events. But Uline was unmoved. In January 1948, under the leadership of Edwin B. Henderson, who, in addition to his involvement with the CIAA, chaired the Citizen's Committee Against Segregation in Recreation (CASR) in Washington, DC, black protesters forced Uline's hand. For years, the District's Golden Gloves Boxing Tournament had been the sole province of white boxers. However, in 1947 black fighters at last were granted the opportunity to take part. Organizers, understandably, envisioned a large African American turnout. Instead, the opposite happened. Heeding Henderson's advice to continue boycotting events at the arena, black residents stayed away. When the tournament's promoter, upset over the lack of black fans, announced that he was considering moving the event in 1948, Uline promptly eliminated the race-based restrictions.

The 1949 tournament at Uline outdrew the three that preceded it—which was no great surprise. The tournament's popularity was growing, and Uline was capable of squeezing in more than 7,000 people, dwarfing the 2,000 capacity of Turner's. By moving the tournament to Uline, the CIAA hoped to reap greater profits. Sadly, it was not to be. While revenues climbed, expenditures did as well. The result was that the association realized a modest $300 increase in profits from the previous year. If the 1949 tournament raised doubts about holding the competition at Uline, the tournament in 1950 confirmed them. That year, the association was able to bank only $147. Both tournaments, however, displayed exciting basketball. In 1949, West Virginia State beat Virginia State, 60–53, to take the tournament. The next year, after downing West Virginia State, 74–70, North Carolina College was crowned champion. The 1949 West Virginia State squad featured Earl Lloyd, a 6'5" forward who, along with Chuck Cooper and Nat "Sweetwater" Clifton, broke the color line in the National Basketball Association (NBA) in 1950. Lloyd played for the Washington Capitols, whose home venue was Uline Arena. That same year, the Capitols inked Harold Hunter, a lightning-quick guard on the 1950 West

Virginia State team and MVP of the CIAA tournament. Unlike Lloyd, Hunter never played in the NBA.[64]

West Virginia State was not just known for producing talented players and winning CIAA championships. In 1949, it did something few schools in the East, let alone HBCUs, had ever done: it traveled to the West Coast to play several games. Jimmy Booker of the *New York Amsterdam News* hailed the West Virginia school as "being the first Negro college basketball team to make an extended tour of the Pacific coast." In an age before jetliners, the great distances separating eastern and western clubs made intersectional matchups difficult to arrange. As an HBCU, however, West Virginia State faced an additional obstacle: the Jim Crow idea that blacks and whites should never compete in sports.[65]

The man most responsible for State's western trip was "Frank Walsh, impresario of San Francisco's Cow Palace"—the Bay Area's then-preeminent sports arena, which also staged livestock exhibits—"who is more generally known as 'Mr. Bow Tie,'" as one United Press journalist put it. According to Herman Hill, the famous *Pittsburgh Courier* editor who, along with other black sportswriters, persuaded the Los Angeles Rams in 1946 to hire two African American players, Kenny Washington and Woody Strode, thereby puncturing the National Football League's color barrier, Walsh had approached Hill several months earlier and inquired about the possibility of having the Yellow Jackets play a handful of teams out west. Hill, presumably, assisted Walsh, and before long, the trip was announced. Walsh, it appears, had been drawn to State because of its exceptional record—in 1947–48, it was 23-0—and because, in the words of Hill, "[Walsh] had also learned how [top-notch black] teams had been stymied in their efforts to show in Madison Square Garden in open competition. He said he was determined to wipe out this injustice."[66]

On the evening of February 5, West Virginia State players departed for the West Coast. In his memoir, *Moonfixer: The Basketball Journey of Earl Lloyd*, Earl Lloyd remembered, "[A]bout two thousand people . . . showed up to see us off." Traveling by train, the Yellow Jackets—whose group included ten players, a manager, and head coach Mark Cardwell—arrived in California four days later. The tour intrigued black and white West Virginians. In a letter to the university a day before the team left, West Virginia governor Okey L. Patterson stated in part: "All West Virginians, I know, are very proud indeed of the West Virginia State team. . . . All power and success to you on your western trip." In the West, commentators called State the "national Negro intercollegiate champion" and "the best Negro college team in the country," and underscored the school's unbeaten streak of thirty-two games (including the twenty-three victories from the season before).[67]

On the trip, State played four games. On February 11, at the Cow Palace, St. Mary's College defeated the travel-weary visitors, 66–52, snapping the Yellow

Jackets' undefeated streak. The following evening, however, the Jackets garnered a 57–44 win over Santa Clara University. Two days later, in Los Angeles, State lost to Loyola University, 65–58. Profits from the game went to West View Hospital, a facility that Herman Hill described as being "interracial, non-sectarian, [and] non-profit." On February 16, Cardwell's team lost again, this time to the University of Nevada. The game was played in Reno.[68]

Despite a disappointing 1-3 record for the trip, the Jackets remained upbeat. In his memoir, Earl Lloyd wrote, "[W]e came back [from the trip] feeling good about ourselves." Sam Lacy of the *Baltimore Afro-American* quoted Cardwell as saying, "I am happy about the whole experience, everyone was swell and many of the [opposing] players expressed satisfaction over the fact they won't have to meet the likes of our Wilson, Clark, Lloyd and the others again." In a development that would have pleased the CIAA founders, State's exemplary behavior drew praise. "[The Yellow Jackets] were good losers and graceful winners," Herman Hill wrote, following the two games in San Francisco. "Their sportsmanship and conduct was highly commendable." Cardwell's players left such a favorable mark that they were invited back the following year. Their record for that trip was 3-3, including a win over a squad of San Quentin inmates. According to West Virginia sports historian Bob Barnett, "The governor of California was so impressed with the State team that he arranged for the Yellow Jackets to play against the San Quentin State Prison basketball team."[69]

In 1951, State finished second at the CIAA basketball tournament. It would be the last CIAA tournament held at Uline Arena. Association officials concluded that the profit margin was too small and moved the tournament to an on-campus site. Morgan State University in Baltimore hosted the 1952 competition. But Morgan State's Hurt Gymnasium was hardly any bigger than Turner's. In November 1952, the CIAA transferred the tournament once more—this time to North Carolina College in Durham. Fans came in droves. Playing games at the college's McDougald Gymnasium, which could hold 5,000 spectators, the CIAA made more than $4,600. Profits rose to $6,349 in 1956, and then to $8,786, two years later. In 1960, the newly constructed War Memorial Coliseum in Greensboro, North Carolina, hosted the event (War Memorial's capacity was 7,100). From 1961 to 1963, the tournament was held on the campus of Winston-Salem State University in North Carolina. The next year, it was moved back to War Memorial.[70]

In all, the success of the CIAA basketball tournament matched that of the association as a whole. Unlike many other separate black sports organizations that were unable to survive integration, the most notable being the Negro Baseball Leagues, the CIAA still exists, and thrives. Now named the Central Intercollegiate Athletic Association—the change took place in 1950 after members determined that "colored" was no longer *de rigueur*—the CIAA consists of twelve public and private institutions ranging in size from 750 to 7,000 students, with schools located mostly in North Carolina, Maryland, and Virginia. Backed by such companies as Toyota, Nationwide Insurance, Coca-Cola, and Russell Athletic, the CIAA holds annual championships in sports ranging from football and baseball to men's and women's basketball to men's and women's tennis. The reasons for the association's continued success are many, but certainly a major factor is due to the founders who, with great foresight and acuity, crafted a durable "Constitution and By-Laws," while implementing high-quality sports programs that outlasted racial and domestic crises, as well as two world wars.

The CIAA is now more than one hundred years old, and still going strong. The founders' efforts at racial uplift have obviously been realized. Affirmation of this reality has come from many sources, including none other than President John F. Kennedy, who in 1962, just a year before his assassination and two years before the passage of the historic Civil Rights Act, cabled CIAA president Leroy T. Walker—who had been John McLendon's assistant in 1946, when North Carolina College won the inaugural CIAA basketball tournament, and who would go on to become the first African American to coach an American Olympic track and field team, in 1976 in Montreal—congratulating him on the fiftieth anniversary of the association. "The long record of service and progress of your conference," wrote Kennedy, "is well known and respected in athletic and academic circles. It deserves the esteem for its continued pursuit of the highest standards, both on the field and in the classroom." The CIAA founders would have indeed been proud.[71]

10

Game, Set, and Separatism

The American Tennis Association, a Tennis Vanguard

Sundiata Djata

By the late nineteenth century, the upper class had adopted tennis, yachting, polo, fox hunting, and golf, "pursuits whose cost put them out of reach of ordinary Americans." Taking up the customs of the British elites, the upper class used these sports to mark themselves off and maintain a level of social prestige.[1] For many of them, tennis was their sport of choice.

Unfortunately, middle- and upper-class African Americans found that their pursuits of such sports as tennis were circumscribed by racial discrimination. They were unable to join white country clubs and were denied participation in the United States Lawn Tennis Association (USLTA), formed in 1881 (later changed to USTA). Moreover, African Americans lacked the opportunity to compete, let alone dominate world-class tournaments because white athletes in tennis (and other sports) were afraid of competing with them on an equal basis.[2] In addition, they were mostly denied entrance onto public tennis courts. As a result of this racial discrimination, a few prominent African American players founded the American Tennis Association (ATA) in 1916 to provide support, services, and competition for those in the black community who played the sport.

African Americans had begun to play tennis by the late 1880s, shortly after the sport was introduced in the United States. In 1887, the *Christian Recorder*, a black-owned newspaper in Philadelphia, featured an ad from Wanamaker's store for tennis goods, including "individual rackets of all the popular makes, $1.25 to $6.00, and *our own special* racket, $4.00."[3] Some northern African Americans were already playing the game when Tuskegee Institute faculty members began to promote tennis at the college in 1890 and hosting tournaments by 1895, becoming the first historically black college and university (HBCU) of record to sponsor such events.

Likewise, African American tennis players in Philadelphia held a tournament in 1898, sponsored by the Chautauqua Tennis Club, won by Thomas Jefferson of Lincoln University. In addition, a group of black players from Philadelphia, led by Rev. W. W. Walker, invited a group of black players from Washington, DC, headed by Dr. Henry Freeman, to compete in team competition in 1898 and 1899.[4] Soon, black tennis clubs developed in New York City, Wilmington, New Rochelle, New Haven, Annapolis, Durham, Charleston, and St. Louis. By the 1930s, several other black clubs had been founded in Florida, Oklahoma, Louisiana, Texas, Alabama, and Georgia.[5]

There were few public tennis facilities for African Americans. For instance, in St. Louis, there was one public court available to blacks.[6] African Americans organized the West Louisville Tennis Club in the early 1920s at Chickasaw Park because they were not permitted to play tennis in other inner-city facilities. African Americans in Chicago played tennis in Washington Park, and in Baltimore they could use Druid Hill Park.

Due to the racial practices of the USLTA, African American players founded the ATA on November 30, 1916, in Washington, DC. The idea was conceived that year during a tournament in New York City between members of the Association Tennis Club of Washington, DC, and the Monumental Tennis Club of Baltimore. Letters were mailed to all known black tennis clubs in the United States. In New York City, a permanent organization was formed, officers and an executive committee were elected, and a committee was appointed to draft a constitution.[7] Present at the formation were Henry Freeman, John F. N. Wilkinson, and Tally Holmes from Washington, DC, and H. Stanton McCard, William H. Wright, B. M. Rhetta, and Ralph Cook from Baltimore. McCard was elected president and Gerald Norman of the Ideal Tennis Club in New York City was elected as the executive secretary. The ATA had four stated goals: to develop tennis among blacks; to encourage the formation of clubs and the building of courts; to encourage the formation of local associations; and, to encourage and develop junior players. In addition, the ATA hoped to improve the standards of existing clubs, appoint referees and officials for events, hold a national championship tournament, and promote the standard of the game among African American men.[8]

Tellingly, the founders avoided using "Colored," "Negro," or any racial identifier in the name of the organization because they took pride in being inclusive. Holmes selected the name, hoping that "enlightened whites ultimately would play under its auspices for a genuine national championship." He assumed, not unexpectedly, that it would be easier to get whites to play in black tournaments than for blacks to be allowed to participate in white organized tennis tournaments. Bruce Schoenfeld, a correspondent, argues that Holmes was idealistic in thinking "enlightened whites" might play in ATA national tournaments, asserting, "It never happened."[9] In reality, it did happen, although only occasionally. Althea Gibson won her first tournament in 1942, defeating Nina Irwin, the daughter of a white Russian immigrant at the Cosmopolitan Club in New York in an ATA event.[10] In later years, not only did nonblack players participate in ATA local and national tournaments, a few won ATA titles.[11]

In addition to being a founder of the ATA, Holmes won eight doubles titles in ATA national tournaments. Like many whose names are chronicled in the early years of black tennis history, Holmes, who attended Dartmouth College, was an accomplished professional. At the time of the ATA formation, he was serving as an intelligence officer in the military. After WWI, he returned to Washington, DC, to teach German, French, Latin, and math at the famous M Street School (later Paul Dunbar High). In addition, he owned the Whitelaw Hotel, the largest in the city to house African Americans.[12]

The Monumental Tennis Club of Washington, DC, hosted the first national ATA championship in 1917 at Druid Hill Park in Baltimore. Three events were played: men's singles won by Tally Holmes; women's singles won by Lucy Slowe; and men's doubles won by Tally Holmes and Sylvester Smith. The following year, mixed doubles were added. The Ideal Tennis Club of New York hosted the event, and "race players from all over the country" were "requested to take part." Clubs wishing to enter representatives had to join the ATA for the purpose of the "preservation of the game of tennis from a point of sportsmanship."[13] Women's doubles and boys' singles were added in 1924 with Isadore Channels and Emma Leonard winning the women's doubles, Nellie Nicholson and B. M. Rhetta winning the mixed doubles event, and Russell Smith winning the boys' title.

On August 21, 1926, Dr. Ivson Hoage, Gerald F. Norman, Kinckle Jones, Laurence C. Dancy, Loaura V. Junior, Lester B. Granger, Richard Hudlin, and W. H. A. Barrett executed a certificate of incorporation for the ATA and filed it in the office of the New Jersey secretary of state on September 1, 1926.[14] By that time tennis had gained greater exposure, although the sport was still associated with the "English upper classes and rich Americans who played on their estates or in their exclusive clubs."[15]

Some prominent African Americans worked to introduce tennis to a broader audience. Dr. Elwood Downing of Roanoke, Virginia; Charles Williams of Hampton Institute; and Cleveland Abbott of Tuskegee Institute worked to increase the participation of African Americans in tennis in their respective areas.[16] In an attempt to capitalize on a growing interest in the sport, the ATA, under the direction of the ATA's Intercollegiate Committee, approved an educational and goodwill tour, and composed of its highest-ranking players, to play at black colleges and high schools in 1937. The following year, the team, which included the outstanding players Lulu Ballard and Ernest McCampbell, visited twenty-one black colleges and eight high schools, offering lectures on keeping fit and demonstrations among members of the team and local stars of promise.[17]

By 1939, 150 black tennis clubs existed with 28,000 players. In addition, there were thirty-five sectional and state tournaments, which led to the ATA National Championships tournament.[18] For example, the Tuskegee Club, composed of Tuskegee faculty and US Veteran's Hospital employees, became affiliated with the ATA in 1930 and hosted the fifteenth ATA National Championships in 1931. Emmett J. Scott, S. E. Courtney, Warren Logan, and E. T. Atwell of Tuskegee Institute; Charles Cook of Howard University; and, Thomas Jefferson of Lincoln University were leading black collegians. The Annual Southern Tennis Championship was also inaugurated in 1930. D. Ivison Hoage, president of the ATA, secured the Williams Cup from James Williams of New York City to present to the ATA as a permanent trophy for the national intercollegiate singles championship. The sterling silver cup from Tiffany was awarded to the winning college and placed in its custody for one year.[19] Despite the claim that African American players at predominately white colleges had more exposure to tennis at a higher level of competition, a player from a black college, Nathaniel Jackson of Tuskegee, defeated Reginald Weir of the City College of New York in 1932 and 1933.[20]

Black players at white colleges were thought to have "the best exposure to serious, high level tennis" because they were "recipients of skilled coaching and intense competition, and they enjoyed the use of modern facilities."[21] A few notable names included Richard Hudlin,[22] who served as captain of the University of Chicago tennis team; Douglas Turner of the University of Illinois; and Weir, who was the team captain at the City College of New York. Dan Kean played at Michigan, and Maceo Hill competed at Ohio State. Later, Desmond Margetson served as captain of the tennis team at New York University and Robert Ryland played two years for Wayne University (now Wayne State). One writer commented on Turner's and Weir's talents, arguing, "Tennis finds in these two lads their greatest reasons for hope that tennis among our players will in the near future approach that of the world's outstanding players. Their form is correct, they are enjoying the advantages of expert coaching and through their play on school and college teams they are meeting players of making in U. S. L. T. A. circles."[23]

It is difficult to assess the playing styles of the earliest African American tennis players. A few notable black players learned from whites. As already mentioned, black players at white colleges and universities had white coaches. Weir also played in Europe as a junior.[24] Margetson, who invented the tennis bubble to allow people to play tennis year around, credits Elwood Cooke, the runner-up in the 1939 Wimbledon Championship, for improving his game. Cooke started coaching him in 1949. Moreover, Margetson played against whites in high school and college. In addition, Edgar Brown, a national champion, studied "under some of the best white players" in the winter of 1922 at the Drake Hotel in Chicago.[25] Others had opportunities to compete against whites. Photos exist of Amanda Falker, taken in 1910, showing her with whites, and also at the Aztec Tennis Club in Chicago.[26] La Jolla, California, was a mecca for tennis players in the 1930s and 1940s. When actor Cliff Robertson attended La Jolla High School, one African American player was on the tennis team.[27] Sonny Jackson played in the Eastern Scholastics tournaments against whites. Jimmy McDaniel and Oscar Johnson were self-taught players, but Johnson watched the top players at other schools and copied what he saw.[28] Few of the ATA champions practiced regularly against whites like Johnson, Lloyd Scott, or Robert Ryland, who played at integrated Tilden Tech High School, where the team won three city championships on public courts in Chicago.[29]

The best players to emerge from the ATA system, Althea Gibson and Arthur Ashe, were taught by African American teachers and coaches. Not only did Gibson have no knowledge of the history of the ATA before being introduced to its circles, "it is also difficult to imagine that she knew anything of substance about the dominant white players."[30] First, Fred Johnson taught Gibson at the Cosmopolitan Club in New York City. As a teenager, he lost an arm in a factory accident. He held the racket and the ball in his only hand; after he tossed the ball, he waited to "swat at it on its way back down." Since he was unable to turn the racket for a

ATA Nationals Cosmopolitan Tennis Club. *Image courtesy of blacktennishistory.com.*

backhand, he used a continental grip. That is what he taught his students. Ashe became interested in tennis by watching Virginia Union University player Ronald Charity practicing at the Brook Field Park. Charity, who played in ATA sanctioned events, offered to teach Ashe and entered him in ATA events.

Top players of the early twentieth century included John F. N. Wilkinson, who played with the DC group mentioned earlier. He was considered the best African American player between 1910 and World War I. Other leading players of note were Rev. W. W. Walker, Edgar Brown, Henry Freeman, E. J. Ridgely, Ralph Cook (Charles Cook's brother), H. Stanton McCard, Gerald F. Norman, Daisy Reid, Dora Cole Norman, and Lucy Diggs Slowe.[31]

A few of the top African American tennis players played other sports. For example, Dora Cole Norman was considered the best basketball player in her day. Eyre Saitch, the 1926 ATA men's champion, played for the New York Renaissance (Rens) Big Five basketball team. Isadore Channels of Chicago, a net rusher who won four ATA titles in the 1920s, played for the famous Romas basketball team. In addition, Ora Washington, who won eight ATA national singles titles between 1929 and 1937, played center for the highly successful Philadelphia Tribune girls basketball team. Althea Gibson played a variety of sports in the 1940s. David Dinkins, the first black mayor of New York City, met her in the mid-1940s, calling her "champ" because she excelled in tennis, paddle tennis, basketball, softball, pool, and "any sport she played."[32] In addition, her father trained her to box. Her coach, Robert Johnson, played football and basketball at Lincoln University.

In 1931 Ora Washington dominated the ATA circuit. "Ora Washington . . . again holds her position as national champion, having gone through the season without a defeat. We don't even recall her losing a set. . . . Her superiority is so evident that her competitors are frequently beaten before the first ball crosses the net."[33] Washington held her racket halfway up the handle and seldom took a full swing. However, she enjoyed amazing foot speed. Lulu Ballard ended Washington's reign in 1936. According to Ryland, Washington was "really angry about never getting a chance to play against the best white women. She'd hear about the white women winning at Wimbledon and the U. S. Nationals, and those other (grand Slam) tournaments, and she'd be saying 'I could beat them,' . . . was angry that 'she was unable to play in the big leagues.'"[34]

Reporters who covered ATA tournaments understood it was difficult to rank black players among better white players; as a result, they compared black players to each other. For example, one writer argued that Tally Holmes was "one of the best tennis stars this country has known among our group."[35] In doubles, sisters Roumania and Margaret Peters of Tuskegee Institute won fourteen ATA doubles titles, unmatched by any doubles team in any event. Other dominant players later emerged. For instance, left-handed George Stewart won seven titles between 1947 and 1964. A student at South Carolina State, Stewart became the first African American to compete in the NCAA championships with Bob Ryland of Wayne State University becoming the second.[36]

There were competing styles of play among black tennis players. Early on, players used chops and spins. When better equipment became available, players used more power. Brothers Nathaniel and Franklin Jackson were baseline experts like white champion Don Budge. They were coached by Cleveland Abbott of Tuskegee, who eventually became an ATA president. R. A. Toney, a member of the Prairie Club of Chicago, had "a slashing drive."

Black players debated styles of play. After Edgar Brown wrote a series of articles for the *Chicago Defender*, promoting his style of play, he drew some criticisms from those who played an entirely different style.[37] Even so, Brown's play in the 1923 national tournament was heralded in an article, "He drove the ball over the net with such an accuracy as never before seen in any of the national tournaments. His placement shots showed skill and beautiful execution and at all times he made his opponent bring the game to him and forced the New Yorker (E. Saitch) to beat himself. As far as tennis is concerned Brown has almost reached the point of perfection, surely he has reached the pinnacle among our own and it will be some time before he will be beaten."[38] Brown was an advocate of the "modern, scientific, top-spin driving game." He applauded the young players, especially Reginald Weir, who followed "the driving example of the world's greatest players—Tilden, La Coste, Cochet, etc."[39]

In Brown's absence (due to a suspension) Tally Holmes won the national championship in 1924, but his win was not received well by Brown, who criticized Holmes's style as "a very ordinary soft chop stroke artist," and asserted that Holmes won because the "western bronco 'busting,' driving enthusiast" was absent. In addition, he asserted that others lost to Holmes because they "persisted in copying most of Holmes' style and failed to use the brain and muscle God gave them to hit the ball and not try to outpat Holmes."[40]

Soon, another style emerged. Jimmy McDaniel of Los Angeles was a serve and volleyer, considered an aggressive style of tennis, developed on fast cement courts. Beginning in 1939, he captured four ATA national championships, and was considered the best black male player of his era. According to Sidney Llewellyn, Jimmy McDaniel was the greatest black tennis player of them all.

Tennis among African Americans was centered on just a few black colleges. A 1926 survey revealed that there was little interest in tennis at fifty-six of the seventy colleges queried, only thirty-six schools having tennis courts and only four of them with coaches. Tennis at black colleges, however, fit neatly within the ATA's middle-class orientation. Black colleges certainly benefited from hosting ATA tournaments because it brought wealthy African American professionals to campus, who could potentially provide funding for the academic institutions. Holding the events at black colleges accomplished two other objectives. Children were made aware of black college campuses at an early age. Furthermore, black colleges provided lodging and meals, particularly important in the South, where public accommodations were racially segregated or nonexistent. According to Clifford Blackman, an original ATA member and official, "We traveled in cars; that was the only way we could get around."[41] In addition, the black athletic conferences provided intercollegiate competition, but also provided players for ATA national tournaments and other events.

Another advantage was that black colleges could host the ATA nationals when the number of participants became too large to host for individual black clubs. Beginning in 1927, Hampton Institute, Morehouse, Lincoln (MO), Wilberforce, Central State, Lincoln (PA), and South Carolina State hosted the nationals. Tuskegee had fourteen courts, one with a covered grandstand that seated 1,000 by 1931, allowing the college to host the nationals. Tuskegee also hosted the 1941 nationals, the year of the ATA's silver jubilee. In 1957 the ATA National Championships tournament was held at Central State College in Wilberforce, Ohio. One observer remarked of the ATA national tournament, "The caliber is improving year by year, several of its members having numerous victories to their credit in major competition all over the world. This too is tennis."[42]

The nationals remained east of the Mississippi River. Wilberforce College in Ohio became the most centrally located due to entries from the West.[43] In 1940 the ATA divided the United States into nine zones, each with a field secretary. The Bahamas and Bermuda formed separate zones, but were included in the national set-up. Nineteen states were represented at the 1939 national tournament, furnishing 208 players.[44] In order to participate in the ATA national events, a player had to belong to clubs that were members of the ATA.

Trophies held a special place in the ATA tournaments. At the 1918 nationals in New York silver cups were donated by Bert Williams, a Vaudeville entertainer, and Lelia (A'Lelia) Walker Robinson, daughter of Madame C. J. Walker and cofounder of the Madame C. J. Walker Manufacturing Company. The single champions were required to win the trophy three times to take personal ownership. Other prizes for the winners included a cake plate, tray, vase, and three cups, all made of Sheffield silverware.[45] In 1923, the winners took multiple trophies in Chicago; the W. McCard trophy for men's singles, the B. M. Rhetta Cup for women's singles (both from Baltimore), the D. I. Hoage trophy (New York) for men's singles, the Roosevelt State Bank trophy (Chicago) for men's singles, the W. B. Ziff trophy (Chicago) for women's singles, the two Chicago Evening American trophies for each winner in the men's doubles, the *Chicago Defender* trophy for women's singles, the Bingo State Bank (Chicago) trophy for winner in men's singles, the

Liberty Life Insurance Co. (Chicago) for men's singles, and other silver trophies. The trophies were on display at Stoball & Hudson's drugstore in Chicago prior to the tournament.[46]

The ATA nationals, like many other sporting events behind the walls of segregation, became grand social affairs, allowing people to meet tennis players and other attendees at the tournaments from different areas of the country. According to Wilbert Davis, a former ATA president, some people scheduled their vacations around the national tournaments, a necessity for some since they were week-long events. In addition to tennis competition, ATA national organizers held dinners, formal dances, and fashion shows, functioning much like a country club for the week.[47] For instance, in 1918 the program included a reception at the music School Settlement in New York, and an annual subscription smoker, while the "main event," a public reception, was held at the Manhattan Casino.[48] The eighth national tournament, held in Baltimore in 1924, featured a welcoming party for the visiting ladies, an open-air dance at the Druid Hill Park swimming pool, a moonlight steamboat excursion down the Chesapeake Bay, a moving picture party at the Regent Theater, a reception and dance, and the annual tournament banquet at the Royal Palace Hotel.[49] When the nationals were held in Bordentown, New Jersey, at an industrial school, the activities included a reception for the ladies, a card party and dance, a moonlight steamboat ride on the Delaware River, a lawn party and dance, and a special dinner for visitors.[50] Hampton featured a musical program, a watermelon feast and lawn party, and a boat sail over Hampton Roads.[51]

Hosting the ATA national tournament became competitive. For instance, Chicago always wanted to host the national tournament and in 1922, O. B. Williams, representing the Prairie Tennis club had the proxies of the Pyramid, Pilgrim Baptist, West Side clubs, all of Chicago, and the LaFon Tennis club of New Orleans. In addition, he had the support of clubs in St. Louis and Indianapolis, and telegrams from the *Chicago Defender* and Chicago black businessmen.[52] The previous year, it was noted in an editorial that players from other cities wanted to see the tournament in Chicago if the players believed "Chicago folks knew how to conduct a tournament." The reply was that "Just vote it out here in the meeting next year at Philly and we'll guarantee that 1923 will see the greatest tournament ever held."[53]

The ATA experienced some problems as well. Despite the progressive nature of the national office, the issue of race became a problem for the ATA in 1940 when the national office stated that "the constitution of the A.T.A. prohibits no player because of color. Our only prohibition of any player is based on proven facts that he is a player of 'ill repute.'" Edward Graysing, white, applied to play in an Englewood (NJ) Tennis Club tournament. An official of the Englewood club insisted that he had Dr. Hoage's word that the ATA would permit Graysing to enter the tournament. The ATA office added, "We have no objection to any white player who is in good standing with a member club, entering any tournament. We believe our players can hold their own against such competition. If the white element wins, so what. It just means that our competition will get stiffer and therefore we will become better players." Ignoring the directive, the New Jersey Tennis Association amended its constitution to ban all white players in any of its tournaments. New Jersey was the only state to raise this issue even though some club members disagreed with the constitutional amendment. Nevertheless, some "champion" players stated this view, "Sure allow whites to enter our tournaments, but only if we can enter theirs."[54]

Another problem involved Edgar Brown, who was suspended by the ATA for the criticism he leveled against the organization in several newspaper articles. Frank A. Young of the *Chicago Defender* defended Brown, arguing that a one-year suspension was sufficient. Young asked, "Did he not have the right, being suspended to seek to earn a living writing articles for newspapers as Wm. Tilden II has done in defiance of the United States Lawn Tennis association?" He continued, "Are the powers that be in the American Tennis association too big to be criticized and are they attempting to dictate to the entire nation who shall and who shall not enter into active competition in tournament play, seeking to rush any player because of ability to play the game above the standard exhibited by the supposed best players now in the association?" The ATA ignored four pages of names who asked for Brown's reinstatement. Moreover, Young complained of the fact that most national tournaments were held in the East, and suggested that Chicago, being centrally located, could "start . . . a new national body, wide in scope and fair in judgement. This is a warning. Don't let the lightning strike."[55]

Black newspapers provided most coverage of the ATA nationals, and it has been suggested that competition in the ATA existed outside the interests of the white-owned print and broadcast media.[56] Although this was true for many white-owned media, the *New York Times*, for example, began reporting on the day-by-day results of the ATA nationals.[57]

Despite the segregation in tennis, overtures were occasionally made across racial lines. For example, in 1921 Dwight F. Davis, donor of the Davis Cup and the secretary of war, umpired the semifinal match between Tally Holmes and Sylvester Smith at the ATA nationals. Davis expressed "his surprise and delight at the excellent playing that he witnessed."[58] In 1940 the president of Wilson Sporting Goods, L. B. Icely, arranged for Donald Budge (the first player to win a grand slam) to play an exhibition match against Jimmy McDaniel at the Cosmopolitan Tennis Club in New York.[59] Budge won 6–1, 6–2. Afterward, Budge teamed with Reginald Weir to play McDaniel and Richard Cohen, the current ATA doubles champions.[60] An estimated 2,000 spectators watched the match, and another 3,000 looked on from apartment windows and fire escapes.[61]

The following year, Icely arranged for Charles E. Hare, a white British player (ranked no. 20 in England), to play Harold Mitchell of the ATA in an exhibition match at Tuskegee Institute during the Silver Jubilee.[62] On occasions, other whites played at the Cosmopolitan Club. Alice Marble played an exhibition match there in 1944. She and Bob Ryland played against Weir and Mary Hardwick.[63] Not only did whites play with blacks, but the fact that two white women were on the court in public with black men, a social taboo, was a major statement on race relations no matter the geographical location. Nevertheless, such exhibitions did nothing to tear down the walls of racial segregation.

The first confrontation between the ATA and the USLTA occurred in 1929 when the USLTA's Junior Indoor event at New York City's Seventh Regiment Armory rejected the entry of Reginald Weir and Gerald Norman Jr. Prior to that event, the relationship between the organizations had been cordial as long as segregation remained unchallenged. When Weir and Norman were told they could not play after having paid their one-dollar entry fee, Norman's father, Gerald Norman Sr. contacted the National Association for the Advancement of Colored People (NAACP). The NAACP assistant secretary, Robert Bagnoll, contacted the USLTA, and was told that the policy of the USLTA was to "decline the entry of colored players in our championships . . . In pursuing this policy we make no reflection upon the colored race but we believe that as a practical matter, the present method of separate associations . . . should be continued."[64]

Some twenty-nine years after the Weir and Norman incident, the USLTA was still resisting integration. In 1948 Oscar Johnson applied to the USLTA National Junior Indoor Championships in St. Louis, but was denied entry when he appeared at the tournament site and USLTA officials discovered that he was black. "The tournament director looked at me and said, 'You won't play here.'" Richard Hudlin and Frank Summers, a black attorney from East St. Louis, had accompanied Johnson, expecting a problem. They sent a telegram to the New York USLTA office, insisting that Johnson be admitted because he had won a national championship. Ultimately, the officials readmitted Johnson.[65] Johnson commented, "Strangely enough, I had no trouble at all with any of the players. In fact, a guy from Texas asked me to be his doubles partner and we reached the semifinals."[66]

The ATA ultimately played an instrumental role in the integration of the USLTA. ATA leadership negotiated with USLTA supporters, particularly "liberal and Jewish" Harold LeBair,[67] after WWII. LeBair had to fight with ultraconservatives like Bill Clothier Jr., "the most conservative man I've ever met," according to Alastair B. Martin, a committee member. In 1950, Dr. Sylvester B. Smith, ATA president; Arthur E. Francis, assistant executive secretary; and Bertram L. Baker, executive secretary, held conferences regarding player eligibility with Dr. S. Ellsworth Davenport Jr. and Alrick H. Man Jr., who represented the USLTA.

Although the conferences were held in private, Alice Marble wrote an editorial about them in *American Lawn Tennis Magazine*, criticizing the USLTA for not accepting Althea Gibson.[68] Marble's editorial was also mentioned in the *New York Herald Tribune, New York Post, Life,* and *Time.*[69] The USLTA had a convenient excuse for denying black players entrance into their national tournaments. A player had to play in several tournaments in order to qualify for the nationals, and those tournaments were generally held at exclusive private clubs that practiced racial segregation. In addition, female players were housed during tournaments at the homes of club members, who were white and unwilling to host blacks. Ultimately, Gibson was accepted for the US National Clay Court Championships, the Eastern Grass Court Championships, and the USLTA National Championships at Forest Hills. An ATA officer had worked to get Gibson accepted at Orange and Chicago tournaments of USLTA. However, some walls of segregation remained standing. Arthur Francis, the assistant to Bertram Baker, sent a note to New Jersey's Maplewood Country Club officials, who sought to keep Gibson out of the tournament, attacking the association's "snobbishness, prejudice, and bad judgements."[70] Even when the race barrier was broken, the USLTA instituted a "quota system" to limit the number of blacks participating in their tournaments. When this news was revealed at the ATA Nationals, some ATA members strongly objected.[71] In addition, the only way blacks could play at the national tournament at Forest Hills was through a recommendation by the ATA.

While the USLTA had no interest in searching for talent in black communities, ATA members worked to find and develop black players.[72] Dr. Walter Robert Johnson, who lived in Lynchburg, Virginia, had a tennis court in his yard and headed the Junior Development Program, which he founded for the ATA. Many youths, including Althea Gibson, worked with Dr. Johnson, developing their skills during the summer.

Although sport historians have chronicled the class aspect of tennis, rarely have they focused on the fact that some middle-class blacks brought poorer blacks into the game, including cross-class line connections in tennis that shaped Gibson's development. A part-time bandleader, Buddy Walker, saw Gibson play paddle tennis, bought her two used rackets, and had her hitting balls against a wall. Juan Serrall (Serrell), a schoolteacher, watched her hit with Walker, and subsequently introduced her to members of the Cosmopolitan Club. The Cosmopolitan Club paid for Gibson's membership and bought her rackets. Gibson had no money to use for tennis, but the ATA became her support system. When she traveled to tournaments, she stayed in homes of ATA members. Dr. Johnson, who became the ATA Middle Atlantic field secretary, trained her and other youths at his home. Other examples include the ATA goodwill tours. ATA players visited high schools, where students were not segregated by economic class, providing opportunities for some poor blacks to be introduced to the sport. There were additional efforts. Ms. C. O. "Mother" Seames, a legendary figure in Chicago tennis circles, taught tennis on a single court at the turn of the century. Edwin B. Henderson, well-known historian of the black athlete and head of the separate health and physical education program in Washington, DC, and Roscoe C. Bruce, the assistant superintendent of Colored Schools of Washington, DC, had introduced tennis to some public school students by the start of WWI. Tuskegee Institute became a tennis power among black colleges despite being an agricultural and industrial college, developing an early tennis history that surpassed more elite black colleges. Although most of the prominent names in the early history of black tennis were elite blacks, some were from the lower class, including the likes of Ora Washington, who worked as a domestic.[73]

African American players could not even dream of making a living at their sport. Unlike the Negro Baseball Leagues, the ATA provided no professional, or monetary competition. Increasingly, the integration of the USTA meant less exposure for the ATA. Some of the ATA and USTA tournaments allowed players to enter tournaments with a membership in either organization. Nevertheless, the ATA remained relevant. In recent years, the national tournament offered more than fifty competitive categories for players eight to eighty.[74] The USTA sent members a free subscription to *Tennis* magazine. Likewise, the ATA extended its members a subscription of *Black Tennis* magazine, founded by Marcus Freeman in 1977. The USTA no longer requires recommendation from the ATA for blacks to play in the US Open. Bertram Baker worked out an arrangement for the ATA national singles champions to have a wild card entry into the US Open. However, the ATA national singles champions no longer receive an automatic wild card into the main draw. Instead, the winners enter the qualifying rounds of the US Open. Other aspects have remained constant. For instance, most of the ATA local affiliates and tournaments are still held east of the Mississippi River. In addition, the national tournaments have continued to be great social affairs with more recent activities including a junior mental toughness workshop, welcome BBQ, HBCU showcase, Greek night, dinner cruise, casino night, youth pizza party, and receptions.

Integration placed blacks within white institutions mostly on the lower and middle rungs, while black institutions dwindled, weakened, or disappeared. After black players were allowed to play in USTA tournaments, the fight for blacks to become lines' persons, and chair umpires for important matches, as well as hold other administrative positions proceeded. As a result of the ongoing debate among black leaders in tennis about the scarcity of black American professionals on the world tour, the ATA has been working with officials in Fort Lauderdale to develop a permanent home for the ATA, which will include a national training facility, ATA offices, and a place to house the history of the organization.

The ATA was born due to racial segregation, but thrived to provide an outlet for black adults and youths who had an interest in tennis. Although turned away from white exclusive country clubs, private facilities, and often public courts, elite blacks formed a tennis community of their own, while embracing black youths from lower classes, who showed the ability to play the sport. Many took pride in their pursuit. Ed McGrogan, writing in the *New York Daily News*, illustrates this pride when describing a 1930 photo of doubles teams at an ATA tournament displayed on the wall of a lounge at the US Tennis Center. There were photos of white tennis greats, "but none of those legends looked quite as immaculate as the four anonymous players, who appeared in another shot. . . . They sport collared white shirts, khaki pant and canvas shoes, and they carry multiple wood frames. Like their better-known white contemporaries, each exudes the easy grace of the amateur sportsman."[75] In all, the ATA led the fight to integrate the USLTA. Nevertheless, the organization survived integration, and expanded its base by including more tournaments. It has been argued that the "ATA was not to tennis, what the Negro League was to baseball, because the ATA is still here. Not as celebrated in the black community as it once was, but still here."[76] It is a testament to the ATA, an organization that welcomed integration of the USTA because of the promises it held out for talented black players, survived in order to continue serving amateur and recreational players. It "became the oldest, continuously operated black sports group in the country, outside of collegiate circles."[77]

11

Pars and Birdies in a Hidden World

African Americans and the United Golfers Association

Raymond Schmidt

Among the most popular sports for African Americans during the Jim Crow era was golf. Because of racial segregation, African Americans established their own golf clubs, which were linked together during the last four decades of Jim Crow through a national organization called the United Golfers Association (UGA). Organized in 1925, the UGA recruited new players to the sport, encouraged the formation of new clubs, staged an annual national tournament, and in many other respects provided the support that helped African American golfers face segregation on and off the course. It is a sporting history worth remembering, and one that finds its antecedents nearly two decades before the organization was founded.

Early Development of African American Golf

During the first two decades of the 1900s racial exclusion was being regularly encountered by African American nonprofessional golfers—almost exclusively men —who sought to play the game for recreation and/or in local tournaments staged on municipal or public courses. Initially the largest number of recreational African American golfers were located in East Coast and Midwest cities that had opened public courses; many of which sought to exclude or severely limit the amount of play by African Americans. The challenges to African American golfers were similar in all of these cities, and Chicago—already one of the major centers of American golf by 1910—was one of those that provide insights as to why the UGA was eventually formed.

Chicago opened its first municipal golf course in Jackson Park in 1899. Within two years the course had been expanded to twenty-seven holes, and by 1913 the city had opened two more courses for its golfers. Since there were no fees for playing, the municipal courses were wildly popular from the very beginning among the city's golfers who were unable to afford the plush and private country clubs or member-only golf clubs. African American golfers were allowed to play at any of the municipal courses without the harassment that typified public courses in so many other cities. This was perhaps the case because there were relatively few African American players—most of them having learned the game while working as caddies in the South before migrating north.

Led by Walter Speedy, there was a small group of very talented African American men players in Chicago during the first decade of the 1900s. Speedy, from Louisiana, moved to Chicago in 1900 at age twenty-two and quickly became one of the top African American men golfers in the city. He was an early activist in seeking competitive playing opportunities for minority golfers, and would remain involved in both national and local matters for the African American game into the 1940s. Sometime prior to 1910, Speedy and a number of African American players organized an informal group called the Pioneer Golf Club. Later in 1910, Speedy and three other African American players sought to enter the Chicago Parks Championship tournament at Jackson Park, but all were barred from playing. The four men challenged park officials in court, but nothing would come of it as the ban on African American players continued until later in the decade.[1]

Frustrated by the inability to compete against a wider range of golfers in formal tournaments, Speedy was among a group of African American men in 1915 who formed another group, this one called the Alpha Golf Club. The movement to organize golf clubs for African American players would gain momentum in the early 1920s as a vehicle for staging tournament competition among interested members, expanding the social contacts and interactions that the sport easily encouraged, and with safety in numbers, hopefully reducing the racially motivated incidents often encountered by individual players. Among the first significant events sponsored by the Alpha Club was a men's tournament held in October 1915, at the city's Marquette Park course. Publicized as the first "Negro National Golf Tournament," the small field of players illustrates this was more of a local event, won handily by Speedy.[2]

Although African American golfers were barred from Chicago's city tournament until near the end of World War I, they did have access to the city's several municipal courses. This was not always a condition that existed in other cities. For example, in 1917 a small group of African American men petitioned the park commissioner of St. Louis to set aside one day each week, or certain hours on several days weekly, for "Race people" to play golf on the city's Forest Park municipal course. The commissioner conceded that while African Americans were entitled to play golf within the city, "until such time as separate links could be provided for them they would not be allowed to play" on the existing Forest Park course. In

Indianapolis in 1915 a local group spearheaded the building of a separate course for African American players, and to lend a sense of distinction to playing the course, the golfers were charged a small fee rather than free access.[3]

Racial segregation continued on golf courses throughout the United States well beyond 1920. In Washington, DC—one of the centers of African American golf—segregation was a major problem on the city-owned courses beginning in the early 1920s. African Americans were allowed to play the East Potomac course exclusively after 3 P.M. every Tuesday and the three-hole West Potomac course only on Wednesday afternoons. In 1925 the city constructed a short and poorly maintained nine-hole course near the Lincoln Memorial for the primary use of African American players. Rulings by federal officials would eventually be necessary to overturn the city's segregated golf courses.[4]

Meanwhile, in 1918, three African American men golfers were allowed to enter and qualified for the Chicago Parks Championship at Jackson Park. One of them, an excellent player named Robert (Pat) Ball, eventually reached the tournament's semifinals, which resulted in renewed opposition to African American golfers being allowed to play in the tournament. During the summer of 1919 Chicago was the site of race riots, which caused concern when Pat Ball attempted to again enter the city parks championship. Eventually, the event organizers announced a ruling that each player seeking to enter the tournament must belong to some regular organized golf club and that the club must formally submit the player's entry and await authentication. The Alpha Golf Club was not recognized as a "regular" club and thus Ball's entry was rejected.[5]

Responding to the latest effort to exclude Chicago's African American golfers, a group that included all the leading players in the city organized a new club in 1920 titled the Windy City Golf Association and obtained a charter that established its legitimacy. Claimed to be the first-ever African American golf club to be granted a charter, similar to most of the minority golf clubs organized throughout the 1920s and 1930s, the group's stated goal was "to create interest and promote enthusiasm in the game of golf"—not just for tournament players but as a social, cultural, and athletic stimulus for all its membership. Almost immediately, V. K. Brown, the new superintendent of Chicago's playgrounds, issued a ruling that only players affiliated with a club that was a member of the Western Golf Association— all white and almost entirely comprised of private country clubs—could participate in the Chicago city tournament. Although attempts were made to overturn this ruling through the courts, the policy would remain in place for several more years.[6]

As the number of African Americans interested in the sport of golf began to grow in the aftermath of World War I and during the growing prosperity of the 1920s, a number of areas in the East became extraordinarily popular among minority players. This included the slow growth of black-owned golf clubs that often included many of the features to be found at white private country clubs. One such venture began in late 1921 when a black-owned realty company purchased a previously segregated nine-hole golf course in New Jersey and renamed it Shady Rest. The club had all the amenities of a private club and it provided a safe haven for African American sport and culture. The membership list included individuals from all classes of black society and one historian has described the club as "the birthplace of African America's golfing independence" and "a haven for black golfers on the East Coast."[7]

By the mid-1920s, there was an increasing interest in organizing golf clubs for African Americans where friendly tournament competition and social interaction could be facilitated, along with group events with neighboring clubs that would expand the athletic and cultural experience for the memberships. In addition to the Windy City Golf Club in Chicago, other big city examples would include the Riverside and Capital City clubs in Washington, DC, the St. Nicholas Club in New York City, the Atwater Golf Club in St. Louis, and the Fairview Golf Club in Philadelphia. In the fall of 1924, the Riverside Club sponsored a tournament at the nine-hole Lincoln Memorial course that featured sand greens, yet it attracted some of the top African American players on the East Coast.[8]

Birth of the UGA

The 1924 Riverside Club event was so successful, that in early 1925 a group of respected African American men met at the 12th Street YMCA in Washington to form a wide-ranging organization of minority golf clubs and players—a press release stating that "the object of the national organization is to gather all colored golfers and golf associations into one body." While there is some uncertainty as to all the individuals involved in this breakthrough meeting, it is apparent that the leadership roles in this effort were provided by Dr. George Adams and Dr. Albert Harris, both physicians in the nation's capital. The new organization was initially called the United States Colored Golf Association (USCGA) and consisted of twenty-six clubs, with a few of them actually owning their own courses. The group's first elected president was Mr. B. C. Gordon, who also headed the Shady Rest Golf Club. In 1929 the group would formally change its name to the United Golfers Association (UGA).[9]

From the beginning, the organization sought to provide a unified voice for African American golfers in an effort to improve playing conditions in the segregated sport. It was also clear from the beginning that the sponsoring of tournaments for the membership was of major interest. These large-scale events would provide a social, competitive, and cultural experience that was far beyond what the local club events could provide and that would parallel to an extent those of the segregated white golf world. They would also serve to generate publicity for the organization and its member clubs while at once providing venues for the better African American golfers to demonstrate and improve their skills.[10]

Although a men's tournament was held in July 1925 at the Shady Rest course—featuring a stirring finish between the winner, Harry Jackson, and John Shippen—the first official Negro National Open (again for men players only) was played on Labor Day weekend of 1926 at the Mapledale Country Club in Stow, Massachusetts. Established near Boston in 1926 by African American businessman Robert H. Hawkins, the club, which also had riding and tennis facilities, welcomed minority players from across all class levels. Although Mapledale would become very popular among African American golfers by hosting the UGA National tournament for three consecutive years, the club ran into financial problems and in 1929 became a municipal course, although African Americans were still able to play there.[11]

The 1926 Negro National Open attracted thirty-eight players from ten states, and despite inclement weather, Harry Jackson won the championship in another well-played event. Mapledale again hosted the tournament in 1927, and that year there was a new champion as Pat Ball of Chicago won by an impressive margin of 20 shots. Ball, secretary of the Windy City Golf Club, had been a top-flight player since his earlier attempts to enter the segregated Chicago municipal parks tournament, and by 1927 his game was beginning to peak. By the late 1920s, Chicago's parks organization was allowing African Americans to enter tournaments with white players, and before the Negro National Open in 1927 Ball had surprised many by winning the city's Cook County Open tournament in a thrilling match against a white two-time former champion named Tommy Thompson.[12]

In 1928 at Mapledale, another Chicago player named Porter Washington outlasted Ball for the championship of the now designated "professional" division of the Negro National Open—which included a modest amount of prize money for the top finishers. The 1928 event was also notable for the formal addition of an "amateur" division for men players—won the first year by Frank Gaskin of Philadelphia—expansion of the tournament to three days, and the addition of qualifying rounds because of the increasing number of entries.[13]

In 1929 the UGA National was played at the Shady Rest club and Pat Ball again won the professional title with an impressive score of 284, following up his repeat victory at the integrated Cook County tournament in Chicago earlier in the summer. Ball, described by one historian as "an integral figure in the formative years" of the UGA, would earn the distinction in 1930 of becoming the first African American golfer to enter the prestigious Western Amateur tournament, although an odd number of entries in the event facilitated scheduling him to play alone during the qualifying round, accompanied by a WGA official.[14]

By the close of 1929, the organization had been renamed the United Golfers Association, and Dr. Ernest J. Ricks of Chicago was elected as the group's first president under its new title. The UGA seemed on firm footing among African

American golfers and it was clear that it would serve to stimulate interest in the game, while the Negro National Open tournament had already garnered a reputation among black society as an elite athletic and social event after only just a few years. Increasingly, the popularity of the UGA National Open tournament would also encourage the formation of additional local clubs and sponsorship of local and regional tournaments around the country as golf's popularity grew for African Americans.[15]

Providing assurances for the UGA's future security was the organized and disciplined manner in which it was structured. The organization was divided into administrative districts comprised of member clubs in the states of each—initially the New England, Eastern, and Midwest districts. As the popularity of golf among African Americans grew nationally and more clubs were organized, the scope of the UGA likewise expanded to eventually add district organizations to cover the Southwest, Central, and Southeast regions of the country. Each district elected officers and sponsored its own golf events, while every two years the UGA member clubs would elect a new slate of national officers and address whatever business might have arisen.[16]

During its initial years, the UGA conducted the annual Negro National Open primarily on municipal golf courses located in the northern part of the country—the 1939 National in Los Angeles being the first-ever west of the Mississippi River. Because of the segregationist policies in the southern states, the UGA for many years would have few member clubs from the South. Yet, despite the limited competitive events, the South still produced several outstanding players and UGA champions during the 1930s, such as John Dendy, Howard Wheeler, and Edison Marshall. Also, an annual tournament for top African American players called the Southern Open began in the early 1930s at the Lincoln Country Club in Atlanta and became a popular stop for black professional players.[17]

Development of Women's Golf

The summer of 1930 witnessed another significant event in the history of the UGA in that for the first time a women's division was added to the Negro National Open, being held that year at the Casa Loma Club in Powers Lake, Wisconsin.[18]

Golf for African American women had always been problematic because of time and economic constraints and working conditions that usually demanded long and stringent hours. Also, African American women encountered the same segregationist policies at the municipal courses as did their male counterparts. Still, there were cities that would eventually produce outstanding African American women players and clubs. Chicago was among the leaders in the advancement of black women's golf. Nettie George, a society reporter for the *Chicago Defender* newspaper, was married to Walter Speedy in 1909 and after learning the game she was reputed to be the first African American woman golfer in Chicago.[19]

The first reports of African American women golfers in the city appeared in the *Chicago Defender* in 1916, and George regularly promoted the sport in her column, billing it as a game for all ages and stressing the health benefits to be realized. The local Pioneer Golf Club, along with the formation of the UGA in 1925, contributed to an interest in the game among women as evidenced by their participation in an increasing number of competitive/social golf events on Chicago's municipal courses.[20]

By the late 1920s, an increasing number of African American women golfers were beginning to receive attention in the black newspapers of various cities, although most of the coverage treated the women's game as primarily a social event. In 1930, with Chicago's Pioneer Club sponsoring the UGA National at Casa Loma, a women's championship was added for the first time. The winner of the initial UGA Women's National was a Chicago player named Marie Thompson, who easily won the eighteen-hole event over a field of sixteen players. In 1931 Thompson successfully defended her title, winning by one shot in the twenty-seven-hole tournament held at the Sunset Hills club south of Chicago, and she continued as one of the top challengers for the UGA Women's National title until 1941. Thompson also achieved additional notoriety as one of the major organizers of the Amateur Golfers' Association club in Detroit in the early 1930s, and won its women's championship four times before the war.[21]

Throughout the 1930s the UGA Women's National tournament was contested for by a relatively small number of players, a reflection of the difficulties women players faced in finding adequate time and opportunities to develop their golf games, much less justifying the travel expense. For most of the decade, African American women players were fortunate to obtain membership in an existing men's golf club. African American men's clubs in some cities often adopted a "men only" organization, a circumstance in which women players struggled to find chances to play and any formal competitive opportunities were virtually nonexistent—the only exceptions being the annual UGA National or the large regional tournaments occasionally sponsored by UGA clubs. In this environment, the UGA Women's National championships from 1930 to 1940 were dominated by just a few top players—four women accumulating nine of the eleven titles during the period. Lucy Williams of Indianapolis was the most successful of the elite group of top women players in the UGA National during this period. Between 1930 and 1940 she won the national championship on three occasions (1932, 1936, and 1937) and also finished runner-up five times.[22]

Conditions began to change for African American women players with the organization in 1937 of the first all-women golf clubs that would soon become members of the UGA organization. On April 22, 1937, a group of thirteen women golfers met in Washington, DC, and formed the Wake-Robin Golf Club, the first African American women's golf club. These women had been enduring all the segregation-oriented problems that typified blacks' efforts to play on the city's public golf courses, made even more difficult by their gender. Although the group would seek to attract more women to the sport—which soon would inspire the formation of African American women's golf clubs in other cities around the East—the other major goals of the Wake-Robin were to conduct local tournaments for its membership and, most significantly, to work for the desegregation of golf in the nation's capitol.[23]

The Wake-Robin club combined its efforts with those of the Royal Golf Club—a UGA men's group in Washington—as the two organizations petitioned and lobbied city officials until their efforts succeeded in bringing about the building of the nine-hole Langston Golf Course for black players in 1939. Built on the site of an old trash dump in northeast Washington not far from RFK Stadium, it featured a sewage ditch running along one of the holes. Despite being poorly maintained, it quickly became apparent that the little nine-hole course was inadequate for handling the large number of African American golfers wanting to play there. The course was the center of significant attention when Joe Louis played there in the 1940 Eastern Golf Amateur tournament before very large crowds. Langston eventually became a first-rate facility after major improvements were made and the course expanded to eighteen holes by the early 1950s, and it was very popular among top-flight African American players and became home to the UGA's prominent Capital City Open tournament. Meanwhile, throughout the 1940s the Wake-Robin and Royal Golf clubs would continue to work toward desegregation of all the public courses in the city.[24]

Another prominent UGA women's club was organized on November 16, 1937, when the Chicago Women's Golf Club (CWGC) was formed under the leadership of the city's leading African American women players, including the club's first president, Anna Mae Robinson, with assistance being provided by Chicago golf pioneers Walter and Nettie Speedy. Among the club's major goals were stimulating interest in the sport, sponsoring competitive events, and developing younger players. After receiving a state charter, the CWGC gained full membership in the UGA. In 1940 the club hosted the UGA National championships and at the annual meeting had two of its members, Geneva Wilson and Elizabeth Mitchell, named to the UGA Golf Championship Committee. The CWGC would continue as one of the major clubs within the UGA well beyond the end of the Jim Crow era, while at the same time the rapid expansion of African American women's golf clubs after the late 1930s would significantly expand the increasing pool of capable women players who competed and flourished as part of the UGA.[25]

Upgrading UGA Competitive Play

While the women's branch of the UGA began to evolve in the late 1930s, the African American men's game was already producing some of the top competitive players during the Jim Crow era. The number of men's clubs in the UGA would continue to increase despite the Depression, and in the 1930s the Negro National Open stood firmly as the premier African American golf event each year. It would eventually serve as the catalyst for the organization of a slate of local and regional championship tournaments around the country. The widespread coverage of the Negro National tournament by the country's major African American newspapers and the organized efforts of the UGA combined to attract many new African American golfers to the sport—estimates placing the number of black golfers during the 1930s at 50,000 players.[26]

The UGA encouraged a growing interest in golf by moving its annual championship tournament around to various cities in the East and Midwest throughout the 1930s, yet the Deep South still held some strong ties for the UGA in the late 1920s and 1930s. It was well recognized that the South produced some excellent African American men golfers as a direct byproduct of their years working at country clubs as caddies and grounds maintenance personnel. These jobs often developed interest in golf beyond just becoming excellent players, and one direct result was the building in the late 1920s of two black-owned golf courses that became the centers of African American golf in the Southeast region. The courses were both named "Lincoln Country Club" and were located in Jacksonville, Florida, and Atlanta, Georgia, and both were nicely maintained and considered quite impressive layouts. The Atlanta club became a center for top-flight African American men players, largely as a result of the annual Southern Open that was played there beginning around 1932. The Atlanta area produced six of the UGA's men's professional national champions between 1932 and 1938, and along with the titles won by Edison Marshall of New Orleans in 1930 and 1931, demonstrates the high quality of African American men players active in the South in the 1930s.[27]

While southern golfers dominated the UGA championships of the 1930s, and a new group of future stars prepared to take over the sport by the 1940s, one of the legends of early African American and UGA men's golf continued to enhance his reputation. Robert "Pat" Ball of Chicago captured his third UGA National Open title in 1934, and in 1938 was named the golf pro at the popular eighteen-hole integrated Palos Park public course located just outside Chicago. Of equal importance was the record Ball established when he was able to play in integrated tournaments. In 1932 and 1934 he won a prominent regional tournament held in Des Moines, Iowa, along with the 1934 Cook County Open in Chicago. In 1932 he successfully filed for an injunction in Common Pleas Court to gain entry to the

USGA-sponsored National Public Links tournament in Philadelphia where he was the only African American player in the event.[28]

With the arrival of the 1940s, the UGA was well into its second decade while African American golfers—frustrated by the difficulties imposed by the Jim Crow era—had evolved into what one historian has described as "a sanctuary for a unique subculture." Under leadership of the UGA, black golfers around the country had available social and sporting events that allowed them to enjoy many of the same approved leisure activities that paralleled those denied to them by segregated society. Black society had a venue for demonstrating and publicizing its athletic and cultural values while the growing numbers of new players attracted to the sport—many from the black business and professional class—helped provide a foundation for the soon-to-be-widespread efforts aimed at desegregating "white only" public golf courses around the country.[29]

By 1940 the UGA had also contributed to a regular slate of tournaments that would be held each summer around the country in leading up to the prestigious Negro National Open. These regionally organized tournaments provided top competition for many African American golfers, but were particularly valuable to black professionals who had no other formal competitive avenue to supplement their incomes because of the segregation policies of the Professional Golf Association (PGA). Segregation had always been enforced in the PGA men's pro tournaments dating back to its 1916 formation, but in 1943 the organization had formally adopted a policy that membership was only open to "Caucasian" men professionals. While tournaments could choose to allow the entry of black players, the PGA regularly applied social and political pressures on the tournaments to allow only white entrants.[30]

The UGA-endorsed regional tournaments thus provided an opportunity for the top African American professionals to improve their games, earn a small supplementary income, and help to popularize the sport further in the African American community. These regional tournaments—which often featured appearances by black celebrities and pro athletes—were major social events that financially benefited local business communities. By 1940, the UGA was assisted by the growing number of competitive events sponsored by regional organizations such as the Eastern Golf Association (EGA), which was based in Washington, DC. Further evidence of the growing maturity of the UGA came with the founding in May 1936 of the official magazine for the organization, entitled *United Golfer*, which included news items about various UGA clubs and articles related to continued discrimination encountered in the sport.[31]

The magazine was initially published by the Fairview Golf Club under the direction of editor John M. Lee, the copies at first selling for 25 cents each. With the white-based national golf magazines almost never giving space to African American golf, *United Golfer* (with its excellent photographs, instructional articles, and coverage of major tournaments) became extremely popular among member clubs. The magazine continued to be published on a fairly regular schedule until 1938 when a new editor took over. At about the same time the magazine began to include coverage of other sports and its name was changed to *The United Golfer and Other Sports*. Soon, the overall quality of the magazine—golf coverage in particular—began to decline and shortly after World War II it ceased publication, a serious loss for UGA member clubs.[32]

The year 1941 is particularly notable in UGA history for several reasons. The highlight of the season was the UGA National Open, which was held that year at the public Ponkapoag golf course near Boston. The 1940 tourney in Chicago had been a very successful event as the entry of heavyweight boxing champion Joe Louis had attracted thousands of spectators to watch him and the rest of the field. In 1941 a field of two hundred golfers were entered—a new record for the event. Pat Ball won the tournament, his fourth UGA National title, by just one stroke. His wife, Cleo Ball, captured the amateur women's championship to complete the sweep for the Chicago golfers.[33]

The tournament also was highlighted by the extensive pre-event publicity that appeared in black newspapers around the country, the gala parties that were integral to the annual event, the careful preparation and grooming of the golf course, and the serving of catered meals in an outdoor dining facility. The 1941 National tournament is considered, moreover, to be a transitional point in black golf history as it marked the final time that most of the major pioneers of African American golf would participate in the event before the new corps of young stars would begin to make their marks in UGA golf. While many local and regional UGA events would continue through the war years, the UGA National Open was suspended from 1942 to 1945. The years following World War II would bring an increasing aggressiveness by UGA members and clubs toward the segregationist conditions in golf, and much of the initiative originated in the early years of the 1940s.[34]

The World War II Years

While the UGA tournament circuit had been gradually adding more regional events leading into the 1940s, the 1941 golf season saw the initiation of a major tournament that served as a fitting warm-up to the National Open. This was the Joe Louis Open—organized and sponsored by the heavyweight champion boxer and an avid golfer—which was first held in Detroit. The tournament, with its attractive prize money, was played just a couple weeks before the UGA National and quickly became the second major African American golf tournament each season; attracting nearly all the top African American players.[35]

Although suspended during the war years of 1942—1944, the Joe Louis Open was played eight times between 1941 and 1951, and Louis considered his tournament an opportunity to further publicize the playing skills of African American golf professionals. One of the highlights of the Louis tournaments was an exhibition match at the close of the event, which pitted two top black players against a pair of local white golf pros. The Joe Louis Open added a women's tournament in 1946, although the event was canceled for 1949 because of a number of disturbances at the 1948 tourney among some of the women players, including an embarrassing dispute over the prize money awarded.[36]

The 1941 golf season also provided a notable event that would launch the late 1940s and 1950s attacks on golf course segregation. The African American golfers of Washington, DC, had long been active in organizing clubs and outings, along with questioning the golf facilities made available to them. Yet the frustration at being unable to play on the city's municipal courses prompted a small group of black golfers from the men's Royal Golf Club to attempt to get on the East Potomac course. The group was soon attacked by rock throwing white players who ultimately had to be removed by the police.[37]

Soon afterward, the Royal Club petitioned the secretary of the interior, Harold Ickes, to intervene with the city administration to open the municipal plots to all players. Ultimately Ickes, on behalf of the federal government, ruled that blacks as taxpayers had a legal right to play on any of the city's public courses. Yet there would be little enforcement against harassment from other players until the mid-1950s when blacks would be allowed to use all of the District's public facilities. Around that time, the black-operated Langston golf course was expanded to eighteen holes and greatly improved, and would soon become home to the prestigious Capital City Open.[38]

During World War II, both the Joe Louis and UGA National tournaments were canceled, which resulted in African American golfers being limited to participating in local and regional events. There were a number of black professionals who were ready to make a mark in golf, yet with PGA sanctions still in place it was extremely difficult for them to earn a living playing the sport. All of the aspiring black golf pros worked at a variety of other jobs, some serving as chauffeurs and teaching pros for golf-minded celebrities such as Joe Louis and Billy Eckstine. Black golf pros also had a well-deserved reputation for their ongoing roles as gamblers and "hustlers" within the sport, which may have reached a peak during the war years as they sought to supplement their income from the game they played.[39]

As the decade progressed, the African American men's game featured four excellent players—any of whom were talented enough to play in PGA tour events if they had been allowed. These notable UGA players of the postwar era were Howard Wheeler (who had already won three UGA Nationals in the 1930s and would eventually capture three more titles), Teddy Rhodes (one of the two best African American golfers produced in the Jim Crow era, who would win five UGA National Opens during his career), Charlie Sifford (eventual winner of five UGA National titles), and Bill Spiller (the most militant of the black golf pros seeking admission to the PGA tour).[40]

Before the war years, black golf pros had been allowed to enter only the US Open, the Los Angeles Open, and the Canadian Open, among the events that comprised the annual tour for white golf pros. In 1942, with the US Open canceled for the duration of the war, the USGA decided to hold a tournament in Chicago to be called the "Hale America National Open." Seven black golf pros attempted to enter the event, but despite the involvement of the more liberal USGA, all were denied places in the event because of the opposition of the host Ridgemoor Club, which had a rule against black players using the course or clubhouse.[41]

Despite this insult, in 1942 the chances for African American pros to compete in white-run events had improved. The year before, a businessman named George S. May had launched a new tournament called the All-American Open at the Tam O'Shanter club just outside Chicago. In the spring of 1942, Chicago alderman Benjamin Grant sent a letter to May, formally asking whether African Americans would be given the opportunity to compete in the annual Tam O'Shanter tournaments. May quickly replied that his tournament would be open to "any American who is willing and able to qualify under the rules of competition." And so in 1942 there were a few African American players who qualified for the All-American, although many of the white pros refused to play in the same groups with their black counterparts. Wheeler shot the lowest four-round total of any of the black players and May awarded him a special purse of $200 as the tournament's "most glamorous player." Within a few years, May added another tournament the week after the All-American and called it the World's Championship with the largest prize money in pro golf at the time, and African American golf pros were always welcome entrants.[42]

In the postwar years of the 1940s, the UGA restored its National Championship with all the social trappings of the earlier years, along with the Joe Louis Open, and in 1948 a new tournament in the East established by middleweight boxing champion Sugar Ray Robinson. Added to these were eight or nine other regional events that were held primarily in the East and Midwest, although there were also tournaments held in Houston and Miami for African American professional players.[43]

The 1946 UGA National Open in Pittsburgh launched the rivalry between Teddy Rhodes and Howard Wheeler for the top spot in African American pro golf. Wheeler captured the title in the 1946 tourney by a mere two shots over Rhodes. He then repeated his UGA championships in 1947 and 1948, with future UGA star Charlie Sifford and Rhodes finishing runner-up in the two events respectively.

Rhodes, then thirty-three years old, did demonstrate his talent in the 1947 Joe Louis Open where he defended his title from the previous summer with a brilliant total of 280 at Detroit's Rackham course.[44]

Rhodes had met Joe Louis during the early war years, and the heavyweight champ eventually offered him a full-time job as teaching pro and traveling companion. The chance to play more golf led to improved results for the stylish Rhodes by 1946. Despite coming up just short in the 1946 UGA, he had captured the Joe Louis event two years running, which set the stage for the top years of his UGA days. Yet, Rhodes first served up widespread notice of his great talent at the 1947 Los Angeles Open against the top PGA players in the country when he shot a 71 in the tourney's first round, which prompted the *Los Angeles Times* to describe Rhodes as "America's greatest Negro golfer." He would go on to win the UGA National title five times; in 1949, 1950, 1951, 1952, and 1957—the 1949 championship captured with a brilliant four-round score of 277 that outdistanced the field by ten shots. In 1949 Rhodes also won the Joe Louis Open, the Ray Robinson Open, and the Sixth City event in Cleveland to establish his top ranking, along with an impressive top-twenty finish in the PGA's World Championship tournament at Tam O'Shanter, which garnered him $300 in prize money.[45]

Women in the Postwar Era

The years from World War II up to the early 1950s brought a number of significant changes for women in the UGA, both on and off the golf course. The women's clubs were to an extent successful in attracting new players to the sport, despite economic considerations that kept many women from taking up golf, inspiring the organization of new all-women groups, and raising money for charitable causes; all of which were among the basic intentions of the earliest women's clubs. One of the more notable new women's clubs formed during this period was the Vernondale Women's Golf Club in Los Angeles, the first black women's golf club on the West Coast, organized in 1947 under the leadership of successful businesswoman Mae Crowder. The club would eventually be renamed the Vernon Crest Golf Club. Crowder would later be one of the organizers of the Western States Golf Association in 1954. A little publicized aspect of the UGA was that not all the member men's clubs were willing to allow UGA women members to participate in their outings and events—the ban on women in the 1949 Joe Louis Open being one example. The UGA executives held that while the national group would urge its member clubs to remove any restrictions regarding women members, the final decision remained the right of the local clubs.[46]

Not unexpectedly, African American women still encountered racial harassment while trying to play at municipal courses. Despite the Department of Interior's 1941 ruling that all Washington, DC, municipal courses were open to all players, the following year at the city's Anacostia Fairlawn course a group of four women from the UGA's Wake-Robin Club were attacked on the third green by a crowd hurling stones. White soldiers also reportedly shouted racial slurs at them. Some of the difficulties encountered by women's clubs were not racial in nature, such as the home Palos course of the Chicago Women's Golf Club being sold in 1943 to the government to serve as a proving ground for military operations.[47]

Despite the opposition of many of the men's clubs comprising the UGA, women members were determined to assume a more active role in the organization. One of the key local women officials was Paris Brown, elected president of the Wake-Robin Club in 1939, followed in 1941 by her election as a vice president of the UGA—the first woman to hold an executive position in the UGA. She was joined in 1944 by Anna Mae Black Robinson of the Chicago Women's Club, who was elected as the fourth vice president of the UGA. Brown was also appointed to the National tournament committee and soon became an assistant tournament director in charge of running the annual women's National tourney.[48]

In 1954 Brown was elected UGA tournament director, a prestigious position she held until 1964 despite ongoing opposition from a small number of men executives of the UGA. During her tenure the event at one point grew to nearly four hundred entries. Brown was a firm believer in strong organization and planning, and was adamantly opposed to gambling by players. As tournament director she produced a long series of successfully run events, while also traveling widely in promoting the sport for African American women. After resigning her post in 1964, Mrs. Brown would continue to serve in other tournament-related activities, and many golf historians consider her the top woman executive ever in the UGA. At the UGA winter meetings in early 1949, women achieved another leadership milestone despite some heavy male opposition with the election of Catherine Dixon of Chicago as assistant secretary of the UGA and a member of the executive committee.[49]

While women in the UGA had expanded their off-course activities substantially during the 1940s, the emergence of several talented women players from different regions of the country was another significant development in the UGA during those years. Just before the suspension of the UGA National during the war years the 1939 and 1940 women's titles were captured by an excellent player named Geneva Wilson of Chicago. Wilson would continue to hold her place near the top of the UGA women's standings with her play in local and regional tournaments, including defeating former national champion Lucy Williams in the 1941 CWGC Women's Midwest Amateur. Indeed, Wilson was so highly regarded at the time that she was among four African American women players invited by George S. May to play in the prominent 1944 All-American tournament at Chicago's Tam

O'Shanter, making her one of the first African American women to play in the tourney. Just days before the 1944 All-American tournament, Mrs. Wilson again won the CWGC's Midwest Women's Amateur event. The other African American women who played in the historic 1944 tournament were Magnolia Gramble and L. Francis Hill Watkins of Washington, DC, and Julia Siler of St. Louis, the UGA Women's National champion in 1933.

While Lucy Williams Mitchum of 1930s fame remained near the top of the UGA women's game and captured her fourth National women's title in 1946, along with the Joe Louis Open championship that same summer, a number of other very good black women players began to emerge near the end of the 1940s. Among the more notable newcomers was Thelma Cowans, who won her first UGA Women's National title in 1947 and would later add four national crowns, along with being invited a number of times to play in the prestigious Tam O'Shanter tournaments. Another top player in UGA women's history was Ethel Funches of Washington, DC, who began seriously competing in the late 1940s and continued to experience success through the rest of the Jim Crow era and beyond. The winner of numerous local and regional UGA tournaments during her career, she captured her first UGA Women's National championship in 1959 and then proceeded to win five more of the prestigious titles in the years of 1960–1969; adding a final national crown in 1973. Considered a good enough golfer to compete in the predominantly white women's major championships, Funches instead chose to limit her tournament play to UGA events where she would not encounter any racial incidents.[50]

It is generally acknowledged that the best woman golfer to ever come out of the UGA was Ann Moore Gregory of Gary, Indiana, and the Chicago Women's Golf Association. Taking up the game of golf while her husband was in the military during World War II, she soon became a very good player and compiled an excellent record in local and regional tourneys. Invited to play in the 1947 All-American event at Tam O'Shanter, it was the start of her career playing in top-flight nonsegregated women's events. The 1950 season was one of the best of Gregory's playing career as she won several tournaments, including the Sixth City Open in Cleveland and the Midwest Amateur, finishing off the summer by capturing her first UGA Women's National title, eventually going on to capture four more UGA National titles in her career. During the 1950 season, Gregory distinguished herself by winning six of the seven tournaments she entered. It is estimated that she captured over a hundred titles in African American women's competition during her twenty-plus years of play.[51]

Opportunities for Gregory to match her golf game against the best white women amateurs in the country improved substantially in 1956 when the Chicago Women's Golf Club succeeded in becoming the first African American club to attain membership in the United States Golf Association (USGA). This gave the club's qualified players the right to enter all USGA-sponsored women's tournaments and paid off for Gregory in 1956 when she became the first African American woman golfer to enter a USGA event—in this case the United States Women's Amateur tourney at Indianapolis. Gregory lost a very close match in the first round, but made a favorable impression on other competitors.[52]

In subsequent years Gregory would play in other US Amateur events, with her best performance coming in the 1959 tournament at Congressional Country Club near Washington, DC, where she advanced to the third round. While playing in USGA tournaments, Gregory still had to face racial intolerance. At the 1959 Amateur at Congressional, club officials barred her from attending the annual player's dinner held the night before the tournament began. At the 1960 Amateur in Tulsa, a white hotel refused to honor her reservation and she was forced to take a room in a rundown hotel for blacks, and at the 1963 Amateur in Massachusetts she was mistaken for a maid by one of the other players. Yet Gregory's career was marked by distinction and success. She won her final UGA Women's National title in 1966 and nearly won the 1971 US Senior Women's Amateur event, remaining active in women's amateur golf until well into her seventies, and closed her playing career by capturing the 1989 US National Senior Olympics championship.[53]

Challenging PGA Discrimination

While women of the UGA were strongly focused on organizational and playing issues from the end of the war up through the 1950s, news on the men's side increasingly focused on challenges by the top UGA men professionals to the segregationist policies that prevented them from playing in nearly all PGA-officiated tournaments. At the center of the bitter controversy were UGA players Teddy Rhodes, Charlie Sifford, and Bill Spiller—all of whom believed they were good enough to earn a living playing on the PGA tour if only allowed to compete.[54]

With the PGA clearly having no intention of easily revoking its Caucasian-only rule or ceasing its opposition to African American players being given exemptions into tournaments, the controversy became an embarrassment for the organization beginning in 1948. That year three black players (including Rhodes and Spiller) had all qualified for entry to a minor tournament in Oakland, California, only to have a PGA official step in and cancel their spots because of the organization's Caucasian clause. The three black players hired an attorney and were prepared to file a lawsuit against the PGA, which officials of the organization quickly attempted to settle out of court with promises of a series of largely meaningless changes to their rules and tournament qualification procedures.[55]

For 1950 the UGA had put together a schedule of fifteen tournaments, although only one—the New Lincoln Open in Atlanta—would be held in the

South. A major problem for black professionals was making a living on the UGA circuit. Prize money in the events was declining and, more seriously, of the fourteen UGA tournaments scheduled in 1951, only four of them were open to men pros. These problems continued with the 1952 UGA schedule.[56]

By 1952 the ongoing attacks on the PGA's discriminatory policies by black newspapers and the UGA was becoming increasingly widespread, and events at the San Diego Open launched the drive that would eventually end the "Caucasian" rule. For the 1952 tournament the sponsors of the San Diego Open initially accepted the applications from amateur Joe Louis, the boxer now having become a very good golfer, and two black pros, Bill Spiller and Eural Clark. Yet the invitations were quickly rescinded because of the PGA's insistence that black players could not compete in the tournament. This action triggered a widespread reaction and spread coverage of the controversy in leading mainstream newspapers over a policy that most observers could no longer accept.[57]

Joe Louis, still extremely popular, did not hesitate to express his views in the major newspapers, and PGA president Horton Smith quickly attempted to defuse the situation. Since Louis was an amateur, he did not have to qualify for the tournament and so the PGA allowed him to play as a special invitee of the San Diego sponsors. Spiller and Clark had been allowed to play in the qualifying round and Spiller had scored well enough to get in. But the PGA stepped in and ruled that it could not waive its rules regarding non-Caucasian players so Spiller was disqualified.[58]

The national uproar over the PGA's racial discrimination continued unabated, and Smith publicly "predicted" that the board would discuss its non-Caucasian clause at the organization's next annual meeting. Spiller responded by again threatening to sue the PGA, which forced Smith to install a new plan that set up a special committee of black golfers who could select one black pro and one black amateur to play in each PGA-sponsored tourney. Of course, the two entries could still be discarded at the discretion of the local sponsors or the host country club. Clearly, this was not going to be a long-term solution to the PGA's discrimination policy. Throughout the rest of the decade, the top African American golf pros were able to only gain entrance to a relatively small number of PGA tournaments.[59]

Racial segregation at the top tournaments was not restricted only to the professional ranks. For example, in 1952 the Miami Country Club informed the USGA that it would not permit black players to compete that year in the US National Public Links tournament, which it was hosting. This was a USGA-sanctioned amateur event, yet the organization would not force the club to allow black players to compete so the ban remained in effect.[60]

Finally, in early 1960 the ongoing controversy over segregation in professional golf tournaments came to the attention of California attorney general Stanley

Mosk. After some research, Mosk notified the PGA that if it continued to discriminate against black golfers it would no longer be able to play its tournaments on any of California's public courses. Apparently not recognizing the evidence that their segregationist policies could not be defended any longer with the majority of Americans, the PGA arrogantly informed California that henceforth it would play its tournaments exclusively at private clubs. Mosk immediately informed the PGA that it would also be prohibited from using California's private courses for its events and then proceeded enlisting the support of attorneys general of other states in a highly publicized campaign against the PGA's policy of discrimination.[61]

With the civil rights movement increasingly gaining momentum nationally, along with the increasing numbers of lawsuits being brought against states and municipalities that were attempting to maintain segregated public golf courses, the PGA realized the futility of its position on African American professionals. At last, during the PGA's annual meeting on November 10, 1961, in Hollywood, Florida, the "Caucasian only" clause was removed from its constitution with no opposition. After fulfilling the qualification requirements, Charlie Sifford—a five-time winner of the UGA National Open—became the first African American playing member of the PGA in 1965. He would win the PGA-sponsored 1967 Greater Hartford Open and the prestigious 1969 Los Angeles Open.[62]

Expanding African American Golf

Through the 1950s and 1960s the UGA continued to operate its annual National championship tournament, assisted with the organization of new all-black golf clubs, endorsed major regional events, and continued its efforts to attract new players to the sport. As such, the UGA was continuing its role of providing the foundation and support for golf among African Americans, and finally the civil rights movement would join the efforts to aggressively oppose discrimination both on and off the golf course. During this period there were two new major regional African American golf organizations formed outside the boundaries of the UGA—the Western States Golf Association and the North American Golfers Association—yet there was no disharmony among the groups and the UGA always remained the only truly national organization for African American golfers.[63]

The first of these two groups was formed in 1954 in Los Angeles as the Western States Golf Association (WSGA) with the purpose of organizing and administering black golf clubs west of the Rockies. The UGA had always maintained a minor presence on the Pacific Coast, despite the Cosmopolitan Club of Los Angeles staging the 1939 UGA National tournaments in that city. By early 1957, the WSGA included eight African American member clubs from the western states region, including four in Southern California and two in the San Francisco area. Also, in the mid-1950s the organization began sponsoring a monthly magazine about the world of African American golf entitled *Tee-Cup*. Published in Los Angeles, the magazine included news about African American golf from around the country, with the majority of its pages devoted to golf in the Los Angeles and San Francisco areas. The editor and publisher of *Tee-Cup* was J. Cullen Fentress.[64]

Through the years the UGA had always encountered difficulties in attracting African American golf clubs from the South as members of the national organization, although the region had produced a relatively large number of outstanding players who had competed in UGA's annual competitions. With the growing civil rights movement and the availability of more public courses to African American golfers in the South, the direct result was a steady increase in organized all-black golf clubs. By the civil rights era of the 1960s most southern states were home to at least one African American golf club and there was plenty of competition available.[65]

In 1954, in a major breakthrough for African American golf, the first North and South tournaments for black professional and amateur players was staged in Jacksonville by a former Harlem teacher named Ray Mitchell. The next year he moved the tournaments to Miami, and with the eventual corporate sponsorship of Schaefer Brewing and Coca-Cola, the tourney began to attract top black golfers from across the country. The event became a major fixture on the African American golf tour and continued into the late 1990s.[66]

In 1964 a businessman named Earl Hill organized the first Southeastern Open tournament at Jekyll Island, Georgia, destined to be the region's largest tourney. Seeking a larger role for the clubs of the South, Hill convened in November 1968 a meeting of representatives of many of the region's black golf clubs and from this came the regional organization known as the North American Golfers Association (NAGA), yet it would not become an affiliated member of the UGA. Soon the NAGA organized a regular schedule of tournaments, which were hosted by member clubs from Alabama to North Carolina; each of the events usually played over fifty-four holes with competitions for professionals, amateurs, and women members, with the Southeastern serving as the culminating event each November.[67]

During the 1960s, the annual UGA National Open tournament was still one of the top social and athletic events among African Americans. Along with the success in ultimately overturning the PGA's segregationist policies, the UGA and its annual tournament schedule was still providing a proving ground for developing up-and-coming young black players. A notable milestone was achieved in 1959 by a young African American player named Bill Wright, who captured the USGA's National Public Links championship at the Wellshire course in Denver after barely qualifying for the match play event, earning the honor of being the first black golfer to win an integrated national championship.[68]

Promotional ad for the 1956 UGA Tournament. *Image courtesy of Raymond Schmidt.*

Decline of the UGA

The ultimate decline of the UGA was a result of organizational and structural issues more than anything else. The UGA had been under the guidance of capable and effective leaders through the years, but by the end of the 1960s the UGA's prestigious place in the African American sporting world began to slowly erode. For many years there had been occasional talk of controversy among various member clubs over matters relating to the conduct of the annual UGA national tournament, along with difficulties in communicating issues consistently to member clubs due to the lack of a permanently based administrative structure. The lack of communication was accelerated when the UGA's regular publication—the *United Golfer*—was discontinued shortly after World War II, removing an effective vehicle for disseminating information to the membership.[69]

Another difficulty for the UGA and its member clubs was the dwindling media coverage their competitions were receiving in black newspapers; a situation that began in earnest by the 1970s. The UGA national tournament always received coverage in black newspapers, but the regular local club events received little coverage. There are sport historians who compare this development to that experienced by the Negro League teams when major league baseball dropped its color line and began signing the top black players. For the UGA and African American golf the parallel had been the PGA dropping its Caucasian-only rule. By 1974 there were ten African American men players on the big-time PGA tour and readers of the black press wanted to read about these players.[70]

By the early 1970s, the UGA included 89 member clubs and nearly 40,000 members. In 1974 the organization included 400-plus self-declared black golf pros, despite the fact that most UGA-sanctioned pro events had been reduced to just one day and prize money had dwindled to almost nothing. In fact, in 1975 the difficulties in raising prize money for the tournaments resulted in the men's professional competition of the UGA National being discontinued. By this time, most of the UGA's member clubs had evolved into social groups that regarded golf as a strictly recreational sport, rather than a crusade against injustices in American culture.[71]

For the UGA and African American golfers, the long and painful struggles through the Jim Crow years of the twentieth century came to a close in 1975. An African American player on the PGA tour named Lee Elder had been a major success in UGA competition for years, dating back to 1951 when as a sixteen-year-old he had lost in the UGA National Amateur final to Joe Louis. Having first learned the game while working as a caddie in Dallas, he eventually moved to Los Angeles where he worked on his game with former UGA great Teddy Rhodes. Throughout the mid-1960s, Elder was one of the top players in UGA tournaments that were still available to black pro golfers, and then in late 1967 he qualified to play on the regular PGA tour. Finally, in 1974 Elder won the PGA's Monsanto Open, which qualified him for an automatic entry into the next year's prestigious Masters tournament. In the spring of 1975 Elder became the first African American golfer to play in the Masters at the Augusta National Golf Club, the ultimate symbol of the exclusive private country clubs of America and the final vestige of white discrimination in American professional golf.[72]

With a different UGA organization evolving in the face of the many changes in golf and American society that had taken place during its first half century of existence, the member clubs returned to most of their original goals. Along with local golf events that always had been important, the clubs now recommitted themselves to charitable fundraising and bringing young African American players into the sport with renewed junior golf programs. The UGA celebrated its seventy-fifth anniversary as it moved into the twenty-first century still pursuing most of its original goals, and the organization had earned a lasting place in sport history with its contributions to golf and American culture.

12

Basement Bowlers

The National Negro Bowling Association and Its Legacy of Black Leadership, 1939–1968

Summer Cherland

On September 11, 1964, Louise Fulton wept when she won the Professional Woman's Bowling Association (PWBA) tournament, held in New Jersey. "The road to the top had been long and lonely," wrote sports correspondent Bill Nunn. Fulton's victory made her the first black woman to win a professional tournament in bowling history, but this was not Fulton's first taste of victory. She had already blazed a trail when she became the first black bowler invited to join a professional league. She had been the first to qualify for a national professional tournament in 1962, and was the first to win one in 1964. Hours after the first day of PWBA competition, Ted Page awoke to a 2:30 A.M. phone call. It was Louise Fulton, calling to excitedly regale Page with details of her performance from the night before. Fulton was unsure how she would do in the next round, but believed that she would be successful if her mentor and friend was there to cheer for her. "She said if I could fly up to Princeton she figured she could finish among the top four. I got on a plane out of Pittsburgh early the next morning."[1] Personifying the familial connections made among NNBA/TNBA members, instructor and student celebrated together when Louise Fulton was crowned the champion after "sudden death" playoff. Thus Nunn, it seemed, was only half correct; the road was indeed long, but never lonely.[2]

In 1962, Fulton earned the title "the most dangerous woman bowler" from sports writer and former Negro Baseball League star Ted Page.[3] Fulton, a friendly bespectacled woman, had likely never been thought of as a threat to anyone until she began breaking records and knocking down racial barriers along with bowling pins. Fulton grew up near Pittsburgh and found her way to bowling as an adult, when she began training at Ted Page's Hillview Lanes.[4] Page and Fulton embarked

on a career-long friendship, and under his coaching, she quickly progressed to
become a danger to the status quo in bowling throughout the 1960s.[5] In 1960,
Fulton and fellow Pennsylvania bowler Sadie Dixon became the first black women
to qualify for the National All-Star Tournament.[6] Four years later, Louise Fulton
solidified her place in bowling history when she became the first black woman to
win a professional championship at the Professional Women's Bowling Association
Open.[7] Fulton's career trajectory, her friendship with Page, and her unexpected
roles as leader and activist by way of her love for bowling are representative of
her membership in what was once called the National Negro Bowling Association
(NNBA). By the time Fulton was breaking racial and gender restrictions in bowling, the NNBA had adopted a new name, The National Bowling Association
(TNBA). This 1944 decision was little more than a renaming, and did not represent a new mission for the organization.[8] Instead, NNBA's founding principles set
the course in 1939 for one of the longest-standing and largest black-owned, black-
led associations in the country.

Meadow Lanes in Pittsburgh 1974, Grand Opening.
Image courtesy of the National Bowling Association.

Scholars of race and sport generally agree that an American Bowling Congress (ABC) tournament in 1951 marked the beginning of integration for the sport. That year, ABC and the Women's International Bowling Congress (WIBC) allowed black bowling teams to compete after a nationwide political campaign to overturn "white's only" requirements. White and black leaders, bowlers, and politicians from across the country joined forces with NNBA, the New York Catholic Youth Organization (CYO), the United Auto Workers-Congress of Industrial Organizations, the National Committee for Fair Play in Bowling, and numerous black newspapers to break open the largest and most significant bowling organizations for keglers, as they called themselves.[9] However, while the ABC overturned its "whites only" membership clause in a board meeting in 1950, segregation remained constant in the sport of bowling throughout the 1960s.[10] Particularly but not exclusively in the South, hotels sponsoring ABC and WIBC tournaments refused black patrons and some owners of private alleys did not allow black bowlers to access their lanes, despite their registration as tournament players.[11] ABC's racial discrimination continued when black bowlers struggled to find open lanes and hotels for competitions held in the South. ABC attempted to shift the blame to the overwhelming "emergence of Negro bowling," but TNBA leaders refused to accept this passive stance. Ted Page wrote, "I might add that there has been and still is a problem in every sport that the Negro has entered and the problem is not created in the South alone."[12] Over the course of their history, the NNBA confronted these issues by boycotting and picketing outside intolerant lanes, taking to the presses, and also creating opportunities for black bowlers to compete on their own terms.

Leading up to the creation of the NNBA in Detroit in 1939, the founders set out to desegregate the sport of bowling. More importantly, NNBA creators committed to a spirit of inclusion among all bowlers across the country. When they drafted NNBA's founding documents, the writers wrote that their "purpose was to foster and promote the game of Ten Pins among BOTH [sic] men and women," and to "serve as a point of entry for minority ethnic bowlers who otherwise would not get the opportunity."[13] In doing so, the NNBA became the first organization open to all bowlers of any race or gender, though black men and women made up a significant majority. Members were urged to take on leadership opportunities within the organization and particularly at the local level. Though they prided themselves on being inclusive despite race, the NNBA emphasized self-reliance, encouraged blacks to seek out black-owned lanes to patronize, and created their own annual national tournament in 1939. Thus the NNBA, and subsequently TNBA trained black bowlers in more than the sport. Their members became activists and leaders, who built and nurtured a national network of allies that would stand the test of time.

Bowling's Popularity and the Burgeoning NNBA

The national bowling craze reached a fever pitch in the United States in the years between World War I and World War II.[14] By 1945, an estimated 12 to 16 million Americans had picked up a ball, making bowling a billion-dollar industry.[15] Scholars attribute the sport's popularity to the expanding middle class and encouragement from the United States military. Bowling had been a popular pastime among black and white servicemen, and following World War I, it was considered a physically healthy and patriotic way for veterans and their families to spend their time.[16]

Bowling is today viewed a democratic sport, bridging social classes, age groups, and skill levels. However, the sport has a racist past, marked by segregation as racial restrictions excluded blacks from alleys across the country and banned them from tournaments.[17] Importantly, the rise of bowling's popularity among African Americans occurred simultaneously alongside increased measures to segregate public accommodations and limit opportunities for blacks to participate in sports and leisure. Black bowlers might have gained limited access to a few alleys thanks to enterprising owners, but those lanes filled quickly and often were open to blacks only after hours.[18] A few owners could be convinced to open their lanes to black bowling alley employees and their teammates. Typically, blacks employed in most of the country's alleys were "pin setters, janitors and custodians," so many of these after-hour bowlers spent their days cleaning and their nights bowling with their friends on those very same lanes.[19] White owners of "discarded lanes," or bowling halls that had closed due to dilapidated facilities or lack of consumers in northern cities were reopened secretly to African American keglers, under the premise of an opportunity for profit. Until 1938, black bowlers used the "hidden" or downstairs alleys in YMCAs, churches, and community centers to welcome them to their hidden or downstairs alleys. Thus, the term "basement bowler" was coined.[20]

Despite these challenges, bowling appealed to African American working-class men and women in part because it seemed inexpensive, was somewhat easy to learn, and was becoming a national trend. Many also considered the sport to be an opportunity to compete and socialize with their friends without spending too much money.[21] Even if they were denied access to ABC competition, black men and women formed their own organizations and tournaments as early as 1920.[22] Likewise, as greater numbers of blacks migrated to northern urban settings like Cleveland, Detroit, New York, and Pittsburgh, the demand for social spaces including restaurants, movie halls, parks, and bowling alleys increased. Black bowlers began searching for lanes that were willing to take their business, even if they were not able to compete nationally with the ABC.[23] As popularity grew and word spread about discarded and after-hour lanes, the number of basement bowlers outnumbered the availability of lanes open to them.

Amid the rising black demand for bowling, a group of Cleveland, Ohio, men met to discuss an all-black league in 1931. Within two years, Oscar McDonald, a Cleveland bookbinder, joined Wynston Brown to form the United Clubs Bowling League (UCBL) with only eight teams.[24] While many bowlers and public figures focused on taking the ABC to court and demanding desegregated tournaments, the UCBL laid the foundation for what was to become the National Negro Bowling Association. Emphasizing black leadership and inclusivity, the men who made up the UCBL began encouraging Cleveland women to form teams. In addition, the UCBL went searching for lanes in Cleveland that would welcome their business and accommodate a sizable tournament.[25] By this time, some alley owners were willing to allow black bowlers, however secretly. In more than one midwestern city, alley owners found it profitable to close their lanes, post signs stating, "Closed: Rented to a Special Party" or "Private Event," and allow black bowlers to enter secretly through the back door.[26]

Black bowlers were eager to form social and competitive connections. In 1936, six teams of black women in Cleveland formed the Ladies Progressive League under the direction of black bowler Viola Crosswhite from Cleveland, Ohio.[27] All the while, membership in the UCBL continued to increase. McDonald, Brown, and the UCBL founders were proud to know that women's leagues were shaping up in their hometown, and men and women were organizing in nearby midwestern cities. In 1939, Wynston Brown took the UCBL to regional presence when he invited teams from Cleveland, Cincinnati, Detroit, Chicago, and Toledo to participate in an inner-city match game. Black men and women from these five cities descended upon the Ontario-St. Claire Avenue Lanes in Cleveland on May 5 and 6 of that year.[28] The coed tournament was considered a rousing success by most of the participants. Having found a community and the opportunity to compete alongside fellow bowlers, the keglers vowed to continue the tradition. They kept their promise to one another. The 1939 class of competitors waited only three months before they organized a meeting in Detroit to discuss forming a national organization.[29]

On Sunday, August 20, 1939, twenty-two men and women voted to form the National Negro Bowling Association. John Smith, Arble J. Woods, Firley Carr, Wynston Brown, Joe Blue, Jack Robinson, J. Elmer Reed, Oscar McDonald, Viola Crosswhite, Issac Rivers, Brownie Cain, Leroy Brown, Henry Hardin, Ernest S. Moore, June Watts, George Porter, James Roden, Richard Benton, James Watt, Lucius Huntley, Dwight Guy, and Clarence King made up the twenty men and two women delegation.[30] They adopted a constitution penned by J. Elmer Reed and devised a plan to recruit nationally, appointing "Senates," or local governing bodies in each region.[31] The delegation identified three founding tenets of the NNBA; sportsmanship, fellowship, and friendship. From 1939 throughout the remainder of NNBA and TNBA's history, these three pillars remained central to the organization's mission. However, the NNBA founders established a tradition of leadership and activism that was as essential to their association as the foundational tenets. Over the course of their seventy-five-year history, the NNBA trained black bowlers for local and national leadership, encouraging men and women to take on prominent roles in their communities and beyond the NNBA's scope. Members perfected their resistance strategies at the same time as they practiced throwing a bowling ball. By focusing on localized leadership, recruiting women and youths, and placing great emphasis on prioritizing black alley ownership, the NNBA became a community of activists in its own right. Finally, the NNBA got its start by nurturing a strong social network among its founders, and the emphasis on a family-like community continued to define the organization throughout the twentieth century.

NNBA and Black Leadership

When Ted Page retired from the National Negro Baseball League 1937, his former teammate Jack Marshall offered him a job at a bowling alley in Pittsburgh. Within a few years, Page became a skilled bowler. In 1941, he bought the business from Marshall, began training other bowlers, and entered local tournaments at every opportunity. Thus began Page's lifelong commitment to black bowling and all that it could do for his friends and community.[32] Page saw bowling as "an inspiration for other Blacks to get together and do something."[33] Under his supervision, Hillview Lanes became a central meeting place for blacks to bowl, socialize, and build connections among their neighbors. When the NNBA incorporated in 1939, Page was one of the first officers and a significant part of the Pittsburgh bowling community.[34]

New members like Page were thrilled with the NNBA and its mission. Though their desegregation efforts received more recognition, the National Negro Bowling Association focused most immediately on creating an organization that would cultivate black leadership. Page approached the NNBA with this strategy when he began writing a bowling column for the *New Philadelphia Courier*. By taking to the presses, Page helped recruit interested black bowlers to NNBA, and he publicized their achievements over the course of his career. It is through Page's column that the longevity of NNBA's foundational principles is evident, even after the renaming of the organization.

The NNBA became one of the largest black-founded, black-led, and black-directed organizations in the country.[35] J. Elmer Reed calculated that by 1942, the NNBA had 1,800 members, with most Senates located in midwestern cities, all headed by black leadership.[36] NNBA members believed this was a significant accomplishment, and the leadership began to reconsider their name to increase exposure. Having earlier decided on the National Negro Bowling Association, several of the founders and NNBA president Jack Robinson discussed a name change in 1943. "When they started, they chose to use the name Negro, but it wasn't restricted," stated TNBA president Wayde Broughton in 2013. But with the encouragement of the NAACP, they decided to change their name because "National Negro seemed exclusive."[37] Since one of their founding principles was to desegregate the sport of bowling, the NNBA recognized that their title was counterintuitive.

The NNBA, however, was considered "the father of Negro Bowling," even after the name was changed.[38] In the course of only five years, the NNBA created a national network of black bowlers, all willing to guide the organization in various ways. As the NNBA looked forward to a new era with a new name, they clung to their founding principles of sportsmanship and fellowship. Local leaders, as a result of their training from building the NNBA, discovered they were sought after to take on responsibilities in the bowling world, beyond their organization's reach. In an article about the rise of black bowling, Memphis author Edgar Cheatham discussed the "ups and downs" of TNBA "as the results of the integration" of the ABC's tournaments. Citing nearly thirty black keglers and alley owners who made bowling history by 1960, Cheatham gave credit to the Chicago Bowling Senate, and the men and women who broke records, recruited other black bowlers to the sport, and were instructors at local black-owned bowling alleys.[39]

NNBA originators laid a foundation that emphasized leadership skills at all levels of membership, and this call remained after 1944. Men and women from a variety of geographical locations were encouraged to take on formal and informal leadership roles. NNBA Senates opened in Michigan, Chicago, Detroit, and Cleveland with enterprising bowlers who had their eyes on progress. Potential new members did not need much convincing to join, but they were greeted with a persistent message that their individual efforts would determine their national organization's success. Marguerite Sparks, who joined the Empire Bowling Senate in Brooklyn, learned quickly that she was expected to speak up and get involved. "You get nothing except what you put into it," she remembered in 1961. She added, "The [N]NBA meant the same as the NAACP and the Bill of Rights to the Negro bowler."[40] Bill Rhodman of Detroit learned that on the lanes he was both a player and a leader. Rhodman began bowling in 1941, joining the Allen Super Market Team. In 1951, Rhodman's team changed history when they "broke the ice for Negro bowlers" by becoming the first black bowlers to compete in the newly desegregated ABC's annual tournament. Rhodman earned the label "the greatest Negro bowler of all time" in 1962.[41] Rhodman's skills as a bowler paired with his willingness to desegregate the ABC set a standard for TNBA members. Rhodman and his teammates inspired other black bowlers to rise in the ranks of their sport in order to challenge racist restrictions in bowling and sports in general.[42]

Women in particular thrived as leaders within NNBA/TNBA. Some, like Louise Fulton, eventually broke color barriers at national championships. Others became youth instructors and officers for their Senates. Rachel Ridley of Chicago used her years of experience to "recruit and organize Negro women bowling leagues."[43] Ridley, an office manager, was already a leader in her community by the time she joined the NNBA in 1939. Having learned leadership skills as a member of the Association of Colored Girls and the Chicago Urban League, Ridley connected and networked among Chicago's blacks from a young age. Not long after she began working for the *Chicago Defender*, the NNBA praised her efforts as a woman who "has done the most" in the Chicago Senate.[44] By focusing on bringing more women to the NNBA, Ridley's prominence within the association increased. Kay Brisson, another accomplished woman bowler, held many formal leadership positions within TNBA which eventually led to national leadership roles in other organizations. Almost immediately after joining the organization in the 1960s, Brisson was appointed to director of Junior Bowling for TNBA. At the time, Brisson was the first black woman to provide instruction in the sport at Harlem Lanes in New York. This position and her experience as a junior bowling instructor led to a new appointment with the New York City Bowling Council. Brisson's work with youth bowlers allowed her to take on formal supervisory positions and break color barriers within the world of bowling, beyond participating in tournaments.[45]

Perhaps the best example of the NNBA's legacy leadership is Eric deFreitas of New York. DeFreitas, born in Trinidad and raised in New York, was introduced to bowling as early as fourteen years old. Like many black teens at the time, deFreitas worked as a pinboy at a local bowling alley and became interested in the sport. From his pinboy days at the New York YMCA, deFreitas advanced within the bowling world to become one of its most significant contributors. He joined the NNBA in 1939 and in 1962 was elected to his third successive term as TNBA president.[46] After joining the NNBA, deFreitas became a bowling instructor, which helped him become a networker and promoter of black bowlers. He helped to organize the United Bowling League of Brooklyn, and was a member of the Greater New York Committee for Fair Play in Bowling, which steered the racial desegregation movement in 1951.[47] Under his guidance, TNBA "ballooned into one of the most vigorous national organizations of modern times."[48] DeFreitas remained committed to his role with TNBA and the well-being of black bowlers for the rest of his life. In 1962, he was recruited by the American Bowling Enterprise (ABE) to serve as a good will ambassador to the South. Due to a flood of black interest in bowling despite the longevity of segregation in the South, the ABE asked deFreitas to oversee a multi-million-dollar construction project for black-owned black-led alleys. This ambassador role led deFreitas to travel and promote the history of black bowling across the country and to other parts of the world.[49]

Activism and Self-Reliance

At the core of TNBA's national significance was its emphasis on economic independence and black solidarity, beginning with its first official tournament. In the face of racial segregation, the NNBA/TNBA has held its own national bowling tournament every year from 1939 until 2013. Though the tournaments were open to all members of the NNBA/TNBA, and membership was not racially exclusive, the NNBA nonetheless resisted segregation practiced by the ABC and WIBC by using strategies of self-reliance. Typically held at black-owned alleys and operated by one of the country's largest black-led organizations, these tournaments were prime examples of racial solidarity and independence. The NNBA encouraged and helped black owners to open alleys in their cities. On Chicago's South side, the NNBA helped to scout out lanes owned by black bowling legends and NNBA founders Charlie Parks, Billy Hampton, and O. H. Harrison.[50]

The organization enjoyed financial success almost immediately and made a commitment to use their financial success to promote bowling and improve member services. As soon as they incorporated, the NNBA embarked on an enterprise to build black-owned and operated alleys. They continued searching for hospitable alleys, but their commitment to invest in black ownership exemplified self-reliance from the birth of the organization. In 1942, J. Elmer Reed documented that the NNBA had "over $450,000 invested in Negro owned and operated alleys." In his list, Reed included four businesses, located in four different cities in three states. Due in part to these efforts in Detroit, Toledo, Cleveland, and Cincinnati, the NNBA made its presence known throughout communities in the Midwest by securing job opportunities for blacks. Reed estimated, "These four alleys have paid salaries to employees over $100,000 in 1942."[51]Reed was among the first to consider the benefits of NNBA investment in black-owned alleys. He approached two investors in Cleveland to discuss buying or building lanes for the sole purpose of creating a black-owned bowling alley. Because of Reed's efforts, his brainstorm, in 1942, United Recreation was built in Cleveland.[52]

That same year, the NNBA asked Ted Page to advise them as they planned to partner with a new bowling alley owner in Washington, DC. Having led a successful business in Pittsburgh, Page seemed an excellent candidate to oversee the opening of DC's "first bowling establishment for Negroes."[53] Page was charged with outfitting the alley in the nation's capital with fourteen lanes, and recruiting staff for the new business. In addition, the NNBA asked Page to promote the sport of bowling among black residents of DC. The Washington, DC, alley opened in

1942 and remained successful for decades. Black bowlers in DC quickly took to the sport and over time became some of the strongest competitors in the country. The NNBA was satisfied with Page's work and began to make more efforts to encourage black ownership of alleys.[54]

NNBA founders believed that black-owned alleys would be successful, predicting that their members would prefer to patronize black-owned businesses. Black alleys experienced moderate success when they first opened, as black bowlers sought out these businesses. J. Edgar Reed asserted that black alleys were successful because "we leave every white alley as soon as a Negro builds one in that city."[55] This NNBA-led endeavor proved a triumph when, in 1961, American Bowling Enterprises (ABE) announced a six-million-dollar project to build another alley "for the Negro bowler." An assumption prevailed that these enterprises were most successful in northern cities, but this was not completely founded. National discourse claimed that rising interest in bowling among black southerners seemed to happen overnight, and black bowlers in the South had fewer basement bowling opportunities. Many struggled to find welcoming houses that would allow them to bowl after hours.[56] Black bowlers, even after the ABC changed their "whites only" clause, were excluded from southern tournaments because many alleys prohibited blacks from entering their establishments. One white owner in Tennessee notified the ABC and TNBA that he vowed no black bowler would ever "roll a ball in that establishment."[57] After a series of such incidents that continued segregation of bowling despite organizational policies, the American Bowling Enterprise enlisted Eric deFreitas, the two-time TNBA president to oversee development of black-owned bowling alleys.[58] His initial project was a bowling house in Nashville that would be the first black-owned and operated alley in the city. Following in the tradition of Atlanta's Fun Bowl, where ABE was headquartered, the Nashville lanes would set the standard for other alleys in seven southern cities. The ABE elected to build these alleys in response to the increased interest in bowling among black southerners, and partnered with deFreitas and NNBA leadership, since their efforts had been so successful in the development of northern houses.[59] Just a year prior, Edgar Cheatham had indicated the benefits of black-owned alleys when he wrote, "The opening new houses gave our bowlers some advantages." Cheatham argued that some blacks could find success in business if they wished to own bowling alleys, and keglers would be better off patronizing these lanes, especially in Chicago.[60]

TNBA and the ABE alike continued to tout the success story of Ted Page. Over the course of nearly twenty years, Meadow Lanes, or Page's Lanes, as the place became known in Pittsburgh, was a center of community, competition, and fellowship among black bowlers.[61] Page's was most widely recognized as the bowling alley where Louise Fulton and Sadie Dixon trained and instructed, but it was home to many bowlers throughout the city as well.[62] Men, women, and children flocked to Page's Lanes, and found social connections through the sport. Members of Pittsburgh's West End AME Zion Church team struggled to find consistency until they began rolling at Page's. Once they began meeting at Meadow, "the group hasn't missed a week since it began to play at Ted's Lanes."[63]

TNBA's success was a product of this blend of activism, community, and racial solidarity. By emphasizing fellowship as well as self-reliance, NNBA founders created a foundation that became TNBA's legacy. Through bowling, blacks created a national network that defined progress as inclusivity, but with an importance placed on autonomy. Ted Page exemplified this mission. A bowling alley owner and active member in the NNBA from the beginning, Page demonstrated the importance of self-reliance. He helped other black owners build successful businesses and promoted their success through his weekly column. As a bowler and an instructor himself, he spent time recruiting and training other athletes. "Ted Page was a proprietor. He had a vision of TNBA being prominent."[64] However, Page's vision for TNBA and the organization's vision for itself always included the best interests of members. On an individual level, TNBA members were encouraged, nurtured, and supported and their recollections indicate that TNBA was a family first and a national association of bowlers second.

Inclusion and Community Building

The emphasis on leadership and activism was successful because of NNBA's effective community building efforts. As a result of these strategies, the NNBA became part of the community building tradition that flourished in black neighborhoods. In the sport of bowling in particular, keglers and business owners fostered strong bonds in the era of segregated sports, and the effect was widespread. Bowling was accessible to professionals and amateurs alike, a sport that welcomed thousands to its ranks. TNBA had 7,000 members in 1962, indicating that the appeal of bowling had reached thousands of households in dozens of cities.[65] But the large numbers only told a small part of the story. From its inception, the NNBA welcomed all bowlers regardless of race or gender, or ability level. Senates, in particular, were charged with creating "family-like" atmospheres among their local members.[66] TNBA members thus, could expect regular, locally organized, good-natured tournaments with nearby Senates. The annual national tournament originated in 1939 was expanded in 1963 to not only the bowling competitions but meetings, special events, fundraising activities, and celebrations honoring TNBA's history.[67] In 1960, TNBA created the King and Queen Contest, an annual competition honoring the organization's top fundraisers and community builders. The contest was designed to enhance TNBA's exposure, and to encourage a healthy spirit of competition among Senates. Surplus money was sent to the United Negro College Fund as well as TNBA's Foundation.[68] A new king and queen have been crowned every year since without fail.[69]

From its inception, NNBA membership was open to women, which stood in stark contrast to the ABC. As a result, women's leadership helped to make TNBA the successful community that it quickly became. When TNBA's prominence grew to rival the previously whites-only ABC and WIBC, women were among the first to encourage blacks to join TNBA. Emphasizing personal connections among the membership, TNBA women sought to demonstrate that TNBA was more than just an organization that would collect dues. "In the NBA there is a personal association in its tournament attractions that the other two organizations don't have," argued Marguerite Sparks of Pittsburgh. Sparks encouraged bowlers to consider joining the other organizations for the tournaments, but not at the cost of their TNBA membership. "You know that next year and the years to come there are going to be many things remembered by many." She went on to say, "You are not just a statistic."[70] Mae Jones McIntosh or "Miss Charlie," as she was known, placed great emphasis on the role of TNBA as a family when the organization faced a brief decline in membership around 1952. Miss Charlie, the secretary of TNBA for a time, "helped saved the NBA" by speaking one-on-one with prospective members, and convincing them of TNBA's benefit to black bowlers. Miss Charlie gave individualized attention to bowlers to demonstrate the personal commitment TNBA made to its members.[71] Throughout her career with TNBA, Miss Charlie personified family-like. She made it her responsibility to console unsuccessful keglers, and she was constantly promoting future TNBA events. In the years following her death, TNBA members continued to reminisce about Miss Charlie's warmth and commitment to the association. "It was strange," wrote Ted Page in 1965, "not seeing the late Miss Charlie around . . . To say she was missed at this annual affair would be putting it mildly."[72]

Another method employed by women to create a strong sense of community in TNBA was the recruitment of black youths. Teens and children who were interested in bowling were recruited to the NNBA/TNBA at a young age. Since the early 1930s, black teens found their way to bowling through employment as pinboys. Some, like James Haynes of Chicago, took on special roles as line judges. Haynes was known for his fair judgment and confidence when moderating matches between judges and lawyers.[73] Many of TNBA's most prominent bowlers and leaders began their careers as pinboys. Len Griffin and C. W. Williams of Detroit both started as pin setters.[74] Renowned president Eric deFreitas first became interested in bowling when he was a pinboy at the New York YMCA.[75] Henry Brooks of Cincinnati joined the NNBA in 1940, after having spent nearly a decade as a pinboy. Brooks went on to win the single's tournament in 1962 at TNBA's annual meeting in Dayton, Ohio.[76] Women played a significant role in formalizing NNBA/TNBA's commitment to youth bowlers, when they helped to organize youth leagues in the 1960s.[77]

For decades, Ted Page facilitated TNBA's reputation as an extended family through his weekly articles about the association's outstanding members. Page regularly promoted TNBA's, and made constant mention of every bowler's membership status. His articles combined personal anecdotes about the keglers, along with bowling scores. In some cases, Page documented the personal lives of bowlers across the country. He praised bowling alley owners for maintaining "beautiful lanes," but also recorded personal tragedies and tribulations of TNBA members that had little to do with bowling.[78] In 1962, Page described a car accident involving four TNBA women, and he included a brief reassurance that all women were "out of danger, now."[79] Page diligently recorded and published individual stories, how individuals found their way to bowling, and what each person was doing for TNBA. He celebrated their achievements and praised their efforts. He assigned each kegler a unique personality, describing his or her appearance and mannerisms in order to give the impression that everyone reading the article was already familiar with the subject. In 1961, Page described Sadie Dixon as "the boxom housewife," and "the little pepperpot from Chester," before explaining that while new bowlers were garnering more attention, Dixon's honorable history was "really something."[80]

On April 14, 1962, Page devoted another article to promoting the accomplishments of two more black women bowlers, Carol Strickland and Carol Brown. He wrote, "The beautiful Miss Strickland was the first bowling personality signed on by the Blatt Company."[81] Page's descriptions were not limited to his favorite women bowlers, however. In 1962, when fellow bowler Merrill Thomas wrote a thank you to Page for an article on TNBA's prominence, Page replied with a summary of Thomas's contributions. After a brief biography Page wrote, "He is especially proud to be remembered as a former member of that once-famous bowling team." and included the names of four more NNBA groundbreaking keglers.[82] Page's articles were widely read among TNBA members, and many relayed messages through him because of it. In 1962, Page published a letter written by Al Rotunnol. Rotunnol's letter commended the *Courier* newspaper for its continued support of TNBA, and praised Page's work. Rotunnol ended, "If you see Louise Fulton, please give her my best regards . . . In my opinion, she is the finest Negro woman bowler that I have seen."[83]

The NNBA continued to succeed as an organization, even after bowling was desegregated in 1951, in part because of the association's commitment to its members. The NNBA's mission to be an organization with familial relationships mirrored efforts for community building evident in nonathletic agencies, schools, and churches during segregation. Like schools and churches, TNBA was open to everyone, despite class, age, gender, race, ability, and location. Bowling, it seemed, was a sport of "kings and commoners."[84] To many members, TNBA membership represented more than an interest in bowling. The organization continued to grow, even when briefly threatened in 1951 when the ABC desegregated. Throughout the 1960s, TNBA remained committed to its purposes of sportsmanship and friendship. These tenets, combined with the organization's commitment to activism and leadership, came to also represent "unity, strength, and solidarity."[85]

The Legacy of NNBA

TNBA continued to enjoy national significance and increasing membership throughout the remainder of the twentieth century. The organization held its annual bowling tournament every summer, and its national reach expanded to include the West. In 1976, a group of black bowlers in Las Vegas organized a TNBA Senate, joining over one hundred local chapters dispersed throughout the country that made up the association. By 1999, the organization boasted a membership of 30,000. TNBA leaders believed that each member had his or her own connection to the national organization because of the local Senates. Some chapters, like the Las Vegas Senate, employed a monthly ritual of wearing "TNBA shirts to show camaraderie and remember the history of black bowling clubs."[86] Long after Ted Page and Louise Fulton passed away, their influence remained a significant part of bowling's history. Fulton's aunt Marjorie Mitchell and sister Karen Fulton-Parks took over as managers of Meadow Lanes in Pittsburgh, which remained a successful black-owned business.[87] It prospered until facing a dramatic economic decline in 2004, when Mitchell began to struggle with a loss of business and increasing repair costs for the aging building. "This place," remembered Fulton-Parks, "has meant so very much to the community because so many young people have gotten their start at Meadow Lanes."[88]

"For African-Americans," a writer for *Ebony* explained in 1994, "that sense of together-ness has directly contributed to TNBA's growth."[89] Nearly sixty-five years after its inception, the ideals upon which the National Negro Bowling Association was founded remained integral to the organization. The central mission remained "sportsmanship, fellowship, and friendship" but expanded, due to its history, to include "unity, strength, progressivism, and solidarity."[90] In 1939, NNBA founders set out to open the lanes for black bowlers, but more importantly, foster a national black-led community based on local leadership, self-reliance, and friendship. The organization's commitment to these ideals remained central throughout bowling's history. After NNBA renamed itself in 1944 to The National Bowling Association, and following the desegregation of the ABC and WIBC in 1951, TNBA flourished instead of floundering, demonstrating a legacy uniquely different from other predominately black sport organizations. By opening officer positions to every single member, demanding local Senates to be self-sustaining and emphasizing future success, NNBA created a legacy of leadership that quickly spread beyond the organization's scope. By emphasizing self-reliance and racial solidarity, the association resisted racist practices and created a system of self-support that remained central to its mission after desegregation. Finally, the founders of NNBA insisted that the association be welcoming and inclusive, with an importance on a family-like community. This legacy remained throughout the organization's history. TNBA membership currently stands at nearly 30,000 members, many of whom believe they are among friends first and bowlers second.

Notes

1. Cuban Giants: Black Baseball's Early Sports Stars

1. Michael Lomax, "Black Baseball's First Rivalry: The Cuban Giants Versus the Gorhams of New York and the Birth of the Colored Championship," *Sports History Review* (1997): 28, 141–42.

2. Michael Lomax, *Black Baseball Entrepreneurs, 1860–1901* (New York: Syracuse University Press, 2003), xx.

3. Rory Costello, "S. K. Govern," http://sabr.org/bioproj/person/af52b171.

4. Booker T. Washington, *The Negro in Business* (Wichita, KS: Devore and Sons, 1992); Jerry Malloy, "The Birth of the Cuban Giants," *Nine: Journal of Baseball History and Social Perspectives 2* (1994): 233–47.

5. "The Cuban Giants Beaten," *New York Times*, October 6, 1885.

6. *Pottsville Daily Republican*, September 30, 1885.

7. Frank Ceresi and Carol McMains, "Original Photo of the 1885– 1886 Cuban Giants," http://www.thenationalpastimemuseum.com/article/ original-photo-1885-1886-cuban-giants-black-baseballs-first-professional-team.

8. "Victory for the Orions," *New York Sun*, September 13, 1882; "Base Ball," *Trenton Evening Times*, May 9, 1886, 8.

9. "The Cuban Giants Released," *Trenton Evening Times*, October 7, 1886, 1.

10. "An Unchanged Record," *Trenton Evening Times*, May 15, 1886, 1; "The Elite Gets Left," *Trenton Evening Times*, May 20, 1886, 1.

11. "Cuban Giants 9; Flushing 7," *Trenton Evening Times*, June 12, 1886, 8.

12. "The Cuban Giants Honored," *Trenton Evening Times*, October 11, 1886, 1.

13. "The Cuban Giants Released," *Trenton Evening Times*, October 14, 1886, 3; "The Cuban Giants," *Trenton Evening Times*, November 18, 1886, 1; "The Cuban Giants," *Trenton Evening Times,* January 20, 1887, 4.

14. *New York Sun*, August 23, 1886.

15. "The Cuban Giants," *Trenton Evening Times*, January 19, 1887, 1; "The Orange and Blacks," *Trenton Evening Times*, April 12, 1887, 3; "Very Badly Left," *Trenton Evening Times*, May 1, 1887, 1; "A One-Sided Ball Game," *Trenton Evening Times*, May 5, 1887, 1; "They Got Sadly Left," *Trenton Evening Times,* May 21, 1887, 1; "Another on the List," *Trenton Evening Times*, May 26, 1887, 6; Sol White, *History of Colored Baseball*, 3d ed. (Lincoln: University of Nebraska Press, 1995).

16. *Trenton Evening Times*, May 11, 13, and 14, 1887.

17. "Ding, Ding, Ding, Ding," *Trenton Evening Times*, June 2, 1887, 1.

18. "The Cuban Giants," *New Haven Register*, June 7, 1887, 1.

19. "Cuban Giants," *Baltimore Sun*, June 15, 1887, 1; "A League Club Beaten," *Trenton Evening Times*, July 21, 1887, 6.

20. "The Color Line in Baseball," *Macon Telegram*, September 16, 1887, 3.

21. "The Tables Turned," *Trenton Evening Times*, June 9, 1887, 6; Paul Browne, *The Coal Barons Played Cuban Giants* (Jefferson, NC: McFarland Publishing, 2013).

22. "A Remarkable Record," *Trenton Evening Times*, July 7, 1887, 2; "Badly Knocked Out," *Trenton Evening Times*, July 7, 1887, 6.

23. "The Orientals Knocked Out," *Trenton Evening Times*, September 6, 1887, 2; "Cuban Giants," *Baltimore Sun*, October 11, 1887, 6; "Cuban Giants," *Cincinnati Enquirer*, October 19, 1887, 2.

24. White, *History of Colored Baseball*, 10.

25. "Cuban Giants to the Front," *Cleveland Gazette*, January 21, 1888, 3; "Opening the Season," *Trenton Evening Times*, April 5, 1888, 3; "The College Boys Win," *Trenton Evening Times*, April 14, 1888, 3; Browne, *The Coal Barons Played Cuban Giants*; "The Ball Field," *Trenton Evening Times*, April 22, 1888, 5; "Cuban Giants Dwarfed," *Chicago Daily Tribune*, June 8, 1888, 8; "On the Diamond," *Trenton Evening Times*, June 10, 1888, 3.

26. "S. K. Govern, Black Baseball's Renaissance Man," http://home.roadrunner.com/~vibaseball/govern.html.

27. "These Are Real Giants," *Detroit Free Press*, October 2, 1888, 8.

28. "Colored Championship Series," http://www.cnlbr.org/Portals/0/RL/Colored%20Championship%20Series%20%281867-1899%29.pdf.

29. Lomax, *Black Baseball Entrepreneurs,* 94–95.

30. Middle States League, Baseball-reference.com.

31. "Two Items of Baseball," *Harrisburg Patriot*, March 14, 1889; *Philadelphia Inquirer*, May 10, 1889; "What Earnest, Active and Capable Team Workers Those Cuban Giants Are," Baseballhistorydaily.com/tag/frank-grant.

32. Browne, *The Coal Barons Played Cuban Giants*; "The Cuban Giants Beaten," *Philadelphia Inquirer*, April 13, 1889, 6; "Second Championship Game," *Lancaster Intelligencer*, May 8, 1889.

33. Browne, *The Coal Barons Played Cuban Giants*; "Shut Out the Visitors," *Trenton Evening Times*, May 15, 1889, 3; "A Short, Sharp Game," *Lancaster Intelligencer,* May 23, 1889; "The Ponies Knocked Out," *Harrisburg Patriot*, May 29, 1889, 1; "Middle States League," *Philadelphia Inquirer*, June 10, 1889, 6; "A Surprise at Burlington," *Philadelphia Inquirer*, July 11, 1889, 6; "Harrisburg 6; Cuban Giants 0," *Philadelphia Inquirer*, July 23, 1889, 6; "Cuban Giants, 9; Harrisburg 2," *Philadelphia Inquirer*, August 9, 1889, 6; "The Cuban Giants Claim," *Philadelphia Inquirer*, October 11, 1889, 6.

34. *New York Sun*, October 11, 1889.

35. "Cuban Giants No Longer," *Cleveland Gazette*, April 5, 1890, 1; "Cuban Giants," *Boston Daily Globe*, May 4, 1890; *Baltimore Sun*, May 6, 1890, 6; "Cuban Giants Beaten at Pottstown," *Philadelphia Inquirer*, May 30, 1890, 2; "Other Games Yesterday," *New York Herald*, August 18, 1890, 8; Lomax, *Black Baseball Entrepreneurs,* 110–11; *New York Sun*, May 6, 1890, June 21, 1890.

36. *Boston Daily Globe*, July 3, 1891, 5; "Cuban Giants Defeat Pottstown," *Philadelphia Inquirer*, July 11, 1891, 3; "Camden vs. Cuban Giants," *Philadelphia Inquirer*, July 25, 1891, 3; Michael Lomax, *Black Baseball Entrepreneurs,* 106, 114–15; *New Haven Journal and Courier,* April 20, 22, and 28, 1891.

37. "Cuban Giants Win," *New York Herald*, May 2, 1892, 5; "Cuban Giants on Top," *New York Herald*, June 27, 1892, 6; "Sunday Baseball on Local Fields," *New York Herald*, September 12, 1892, 8; "Fultons Kick Fruitlessly While the Cuban Giants Win," *New York Herald*, October 3, 1892, 5.

38. "Cuban Giants Defeat Easton," *Philadelphia Inquirer*, May 1, 1893, 2.

39. "Cuban Giants Victorious," *New York Herald*, June 26, 1893, 8; *New York Sun*, August 30, 1893.

40. "Best Williams," *Boston Daily Globe*, May 6, 1894; *Statistics of Intercollegiate Contests*, 10.

41. Karl Lindholm, "A Century and a Half of Middlebury Baseball" (N.p.: 2006), 3.

42. "The Cuban Giants," *Cornell Daily Sun*, May 3, 1894.

43. Lomax, *Black Baseball Entrepreneurs*.

44. "Cuban Giants," *Boston Daily Globe*, May 3, 1895; "Cuban Giants," *Boston Daily Globe*, May 15, 1895; "Beat Newport," *Boston Daily Globe*, July 19, 1895, 4.

45. *Boston Daily Globe*, April 25, 28, and 29, 1896; *Baltimore Sun*, March 9, 1896, 6; *Boston Daily Globe*, June 16, 1896; "Cuban Giants Are Done," *Chicago Daily Tribune*, September 18, 1896, 8; "Giants Vs. Giants," *Detroit Free Press*, September 23, 1896, 6.

46. Lomax, *Black Baseball Entrepreneurs*, 152–53; *Boston Daily Globe*, April 27, 1897; "Colored Champs Here," *New Haven Register*, October 6, 1897, 11.

47. "Cuban Giants Engaged in War," *Trenton Evening Times*, March 30, 1898, 6; *Chicago Inter Ocean*, September 11, 12, and 17, 1898; *New York Sun*, September 17, 20, 1898, and October 3, 1898.

48. "Unions Defeat Cuban Giants," *Chicago Daily Tribune*, June 12, 1899; "Unions Defeat the Giants," *Chicago Daily Tribune*, June 19, 1899, 4; "Unions 8, Cuban Giants, 7," *Chicago Daily Tribune*, June 20, 1899, 4; "Unions Are Defeated Again," *Chicago Daily Tribune*, June 26, 1899, 4; "Cuban Giants 7, Columbias 4," *Chicago Daily Tribune*, September 11, 1899, 10; "Baseball," *Detroit Free Press*, September 14, 15, and 16, 1899, 6.

49. "Among the Amateurs," *Chicago Daily Tribune*, June 24, 1900, 18.

50. *Cincinnati Enquirer*, April 16, 1902, and June 10, 1902; *Boston Daily Globe*, June 1, 1904; *Baltimore Afro-American*, October 8, 1904, 10; "For Colored Championship," *Chicago Daily Tribune*, September 11, 1904, A2; "Cuban Giants Win, 6 to 1," *Chicago Daily Tribune*, September 12, 1904, 9; "Other Local Games Today," *Chicago Daily Tribune*, September 18, 1904, A2; "Barons Again Down the Cuban Giants," *Wilkes-Barre Times-Leader*, April 24, 1908, 11; "Cuban Giants Mere Pygmies," *Chicago Broad Ax*, July 11, 1908, 2; "Victory to Logan Squares," *Chicago Daily Tribune*, July 20, 1908, 8.

51. "Lightning Kills Player on a Baseball Diamond," *Chicago Daily Tribune*, August 27, 1909, 2.

52. "Cuban Giants as Helpless as Babies," *Trenton Evening Times*, May 1, 1911, 11.

53. "Arkadelphia Cuban Giants," *Arkansas Baseball Encyclopedia*, http://arkbaseball.com/tiki-index.php?page=Arkadelphia+Cuban+Giants+%281910%29 (accessed October 31, 2013).

54. *Chicago Defender*, June 21, 1941, 23; "Clowns Drive Satchel Paige to Showers," *Chicago Defender*, July 5, 1941, 23; *Cleveland Call and Post*, September 6, 1941, 7A.

55. Rich MacAlpine, "The Penn Yan Cuban Giants," *Yates Post* (July 2007), Yates County History Center; Penn Yan Cuban Giants File, Yates County History Center.

56. MacAlpine, "The Penn Yan Colored Giants," *Yates Post* (September 2007), Yates County History Center; Penn Yan Colored Giants File, Yates County History Center.

2. Smilin' Bob Douglas and the Renaissance Big Five

1. The first two professional black teams included the Incorporators of New York in 1911 under Will Anthony Madden, and Loendi of Pittsburgh in 1913 under Cumberland Posey.

2. Nomination form, "Robert L. Douglas" file, Naismith memorial Basketball Hall of Fame; James Douglas, phone interview with writer, June 26, 1994.

3. *New York Amsterdam News*, June 12, 1948, July 21, 1979; Edna and Art Rust, *Art Rust's Illustrated History of the Black Athlete* (Garden City, NY: Doubleday, 1985), 298–99.

4. *New York Age*, April 9, 1921, April 16, 1921, April 23, 1921. The nine-member MBA included Alpha PCC, Borough AC, St. Christopher, Spartan FC, St. Mark's, Dunbar AC, Titan AC, Salem-Crescent AC, and Oriental AC.

5. *New York Amsterdam News*, December 20, 1922, January 3, 1923.

6. *New York Age*, November 4, 1922.

7. *New York Amsterdam News*, October 24, 1923; Bruce Newman, "Yesterday," *Sports Illustrated,* October 22, 1979, 1.

8. *New York Amsterdam News,* December 16, 1944.

9. Ibid., November 7, 1923.

10. See Susan Rayl, "African American Ownership: Bob Douglas and the Rens," in *Basketball Jones,* ed. Todd Boyd and Kenneth L. Shropshire (New York: New York University Press, 2000), 104–22.

11. *New York Age*, March 1, 1924; March 15, 1924.

12. *Pittsburgh Courier*, October 25, 1924.

13. *New York Amsterdam News*, January 28, 1925; October 7, 1925.

14. For an excellent history of the Original Celtics, see Murry Nelson, *The Originals: The New York Celtics Invent Modern Basketball* (Bowling Green, OH: Bowling Green State University Popular Press), 1999.

15. *Pittsburgh Courier*, January 24, 1925; *Interstate Tattler*, March 27, 1925. A second match-up with the Original Celtics at the Renaissance Ballroom drew a record crowd, despite a 49–38 loss. *New York Amsterdam News*, December 9, 1925. The Rens lost to the Original Celtics, 31–29, at the Orange Armory in New Jersey. Still, approximately 3,000 spectators attended, one-sixth of whom were black.

16. *New York Amsterdam News*, December 23, 1925. In a portion of an article from the *Daily Mirror*, a white newspaper, reprinted by the *Amsterdam News*, Douglas is referred to as "wily" and "the sheik of West 131st street."

17. *New York Amsterdam News*, February 3, 1926. The teams played at the Orange Armory in New Jersey, with the Rens winning, 32–28; February 24, 1926. In this game the Rens did not stand a chance against the bigger, taller, and more talented Celtic squad.

18. *Pittsburgh Courier*, March 7, 1925.

19. *New York Amsterdam News*, November 18, 1925. The Rens lost to the Nonpareils, 37–34.

20. Ibid., September 3, 1925. Douglas catered to the public while limiting his own financial gain.

21. Ibid., February 10, 1926.

22. Ibid., April 21, 1926; *Chicago Defender*, April 24, 1926.

23. *Pittsburgh Courier*, December 1, 1928.

24. *New York Amsterdam News*, August 25, 1926; October 20, 1926.

25. Ibid., March 30, 1927.

26. Ibid., November 2, 1927. The Rens lost to the Brooklyn Dodgers, 36–29.

27. Ibid., January 18, 1928; January 25, 1928. By mid-January 1928, however, the team played without the services of Hilton Slocum, who had pneumonia; Fats Jenkins, who had the flu; and William Sanders, who suffered with a badly sprained ankle. Harold Mayers

played with an injured finger, and George Fiall displayed several bruises; April 18, 1928; *Pittsburgh Courier*, February 11, 1928, 2nd sec.

28. *New York Amsterdam News*, January 16, 1929,

29. Ibid., February 6, 1929; *Interstate Tattler*, February 8, 1929.

30. *Chicago Defender*, February 9, 1929.

31. Ocania Chalk, *Pioneers of Black Sport* (New York: Dodd, Mead, 1975), 94.

32. Gilbert Osofsky, *Harlem: The Making of a Ghetto* (New York: Harper & Row, 1963), 6–137, 140.

33. *New York Amsterdam News*, August 14, 1929.

34. Ibid., October 23, 1929. The Central Opera House owned the Original Celtic team at this time.

35. See Susan Rayl, "The New York Renaissance Professional Black Basketball Team 1923–1950" (Doctoral diss., Pennsylvania State University, 1996), 6–189, 491–93.

36. *Pittsburgh Courier*, November 14, 1931, 2nd sec.; *New York Amsterdam News*, February 24, 1932. The Rens defeated the New Jersey Hebrews, 37–24, March 2, 1932.

37. *Chicago Defender*, January 21, 1933; February 4, 1933; *Pittsburgh Courier*, January 28, 1933.

38. *New York Amsterdam News*, April 13, 1932. The Rens defeated George Gregory's team, 39–21; *New York Age*, April 23, 1932; May 7, 1932.

39. *New York Age*, January 20, 1934; Bruce Newman, "Yesterday," *Sports Illustrated*, October 22, 1979, 1; *The (Moorestown, NJ) News Chronicle*, July 25, 1963.

40. James Douglas, phone interview with author, June 26, 1994.

41. *New York Amsterdam News*, January 11, 1933, January 18, 1933; February 1, 1933; *Pittsburgh Courier*, January 28, 1933, 2nd sec.; February 4, 1933, 2nd sec.; *Chicago Defender*, January 28, 1933; February 4, 1933.

42. *New York Amsterdam News*, March 1, 1933; *Pittsburgh Courier*, March 4, 1933, 2nd sec. As a result of the accident, Johnny Holt was injured and unable to play the rest of the season.

43. *New York Amsterdam News*, March 8, 1933; March 15, 1933; *Pittsburgh Courier*, March 11, 1933; March 18, 1933.

44. *New York Amsterdam News*, March 29, 1933; April 5, 1933.

45. John Isaacs, interview with the writer, May 14, 1994, Bronx, New York.

46. Stephen Land and George Veras, executive producers, *Basketball: The Dream Teams* (Veras Communications, 2000), first aired June 6, 2000, History Channel.

47. *New York Amsterdam News*, February 2, 1935; *Chicago Defender*, February 2, 1935; John Isaacs, interview with writer, May 14, 1994.

48. *Pittsburgh Courier*, February 15, 1936.

49. Ibid., September 19, 1936, 2nd sec.

50. *Pittsburgh Courier*, December 19, 1936, 2nd sec. From Philadelphia, Clayton had played basketball for Savoy of Chicago, and also first base for the Chicago American Giants in 1935; *New York Amsterdam News*, January 2, 1937. A star for Textile High School and named to the 1936 *World Telegram* All-City Team, Isaacs stood six feet and weighed 190 pounds. "His playing ability and temperament fits him to become an important cog in the fast moving Rennie team," stated Romeo Dougherty about Issacs; November 27, 1937. At 5'7" and 148 pounds, the twenty-year-old Badger was quick on the floor and an accurate shooter. He had played with several teams, including the Marvels, the New York Collegians, the Red Wings, and the Passaics; *Chicago Defender*, November 27, 1937. Al Johnson had been a star player for the University of Illinois.

51. *New York Amsterdam News*, October 15, 1938; October 29, 1938; November 5, 1938; *Pittsburgh Courier*, April 23, 1938; November 19, 1938. An All-New York City center, Gates had graduated in the spring from Ben Franklin High, where he played varsity basketball for four years and served as captain for three. At twenty-one years of age, 6'2" and 191 pounds, Gates had played basketball for ten years with the Harlem YMCA Seniors, the Passaic Crescents, and the Harlem Yankees. Plans to play for Clark University in Atlanta fell through when he decided to return home after just a few days into the semester. Prior to the Rens, Puggy Bell played basketball for nine years with the Harlem YMCA Midgets team, the Harlem YMCA Seniors, the Passaic Crescents, and the Harlem Yankees. Bell was twenty-three years old, 6'0" and 175 pounds.

52. *Chicago Defender*, January 9, 1937; January 16, 1937. The Rens defeated Kentucky State, 50–33; January 23, 1937.

53. John Isaacs, interview with the writer, May 14, 1994.

54. *New York Amsterdam News*, October 29, 1938; November 19, 1938; *Pittsburgh Courier*, April 23, 1938.

55. *Chicago Defender*, December 10, 1938; December 24, 1938; *New York Amsterdam News*, December 17, 1938.

56. *Pittsburgh Courier*, January 7, 1939.

57. *Chicago Defender*, January 28, 1939; February 4, 1939; March 4, 1939.

58. John Isaacs, presentations at Cortland College, New York, April 1987 and May 1988.

59. John Isaacs, interview with the author, May 14, 1994.

60. *Chicago Defender*, March 4, 1939.

61. *Pittsburgh Courier*, February 11, 1939.

62. *Pittsburgh Courier*, March 18, 1939. Douglas requested a $150 guarantee and 40 percent of the profits, which Saperstein viewed as unreasonable, and offered a game with Saperstein's team on March 14 or 21, but the Globetrotters were reportedly booked on those two dates; *Chicago Defender*, March 18, 1939. The Globetrotters defeated the Celtics, 37–24.

63. *Chicago Herald and Examiner*, March 15, 1939; *Sheboygan Press*, March 22, 1939. The twelve teams included the Chicago All-Americans (Harmons), New York Yankees, Harlem Globetrotters, Clarksburgh Oilers, Illini Grads, New York Renaissance, Michigan House of David, Sheboygan Redskins, Fort Wayne Harvesters, Cleveland White Horses, Oshkosh All-Stars, and the New York Celtics. For an excellent year-by-year history of the World Professional Tournament, see John Schleppi, *Chicago's Showcase of Basketball: The World Tournament of Professional Basketball and the College All-Star Game* (Haworth, NJ: St. Johann Press, 2008).

64. *Oshkosh Daily Northwestern*, March 27, 1939.

65. *Sheboygan Press*, March 28, 1939; *Chicago Daily Tribune*, March 28, 1939; *Pittsburgh Courier*, April 1, 1939.

66. *Oshkosh Daily Northwestern*, March 29, 1939. Gates, Cooper, Smith, Bell, Saitch, Clayton, and Isaacs played in the championship game. The Renaissance team won $1,000 in prize money.

67. *Chicago Defender*, April 8, 1939; *New York Amsterdam News*, April 8, 1939, 19. Winning the World Professsional Tournament gave the Rens a 112-7 season.

68. *New York Amsterdam News*, November 4, 1939. The 1939–40 Renaissance team included Eyre Saitch—captain, Tarzan Cooper, Willie Smith, John Isaacs, Pop Gates, Puggy Bell, and Zach Clayton; *Chicago Defender*, December 16, 1939.

69. *New York Amsterdam News*, January 6, 1940; *Afro-American*, January 6, 1940; January 13, 1940.

70. *Afro-American*, January 13, 1940; *Pittsburgh Courier*, January 20, 1940; February 3, 1940; *New York Amsterdam News*, February 10, 1940; *Chicago Defender*, February 10, 1940.

71. *Oshkosh Daily Northwestern*, March 19, 1940; March 20, 1940; March 21, 1940; *Chicago Defender*, March 23, 1940; March 30, 1940. Approximately 10,000 fans attended the final games.

72. James Douglas, telephone interview with the writer, June 26, 1994.

73. *Pittsburgh Courier*, December 14, 1940; *New York Amsterdam News*, February 22, 1941, 19; *Chicago Defender*, March 1, 1941.

74. *Afro-American*, November 2, 1940; *New York Amsterdam News*, November 2, 1940.

75. *Pittsburgh Courier*, December 14, 1940; December 21, 1940.

76. *Chicago Defender*, March 1, 1941; March 8, 1941, 24.

77. *Chicago Defender*, March 8, 1941. The other thirteen teams were the Chicago Bruins, Oshkosh All-Stars, Sheboygan Redskins, Kenosha Royals, Newark NY Elks, Rochester Seagrams, Dayton Sucher Wonders, Indianapolis Kautskys, Fort Wayne Zollners, Davenport Iowa Rockets, Detroit Eagles, Bismarck North Dakota Phantoms, and the SPHAs.

78. *Oshkosh Daily Northwestern*, March 17, 1941; March 18, 1941. The Globetrotters defeated the Newark Elks, but were eliminated by the Detroit Eagles, while the Rens defeated the Dayton Suchers and the Kenosha Royals.

79. *Oshkosh Daily Northwestern*, March 19, 1941; March 20, 1941; *New York Amsterdam News*, March 29, 1941. Before 12,000 spectators, the Detroit Eagles won the pro tournament by defeating Oshkosh, the NBL champions, 39–37, in a heartbreaking game.

80. *Afro-American*, June 21, 1941.

81. John Isaacs, interview with the writer, May 14, 1994; James Douglas, phone interview with the writer, June 26, 1994. Bob Douglas served as a member of a local draft board in New York City.

82. *New York Amsterdam News*, November 1, 1941; *Pittsburgh Courier*, November 1, 1941. Hillary Brown, a tall and powerful pivot player from Chicago, was good under the basket, and excellent on defense, while Sonny Boswell was a tall, wiry, accurate shooter. Boswell replaced Wilmeth Sidat-Singh who worked at the USO at the 12th Street Branch YMCA in Washington, DC, as a recreation advisor. Sonny Woods, short, stocky, and fearless, had recently turned professional. Returning players included John Isaacs, Zach Clayton, Puggy Bell, Charlie Isles, and Willie Smith, the captain.

83. *Afro-American*, December 20, 1941.

84. *Pittsburgh Courier*, December 6, 1941; *Chicago Defender*, December 6, 1941; December 13, 1941.

85. *Pittsburgh Courier*, February 28, 1942; *New York Amsterdam News*, February 28, 1942.

86. *New York Amsterdam News*, March 21, 1942.

87. Ibid., March 28, 1942. The Rens beat Fort Wayne, 63–61; East Liverpool, 63–45; and the Bruins, 62–51. The Rens won $5,000 for their efforts.

88. *The Afro-American*, April 18, 1942; John Isaacs, interview with the writer, August 17, 1995.

89. *New York Amsterdam News*, December 19, 1942, 18; *Chicago Defender*, December 19, 1942. The Rens defeated the College All-Stars, 41–31.

90. *New York Amsterdam News*, December 26, 1942; *People's Voice*, January 2, 1943.

91. *New York Amsterdam News*, March 27, 1943. Dolly King, Bricktop Wright, Pop Gates, Zach Clayton, Johnny Isaacs, Sonny Woods, Charlie Isles, Tarzan Cooper, and Puggy Bell played for the Washington Bears; *Pittsburgh Courier*, April 10, 1943.

92. *People's Voice*, October 23, 1943; *New York Amsterdam News*, October 23, 1943, B; October 30, 1943, B. The 1943–44 Rens included Clarence "Puggy" Bell and Pop Gates as the nucleus of the team, as well as Zach Clayton, Charlie Isles, Eddie Wright, Hank DeZonie, Benny Garrett, and John Wilson. Willie Smith came from Cleveland to play for the Rens against the Celtics, the 156th meeting between the two teams.

93. *People's Voice*, November 13, 1943; *New York Amsterdam News*, November 13, 1943, B. DeZonie had played for the YMCA and Clark College; November 20, 1943, B; November 18, 1944, B; December 2, 1944, B.

94. *New York Amsterdam News*, March 16, 1944, B; March 31, 1945, A.

95. Ibid., April 8, 1944, B. The Rens lost to Fort Wayne, 42–38, and to the Globetrotters, 37–29. Fort Wayne won the sixth annual pro tourney by defeating the Brooklyn Eagles, 50–33.

96. Ibid., March 31, 1945, A. Playing for the Rens were Eddie Wright, Bricktop Wright, Zach Clayton, Benny Garrett, Lenny Pearson, Hank DeZonie, and Willie Smith; *Afro-American*, March 31, 1945; *People's Voice*, March 31, 1945. The Rens defeated the Indianapolis Stars, 67–59, and the Pittsburgh Raiders, 61–52, in the first two rounds. The Rens lost in the semifinals to the Fort Wayne Zollners, 68–45. In the final games, Fort Wayne defeated the Dayton Acme Aviators, 78–52, and in the consolation game the Chicago Gears beat the Rens, 64–55.

97. *Pittsburgh Courier*, March 31, 1945.

98. *New York Amsterdam News*, October 27, 1945; November 3, 1945. Puggy Bell, Zach Clayton, Hank DeZonie, and Eddie Younger were the core of the team. Douglas looked forward to the return of Sonny Woods from the army at Thanksgiving, and he allowed players who had previously left the Rens to rejoin the team.

99. *People's Voice*, November 17, 1945; December 1, 1945; December 8, 1945; December 15, 1945; January 22, 1945.

100. Ibid., March 16, 1946.

101. *Oshkosh Daily Northwestern*, March 28, 1946. Hank DeZonie led the Rens over Toldeo with 21 points. Dayton held the previous record with 80 points over the Chicago Gears in the 1945 tournament; March 30, 1946. Members of the Rens included King, Bell, Isles, Younger, DeZonie, Wood, Gates, and Cumberland. Pop Gates was the high scorer with 15 points. The score was 21–20 at the half; *Chicago Defender*, April 6, 1946. The Rens had gone out to celebrate, after they broke the tournament record on Wednesday in their defeat of Toledo. Renaissance players were observed at the El Grotto nightclub until 4 A.M. and others were out late the next night, while Oshkosh players observed strict training rules. No Ren players were named to the all-tournament team.

102. *New York Amsterdam News*, October 19, 1946.

103. Ibid., December 21, 1946.

104. *People's Voice*, February 15, 1947.

105. *New York Amsterdam News*, November 2, 1946, 13. Clifton at 6'8" and 230 pounds, had played for Wendell Phillips High School in Chicago and Xavier University in New Orleans. At least six teams bid for Clifton, including Abe Saperstein of the Globetrotters, but reportedly Clifton wanted to come to New York. Usry served as captain of his Lincoln University team during his junior and senior years (separated by World War II), and led the team to the CIAA Championship in 1946. The CIAA named Usry to their All-Tournament team that year. Douglas carried a large team at first and planned on making cuts as time passed.

106. Ibid., January 4, 1947, 20; *People's Voice*, January 25, 1947; *Pittsburgh Courier*, February 8, 1947.

107. *New York Amsterdam News*, November 23, 1946. The Red Devils featured an integrated team with three black starters, Robinson, George Crowe (Indiana), and Ziggie Marcell (former Globetrotter), and two whites, Eddie Oran (UCLA) and Art Stoefer.

108. http://www.blackfives.org/los-angeles-red-devils/ (retrieved January 20, 2015); *People's Voice*, November 2, 1946.

109. *People's Voice*, March 8, 1947; *New York Amsterdam News*, March 8, 1947.

110. *People's Voice*, March 1, 1947; *New York Amsterdam News*, March 15, 1947; April 5, 1947.

111. *Oshkosh Daily Northwestern*, April 4, 1947; *Chicago Defender*, April 12, 1947. Sonny Woods was the top scorer for the Rens with 16 points, followed by Hank DeZonie with 12 against Toledo.

112. Richard E. Lapchick, *Five Minutes to Midnight: Race and Sport in the 1990s* (New York: Madison Books, 1991), 4–196. Bruce Newman, "Yesterday," *Sports Illustrated*, October 22, 1979, 1–106.

113. *New York Amsterdam News*, October 25, 1947; Pop Gates, phone interview with the writer, July 21, 1994. Clarence "Puggy" Bell retired from the Rens and became a policeman in the Riverton Housing Project. Hank DeZonie, Eddie Younger, Sonny Woods, George Crowe, Jim Usry, and Tom Sealy rounded out the 1947–48 team. Eric Illidge returned as road manager.

114. *New York Amsterdam News*, November 15, 1947; November 22, 1947; December 20, 1947; *People's Voice*, January 31, 1948.

115. *People's Voice*, January 31, 1948; *New York Amsterdam News*, March 6, 1948.

116. *New York Amsterdam News*, April 17, 1948.

117. *Chicago Defender*, August 7, 1948; *New York Amsterdam News*, October 23, 1948.

118. *New York Amsterdam News*, November 6, 1948. The 1948–49 Renaissance team included captain Pop Gates, Dolly King, George Crowe, Hank DeZonie, Duke Cumberland, Jim Usry, Tom Sealy, Sonny Woods, Puggy Bell, and John Williams.

119. *Dayton Journal*, November 13, 1948. Glass backboards were used in the Dayton Coliseum for the first time; November 15, 1948; November 22, 1948; *Chicago Defender*, December 11, 1948.

120. Murry R. Nelson, *The National Basketball League: A History, 1935–1949* (Jefferson, NC: McFarland & Company, 2009), 3; NBL "Dayton Rens" program, William "Pop" Gates File, Naismith Memorial Basketball Hall of Fame Library, Springfield, Massachusetts.

121. *Dayton Journal*, December 18, 1948; *New York Amsterdam News*, December 25, 1948; *Pittsburgh Courier*, December 25, 1948.

122. *Dayton Journal*, December 20, 1948; December 23, 1948.

123. Ibid., December 28, 1948. George Crowe was in a Dayton hospital with the flu, Victor Craft went to a Milwaukee hospital for treatment of eye bruises, and Jim Usry was out for another week recuperating. *New York Amsterdam News*, January 1, 1949.

124. *Dayton Herald Journal*, January 13, 1949; February 9, 1949; February 10, 1949; February 14, 1949; February 19, 1949; March 24, 1949,

125. *Oshkosh Daily Northwestern*, April 1, 1949. The Rens earned a 14-26 record. Added to the 2-17 record of Detroit, the combined record for the season was 16-43; Pop Gates, phone interview with the writer, July 21, 1994; *Chicago Defender*, May 28, 1949.

126. *Chicago Defender*, May 28, 1949; *N.Y. Rens vs. Eastern College All-Stars program*,

November 4, 1952, Johnny Walker File, The Schomburg Center for Research in Black Culture, Harlem, New York; *New York Amsterdam News*, November 29, 1952.

127. See *New York Amsterdam News*, March 8, 1952; November 29, 1952; January 10, 1953; January 31, 1953; December 19, 1953.

128. http://www.hoophall.com/hall-of-famers-index/ (retrieved June 22, 2016).

3. The Philadelphia Tribune Newsgirls: African American Women's Basketball at Its Best

1. Charles Ashley Hardy III, "Race and Opportunity: Black Philadelphia during the Era of the Great Migration, 1916–1930" (PhD diss., Temple University, 1989), 70ff, 135.

2. Stephanie Yvette Felix, "Committed to Their Own: African American Women Leaders in the YWCA: The YWCA of Germantown, 1870–1970" (PhD diss., Temple University, 1999), 95ff.

3. *Philadelphia Tribune*, September 19, 26, 1929, October 3, 1929; US Census Manuscript, Philadelphia County, 1920, ED 1477; 1930, ED 21–243.

4. *Philadelphia Tribune*, November 14, 1929, March 13, 1930, April 3, 1930.

5. Ibid., October 16, 1930; Pamela Grundy, "Ora Washington, the First Black Female Athletic Star," in *Out of the Shadows: A History of African American Athletes,* ed. David K. Wiggins (Fayetteville: The University of Arkansas Press, 2006), 84–85; US Census Manuscript, Caroline County, VA, 1910, ED 17; Philadelphia County, 1930, 51–780; Telephone interview, James Bernard Childs, May 29, 2014.

6. *Philadelphia Tribune*, February 12, February 26, 1931.

7. Ibid., April 2, April 9, 1931.

8. Ibid., November 28, 1929, December 5, 1929, November 5, 1931.

9. Ibid., January 22, 1931.

10. Pamela Grundy and Susan Shackelford, *Shattering the Glass: The Remarkable History of Women's Basketball* (New York: New Press, 2005), 68.

11. US Census Manuscript, Philadelphia County, 1920, ED 632.

12. *Chicago Defender*, November 21, 1931; *Philadelphia Tribune*, November 12, 1931, December 24, 1931, January 14, January 28, 1932.

13. *Philadelphia Tribune,* February 18, 1932.

14. Ibid., February 25, 1932.

15. Ibid., March 10, March 17, 1932.

16. Ibid., March 31, 1932, April 7, 1932; Grundy and Shackelford, *Shattering the Glass*, 67–68.

17. *Philadelphia Tribune*, October 3, 1932, November 24, 1932.

18. Ibid., January 19, 1933.

19. *Pittsburgh Courier*, January 7, January 28, 1933; *Philadelphia Tribune*, January 19, January 26, 1933, March 2, 1933.

20. *Philadelphia Tribune,* March 2, March 16, March 30, 1933, April 6, April 13, April 20, 1933; *Amsterdam News*, April 5, 1933; *Chicago Defender*, April 29, 1933; *Pittsburgh Courier*, April 29, 1933.

21. *Philadelphia Tribune*, October 19, November 9, November 23, 1933.

22. Ibid., November 23, 1933; December 7, December 23, 1933.

23. Ibid., November 23, 1933, November 30, 1933, January 26, 1934, February 3, 1934, March 3, 1934.

24. Ibid., January 18, January 25, 1934, February 22, 1934.

25. Ibid., February 1, 1934, March 1, 1934.

26. As quoted in Rita Liberti, "'We Were Ladies, We Just Played Like Boys': African American Womanhood and Competitive Basketball at Bennett College, 1928–1942," *Journal of Sport History* 26, no. 3 (Fall 1999): 573–74; *Philadelphia Tribune*, March 22, 1934.

27. *Philadelphia Tribune*, March 22, 1924; *Chicago Defender*, March 24, 1934.

28. *Philadelphia Tribune*, March 29, 1934.

29. *Philadelphia Tribune*, April 12, April 19, April 26, 1934, May 3, 1934; *Pittsburgh Courier*, April 28, 1934. The *Courier* reported the completion of the suspended game on Friday, April 20 with Tribs winning, 18–17.

30. *Philadelphia Tribune*, October 25, 1934, November 15, 1934.

31. Ibid., December 6, 1934; *Chicago Defender*, December 8, 1934.

32. Duke Hill has been referred to as Dickie Hill earlier in this essay.

33. *Philadelphia Tribune*, December 20, 1934, January 3, January 24, January 31, 1935; *Chicago Defender*, December 22, 1934.

34. *Philadelphia Tribune*, February 28, 1935, *Amsterdam News*, March 23, 1935; Grundy, "Ora Mae Washington," 84.

35. *Amsterdam News,* April 20, 1935.

36. *Philadelphia Tribune*, January 16, 1936; *Chicago Defender,* February 22, 1936.

37. *Philadelphia Tribune* January 9, February 13, 1936; *Atlanta Daily World,* April 9, 1936.

38. *Philadelphia Tribune,* March 28, May 14, 1936.

39. Ibid., October 31, 1935.

40. Ibid., September 5, November 28, December 5, December 12, 1935; March 5, March 12, 1936; *Atlanta Daily World,* January 12, 1936.

41. *Philadelphia Tribune,* September 17, November 12, November 19, December 3, 1936; *Atlanta Daily World*, December 2, 1936; *Amsterdam News*, December 5, 1936.

42. *Philadelphia Tribune*, January 7, January 28, 1937.

43. Ibid., November 25, December 2, December 30, 1937; *Atlanta Daily World*, February 25, 1938.

44. *Philadelphia Tribune,* December 23, December 30, 1937, January 6, 1938.

45. Ibid., October 21, October 28, 1937.

46. Ibid., January 7, January 14, January 28, February 11, March 4, 1937.

47. Ibid., February 3, February 10, February 17, February 24, 1938

48. *Pittsburgh Courier*, February 5, 1938; *Atlanta Daily World,* February 15, March 20, 1938.

49. *Atlanta Daily World*, February 20, February 21, February 25, February 27, 1938; March 3, March 4, 1938.

50. *Pittsburgh Courier*, February 5, 1938.

51. Grundy and Shackelford, *Shattering the Glass,* 82–83.

52. *Philadelphia Tribune*, March 31, 1938, April 7, April 9, 1938.

53. Ibid., October 27, November 10, 1938.

54. Ibid., November 30, 1939, January 4, January 11, 1940, March 14, March 21, March 28, 1940; *Atlanta Daily World*, December 1, 1938, December 2, 1939; *Amsterdam News,* February 15, 1940.

55. *Philadelphia Tribune,* November 1, November 8, 1941, December 6, 1941; *Chicago Defender,* August 16, 1941, October 25, 1941.

56. *Philadelphia Tribune,* December 13, December 20, December 27, 1941, April 4, April 18, 1942, November 21, 1942.

57. *Chicago Defender*, November 6, 1943.

58. US Census Manuscripts, Caroline County, VA, 1910, ED 17; Philadelphia County, 1920, ED 632; Cook County, IL, 1930, ED 16–186; Philadelphia County, 1940, ED 51–1,000.

59. Telephone interview, James Bernard Childs and Brenda Hogue, May 29, 2014.

60. US Census Manuscript, Philadelphia County, 1930, ED 51–780.

61. US Census Manuscript, Philadelphia County, 1920, ED 1477; 1930, ED 51–243.

62. US Census Manuscript, Philadelphia County, 1940, ED 51–313; Pennsauken Twp, Camden County, NJ, 1940, ED 4–105; Woodbury, Gloucester County, NJ, ED 8–63; Montclair, Essex County, NJ, ED 7–538.

4. The Tennessee State Tigerbelles: Cold Warriors of the Track

1. Bobby L. Lovett, "Rudolph, Wilma and the TSU Tigerbelles," *Tennessee Encyclopedia of History and Culture*, ed. Carroll Van West, Connie L. Lester et al. (Nashville: Tennessee Historical Society, 1998), 813–14; Wilma Rudolph of the Tigerbelles racing in the 1960 Rome Olympics is one of the cover images of the state encyclopedia.

2. Tracey M. Salisbury, "First to the Finish Line: The Tennessee State Tigerbelles 1944–1994" (PhD diss., University of North Carolina, Greensboro, 2009); David Maraniss, *Rome 1960: The Olympics That Changed the World* (New York: Simon and Schuster, 2008), 338–39; Jennifer H. Lansbury, *A Spectacular Leap: Black Women Athletes in Twentieth-Century America* (Fayetteville: The University of Arkansas Press, 2014), 133–34.

3. Bobby L. Lovett, *"A Touch of Greatness": A History of Tennessee State University* (Macon, GA: Mercer University Press, 2012), 288–89.

4. Jennifer H. Lansbury graciously shared a transcript of her July 17, 2007, Nashville interview with Ed Temple with the author.

5. Salisbury, "First to the Finish Line," 97.

6. Lansbury interview; Lovett, *"A Touch of Greatness,"* 293.

7. Earl Clanton III, "Bragg, Daniels and Jenkins Star in Washington Indoor Track Meet," *Chicago Defender*, February 5, 1955.

8. Lovett, *"A Touch of Greatness,"* 292–93.

9. Earl Clanton III, "Consider Temple for Olympic Job," *Chicago Defender*, January 21, 1956.

10. "Tigerbelles Win Tuskegee Relays," *Chicago Defender*, May 19, 1956.

11. Lansbury interview; Salisbury, "First to the Finish Line," 92.

12. Salisbury, "First to the Finish Line," 93.

13. Lovett, *"A Touch of Greatness,"* 293.

14. Tennessee A&I teams in football and basketball achieved national significance in the 1960s and several star players had Hall of Fame careers in the National Football League and the National Basketball Association.

15. Lansbury interview.

16. Thomas Borstelmann, *The Cold War and the Color Line: American Race Relations in the Global Arena* (Cambridge, MA: Harvard University Press, 2001), 122.

17. "U.S. Women Fall Behind in Track," *Washington Post and Times Herald*, September 7, 1958.

18. Lovett, *"A Touch of Greatness,"* 294.

19. Salisbury, "First to the Finish Line," 135.

20. "Tennessee Gals Win 4th Indoor Track Meet," *Chicago Defender*, April 5, 1958.

21. "U.S. Womens [*sic*] Olympic Prospects Look Good," *Chicago Defender*, July 12, 1960.

22. This theme dominates Maraniss's narrative in *Rome 1960*; see chapter 2 in particular, quote is from p. 24.

23. Fred Russell, "Wilma Wins 2nd Gold Medal," *Nashville Banner*, September 5, 1960; "A&I Girls Set Relay Mark," ibid., September 7, 1960; "A&I Girls Win Relay Gold Medal," ibid., September 8, 1960.

24. "Wilma Getting Taste of Fame," *Chicago Defender*, September 12, 1960.

25. "Double Spring Champion Hurries Only on Track," *New York Times*, September 6, 1960.

26. "World Speed Queen," *New York Times*, September 9, 1960.

27. Rob Bagchi, "50 Stunning Olympic Moments No. 35: Wilma Rudolph's Triple Gold in 1960," *Guardian*, June 1, 2012.

28. Ibid.

29. "Wilma Rudolph Pauses Briefly for Medal, Visit and Plaudits," *New York Times*, September 27, 1960.

30. Lovett, *"A Touch of Greatness*," 295.

31. John Steen, "Wilma Rudolph Earns Grant for Her College," *Washington Post Times Herald*, April 14, 1961.

32. Photographs of Kennedy-Johnson meeting with Wilma Rudolph, images AR6512-A and AR6512-B, John F. Kennedy Presidential Library.

33. Lansbury interview; photographs of the Kennedy-Johnson-Rudolph Oval Office meeting are at John F. Kennedy Presidential Library, images AR6512-A and AR6512-B.

34. Lansbury interview; "Wilma Rudolph Gets Sullivan Sportsmanship Award," *New York Times*, February 26, 1962.

35. Maureen M. Smith, *Wilma Rudolph: A Biography* (Westport, CT: Greenwood Press, 2006), 72. Also see the autobiography, *Wilma: The Story of Wilma Rudolph* (New York: Signet, 1977). Based on the autobiography is a 1977 TV-movie, also titled *Wilma*.

36. A. S. "Doc" Young, "Track for Girls Now 'In,'" *Chicago Defender*, August 22, 1964.

37. Lansbury interview.

38. Salisbury, "First to the Finish Line," 146.

39. "TSU Tigerbelles Continue as Top Women's Track Team," *Chicago Defender*, May 4, 1968.

40. Sara M. Evans, *Personal Politics: The Roots of Women's Liberation in the Civil Rights Movement and the New Left* (New York: Knopf, 1979), is a classic study on this theme. Also see Kenneth Denlinger, "Now It Takes a Sermon: Tiger Bell Tradition to Remain Swift," *Washington Post*, June 27, 1976.

41. "Tennessee State Honors Coach with a New Track," *New York Times*, April 9, 1978; Lovett, *"A Touch of Greatness*," 298.

42. Lovett, *"A Touch of Greatness*," 298–99.

43. Ibid., 300–301.

44. Ira Kerknow, "Forever the Regal Champion," *New York Times*, November 13, 1994.

45. Athelia Knight, "Olympic Track Star Wilma Rudolph Dies," *Washington Post*, November 13, 1994.

46. Richard Goldstein, "Mae Faggs Starr, Champion and Track Mentor, Dies at 67," *New York Times*, February 11, 2000.

47. Salisbury, "First to the Finish Line," 160.

48. Ibid., 166.

49. Dwight Lewis, "Legendary TSU Coach Ed Temple's Impact Is Undeniable," *Nashville Tennessean*, June 26, 2014.

5. The National Interscholastic Basketball Tournament: The Crown Jewel of African American High School Sports during the Era of Segregation

1. Robert N. Mattingly, "History of the I.S.S.A.A.," in *Official Handbook, Inter-Scholastic Athletic Association of the Middle Atlantic States*, ed. William A. Joiner and Edwin B. Henderson (New York: American Sports Publishing, 1910), 15–23.

2. Charles Herbert Thompson, "The History of the National Basketball Tournaments for Black High Schools" (PhD diss., Louisiana State University, 1980), 10–12.

3. Bob Koska, *Hot Potato* (Charlottesville: University of Virginia Press, 2004), 11–21; Mattingly, "History of the I.S.S.A.A."; Edwin Bancroft Henderson, *The Negro in Sports,* rev. ed. (Washington, DC: Associated Publishers, 1939), 238, 273–75; Thompson, "The History of the National Basketball Tournaments for Black High Schools," 12–13.

4. W. H. J. Beckett, "The Place of Athletics in Secondary Schools," *Official Handbook, Inter-Scholastic Athletic Association of the Middle States*, ed. William A. Joiner and Edwin B. Henderson (New York: American Sports Publishing, 1910), 71–72.

5. Lewis E. Johnson, "Basket Ball in Washington," in *Spalding's Official Handbook, Inter-Scholastic Athletic Association of the Middle Atlantic States*, ed. William A. Joiner and Edwin B. Henderson (New York: American Sports Publishing, 1910), 67–68; Koska, *Hot Potato,* 3 and 26.

6. Edwin B. Henderson, "Report of Secretary of the Public Schools Athletic League of Washington, DC," in *Official Handbook, Inter-Scholastic Athletic Association of the Middle Atlantic States*, ed. Edwin B. Henderson and William A. Joiner (New York: American Sports Publishing, 1911), 17–27; *Washington Post*, March 12, 1911; *Chicago Defender*, November 26, 1925; *Chicago Defender*, December 6, 1930; David K. Wiggins, "Edwin B. Henderson: Physical Educator, Civil Rights Activist, and Chronicler of African American Athletes," *Research Quarterly for Exercise and Sport* 70, no. 2 (June 1999): 90.

7. C. Robert Barnett, "'The Finals': West Virginia's Black Basketball Tournament, 1925–1927," *Goldenseal* 9, no. 2 (Summer 1983): 30–36; *Chicago Defender*, March 20, 1926; *Chicago Defender*, March 27, 1926; *Afro-American*, June 5, 1937.

8. *Chicago Defender*, April 2, 1921; *Chicago Defender* (nat. ed.), March 7, 1925; *Chicago Defender*, March 19, 1927; *Chicago Defender*, February 25, 1928. Thompson, "The History of the National Basketball Tournaments for Black High Schools," 14–15.

9. Richard B. Pierce, "More Than a Game: The Political Meaning of High School Basketball in Indianapolis," in *Sport and the Color Line: Black Athletes and Race Relations in Twentieth-Century America*, ed. Patrick B. Miller and David K. Wiggins (New York: Routledge, 2004), 191–209; *Chicago Defender*, January 31, 1920; *Chicago Defender* (nat. ed.), March 28, 1925; *Chicago Defender* (nat. ed.), May 11, 1929; Charles W. Whitten, "The Colored High Schools of Illinois," *Interscholastics: A Discussion of Interscholastic Contests* (Chicago: Illinois High School Association, 1950), 134–39; Thompson, "The History of the National Basketball Tournaments for Black High Schools," 18.

10. Whitten, "The Colored High Schools of Illinois," 136–37.

11. *Chicago Defender*, May 21, 1921; *Chicago Defender*, May 17, 1924.

12. *Chicago Defender*, March 25, 1922; *Chicago Defender*, May 17, 1924; *Chicago Defender*, May 22, 1926.

13. *Chicago Defender*, May 3, 1930; *Chicago Defender*, April 25, 1931; *Chicago Defender*, May 16, 1931; *Chicago Defender* (nat. ed.), March 17, 1934.

14. Robert Pruter, *The Rise of American High School Sports and the Search for Control: 1880–1930* (Syracuse, NY: Syracuse University Press, 2013), 68–69; Mattingly, "History of the I.S.S.A.A.," 15–23; *Chicago Defender*, March 28, 1931.

15. Thompson, "The History of the National Basketball Tournaments for Black High Schools," 20–26; *Chicago Defender*, February 9, 1929.

16. *Chicago Defender*, March 10, 1928; *Chicago Defender*, March 18, 1931; Thompson, "The History of the National Basketball Tournaments for Black High Schools," 19, 26–27.

17. *Chicago Defender*, March 22, 1930; *Chicago Defender*, March 22, 1930; *Chicago Defender*, March 29, 1930; Thompson, "The History of the National Basketball Tournaments for Black High Schools," 163.

18. *Chicago Defender*, March 28, 1931; Thompson, "The History of the National Basketball Tournaments for Black High Schools," 163.

19. Thompson, "The History of the National Basketball Tournaments for Black High Schools," 28–29.

20. *Chicago Defender*, May 31, 1934; *Chicago Defender* (nat. ed.), April 7, 1934; *Chicago Defender* (nat. ed.), March 23, 1935; Thompson, "The History of the National Basketball Tournaments for Black High Schools," 30–38, 171.

21. Thompson, "The History of the National Basketball Tournaments for Black High Schools," 36–37, 52.

22. Louis Stout, *Shadows of the Past: A History of the Kentucky High School Athletic League* (Lexington, KY: Host Communications, 2006), 10, 36, 39, 51, 54.

23. Milton Golden, "Rosenwald, Julius," *American National Biography Volume 18* (New York: Oxford, 1999), 893–95.

24. Stout, *Shadows of the Past*, 10–13, 67, 74; "Maysville Girls Win State Title," *Chicago Defender*, March 31, 1934.

25. *Chicago Defender* (nat. ed.), April 11, 1936; *Chicago Defender* (nat. ed.), March 18, 1939; Thompson, "The History of the National Basketball Tournaments for Black High Schools," 18, 39–52.

26. *Afro-American,* December 11, 1937; *Afro-American*, December 11, 1937; *Afro-American*, January 7, 1939; *Afro-American*, March 25, 1939; *Afro-American*, April 9, 1940; Thompson, "The History of the National Basketball Tournaments for Black High Schools," 163–97.

27. *Chicago Defender* (nat. ed.), March 16, 1935; *Chicago Defender* (nat. ed.), March 28, 1936; *Chicago Defender* (nat. ed.), April 3, 1937; *Chicago Defender* (nat. ed.), March 18, 1939; *Chicago Defender* (nat. ed.) April 1, 1939; Thompson, "The History of the National Basketball Tournaments for Black High Schools," 56–59, 63–65, 184.

28. Fay Young, *Chicago Defender*, March 16, 1929; *Chicago Defender* (nat. ed.), March 19, 1938; *Chicago Defender* (nat. ed.), April 13, 1940.

29. *Chicago Defender* (nat. ed.), April 20, 1940.

30. Whitten, "The Colored High Schools of Illinois," 134–39; Thompson, "The History of the National Basketball Tournaments for Black High Schools," 188.

31. Whitten, "The Colored High Schools of Illinois," 137–38; *Peoria Journal-Star*, March 4, 1973; Pat Heston, "More Than a Game: High School Basketball's Victory Over

Segregation," in *100 Years of Madness: The Illinois High School Association Boys' Basketball Tournament* (Bloomington: Illinois High School Association, 2006), 58–61; Taylor H. A. Bell, *Sweet Charlie, Dike, Cazzie, and Bobby Joe* (Urbana: University of Illinois Press, 2004), 41–44.

32. Troy D. Paino, *Journal of Sport History* 28, no. 1 (Spring 2001): 66–72; Thompson, "The History of the National Basketball Tournaments for Black High Schools," 192–93.

33. *Chicago Defender* (nat. ed.), March 23, 1935; *Chicago Defender*, March 27, 1937; Thompson, "The History of the National Basketball Tournaments for Black High Schools," 66–67.

34. *Chicago Defender* (nat. ed.), March 22, 1941; *Chicago Defender* (nat. ed.), April 4, 1942; Thompson, "The History of the National Basketball Tournaments for Black High Schools," 68–69, 193; The participation figures Thompson uses may be problematic, when one examines his Tournament Summary for 1942.

35. *Chicago Defender* (nat. ed.), March 16, 1935; *Chicago Defender* (nat. ed.), January 25, 1941; Thompson, "The History of the National Basketball Tournaments for Black High Schools," 49, 192, 197.

36. *Chicago Defender* (nat. ed.), March 24, 1945; *Chicago Defender* (nat. ed.), April 7, 1945; Thompson, "The History of the National Basketball Tournaments for Black High Schools," 70–72, 85; Linda T. Wynn, "Pearl High School Basketball: National and State Championships," Profiles of American Americans in Tennessee, Nashville Conference on African-American History and Culture, Tennessee State University, 2007, http://www.tnstate.edu/library/digitalresources/profiles_of_african_americans_in_tennessee.aspx.

37. Thompson, "The History of the National Basketball Tournaments for Black High Schools," 72–73.

38. *Chicago Defender* (nat. ed.), April 20, 1946; *Chicago Defender* (nat. ed.), April 19, 1947; Gerald R. Gems, *Windy City Wars: Labor, Leisure, and Sport in the Making of Chicago* (Lanham, MD: Scarecrow Press, 1997), 181–82; Thompson, "The History of the National Basketball Tournaments for Black High Schools," 75–78, 199–201.

39. Thompson, "The History of the National Basketball Tournaments for Black High Schools," 78–79.

40. "National Prep. Cage Play on March 25–27," *Chicago Defender* (nat. ed.), March 7, 1948; "St. Elizabeth Will Play in Nat'l Tourney," *Chicago Defender* (nat. ed.), March 20, 1948; *Afro-American*, April 4, 1950; Thompson, "The History of the National Basketball Tournaments for Black High Schools," 81–85.

41. *Afro-American*, March 25, 1947; *Afro-American*, March 23, 1948; *Afro-American*, March 22, 1949; *Afro-American*, March 29, 1949.

42. "Southern Trip," *The 1951 Elizabethan* (Chicago: St. Elizabeth High School, 1951), unpaginated; *Afro-American*, April 4, 1951; *Afro-American*, April 10, 1951; Thompson, "The History of the National Basketball Tournaments for Black High Schools," 86–88.

43. *Afro-American*, March 25, 1952; *Afro-American*, March 24, 1953; *Afro-American*, March 31, 1953; Thompson, "The History of the National Basketball Tournaments for Black High Schools," 89–90.

44. *Afro-American*, March 29, 1955; *Afro-American*, March 26, 1956; Barnett, "'The Finals,'" 33–35; Thompson, "The History of the National Basketball Tournaments for Black High Schools," 100–101, 223.

45. *Chicago Tribune*, March 26, 1955; *Chicago Tribune*, March 21, 1957; *Chicago Defender* (nat. ed.), April 13, 1957; "By Their Fruits You Shall Know Them," *'57 Seniorama*

(Chicago: St. Elizabeth, 1957): 17; "The Memory Lingers On . . . ," *1961 Spirit* (Chicago: St. Elizabeth, 1961), unpaginated; Thompson, "The History of the National Basketball Tournaments for Black High Schools," 101–2, 211, 214, 217.

46. Wynn, "Pearl High School"; Thompson, "The History of the National Basketball Tournaments for Black High Schools," 102–3.

47. *Chicago Defender* (nat. ed.), April 11, 1959; Thompson, "The History of the National Basketball Tournaments for Black High Schools," 104–5.

48. *Pittsburgh Courier*, January 26, 1963.

49. Mike Lenehan, *Ramblers: Loyola Chicago 1963—The Team That Changed the Color of College Basketball* (Chicago: Midway, 2013), 79, 85, 89–93.

50. *Tri-State Defender*, April 7, 1961; *Tri-State Defender*, March 24, 1962; Earl S. Clanton III, *Pittsburgh Courier*, March 23, 1963; Thompson, "The History of the National Basketball Tournaments for Black High Schools," 105–9.

51. *Tri-State Defender*, March 24, 1964; Wynn, "Pearl High School"; Gene Peirce, "Nashville Pearl's Short Road to Glory," Tennessee Secondary School Athletic Association, www.tssaa.org/2005Champions/StateBBasketball/Pearl.pdf (accessed December 25, 2012).

52. Thompson, "The History of the National Basketball Tournaments for Black High Schools," 111–15.

53. Ibid., 116–18, 245.

54. Ibid., 118–19.

6. The Black Heart of Dixie: The Turkey Day Classic and Race in Twentieth-Century Alabama

1. *Pittsburgh Courier*, November 25, 1967, 11.

2. For more on the Howard-Lincoln game, see David K. Wiggins, "The Biggest 'Classic' of Them All: The Howard and Lincoln Thanksgiving Day Football Games, 1919–1929," in *Rooting for the Home Team: Sport, Community, and Identity*, ed. Daniel A. Nathan (Urbana: University of Illinois Press, 2013), 36–53. For more on the classic as a staging ground for black success and a theater for black political, cultural, and social disagreements, see Thomas Aiello, *Bayou Classic: The Grambling-Southern Football Rivalry* (Baton Rouge: Louisiana State University Press, 2010).

3. For its part, Howard would also leave Marion in 1887, heading to Birmingham to take advantage of the booming Gilded Age iron economy. Howard would remain affiliated with the Baptist church, and in 1965 the school would change its name to Samford University. "William B. Paterson to Booker T. Washington," in *The Papers of Booker T. Washington*, vol. 2, *1860–1889*, ed. Louis Harlan (Urbana: University of Illinois Press, 1972), 319–20.

4. "William B. Paterson to Booker T. Washington," in *The Papers of Booker T. Washington*, vol. 2, 319–20; and "Booker T. Washington to Warren Logan," in ibid., 331–32.

5. "Booker T. Washington to Warren Logan," in ibid., vol. 2, 332.

6. Seay, for his part, was seeking "Montg Col. people to offer some induc[e]ment in money to get it saying that Birmingham wants it also & will make a good offer for it." His was less a concern about race and religion and more a concern about money. "Booker T. Washington to Arthur L. Brooks," in ibid., 343–44; "Booker T. Washington to Arthur L. Brooks," in ibid., 344; and "Cornelius Nathaniel Dorsette to Booker T. Washington," in ibid., 321–22.

7. "William B. Paterson to Booker T. Washington," in ibid., 346–47.

8. "Warren Logan to Booker T. Washington," in ibid., 373; "Booker T. Washington to Warren Logan," in ibid., 376; "Booker T. Washington to Warren Logan," in ibid., 376; and "T. W. Coffee to Booker T. Washington," in ibid., 376–77.

9. "Booker T. Washington to William Hooper Councill," in ibid., 307–8.

10. "Cornelius Nathaniel Dorsette to Booker T. Washington," in ibid., 387; and "William Jenkins to Booker T. Washington," in ibid., 459.

11. "Booker T. Washington to William Hooper Councill," in *The Papers of Booker T. Washington*, vol. 3, *1889–1895*, ed. Louis Harlan (Urbana: University of Illinois Press, 1974), 77–78; "Warren Logan to Booker T. Washington," in ibid., 99–100; and "Warren Logan to Booker T. Washington," in ibid., 122–23.

12. "William Burns Paterson to Booker T. Washington," in *The Papers of Booker T. Washington*, vol. 4, *1895–1898*, ed. Louis Harlan (Urbana: University of Illinois Press, 1975), 325.

13. Matthews would go on to Harvard and Boston University Law. A standout athlete, he starred on Harvard's baseball team, became the only black player in the minor Northern League, and then eventually went on to become an assistant US attorney in Boston. He would serve as Marcus Garvey's lawyer and a leading black figure in Republican politics in the 1920s. After the election of Calvin Coolidge, the new president appointed him as an assistant attorney general. For more on Matthews, see Karl Lindholm, "William Clarence Matthews: Brief Life of a Baseball Pioneer, 1877–1928," *Harvard Magazine* (September–October 1998), http://harvardmagazine.com/1998/09/vita.html (accessed June 23, 2013).

14. "James B. Washington to Booker T. Washington," in *The Papers of Booker T. Washington*, vol. 5, *1899–1900*, ed. Louis Harlan (Urbana: University of Illinois Press, 1977), 268; "Booker T. Washington to Warren Logan," in ibid., 270–71.

15. "Tuskegee Yearly Results," College Football Data Warehouse, http://www.cfbdatawarehouse.com/data/div_ii/siac/tuskegee/yearly_results.php?year=1900 (accessed February 14, 2013).

16. Ibid.

17. Quote from *Tuskegee News*, November 7, 1901. See also R. Volney Riser, "Disfranchisement, the US Constitution, and the Federal Courts: Alabama's 1901 Constitutional Convention Debates the Grandfather Clause," *American Journal of Legal History* 48 (July 2006): 237–79; and *Tuskegee News*, November 14, 1901; November 21, 1901; November 2, 1901.

18. "Alabama State Yearly Results," College Football Data Warehouse, http://www.cfbdatawarehouse.com/data/div_iaa/southwestern/alabama_state/yearly_results.php?year=1901 (accessed February 14, 2013); and "Tuskegee University: Golden Tiger Pregame Notes—Game 11," Tuskegee University, athletics.tuskegee.edu/sites/.../Football%20Pre-Game%20Notes.PDF (accessed February 14, 2013).

19. "Leaving Booker T. Washington," *New York World*, October 23, 1904, in *The Papers of Booker T. Washington*, vol. 8, *1904–1906*, ed. Louis Harlan (Urbana: University of Illinois Press, 1979), 105–7.

20. "Tuskegee Yearly Results," College Football Data Warehouse; "Alabama State Yearly Results," College Football Data Warehouse; and "Tuskegee University: Golden Tiger Pregame Notes—Game 11," College Football Data Warehouse.

21. "Tuskegee University: Golden Tiger Pregame Notes—Game 11"; "Booker T. Washington to William Burns Paterson," in *The Papers of Booker T. Washington*, vol. 10,

1909–1911, ed. Louis Harlan (Urbana: University of Illinois Press, 1981), 16; "Booker T. Washington to William Burns Paterson," in ibid., 27–28; and "Booker T. Washington to John William Beverly," in *The Papers of Booker T. Washington,* vol. 13, *1914–1915,* ed. Louis Harlan (Urbana: University of Illinois Press, 1984), 256.

22. United States Federal Census, 1880, Roll 589, Film 1254589, Page 235A; *Montgomery City Directory, 1891* (Montgomery: CJ Allardt and Co., 1891); *Montgomery City Directory, 1893* (Montgomery: Walter Howard, 1893); United States Federal Census, 1910, Roll T624_29, FHL microfilm 1374042, Page 14B; United States Federal Census, 1920, Roll T625_37, Page 1B; and United States Passport Applications, January 2, 1906–March 31, 1925, ARC Identifier 583830/MLR Number A1 534, National Archives and Records Administration, Series M1490, Roll 1611.

23. *Montgomery Advertiser,* February 9, 1921; and Tommy Fields, "The Cramton Conversion," *More,* http://mymaxmore.com/index.php?option=com_content&view=article&id=120:the-cramton-conversion&catid=1:current&Itemid=32 (accessed February 15, 2013).

24. United States Federal Census, 1900, Roll 200, FHL microfilm 1240200, Page 12B; United States Federal Census, 1910, Roll T624_28, FHL microfilm 1374041, Page 3A; United States World War I Draft Registration Cards, 1917–1918, National Archives and Records Administration, M1509, Roll 1509445; Alabama Military Card Files, 1917–1918, Alabama Department of Archives and History, SG017111-3; and United States Federal Census, 1920, Roll T625_36, Page 1B.

25. "Tuskegee University: Golden Tiger Pregame Notes—Game 11."

26. Abbot would continue coaching the Tigers until 1954, the year prior to his death. In that time he would compile 205 wins, far and away the most by any coach in the school's history. Abbott also created the school's women's track and field program in 1937, a program that would go undefeated from its creation until 1942 and would generate six Olympic athletes. *Pittsburgh Courier,* November 22, 1924; *Atlanta Daily World,* November 26, 1957; "Tuskegee Yearly Results," College Football Data Warehouse; "Tuskegee University: Golden Tiger Pregame Notes—Game 11"; "Tuskegee Coaching Records," College Football Data Warehouse, http://www.cfbdatawarehouse.com/data/div_ii/siac/tuskegee/coaching_records.php (accessed February 15, 2013); and "Abbott, Cleveland Leigh (1892–1955)," http://www.blackpast.org/?q=aah/abbott-cleveland-leigh-1892-1955 (accessed June 24, 2013).

27. For more on classics and their role in black collegiate athletics and the black community in general, see Michael Hurd, *Black College Football, 1892–1992: One Hundred Years of History, Education, and Pride* (Marceline, MO: Walsworth Publishing, 2000); David K. Wiggins, "The Biggest 'Classic' of Them All: The Howard and Lincoln Thanksgiving Day Football Games, 1919–1929," in *Rooting for the Home Team: Sport, Community, and Identity,* ed. Daniel A. Nathan (Urbana: University of Illinois Press, 2013), 36–53; Hasan Kwame Jeffries, "Fields of Play: The Mediums through Which Black Athletes Engaged in Sports in Jim Crow Georgia," *Journal of Negro History* 86 (Summer 2001): 264–75; Samuel G. Freedman, *Breaking the Line: The Season in Black College Football That Transformed the Sport and Changed the Course of Civil Rights* (New York: Simon and Schuster, 2013); and Thomas Aiello, *Bayou Classic: The Grambling-Southern Football Rivalry* (Baton Rouge: Louisiana State University Press, 2010).

28. Will Rogers, "Football Needs Plenty of Color," *Washington Post,* November 29, 1925.

29. "Tuskegee Yearly Results," College Football Data Warehouse; "Alabama State Yearly Results," College Football Data Warehouse; "Tuskegee University: Golden Tiger

Pregame Notes—Game 11"; *Atlanta Daily World*, October 31, 1932; November 26, 1957; *Chicago Defender*, October 13, 1928; November 24, 1928; and *New York Amsterdam News*, November 14, 1928.

30. "Tuskegee Yearly Results," College Football Data Warehouse; "Alabama State Yearly Results," College Football Data Warehouse; "Tuskegee University: Golden Tiger Pregame Notes—Game 11"; and *Atlanta Daily World*, November 28, 1952.

31. *McLaurin v. Oklahoma State Regents*, 339 US 637 (1950); *Sweatt v. Painter*, 339 US 629 (1950); *Brown v. Board of Education of Topeka*, 347 US 483 (1954); and *Brown v. Board of Education II*, 349 US 294 (1955). The literature on Emmett Till is obviously vast. For strong general accounts, see Stephen Whitfield, *A Death of the Delta: The Story of Emmett Till* (Baltimore: Johns Hopkins University Press, 1991); and Christopher Mettress, *The Lynching of Emmett Till: A Documentary Narrative* (Charlottesville: University of Virginia Press, 2002).

32. *Browder v. Gayle*, 142 F. Supp. 707 (1956).

33. Randolph Hohle, "The Color of Neoliberalism: The 'Modern Southern Businessman' and Postwar Alabama's Challenge to Racial Desegregation," *Sociological Forum* 27 (March 2012): 142–62. For more on activism in Alabama and the frustrated white response, see David Alan Horowitz, "White Southerners' Alienation and Civil Rights: The Response to Corporate Liberalism, 1956–1965," *Journal of Southern History* 54 (May 1988): 173–200. The story of the work of Alabama activists in the creation of the Montgomery bus boycott is ubiquitous. David J. Garrow's *Bearing the Cross: Martin Luther King, Jr., and the Southern Christian Leadership Conference* (New York: HarperCollins, 1988), for example, carries a thorough description of the boycott and its antecedents, as do many others.

34. Joel Rosenthal, "Southern Black Student Activism: Assimilation vs. Nationalism," *Journal of Negro Education* 44 (Spring 1975): 114–18; and William P. Fidler, "Academic Freedom in the South Today," *AAUP Bulletin* 51 (Winter 1965): 415. For more on this phenomenon, see Thomas Aiello, "Violence Is a Classroom: The 1972 Grambling and Southern Riots and the Trajectory of Black Southern Student Protest," *Louisiana History* 53 (Summer 2012): 261–91.

35. Such is relatively common fare in studies of civil rights, but one of the most accomplished historians of this subject is Michael J. Klarman, whose studies have informed the author's thinking about such matters. See Michael J. Klarman, "*Brown*, Racial Change, and the Civil Rights Movement," *Virginia Law Review* 80 (February 1994): 7–150; and Michael J. Klarman, "How *Brown* Changed Race Relations: The Backlash Thesis," *Journal of American History* 81 (June 1994): 81–118.

36. Frank "Fay" Young was friends with Cleve Abbott before his old friend passed away. He was also close with B. T. Harvey, who was, as of the mid-1950s, commissioner of the Southern Intercollegiate Athletic Conference. In May 1956, the end of the school year that featured the 1955 Classic, Tuskegee gave Young an honorary degree. *Chicago Defender*, December 17, 1955; and *Atlanta Daily World*, May 22, 1956.

37. "Alabama State Yearly Results," College Football Data Warehouse.

38. See Jo Ann Gibson Robinson, *The Montgomery Bus Boycott and the Women Who Started It: The Memoir of Jo Ann Gibson Robinson*, ed. David J. Garrow (Knoxville: University of Tennessee Press, 1987); Stewart Burns, *Daybreak of Freedom: The Montgomery Bus Boycott* (Chapel Hill: University of North Carolina Press, 1997); Jeanne Theoharis, *The Rebellious Life of Mrs. Rosa Parks* (Boston: Beacon Press, 1913); Douglas Brinkley, *Rosa Parks: A Life* (New York: Penguin, 2005); and Rosa Parks, *Rosa Parks: My Story* (New York: Puffin, 1999).

39. To organize the boycott, Nixon and others created a new organization, the

Montgomery Improvement Association, to coordinate the protest. And coordinate it did. The group organized a massive car pool service to help people get to and from work. Many chose to walk to work, some for miles every day. There were community meetings almost nightly to keep people informed and to keep their spirits up. His two principal helpers were Fred Shuttlesworth and Ralph Abernathy, local ministers who had been working in Montgomery for years. For citations, see notes 32, 34, and 37.

40. *Pittsburgh Courier*, December 15, 1956; and *Montgomery Advertiser*, November 22, 1956.

41. The *Advertiser* estimated the crowd at the Klan rally at one thousand, not seven thousand. The paper devoted a large portion of its first two pages the day following the rally to the KKK, including a series of articles and several pictures of the event. Significantly, however, and keeping with the general trend, the same paper reported on the Turkey Day Classic both before and after the game, making coverage of the event central to its holiday sports coverage. "Alabama State Yearly Results," College Football Data Warehouse; *Pittsburgh Courier*, December 29, 1956; and *Montgomery Advertiser*, November 22, 1956; November 23, 1956; November 24, 1956; November 25, 1956.

42. *Browder v. Gayle*, 142 F. Supp. 707 (1956). See also notes 32 and 37.

43. "Tuskegee Yearly Results," College Football Data Warehouse; and *Atlanta Daily World*, December 1, 1957.

44. Donnie Williams and Wayne Greenhaw, *The Thunder of Angels: The Montgomery Bus Boycott and the People Who Broke the Back of Jim Crow* (Chicago: Lawrence Hill, 2006), 260–61; and *Los Angeles Sentinel*, December 1, 1960.

45. *Los Angeles Sentinel*, December 1, 1960; *Boston Globe*, November 25, 1960; *Los Angeles Times*, November 25, 1960; and *Washington Post*, November 25, 1960.

46. *Los Angeles Times*, November 25, 1960; *Washington Post*, November 25, 1960; and Williams and Greenhaw, *The Thunder of Angels*, 264.

47. Ralph Abernathy denounced Sullivan in the strongest terms for suggesting cancellation of the football game. *Los Angeles Sentinel*, December 1, 1960; *Baltimore Afro-American*, October 22, 1960; and *Chicago Defender*, November 28, 1960.

48. "Tuskegee Yearly Results," College Football Data Warehouse; "Alabama State Yearly Results," College Football Data Warehouse; "Tuskegee University: Golden Tiger Pregame Notes—Game 11"; and *Atlanta Daily World*, November 16, 1971; November 21, 1971.

49. *Atlanta Daily World*, December 6, 1987; October 23, 1988; "Tuskegee Yearly Results," College Football Data Warehouse; "Alabama State Yearly Results," College Football Data Warehouse; and "Tuskegee University: Golden Tiger Pregame Notes—Game 11."

50. *Baltimore Afro-American*, August 15, 1987; "Alabama State Dedicates Markham Football Complex," November 23, 2011, Southwestern Athletic Conference, http://www.swac.org/ViewArticle.dbml?%20DB_OEM_ID=27400&ATCLID=205338314 (accessed June 27, 2013); and "Tuskegee University: Golden Tiger Pregame Notes—Game 11."

51. "Tuskegee University: Golden Tiger Pregame Notes—Game 11"; *Atlanta Daily World*, September 25, 1990; December 7, 1997; and "88th Turkey Day Classic Set for ESPNU," Alabama Media Group, http://www.al.com/sports/index.ssf/2011/07/88th_turkey_day_classic_set_for.html (accessed February 17, 2013).

52. Nick Birdsong, "Turkey Day Classic: Tuskegee Spoils Alabama State's New Stadium Opening in 27–25 Win," Alabama Media Group, http://www.al.com/sports/index.ssf/2012/11/turkey_day_classic_tuskegee_sp.html (accessed February 17, 2013).

53. *Cleveland Call and Post*, November 18, 1993.

7. Gold and Glory Sweepstakes: An African American Racing Experience

1. Rob Schneider, "A City of Promise," *Indianapolis Star*, February 6, 1999, D6.
2. Ibid., D6–7.
3. Ed Bodenhamer and Robert G. Barrows, eds., *Encyclopedia of Indianapolis* (Indianapolis: Indiana University Press, 1994), 22–38.
4. William F. Nolan, *Barney Oldfield: The Life and Times of America's Legendary Speed King* (New York: G. P. Putnam Sons, 1961), 107.
5. Ibid.
6. Ibid., 108.
7. Ibid., 109.
8. *Chicago Defender*, July 27, 1924.
9. *Indianapolis Freeman*, August 2, 1924.
10. *Chicago Defender*, August 2, 1924.
11. Ibid.
12. Ibid.
13. Ibid.
14. *Indianapolis Freeman*, August 9, 1924.
15. Ibid.
16. *Chicago Defender*, August 7, 1926.
17. *Indianapolis Recorder*, August 14, 1926.
18. *Chicago Defender*, August 14, 1926.
19. *Indianapolis Recorder*, October 8, 1927.
20. *Chicago Defender*, August 9, 1924.
21. *Indianapolis Recorder*, July 13, 1929.
22. Ibid.
23. Ibid., September 19, 1936.
24. Ibid.
25. Ibid., August 29, 1936.
26. *Chicago Defender*, July 31, 1926.

8. The East West Classic: Black America's Baseball Fiesta

1. William G. Nunn, *Pittsburgh Courier*, September 1, 1934. The indispensable source for research on the East West Classic remains Larry Lester, *Black Baseball's National Showcase: The East-West All-Star Game, 1933–1953* (Lincoln: University of Nebraska Press, 2001).
2. I want to thank Rory Szeto, my undergraduate research assistant at the University of Pittsburgh, for the indispensable research he contributed to this piece.
3. Quoted in Neil Lanctot, *Negro League Baseball: The Rise and Ruin of a Black Institution* (Philadelphia: University of Pennsylvania Press, 2004), 38.
4. Roberto González Echevarría's masterful *Cuban Fiesta* (New Haven, CT: Yale University Press, 2010) describes the components of a festival and why these exuberant displays matter to a society. His thinking has influenced my take on the East West Classic.
5. Buck O'Neil, with Steve Wulf and David Conrads, *I Was Right on Time: Buck O'Neil* (New York: Simon & Schuster, 1996), 121.
6. Rob Ruck, *Sandlot Seasons: Sport in Black Pittsburgh* (Champaign-Urbana: University of Illinois Press, 1987), 137–69.
7. Lanctot, *Negro League Baseball*, 22–23; O'Neil, with Wulf and Conrads, *I Was Right on Time*, 122.

8. Nicholas Lemann, *The Promised Land: The Great Black Migration and How It Changed America* (New York: Vintage Books, 1992), is a solid study of the great migration with a focus on Chicago. Page 70 offers some population numbers.

9. O'Neil, with Wulf and Conrads, *I Was Right on Time*, 123.

10. Ibid., 123.

11. Lacy quoted in Lester, *Black Baseball's National Showcase*, 3–4.

12. O'Neil, with Wulf and Conrads, *I Was Right on Time*, 121.

13. Donn Rogosin, *Invisible Men: Life in Baseball's Negro Leagues* (New York: Atheneum, 1983), 11, 26–27.

14. Ibid., 26.

15. Adrian Burgos Jr., *Cuban Star: How One Negro-League Owner Changed the Face of Baseball* (New York: Hill and Wang, 2011), 162–63; Lanctot, *Negro League Baseball*, vii.

16. Quoted in Lanctot, *Negro League Baseball*, 190.

17. *Pittsburgh Courier*, August 18, 1934, 52–53.

18. O'Neil, with Wulf and Conrads, *I Was Right on Time*, 122–23.

19. Quoted in Lanctot, *Negro League Baseball*, 188.

20. *Burlington Free Press*, August 8, 1935, 15.

21. Rob Ruck, *Raceball: How the Major Leagues Colonized the Black and Latin Game* (Boston: Beacon Press, 2011), 83; O'Neil, with Wulf and Conrads, *I Was Right on Time*, 123–24.

22. Echevarria, *Cuban Fiesta*, 2.

23. Lester, *Black Baseball's National Showcase*, 459.

24. Burgos Jr., *Cuban Star*, 164–65.

25. *Pittsburgh Courier*, June 21, 1937.

9. Creating Order in Black College Sport: The Lasting Legacy of the Colored Intercollegiate Athletic Association

1. Ocania Chalk, *Black College Sport* (New York: Dodd, Mead, 1976). Patrick B. Miller, "Slouching toward New Expediency: College Football and the Color Line during the Depression Decade," *American Studies* 40 (Fall 1999): 5–30. Patrick B. Miller, "To 'Bring the Race Along Rapidly': Sport Student Culture and Educational Mission at Historically Black Colleges during the Interwar Years," *History of Education Quarterly* 35 (Summer 1995): 111–33. Raymond Schmidt, *Shaping College Football: The Transformation of an American Sport, 1919–1930* (Syracuse, NY: Syracuse University Press, 2007).

2. S. H. Archer, "Football in Our Colleges," *Voice of the Negro* 3 (1906): 202.

3. J. B. Watson, "Football in Southern Negro Colleges," *Voice* 4 (1907): 169.

4. Earl Henry Duval Jr., "An Historical Analysis of the Central Intercollegiate Athletic Association and Its Influence on the Development of Black Intercollegiate Athletics: 1912–1984 (Unpublished doctoral diss., Kent State University, 1985). Charles H. Williams, "Twenty Year's Work of the C.I.A.A.," *Southern Workman* 61 (1932): 65–76. Another regional conference, the Georgia-Carolina Athletic Association, was founded in 1910. Four years earlier, in 1906, Edwin Bancroft Henderson established the Interscholastic Athletic Association of Middle Atlantic States, which provided needed organizational structure to African American sport prior to the creation of the CIAA.

5. For an excellent work on African Americans and racial uplift, see Kevin K. Gaines, *Uplifting the Race: Black Leadership, Politics, and Culture in the Twentieth Century* (Chapel Hill: University of North Carolina Press, 1996). See also Miller, "To 'Bring the Race Along Rapidly,'" 111–33.

6. Colored Intercollegiate Athletics Association, "Constitution and Bylaws," 1912, n.p.

7. Ibid.

8. Ibid.

9. See http://www.Theside.com/sports2010/2/2gen_0202103837.aspx., and http://en.wikipedia.org/wiki/southernwestern_athletic_conference. Retrieved February 8, 2014.

10. Williams, "Twenty Years' Work of the C.I.A.A.," 69.

11. *C.I.A.A. Bulletin*, 1925, 11.

12. Ibid.

13. Ibid. See also, "Putting Lincoln out Unfair," *Chicago Defender*, April 4, 1925. 10; "Gideon Smith Gives Us Some Light on the C.I.A.A. Controversy," *Chicago Defender*, April 18, 1925; Duval Jr., "An Historical Analysis of the Central Intercollegiate Athletic Association and Its Influence on the Development of Black Intercollegiate Athletics"; and Miller, "To 'Bring the Race Along Rapidly,'" 111–33.

14. *C.I.A.A. Bulletin*, 1942, 16.

15. Ibid.

16. Full collection of *C.I.A.A. Bulletin* is located at Virginia State University in Petersburg, Virginia, and Virginia Union University in Richmond, Virginia.

17. Like many other professional organizations, leaders in the CIAA often held multiple offices over their lifetime.

18. *C.I.A.A. Bulletin*, 1924, 5.

19. Ibid., 30.

20. Ibid. Essays ranged from two to five pages in length.

21. *C.I.A.A. Bulletin*, 18.

22. Ibid., 22.

23. The CIAA occasionally extended invitations to well-known individuals from the world of physical education and sport to speak at their annual meetings. For example, Jay B. Nash, the famous physical educator from New York University, spoke at the association's annual meeting in 1944. Nash's talk was titled "Athletic Competition in Physical Fitness for Post-War America." See *C.I.A.A. Bulletin*, 1945, 14–15.

24. An important group that had a close connection with the C.I.A.A. was the Eastern Board of Officials (EBO). Founded in 1906 by Edwin B. Henderson, a well-known educator, civil rights activist, and historian of African American athletes, the EBO is still in existence and reorganized as the oldest predominately black sports officiating group in the United States. See David K. Wiggins, "Edwin Bancroft Henderson: Physical Educator, Civil Rights Activist and Chronicler of African American Athletes," *Research Quarterly for Exercise and Sport* 70 (June 1999): 91–112; and www.eboinc.org/history-of-the-board.

25. For information on the black press, see Frederick G. Detweiler, *The Negro Press in the United States* (Chicago: University of Chicago Press, 1922), and Roland E. Wolseley, *The Black Press U.S.A.* (Ames: Iowa State University Press, 1974).

26. *C.I.A.A. Bulletin*, 1936, 15.

27. Ibid., 1938, 31.

28. Ibid., 1943, 25–27.

29. Duval Jr., "An Historical Analysis of the Central Intercollegiate Athletic Association and Its Influence on the Development of Black Intercollegiate Athletics," and Williams, "Twenty Years' Work of the C.I.A.A."

30. CIAA official website of the Central Intercollegiate Athletic Association. Retrieved February 14, 2014, from http://www.theciaa.com/information/about_ciaa/index. Duval Jr.,

"An Historical Analysis of the Central Intercollegiate Athletic Association and Its Influence on the Development of Black Intercollegiate Athletics"; Williams, "Twenty Years' Work of the C.I.A.A."

31. *C.I.A.A. Bulletin*, 1932, 15.

32. Ibid., 1933, 9.

33. Ibid., 1943, 12.

34. Ibid., 13.

35. Ibid., 1944, 11.

36. Ibid.

37. For details on the Dickinson system, see Duval Jr., "An Historical Analysis of the Central Intercollegiate Athletic Association and Its Influence on the Development of Black Intercollegiate Athletics," 59–60.

38. See David K. Wiggins, "'The Biggest 'Classic' of Them All:' The Howard University and Lincoln University Thanksgiving Day Football Games, 1919–1929," in *Rooting for the Home Team: Sport, Community, and Identity*, ed. Daniel A. Nathan (Urbana: University of Illinois Press, 2013), 36–53, and Schmidt, *Shaping College Football*.

39. Williams, "Twenty Years' Work of the C.I.A.A.," 74. "Hampton Opens New Athletic Field May 20, with Track Meet," *Chicago Defender*, March 25, 1922, and "Track Meet to Open New Field," *Christian Science Monitor*, May 10, 1922.

40. "Twenty-First C.I.A.A. Track Meet Is on May 16," *Chicago Defender*, May 16, 1942.

41. Williams, "Twenty Years' Work of the C.I.A.A.," 74–75; Sundiata Djata, *Blacks at the Net: Black Achievement in the History of Tennis*, vol. I (Syracuse, NY: Syracuse University Press, 2006), and Sundiata Djata, *Blacks at the Net: Black Achievement in the History of Tennis*, vol. II (Syracuse, NY: Syracuse University Press, 2008).

42. Williams, "Twenty Years' Work of the C.I.A.A.," 75.

43. Paula Giddings, *When and Where I Enter: The Impact of Black Women on Race and Sex in America* (New York: Bantam Books, 1984), and Mary Church Terrell, *A Colored Woman in a White World* (New York: G. K. Hall, 1940).

44. Rita Liberti, "We Were Ladies, We Just Played Basketball Like Boys': African American Womanhood and Competitive Basketball at Bennett College, 1928–1942," *Journal of Sport History* 26 (Fall 1999): 575.

45. Carroll L. L. Miller and Anne S. Pruitt-Logan, *Faithful to the Task at Hand: The Life of Lucy Diggs Slowe* (Albany: State University of New York Press, 2012); Linda M. Perkins, "Lucy Diggs Slowe: Champion of the Self-Determination of African American Women in Higher Education," *Journal of Negro History* 81 (Winter–Autumn 1996): 89–104.

46. Susan K. Cahn, *Coming on Strong: Gender and Sexuality in Twentieth-Century Women's Sport* (New York: Free Press, 1994), and Cindy Himes-Gissendanner, "African American Women and Competitive Sport, 1920–1960," in *Women Sport and Culture,* ed. Susan Birrell and Cheryl L. Cole (Champaign, IL: Human Kinetics, 1994), 81–92.

47. Rita Liberti, "'We Were Ladies, We Just Played Basketball Like Boys,'" 567–84.

48. "Howard Five Lists 12-Game Schedule," *Washington Post*, December 17, 1933, and "Lincoln Eyed as Favorite in CIAA Cage Tournament," *Baltimore Afro-American*, March 9, 1946. For North Carolina College records, see John B. McLendon, *The First CIAA Championship Basketball Tournament* (Downers Grove, IL: Maxaid, 1988), 51.

49. See "L.I.U. Meets Morgan Five on Saturday," *Chicago Defender*, March 26, 1938; "Long Island U All Set for Union," *Chicago Defender*, March 25, 1939; "Union Five Beats Long Island U.," *Chicago Defender*, April 1, 1939; "Union Did Not Defeat Long Island U.

Varsity," *Chicago Defender* (national ed.), April 8, 1939; "White College Team to Play VA Union," *Chicago Defender*, December 7, 1940; and "Brooklyn College Loses," *New York Times*, December 28, 1940.

50. Bell quoted in L. Douglas Wilder Library, Virginia Union University, Archives-AR-0005 (cited hereafter as VUUA), Athletics Department, Box 1/3, Folder: CIAA Basketball Tournament Programs 1971, 1973, 1977, 1978, Richmond, Virginia. For more on the CIAA tournament, see Pamela Grundy, *Learning to Win: Sports, Education, and Social Change in Twentieth-Century North Carolina* (Chapel Hill: University of North Carolina Press), 183–85, and Milton S. Katz, *Breaking Through: John B. McLendon, Basketball Legend and Civil Rights Pioneer* (Fayetteville: University of Arkansas Press, 2007), 46–53.

51. "Cage Capers," *Baltimore Afro-American*, April 5, 1941. "R. B. Atwood Abandons Cage Tourney Idea," *Norfolk Journal and Guide*, January 10, 1942.

52. Origins of tournament in "To Limit the Number of Cages Games," *Norfolk Journal and Guide*, February 13, 1937; "CIAA Votes Tournament Plan on Experimental Basis," *Baltimore Afro-American*, December 21, 1940, and McLendon, *The First CIAA Championship Basketball Tournament*, 26–28. The Virginia Union Archives at the L. Douglas Wilder Library in Richmond, Virginia, has a copy of McLendon's work.

53. Figure in 1945 *CIAA Bulletin*, VUAA, Athletics Department, Box 1/3, Folder: Athletics Department, CIAA Bulletins, 1942–1947.

54. For information on singers and musicians who performed at Turner's, see "500 Hear Robeson on Peace Program," *Philadelphia Tribune*, September 26, 1940; "Bands on Tour," *Chicago Defender*, September 13, 1941; "Capitol Comments," *Atlanta Daily World*, March 21, 1943; "'Dirty Gertie' Is Mad; 'Send Me to Hades,'" *Baltimore Afro-American*, September 25, 1943; and "Sports, Entertainment, Politics Were at Home at Turner's Arena," *Washington Post*, June 16, 1964.

55. McLendon, *The First CIAA Championship Basketball Tournament*, 32–34.

56. Ibid.

57. *Norfolk Journal and Guide*, March 16, 1946, and *Baltimore Afro-American*, March 16, 1946. For more on the game, see McLendon, *The First CIAA Championship Basketball . Tournament*, 43–46, 49–50.

58. Figure in 1946–47 *CIAA Bulletin*, VUAA, Athletics Department, Box 1/3, Folder: Athletics Department, CIAA Bulletins, 1942–1947.

59. "Lincoln Coach Blasts CIAA Prexy Burr; Says 'Weak-Kneed' Policy Robbed Lions," *Baltimore Afro-American*, March 16, 1946.

60. Ibid.; "Looking 'Em Over," *Baltimore Afro-American*, March 23, 1946; "Lively Session Forecast for CIAA Meet This Week," *Baltimore Afro-American*, December 14, 1946; "CIAA Officials Hold Successful Meeting at West Virginia State, *Atlanta Daily World*, December 20, 1946; and "CIAA Gives Lincoln Cage Title; Suspends Two Officials," *Norfolk Journal and Guide*, December 21, 1946.

61. Figures in article of 1954 *C.I.A.A. Bulletin*, VUAA, Athletics Department, Box 1/3, Folder: Athletics Department, CIAA Bulletin, 1949–1954. According to the article, the sums were recalculated because early tabulations had not subtracted the $500 advance that the association gave tournament planners each year. The figures reflect the subtraction of money. CIAA programs in Moorland-Spingarn Research Center, Manuscript Division, Art Carter Papers (cited hereafter as ACP), Box 170-24, Folder: 24, 25, Howard University, Washington, DC.

62. Burr quoted in 1947 program, ACP, Folder: 24. *Norfolk Journal and Guide*, March 20, 1948.

63. This and the next paragraph in Wiggins, "Edwin Bancroft Henderson: Physical Educator, Civil Rights Activist, and Chronicler of African-American Athletes," 99–101, and Justine Christianson, "The Uline Arena/Washington Coliseum: The Rise and Fall of a Washington Institution," *Washington History* 16 (Spring/Summer 2004): 24–26.

64. Figures in *CIAA Bulletin* from 1949, 1950, and 1951, VUAA, Athletics Department, Box 1/3, Folder: Athletics Department, CIAA Bulletins, 1949–1954.

65. "Here's the Story of the Campaign to Get Negro Five in Invitation Tourney," *New York Amsterdam News*, February 19, 1949.

66. "Colored West Virginia State Five to Meet Gaels, Broncos," *Bakersfield Californian*, February 11, 1949. Herman Hill, "Courageous Cage Promoter Who Booked W.Va. on Coast Praised," *Pittsburgh Courier*, January 29, 1949.

67. Lloyd quoted in Earl Lloyd and Sean Kirst, *Moonfixer: The Basketball Journey of Earl Lloyd* (Syracuse, NY: Syracuse University Press, 2010), 57. Patterson letter in "State Quintet Leaves Tonight for California," *Charleston Gazette*, February 5, 1949. Patterson's letter was also reprinted in the *Baltimore Afro-American*, February 12, 1949. "Dons Play Bradley," *San Francisco Examiner*, February 11, 1949, and "Nevada Cagers Meet Yellow Jackets of West Virginia Here Tonight," *Reno Evening Gazette*, February 16, 1949.

68. Herman Hill, "Courageous Cage Promoter Who Booked W.Va. on Coast Praised," *Pittsburgh Courier*, January 29, 1949. Newspapers in each of the three cities covered the games. For instance, see *San Francisco Chronicle*, February 12, 1949, and February 13, 1949; *Los Angeles Times*, February 15, 1949; and *Nevada State Journal*, February 17, 1949. The black also reported the scores. See *Norfolk Journal and Guide*, February 19, 1949; *Atlanta Daily World*, February 22, 1949; *Baltimore Afro-American*, February 26, 1949; and *Cleveland Call and Post*, February 26, 1949.

69. Lloyd and Kirst, *Moonfixer*, 58. "From A to Z," *Baltimore Afro-American*, February 26, 1949. "West Virginia Cagers Win, Lose on Coast," *Pittsburgh Courier*, February 19, 1949. Bob Barnett, *Hillside Fields: A History of Sports in West Virginia* (Morgantown: West Virginia University Press, 2013), 162. In the book, Barnett also discusses the 1949 trip. See pages 159–60.

70. Figures in *CIAA Bulletin* from 1954, 1956, and 1958, VUAA, Athletics Department, Box 1/3, Folder: Athletics Department, CIAA Bulletins, 1949–1954, and Folder: Athletics Department, CIAA Bulletins, 1955–59, 1962.

71. Kennedy telegram in McLendon, *The First CIAA Championship Basketball Tournament*, 53.

10. Game, Set, and Separatism: The American Tennis Association, a Tennis Vanguard

1. See Donald Mrozek, *Sport and American Mentality, 1880–1910* (Knoxville: University of Tennessee Press, 1983), 103–35.

2. See Paul Fein, "20th Century Retrospective," *Tennis Week*, November 18, 1999.

3. Wanamaker's ad, *Christian Recorder*, April 25, 1887. John Wanamaker owned a grand depot in Philadelphia.

4. Arthur R. Ashe Jr., *A Hard Road to Glory: A History of the African-American Athlete 1919–1945* (New York: Amistad, 1993 [1988]), 59.

5. "Southern Tennis Given Stimulus through A. T. A. Title Play at Tuskegee," *Chicago Defender*, July 25, 1931.

6. Edwin B. Henderson, *The Negro in Sports* (Washington, DC: Associated Publishers, 1949), 312.

7. Bertram Barker, "A Black Tennis Association: Active since 1916," in *American Tennis Association National Rankings 1983–1984* (Philadelphia: American Tennis Association, 1984), 60.

8. Ibid.; see also Ashe, *A Hard Road to Glory,* 60.

9. Bruce Schoenfeld, *The Match: Althea Gibson and a Portrait of a Friendship* (New York: Amistad, 2005 (2004),18.

10. Doug Smith, *Whirlwind, the Godfather of Black Tennis: The Life and Times of Dr. Robert Walter Johnson* (Washington, DC: Blue Eagle Publishing, 2004), 55. Irwin's mother took tennis lessons from Fred Johnson at the Cosmopolitan Club.

11. For example, Lisa DeAngeles won the women's title in 1983, and Donovan September of South Africa won the singles title in 1996 and 2001. ATA records, reprinted in appendix A in Cecil Harris and Larryette Kyle-DeBose, *Charging the Net: A History of Blacks in Tennis from Althea Gibson and Arthur Ashe to the Williams Sisters* (Chicago: Ivan R. Dee, 2007), 241, 243.

12. Schoenfeld, *The Match,* 19; see also Henry S. Robinson, "The M Street High School 1891–1916," *Historical Society of Washington, DC* 51 (1984): 119–43.

13. *Chicago Defender*, July 27, 1918.

14. Barker, "A Black Tennis Association," 60.

15. Benjamin G. Rader, *American Sports: From the Age of Folk Games to the Age of Televised Sports* (Englewood Cliffs, NJ: Prentice-Hall, 1996), 190.

16. Ashe, *A Hard Road to Glory,* 61.

17. "History of Tennis at Tuskegee University," unpublished manuscript, Tuskegee University Sports Information Office, 1977, 6.

18. Douglas A. Noverr and Lawrence E. Ziewacz, *The Games They Played: Sports in American History 1865–1980* (Chicago: Nelson Hall, 1983), 132.

19. "Gerald Norman, Eastern Net Champ, May Play Nat Jackson in Meet at Tuskegee Aug. 17," *Chicago Defender,* August 1, 1931.

20. "History of Tennis at Tuskegee University."

21. Steven M. Tucker, "Against all Odds," *Racquet* (Fall 1991): 58.

22. Hudlin won the Freshman Championships at the University of Chicago in 1923, becoming the first black player in university history to win it. "Tennis Players Begin to Arrive for 'Nationals,'" *Chicago Defender,* June 16, 1923. Only males have been found in the annals of the early history of black players at predominantly white institutions.

23. Ibid., July 28, 1928.

24. Ibid., August 10, 1929.

25. Ibid., June 16, 1923.

26. See the *Chicago Daily News* negatives collection at the Chicago History Museum. It is unclear if these photos were published, but a *Daily News* photographer took them.

27. "Remember the Good Times," *World Tennis*, October 1980, 49.

28. Ashe, *A Hard Road to Glory,* 52.

29. Kenny Lucas, "First Black Pro Makes a Racket: Ryland Serves Life Lessons to Stars of Today," *New York Daily News*, March 7, 2000. Ryland won two ATA men's national championships in 1955 and 1956, and a junior championship in 1939.

30. Schoenfeld, *The Match,* 19.

31. Ashe, *A Hard Road to Glory,* 60.

32. Quoted in Harris and Kyle-DeBose, *Charging the Net*, 53. Later, Dinkins sponsored her on the golf tour in the late 1960s; see Schoenfeld, *The Match*, 265.

33. *Chicago Defender*, March 14, 1931.

34. Cited in Harris and Kyle-DeBose, *Charging the Net*, 109.

35. *Chicago Defender*, August 20, 1921.

36. In 1945 Ryland advanced to the NCAA quarterfinals.

37. *Chicago Defender*, June 16, 1923.

38. Ibid., September 1, 1923.

39. *Chicago Tribune*, September 1, 1928.

40. *Chicago Defender*, August 30, 1924.

41. Smith, *Whirlwind, the Godfather of Black Tennis*, 44, 45.

42. Parke Cummings, *American Tennis: The Story of the Game and Its People* (Boston: Little Brown, 1957), 17.

43. Many writers considered Illinois, Ohio, and Indiana as being in the West.

44. *Chicago Defender*, April 6, 1940. In addition, nine schools from eight states participated, mostly black colleges, and Dorchester Academy in Georgia.

45. *Chicago Defender*, July 27, 1918.

46. Ibid., August 18, 1923.

47. A photo of models in an ATA fashion show appears in *World Tennis*, January 1957, 64.

48. *Chicago Defender*, July 27, 1918.

49. Ibid., July 19, 1924.

50. Ibid., August 15, 1925.

51. Ibid., April 9, 1927.

52. Ibid., August 26, 1922.

53. Ibid., September 10, 1921.

54. *Chicago Tribune*, July 27, 1940.

55. *Chicago Defender*, August 30, 1924. For information on Tilden's fight with the USLTA, see "Tilden in Revolt; Defies Tennis Body," *New York Times*, February 25, 1926.

56. Harris and Kyle-DeBose, *Charging the Net*, 106.

57. See, for example, *New York Times*, August 20, 1944; August 17, 1954; and August 21, 1955.

58. *Chicago Defender*, September 3, 1921.

59. Caribbean Americans, mainly from Barbados, Trinidad, and St. Kitts, ran the Cosmopolitan Club, which consisted of five clay courts, and a club house. Considered New York's center for black tennis, it was the "only place for serious players to compete." The Caribbean influence gave the club a "certain colonial air." Even so, nonmembers could rent courts on an hourly basis. Moreover, there was a junior program, which raised money for promising youths to compete in ATA events. See Schoenfeld, *The Match*, 21. Gibson argued that she was uncomfortable at the club, maintaining that "they were probably stricter than white people of similar position." See Gibson's autobiography, and Ed McGrogan, "Stirring Up a Breeze," *New York Daily News*, August 23, 2010.

60. *New York Herald Tribune*, June 30, 1940; Ed Hughes, [no title], *Brooklyn Daily Eagle*, July 30, 1940.

61. Tucker, "Against all Odds," 60; See also Peter Horner, "ATA: The Best Kept Secret in Tennis?" *Tennis USTA*, July 1991, 11. One columnist was unimpressed with the exhibition, maintaining, "Since it is not the first time that Negroes have played with whites and against

whites, even in the state of Missouri, there is nothing unusual about this particular match other than the prominence of the people taking part." See "Don Budge to Play with Reggie Weir against Cohen and McDaniel in Harlem," *Chicago Defender*, July, 27, 1940.

62. See a photo of Hare in "American Tennis Ass'n Silver Jubilee Scenes," *Chicago Defender*, September 6, 1941.

63. See Harris and Kyle-DeBose, *Charging the Net,* 111, for interview with Bob Ryland. See also Kenny Lucas, "First Black Pro Makes a Racket."

64. *Montgomery Advertiser*, December 28, 1929.

65. He lost in the quarterfinals to Tony Trabert, who became a tennis professional and commentator.

66. Barry Meadow, "What's White . . . and Whit . . . And White . . . and Why?" *World Tennis,* March 1984, 58; Brief, *World Tennis,* April 1956, 36; Interview of Oscar Johnson in Ashe, *A Hard Road to Glory,* 161.

67. Schoenfeld, *The Match,* 59. LeBair put the first woman in an umpire chair at Forest Hill.

68. Alice Marble, editorial, *American Lawn Tennis,* July 1, 1950. See also Althea Gibson, *I Always Wanted to Be Somebody* (New York: Harper and Brothers, 1958), 62–66.

69. See, for example, "Ladies & Gentlemen . . . ," *Time,* July 17, 1950, 74.

70. Ibid., 68.

71. Ed Fitzgerald, ed., "Round Table Discussion: The Negro in American Sport," *Negro History Bulletin* 24 (1960): 28.

72. Harris and Kyle-DeBose, *Charging the Net,* 4.

73. Ibid., 109.

74. www.americantennisassociation.org.

75. Ed McGrogan, "Stirring Up a Breeze," *New York Daily News,* August 23, 2010. The players in the photo were Eyre Saitch, Sylvester Smith, John McGriff, and Elwood Downing.

76. Ibid.

77. Ashe, *A Hard Road to Glory,* 60.

11. Pars and Birdies in a Hidden World: African Americans and the United Golfers Association

1. Tom Govedarica, *Chicago Golf: The First 100 Years* (Chicago: Eagle Communications Group, 1991), 58–59; Calvin Sinnette, *Forbidden Fairways: African Americans and the Game of Golf* (Chelsea, MI: Sleeping Bear Press, 1998) 13–15, 53, 56.

2. Sinnette, *Forbidden Fairways,* 56; *Chicago Defender*, October 16, 1915.

3. *Chicago Defender*, October 6, 1917; Pete McDaniel, *Uneven Lies: The Heroic Story of African-Americans in Golf* (New York: American Golfer, 2000), 62.

4. McDaniel, *Uneven Lies,* 62.

5. *Chicago Defender*, August 5, 1922; September 27, 1919.

6. Ibid., July 31, 1920; August 5, 1922.

7. McDaniel, *Uneven Lies,* 60–61.

8. Ibid., 49, 55, 70; Sinnette, *Forbidden Fairways,* 55; *Washington Post*, May 28, 1997.

9. John H. Kennedy, *A Course of Their Own: A History of African American Golfers* (Lincoln, NE: Bison Books, 2005), 21–22; McDaniel, *Uneven Lies,* 51, Sinnette, *Forbidden Fairways,* 57–58.

10. McDaniel, *Uneven Lies*, 50–51—this work describes the 1925 tournament as the first National Colored championship, while 1926 is the more widely accepted date. Ibid., 62.

11. Ibid., 50; Sinnette, *Forbidden Fairways*, 62.

12. McDaniel, *Uneven Lies*, 50–51; *Chicago Defender*, September 1, 1926; Marvin P. Dawkins and Graham C. Kinloch, *African American Golfers during the Jim Crow Era* (Westport, CT: Praeger Publishers, 2000), 40–44. Dawkins and Kinloch provide an excellent overview of the first decade of the Negro National tournaments, along with a listing of yearly men and women champions from 1926 to 1962 on page 41. Unfortunately, this listing contains a major error relating to the 1952 tournament, which has been picked up and widely spread in literature on men's African American golf. See note 45 below for details. "Golf Championship Goes to Jackson Park Player," *Chicago Defender*, August 6, 1927.

13. Dawkins and Kinloch, *African American Golfers during the Jim Crow Era*, 44.

14. Ibid., 44–45; McDaniel, *Uneven Lies*, 51.

15. McDaniel, *Uneven Lies*, 51–52; Sinnette, *Forbidden Fairways*, 58.

16. McDaniel, *Uneven Lies*, 52.

17. Ibid., 52–53.

18. *Chicago Defender*, September 6, 1930; Sinnette, *Forbidden Fairways*, 98.

19. Sinnette, *Forbidden Fairways*, 13; Lenwood Robinson Jr., *Skins & Grins: The Plight of the Black American Golfer* (Chicago: LENROB Publishers, 1997), 87.

20. *Chicago Defender*, January 22, 1916; April 27, 1918.

21. Sinnette, *Forbidden Fairways*, 98; Dawkins and Kinloch, *African American Golfers during the Jim Crow Era*, 41, 46. Both Sinnette (p. 98), along with Dawson and Kinloch (p. 46), are historians who have noted the expanded and more serious coverage given to women's golf by African American newspapers. (An example of the essentially "social" coverage given to early women's golf is found in *Chicago Defender*, August 31, 1918, which describes a "delightful golf party" held at Jackson Park.) *Chicago Defender*, September 6, 1930; "Miss Marie Thompson Retains Crown," *Chicago Defender*, September 12, 1931; M. Mikell Johnson, *The African American Woman Golfer: Her Legacy* (Westport, CT: Praeger Publishers, 2008), 75.

22. Sinnette, *Forbidden Fairways*, 102; Dawkins and Kinloch, *African American Golfers during the Jim Crow Era*, 41; Johnson, *The African American Woman Golfer*, 70, 177.

23. Johnson, *The African American Woman Golfer*, 43–44.

24. Ibid.; McDaniel, *Uneven Lies*, 66, 67; "Black Golfers' Best Club," *Washington Post*, May 28, 1997; Sinnette, *Forbidden Fairways*, 123, 147.

25. Johnson, *The African American Woman Golfer*, 44–46; Robinson, *Skins & Grins*, 86–88; Sinnette, *Forbidden Fairways*, 100.

26. Dawkins and Kinloch, *African American Golfers during the Jim Crow Era*, 45–46; Sinnette, *Forbidden Fairways*, 75.

27. Dawkins and Kinloch, *African American Golfers during the Jim Crow Era*, 48–50.

28. Ibid., 50–51.

29. McDaniel, *Uneven Lies*, 54; Dawkins and Kinloch, *African American Golfers during the Jim Crow Era*, 27, 51; Dawkins, "In the Age of Jim Crow," 44.

30. Dawkins, "In the Age of Jim Crow," 44; George B. Kirsch, *Golf in America* (Urbana: University of Illinois Press, 2009), 156.

31. Dawkins and Kinloch, *African American Golfers during the Jim Crow Era*, 51; Sinnette, *Forbidden Fairways*, 74–75.

32. Sinnette, *Forbidden Fairways*, 74–75.

33. Dawkins and Kinloch, *African American Golfers during the Jim Crow Era,* 52–54.

34. Ibid., 54, 57.

35. Dawkins, "In the Age of Jim Crow," 45; McDaniel, *Uneven Lies,* 67.

36. Dawkins and Kinloch, *African American Golfers during the Jim Crow Era,* 69–79; "Louis Ups Golf Monies, Bars Gals," *Chicago Defender,* May 31, 1949.

37. McDaniel, *Uneven Lies,* 67.

38. Ibid., 67.

39. Ibid., 54–55.

40. Dawkins and Kinloch, *African American Golfers during the Jim Crow Era,* 41; Kennedy, *A Course of Their Own,* 38–48. This new essay accurately credits Teddy Rhodes and Charlie Sifford with five UGA National Open championships each during their careers. This information is the correction of a major error relative to the 1952 tournament's professional division winner that is included in the table of UGA champions from 1926 to 1962 in the widely consulted book by Dawkins and Kinloch (*African American Golfers during the Jim Crow Era*). The table in Dawkins and Kinloch incorrectly lists Charlie Sifford as the winner of the 1952 UGA National Open and thus credits him with winning the tourney six times during his career, including consecutive victories from 1952 to 1956. This erroneous information from Dawkins and Kinloch has obviously been often used in research writings, as the mistakes appear in many books and articles dealing with African American men's golf. To make matters worse, in his autobiography (*Just Let Me Play: The Story of Charlie Sifford, the First Black PGA Golfer* [Latham, NY: British American Publishing, 1992]), Sifford claims that he won his first UGA National Open in 1952 as part of his "six" lifetime titles (p. 43), and he even includes a paragraph describing how he beat Teddy Rhodes out for the title in the 1952 UGA played in "Detroit" (p. 60). The correct facts—that Teddy Rhodes won the 1952 UGA National with a score of 280 in the tourney that was played in Pittsburgh, while Sifford finished in sixth place—were discovered in the *Chicago Defender*'s coverage of the tournament while doing research for this article. Confirmation was obtained in the 1952 tournament coverage of the *Pittsburgh Courier* and another Pennsylvania newspaper, while other eastern papers were seen to also correctly report Rhodes as winning the 1952 UGA event. Also, in following years several article references were found that correctly named Rhodes as the 1952 champion and mentioned how many national titles each man had won. It appears that Sifford started the problem with his erroneous claim in the 1992 autobiography, with Dawkins and Kinloch somehow picking it up for their table and other writers then starting to propagate it around. Coverage of Rhodes winning the 1952 UGA National Open can be seen in "Ann Gregory Upset in Finals," *Chicago Defender,* September 6, 1952; "Only Two Champions Survive Tough Play in 1952 Nationals," *Courier,* September 6, 1952; "Ted Rhodes Again Wins Golf Title," *Bradford Era,* August 30, 1952.

41. Kennedy, *A Course of Their Own,* 25, 100.

42. Ibid., 26, 32; Sinnette, *Forbidden Fairways,* 163–65.

43. Kennedy, *A Course of Their Own,* 38.

44. Dawkins and Kinloch, *African American Golfers during the Jim Crow Era,* 58; "Joe Louis Open Top Prize to Ted Rhodes," *Chicago Defender,* August 30, 1947; "Wheeler Wins National Title," *Chicago Defender,* September 6, 1947; "Wheeler Wins Golf Tourney," *Chicago Defender,* September 4, 1948.

45. Kennedy, *A Course of Their Own,* 45–48; *Los Angeles Times,* January 4, 1947; "Rhodes Wins UGA," *Chicago Defender,* September 3, 1949; "Teddy Rhodes Sets New Mark," *Chicago Defender,* August 6, 1949; "Golf Crowns," *Chicago Defender,* July 16, 1949;

"Demaret Ties Palmer at Tam," *Chicago Tribune*, August 15, 1949. Probably the best round Rhodes ever recorded in a PGA tournament came at the 1953 St. Paul Open when he shot a score of 66 to share the first-round lead. He also posted scores of 67 at both the 1952 All-American at Tam O'Shanter and the 1956 St. Paul Open. *Official PGA Tournament Record Book: Consolidated 1950–1958 Supplement* (Chicago: PGA, 1959), 56, 76, 151.

46. Johnson, *The African American Woman Golfer*, 65, 133; Sinnette, *Forbidden Fairways*, 103.

47. Johnson, *The African American Woman Golfer*, 30; "Down the Fairway," *Chicago Defender*, July 29, 1950; Robinson, *Skins & Grins*, 88.

48. Sinnette, *Forbidden Fairways*, 111–12; McDaniel, *Uneven Lies*, 73–74.

49. Sinnette, *Forbidden Fairways*, 112–14; "Along the Fairways," *Chicago Defender*, March 12, 1949.

50. "National Champ Is in Form," *Chicago Defender*, July 12, 1941; "Mrs. Wilson Tops Women's Bracket," *Chicago Defender*, August 26, 1944; "Sailor Shoots 76 in Tam O'Shanter Open," *Chicago Defender*, August 26, 1944; McDaniel, *Uneven Lies*, 70; Johnson, *The African American Woman Golfer*, 70, 178; Sinnette, *Forbidden Fairways*, 115, 165.

51. McDaniel, *Uneven Lies*, 70–71; Sinnette, *Forbidden Fairways*, 104–6; "Golf Experts Believe Ann Gregory Is Greatest of the Women Champs," *Chicago Defender*, October 14, 1950.

52. Sinnette, *Forbidden Fairways*, 106–7; McDaniel, *Uneven Lies*, 71–72.

53. McDaniel, *Uneven Lies*, 72; Sinnette, *Forbidden Fairways*, 107–10; Robinson, *Skins & Grins*, 94–95.

54. Kennedy, *A Course of Their Own*, 50–51.

55. McDaniel, *Uneven Lies*, 87; Dawkins and Kinloch, *African American Golfers during the Jim Crow Era*, 58–59; Kennedy, *A Course of Their Own*, 54–55.

56. Dawkins and Kinloch, *African American Golfers during the Jim Crow Era*, 59–62.

57. Ibid., 81; Sinnette, *Forbidden Fairways*, 127.

58. McDaniel, *Uneven Lies*, 88; Dawkins and Kinloch, *African American Golfers during the Jim Crow Era*, 81–83; Kennedy, *A Course of Their Own*, 80–81; Sinnette, *Forbidden Fairways*, 129–31.

59. Dawkins and Kinloch, *African American Golfers during the Jim Crow Era*, 81–83; Kennedy, *A Course of Their Own*, 82–83.

60. Kennedy, *A Course of Their Own*, 100.

61. Sinnette, *Forbidden Fairways*, 131–32.

62. Ibid., 132; McDaniel, *Uneven Lies*, 90. One of the early legal decisions going against municipalities that were segregating their golf courses came in late 1955 when the United States District Court in Atlanta insisted that the city must abide by a Supreme Court decision against golf course segregation. While the state's governor was disappointed at the city of Atlanta obeying the law, the city's mayor disclosed that to do otherwise would have forced Atlanta to sell its park courses and land and so lose nearly one hundred employees their jobs. "Atlanta to Open Links," *New York Times*, December 24, 1955.

63. McDaniel, *Uneven Lies*, 56–57.

64. Ibid., 56; "WSGA Directory," *Tee-Cup*, June 1957.

65. McDaniel, *Uneven Lies*, 56.

66. Sinnette, *Forbidden Fairways*, 157–58; McDaniel, *Uneven Lies*, 56.

67. Sinnette, *Forbidden Fairways*, 157–58; McDaniel, *Uneven Lies*, 56.

68. McDaniel, *Uneven Lies*, 103; Kennedy, *A Course of Their Own*, 97–105.

69. Sinnette, *Forbidden Fairways*, 180–82.

70. Calvin Sinnette has studied the difficulties encountered by the UGA and Negro League baseball after true competitive integration in their previously white-only sporting counterparts came about, and has concluded that while the "situations were not identical, there were similarities in the problems faced" by the two sports. Sinnette, *Forbidden Fairways*, 171–72, 182; Robinson, *Skins & Grins,* 46–47; Robert Peterson, "Vanishing Almost before He's Been Seen," *New York Times Magazine*, August 25, 1974.

71. "UGA's 46th Meet to Open Monday," *Chicago Defender*, August 19, 1972; Sinnette, *Forbidden Fairways*, 180–81.

72. "Ted Rhodes Fires 280 to Win," *Chicago Defender*, September 8, 1951; Sinnette, *Forbidden Fairways*, 171–72; Peterson, "Vanishing Almost Before He's Been Seen," 32; Kennedy, *A Course of Their Own*, 221–25, 228–30.

12. Basement Bowlers: The National Negro Bowling Association and Its Legacy of Black Leadership, 1939–1968

1. *New Pittsburgh Courier,* September 12, 1964.

2. Ibid.

3. Ibid., November 24, 1962.

4. *New Pittsburgh Courier City Edition,* March 28, 2004.

5. *Old Post Gazette, Sports,* November 26, 2000: sports. http://old.post-gazette.com/sports/notebooks/20001126bowl.asp (accessed May 10, 2013).

6. *New Pittsburgh Courier,* November 19, 1960.

7. Ibid., September 12, 1964.

8. Because of this, I will use National Negro Bowling Association primarily, even when discussing events after 1944.

9. For more on the desegregation of the ABC, see John C. Walter and Malina Iida, "The State of New York and the Legal Struggle to Desegregate the American Bowling Congress, 1944–1950," *Afro-Americans in New York Life and History* 35, no. 1 (January 2011): 7–32; James H. Rigali and John C. Walter, "The Integration of the American Bowling Congress: The Buffalo Experience," *Afro-Americans in New York Life and History* 29, no. 2 (July 2005): 7–24. For information on the role of black newspapers in the campaign, see Patricia L. Dooley, "Jim Crow Strikes Again: The African American Press Campaign against Segregation in Bowling during World War II," *Journal of African American History* 97, no. 3 (Summer 2012): 270–90. For extensive work on the role of UAW-CIO in civil rights and desegregation efforts, see Robert H. Zieger, *The CIO 1935–1955* (Chapel Hill: University of North Carolina Press, 1995).

10. *Chicago Daily Tribune,* May 27, 1950.

11. The National Bowling Association, Inc., "The Beginning, The Present, The Future" brochure acquired at regional tournament in Las Vegas, 2012.

12. *New Pittsburgh Courier,* October 6, 1962.

13. TNBA President Notes, "A Brief Look at the Early Years of TNBA," acquired by author, September 10, 2012.

14. *Tri-State Defender* (Memphis, Tennessee), March 26, 1960; Al Matzelle and Jerry Schneider, *History of the American Bowling Congress: Celebrating 100 Years of Service to the Sport of American Tenpins* (Milwaukee: American Bowling Congress, 1995), 24–27.

15. Rigali and Walter, "The Integration of the American Bowling Congress."

16. Dooley, "Jim Crow Strikes Again," 275; Walter and Iida, "The State of New York," 7.

17. In 1995, Robert Putnam's "Bowling Alone" and the subsequent book with the same title claimed that the cooperation experienced in leisure activities like bowling created a unique social capital necessary for progress in liberal and modern communities. Putnam's lament on the declining interest in team sports in America would ultimately threaten democracy. Robert Putnam, "Bowling Alone: America's Declining Social Capital," *Journal of Democracy* 6 (January 1995): 65–78.; Robert Putnam, *Bowling Alone: The Collapse and Revival of American Community* (New York: Simon and Schuster, 2000).

18. TNBA President Notes, "A Brief Look at the Early Years of TNBA," acquired by author, September 10, 2012.

19. Ibid.

20. The National Bowling Association, Inc., "The Beginning, The Present, The Future" brochure acquired at regional tournament in Las Vegas, 2012.

21. Roi Ottley, "Negro's First Sport, Turf Now Trails," *Chicago Daily Tribune,* October 31, 1954.

22. *Tri-State Defender,* March 26, 1960; *New Pittsburgh Courier,* August 17, 1963.

23. *Chicago Daily Tribune,* October 18, 1953.

24. One author contends that "the oldest leagues took shape among men of Chicago in the Kingpin League during 1938," though TNBA records credit UCBL with being the first. "Bowling Unified in 1939," *New Pittsburgh Courier,* August 17, 1963; TNBA President Notes, "A Brief Look at the Early Years of TNBA," acquired by author, September 10, 2012; *Cleveland Call and Post,* December 5, 1943.

25. *Cleveland Call,* December 5, 1943.

26. The National Bowling Association, Inc., "The Beginning, The Present, The Future" brochure acquired at regional tournament in Las Vegas, 2012.

27. "Bowlers Charter Course for Chicago Tourney," *Cleveland Call and Post,* November 23, 1939.

28. TNBA President Notes, "A Brief Look at the Early Years of TNBA," acquired by author, September 10, 2012.

29. Ibid.; The National Bowling Association, Inc., "The Beginning, The Present, The Future" brochure acquired at regional tournament in Las Vegas, 2012.

30. TNBA President Notes, "A Brief Look at the Early Years of TNBA," acquired by author, September 10, 2012. See also The National Bowling Association, Inc. "Founders and Past Officers," http://www.tnbainc.org/about-us-founders-and-past-officers (accessed September 10, 2012).

31. The National Bowling Association, Inc., "The Beginning, the Present, the Future" brochure acquired at regional tournament in Las Vegas, 2012.

32. "Ted Page: Theodore Roosevelt Page (Terrible Ted)," *Baseball-Reference.* http://www.baseball-reference.com/bullpen/Ted_Page (Sports Reference LLC, 2000–2013) (accessed May 5, 2013); "Ted Page," *Negro Leagues Baseball Museum eMuseum* (Negro Leagues Baseball Museum and Kansas State University College of Education, 2006) (accessed May 1, 2013); "Negro Leaguer of the Month: Ted Page," *Pitch Black Baseball.* http://www.pitchblack baseball.com/nlotm_Ted_Page.html (McNary Publishing, 2010). (accessed May 1, 2013).

33. *New Pittsburgh Courier, City Edition,* March 28, 2004.

34. The National Bowling Association, Inc., "Founders and Past Officers," http://www.tnbainc.org/about-us-founders-and-past-officers (accessed September 9, 2012).

35. The National Bowling Association, Inc., "The Beginning, the Present, the Future" brochure acquired at regional tournament in Las Vegas, 2012.

36. J. Elmer Reed, *The Unlevel Playing Field: A Documentary History of the African American Experience in Sport,* ed. David K. Wiggins and Patrick Miller (Urbana: University of Illinois Press, 2003): 109.

37. Wayde Broughton, interview with author, May 15, 2013.

38. J. Elmer Reed, *The Unlevel Playing Field,* 109.

39. *Tri-State Defender,* March 26, 1960.

40. *New Pittsburgh Courier,* April 7, 1962.

41. *New Philadelphia Courier,* May 12, 1962.

42. Ibid.

43. *Chicago Daily Tribune,* August 24, 1958.

44. Ibid.

45. Ibid.

46. *Tri-State Defender,* August 11, 1962. Date taken from "Plan Huge $Million Project," *New Pittsburgh Courier,* September 6, 1961.

47. *Tri-State Defender,* August 11, 1962.

48. *New Pittsburgh Courier: National Edition,* August 17, 1963.

49. *New Pittsburgh Courier,* February 24, 1962.

50. *Tri-State Defender,* March 26, 1960.

51. J. Elmer Reed, *The Unlevel Playing Field,* 109.

52. One of the three additional bowling alleys mentioned was famous heavyweight boxer Joe Louis's enterprise, Paradise Bowl in Detroit. TNBA President Notes, "A Brief Look at the Early Years of TNBA," acquired by author September 10, 2012.

53. *New Pittsburgh Courier,* August 11, 1962.

54. Ibid.

55. J. Elmer Reed, *The Unlevel Playing Field,* 109.

56. *New Pittsburgh Courier,* October 6, 1962.

57. Ibid., March 30, 1962.

58. Ibid., October 6, 1962; March 30, 1963; April 6, 1963.

59. Ibid., September 6, 1961.

60. *Tri-State Defender,* March 26, 1960. Another black-owned bowling alley example can be found in the story of Leroy Shepard, of Warren, Michigan. Shepard approached TNBA to support him in building and operating Great Lakes Central, which he eventually opened in 1977 until it was burned down by an arsonist in 1980. Shepard went on to open two more alleys. *Michigan Chronicle,* November 9, 2011.

61. Sometime before 1965, Hillview Lanes was renamed Meadow Lanes, as evidenced in an article about Louise Fulton's career. *New Pittsburgh Courier,* July 7, 1962; March 28, 2004.

62. After a successful streak of bowling competitions, Louise Fulton joined Ted Page's staff at Meadow Lanes in Pittsburgh and continued the tradition of inclusiveness.

63. *New Pittsburgh Courier,* May 13, 1961.

64. Wayde Broughton, interview with author, May 15, 2013.

65. *Tri-State Defender,* August 11, 1962.

66. *Examiner,* July 9, 2010.

67. *New Pittsburgh Courier,* May 4, 1963.

68. Ibid., April 14, 1962.

69. Wayde Broughton, interview with author, May 15, 2013.

70. *New Pittsburgh Courier,* April 7, 1962.

71. Ibid., January 30, 1965.

72. Ibid., June 5, 1965.

73. *Chicago Daily Tribune,* December 16, 1946.

74. *New Pittsburgh Courier,* May 12, 1962.

75. *Tri-State Defender,* August 11, 1962.

76. *New Pittsburgh Courier,* November 17, 1962.

77. Wayde Broughton, interview with author, May 15, 2013.

78. *New Pittsburgh Courier,* June 30, 1962.

79. Ibid., July 28, 1962.

80. Ibid., June 14, 1961; February 4, 1961.

81. Ibid., April 14, 1962.

82. Ed Rollins, Chester Hodo, George Walker, Poindexter Orr, and Merrill Thomas made up the Henry C. Taylor bowling team. *New Pittsburgh Courier,* April 21, 1962.

83. Ibid., October 27, 1962.

84. *Tri-State Defender,* March 26, 1960.

85. The National Bowling Association, Inc., "TNBA 'A Hard Road to Glory,'" http://www.tnbainc.org/aboutus-glory (accessed September 10, 2012).

86. *Las Vegas Review Journal,* March 24, 1999.

87. *New Pittsburgh Courier,* March 28, 2004.

88. Ibid.

89. "The Other N.B.A.," *Ebony,* December 1994, 102–8.

90. The National Bowling Association, Inc., "TNBA 'A Hard Road to Glory,'" http://www.tnbainc.org/aboutus-glory (accessed September 10, 2012).

Contributors

David K. Wiggins is professor and codirector of the Center for the Study of Sport and Leisure in Society at George Mason University. His primary research interest is issues of race and sport. He has published numerous essays and written or edited several books, including *Glory Bound: Black Athletes in a White America* and *Rivals: Legendary Matchups That Made Sport History*. He is the former editor of *Quest* and the *Journal of Sport History*.

Ryan Swanson is an assistant professor of history in the Honors College at the University of New Mexico. His primary research areas are sports, reconstruction, and segregation. He also serves as the director of the Lobo Scholars Program. This program is a joint venture between the UNM Honors College and Athletics Department designed to serve very high achieving student-athletes. Swanson's first book, *When Baseball Went White: Reconstruction, Reconciliation, and Dreams of a National Pastime* (2014), explores how baseball became segregated after the Civil War. The book won SABR's 2015 Research Award.

Thomas Aiello is an associate professor of history and African American studies at Valdosta State University. He is the author of *Jim Crow's Last Stand: Nonunanimous Criminal Jury Verdicts in Louisiana* (2015), *Model Airplanes Are Decadent and Depraved: The Glue-Sniffing Epidemic of the 1960s* (2015), and *The Kings of Casino Park: Race and Race Baseball in the Lost Season of 1932* (2011), among several other books. He has published dozens of articles on American history, philosophy, religion, linguistics, and culture.

Summer Cherland earned her PhD in American history from University of Nevada, Las Vegas. She has published articles regarding historic preservation, teaching and learning, and black leadership. Her specialties include African American, Chicano, women's and gender history, and the urban West. She currently teaches American history at Gate Way Community College in Phoenix, Arizona.

Sundiata Djata is an independent scholar who teaches and researches topics in African, African American, Caribbean, and Latin American histories. His publications include *The Bamana by the Niger: Kingdom, Jihad and*

Colonization, 1712–1920, and *Blacks at the Net: Black Achievement in the History of Tennis* (2 volumes).

Chris Elzey teaches in the History/Art History Department at George Mason University. He also oversees the Sport and American Culture Minor and codirects the Center for the Study of Sport and Leisure in Society at George Mason. He is the coeditor of *DC Sports: The Nation's Capital at Play*.

Todd Gould, a graduate of Indiana University, is a freelance writer, producer, and director. A ten-time Emmy Award winner, he has produced documentaries and features for PBS, BBC, ESPN, and the Learning Channel. He is the author of two books, *Pioneers of the Hardwood: Indiana and the Birth of Professional Basketball* and *For Gold and Glory*.

Leslie Heaphy is an associate professor of history at Kent State University at Stark. She has a particular interest in the Negro Leagues and women's baseball. Among her publications are *The Negro Leagues* (reprint 2013); *Black Ball*—journal on the Negro Leagues published annually; *Encyclopedia on Women and Baseball*, ed. (2006); *Black Baseball and Chicago*, ed. (2006), and *Satchel Paige and Company*, ed. (2007).

J. Thomas Jable is Professor Emeritus, Department of Kinesiology, William Paterson University. His primary work in sport history has focused on nineteenth-century Philadelphia. His research has appeared in the *Journal of Sport History, Pennsylvania Magazine of History and Biography, Pennsylvania History,* and the *Research Quarterly of Sport and Exercise.* He served as president of the North American Society for Sport History, 1985–87, and editor of the *Journal of Sport History,* 2005–7.

Robert Pruter is the government and reference librarian at Lewis University in Romeoville, Illinois. He has a particular interest in the history of high school sports and early amateur sports in the United States, and has contributed articles and reviews to such journals as *Journal of Sport History, Nishim: A Journal of Jewish Women's Studies & Gender Issues, The International Journal of the History of Sport,* and *Sport History Review.* He is the author of *The Rise of American High School Sports and the Search for Control: 1880–1930* (2013).

Susan J. Rayl is an associate professor in the kinesiology department at the State University of New York at Cortland. She teaches courses on the history and philosophy of sport, and her research focuses on the African American sporting experience.

Rob Ruck is a professor in the Department of History at the University of Pittsburgh, where he teaches and writes about sport. His work focuses on how people use sport to tell a collective story about who they are to themselves and the world. Among his publications are *Sandlot Seasons: Sport in Black Pittsburgh* (1987), *The Tropic of Baseball: Baseball in the Dominican Republic* (1991), *Rooney: A Sporting Life* (2010) and *Raceball: How the Major Leagues Colonized the Black and Latin Game* (2011), and two documentaries, *Kings on the Hill: Baseball's Forgotten Men* (1993) and *The Republic of Baseball: Dominican Giants of the American Game* (2006).

Raymond Schmidt is an independent historian living in Ventura, California, now retired from his career in computer systems development. He is interested in the history of all major American sports, with particular emphasis on college football and golf. Among his publications are *Two-Eyed League: The Illinois-Iowa of 1890–1892* (1994); *Football's Stars of Summer: A History of the College All-Star Football Game Series* (2001); and *Shaping College Football: The Transformation of an American Sport, 1919–1930* (2007). He has also written many articles for various historical journals and reference works.

Carroll Van West is a professor of history and director of the Center for Historic Preservation at Middle Tennessee State University. In 2013 he was appointed Tennessee state historian. His most recent book is *Nashville Architecture* (2015).

Index

Abbott, Cleve, 100, 155, 167
Abbott, George, 19
Abbott, Jessie, 61
activism, 101–5, 175–76, 195–97, 205, 211–13
Adams, Dr. George, 182
A. G. Spalding & Bros., 80
Akron Firestone, 29
Alabama A&M, 95
Alabama Colored People's University, 94
Alabama Journal (newspaper), 102
Alabama State College, 92; Thanksgiving Day
  football rivalry against Tuskegee Institute,
  93–108
Alcorn A&M College, 102
Alexander, Henry, 105
Alexander, Walter G., 151–52
All-American Open, 191
Allen Super Market Team, 209
Alpha Golf Club, 180–81
Alpha Kappa Sorority, 155
Amateur Athletic Union (AAU), 62–63; national
  championships, 69; and Tuskegee women's
  track team, 155
Amateur Golfers Association, 185
American Association of University Professors
  (AAUP), 102
American Automobile Association (AAA), 113
American Basketball League (ABL), 22, 29
American Bowling Congress (ABC), xvi, 205–7,
  209, 211, 214, 216
American Bowling Enterprise (ABE), 210, 212
American Lawn Tennis Magazine, 176
American Tennis Association (ATA), xvi, 22,
  154–55, 165–78
Amherst College, 9
Anderson, Barney, 122
Anderson, Zack, 20
Anderson Indiana Duffy Packers, 34–35
Archer, Samuel H., 145–46
Ardee, W., 46
Argyle Athletics, 4
Argyle Hotel, 4
Armstrong, Henry, 135
Armstrong, Louis, 134
Armstrong Field, 154
Armstrong High School, 77, 80, 87–88
Ashe, Arthur, 169–70

Associated Negro Press, 30
Association Tennis Club, 166
Assumption Triangles, 21
Astley Belt, xiii
Atkins, W. E., 146
Atlanta Daily World (newspaper), 54, 106
Atlanta Ladies Tennis Club, 54
Atlanta's Fun Bowl, 212
Atlanta University, 96
Atlantic City Buccaneers, 22
Atwater Golf Club, 182
Atwell, A. T., 168
Aztec Tennis Club, 169
Augusta National Golf Club, 201

Badger, Louis, 26
Bagnoll, Robert, 175
Baker, Bertram, L., 175–77
Baker, C. C., 108
Ball, Robert (Pat), 181, 183, 187
Ballard, Dorothy, 49, 59
Ballard, Lula, 39, 49, 54, 59, 167, 170
Baltimore Afro-American (newspaper), 89, 131,
  136, 150, 154, 156, 158, 163
Baltimore Athenians, 23
Barco, J. W., 146
Barlow, Reggie, 107
Barnett, Bob, 163
Barnett, W. H. A., 167
barnstorming: Cuban Giants, 6–7, 16–17;
  New York Renaissance Five, 23–27, 35–36;
  Philadelphia Tribune Newsgirls, 46–47, 54–55
Bartley, Lula, 61
baseball: Cuban Giants, 3–18; East West Classic,
  129–41
basketball: New York Renaissance Five, 19–36;
  Philadelphia Tribune Newsgirls, 37–60;
  National Interscholastic tournament, 75–92;
  CIAA tournament, 156–64
Basketball Association of America (BAA), 32–34
"Basketball, Inc.," 30
Bateman, Paul, 111–12, 115, 128
Baxter, Brad, 107
Beasley, Herb, 35
Bedford, William, 17
Bee, Clair, 156
Bell, Cool Papa, 129–30, 132

McCard, H. Stanton, 166, 170
McClendon, John B., 91, 156–58, 164
McDaniel, Jimmy, xv, 169, 171, 174
McDaniel, Otis, 105
McDonald, Oscar, 207
McDougald Gymnasium, 163
McGrogan, Ed, 178
McIntosh, Mae "Miss Charlie," 214
McKinley High School, 89
McMahon brothers, 20
McMillan, Kathy, 69–70
Meadow Lanes (Pages Lanes), 212–13, 216
Metcalfe, Tristram Walker, 156
Metropolitan Basketball Association (MBA), 19–20
Miami Country Club, 196
Michigan All-Star Five, 29
Middle States League, 8, 10–13
Middle Tennessee Athletic Association, 91
Middle Western Interscholastic, 79
Midwest Amateur, 194
Mid-Western Athletic Association, 154
Mikan, George, 34
Miller, Robert: eligibility issue and the CIAA, 147–48
Minoso, Orestes, 140
Mississippi Valley Interscholastic Athletic Association, 78
Missouri Valley Interscholastic Athletic Association (MVIAA), 78
Mitchell, Elizabeth, 186
Mitchell, Harold, 175
Mitchell, Marjorie, 216
Mitchell, Ray, 198
Monde, Leon, 20
Monroe, Al, 50
Monsanto Open, 200
Monte, Hy, 20
Montgomery Advertiser (newspaper), 102
Montgomery Voters League and Women's Political Council, 103
Montreal Royals, 33
Monumental Tennis Club, 166–67
Mooch, Freddie, 56
Moonfixer: The Basketball Journey of Earl Lloyd (book), 162
Moore, Archie, 157
Moore, Ernest, 207
Moore, Lavinia, 53, 59
Morehead, Brenda, 70
Morehouse College (University), xiii, 145–46, 172
Morgan State University, 152, 154, 156–57, 163
Morris Brown College (University), 100
Mosk, Stanley, 196–97
Moss, Zefross, 107
Moton, Robert Russa, 93
Moton, Speaks, 22
M Street School, 77, 167

Murphy, Carl J., 154
Murphy, Isaac, xiii
Murphy, John P., 12
Myles, Eddie, 90

Naismith Memorial Basketball Hall of Fame, 24
Nashville Banner (newspaper), 65
Nashville Tennessean (newspaper), 64, 71
National Agreement, 9
National All-Star Tournaments, 204
National Association for the Advancement of Colored People (NAACP), 175
National Association of College Women (NACW), 155
National Baseball Hall of Fame, 3
National Basketball Association (NBA), 36, 161–62
National Basketball League (NBL), 19, 129–30, 32–33, 35–36
National Bowling Association, 216
National Collegiate Athletic Association (NCAA), xvi, 90–91, 145, 147, 149, 159
National Colored Girls Basketball Championship, 37
National Federation of State High School Athletic Associations, 82, 86
National High School Athletic Association (NHSAA), 86–92
National Interscholastic Athletic Association (NIAA), 82
National Interscholastic Basketball Tournament (NIBT), xvi, 75–92
National Invitational High School Basketball Tournament (NIHSBT), 86–88
National Invitational Intercollegiate Basketball Tournament (NIIBT), 156–57
National Invitation Tournament (NIT), 156
National League, 8
National League of Colored Baseball Players, 7, 18
National Negro Bowling Association (NNBA), 203–17
National Negro Women's Basketball Championship, 40, 42
National Police Gazette (magazine), 9
Negro American League, 141
Negro League Baseball, xiv–xv; East West Classic, 129–41, 163, 177, 200
Negro League World Series, xv, 136, 138
Negro National League (NNL), 3, 111, 130–31, 137, 141
Netti, George (Speedy), 184–86
Newark American Association, 12
Newark Little Giants, 8
New Haven Register (newspaper), 8
New Jersey Hebrews, 24
New Jersey Tennis Association: banning of white players, 173–74